FEDERAL
PUBLIC POLICY

**Personal Accounts of Ten
Senior Civil Service Executives**

Theodore W. Taylor
Editor

David S. Brown (W.A. Jump)
James W. Greenwood, Jr.
Martin Kriesberg
Michael S. March
Rufus E. Miles, Jr.

John R. Provan
Theodore W. Taylor
William C. Valdes
Edward Wenk, Jr.
John D. Young

Theodore Lownik Library
Illinois Benedictine College
Lisle, Illinois 60532

Lomond Publications, Inc.
Mt. Airy, Maryland
1984

353
F293

Copyright © 1984 by Lomond Publications, Inc.
All rights reserved.

Library of Congress Catalog Number: 83-81947

ISBN: 0-912-338-47-4 (Clothbound)
       0-912-338-48-2 (Microfiche)

Printed in the United States of America.

Published by
Lomond Publications, Inc.
P.O. Box 88
Mt. Airy, Maryland 21771

TABLE OF CONTENTS

INTRODUCTION

Theodore W. Taylor

The primary purpose of this book is to reveal the Federal policy process through real-life accounts of several senior civil service executives. The authors not only have a rich experience to sample from and report, but also have a special insight which enables them to interpret as well as relate events.

One cannot read the chapters that follow without being emotionally moved and mentally exhilarated. The drama of persons of ability, character, and can-do attitude overcoming the challenges interposed to effective government action is fascinating. This is especially true as the subjects discussed—food, jobs, communication, defense, payments to veterans, space, and national budgetary commitments—are central to the nation's welfare. Members of government agencies cease to be nameless, faceless bureaucrats and become true-to-life flesh and blood individuals doing vital work.

Whether civil servants, political officials appointed by the president, or elected officials, our authors bring these individuals to life as human beings with the same challenges and frustrations as the rest of us. What is electrifying is the acceptance of the challenges, the working around obstacles, and the achievement of national policy objectives by the outstanding individuals who tell their stories in the pages that follow. Some obstacles are the officials who lack creative impulses or knowledge, or individuals insensitive to the nature of our constitutional system, and persons whose primary motivation is private gain at the taxpayer's expense. In short, our career civil servants and our elected and politically appointed leaders are products of our society, and some of the best characteristics of our society are reflected in the people who are part of this book.

Innovative and tenacious staff work by civil servants can be used by appointed and elected officials to create or modify policy in the public interest, and this is dramatically set forth in the vignettes by Miles, March, Brown, Valdes, Wenk, and Young. The authors describe many dedicated public servants interested in carrying out the public interest, often against tough odds. Robert McNamara, Omar Bradley, William Jump, and Congressman Olin Teague are just a few of the talented public servants described in the following pages. Reading these chronicles, it is understandable that many corporate executives find public service rewarding, though often more frustrating and less remunerative than their private employments, as noted by Marver Bernstein in his 1950s studies.

On the other hand, the papers sharply etch the damage to a policy or a process by substituting a Spiro Agnew for a Hubert Humphrey (Wenk), the appointment of a Veterans Administration official who did not think it his responsibility to suggest solutions to the states or the Congress to stop the hemorrhaging of funds under the G.I. Bill (Miles), and the patronage-grabbing Senator from New Jersey who deprived the Federal Mediation and Conciliation Service of the best candidate for director (Greenwood). The reader may well conclude that the kind of people we raise and the quality of those we elect and appoint to positions of responsibility in government will have a make-or-break relationship to the creation of effective policy and its implementation for the well-being of our country.

It is obvious that a James Webb, Admiral E. L. Cochrane, Cyrus Ching, Omar Bradley, or a Dillon Myer have a capacity for leadership and clearly relating programs and operations to the central purpose of their agencies. They set the tone for the entire organization, recruit capable personnel, delegate authority, and back up subordinates; reject attempts to weaken their organization through unwise use of patronage or preference hiring; imbue their co-workers, the public, and other cooperating institutions with enthusiasm and a spontaneous outpouring of effort to achieve the organization's publicly assigned objective. They stand firm when others seek to deflect them from their goal. Many of the writers have seen government organizations tightly run, productive, with high morale. They have also seen the opposite.

Individuals in government bureaus are important. The ethics, work habits, and understanding of the relation of public service to our democracy are important factors in an agency's operation and its policy creation and execution. Charles Rovin's innovation of a Tribal Work Experience Program in Indian Affairs, Michael March's persistence in calling attention to the long-run fiscal impact of veterans pension plans, Rufus Miles' initiative in cutting off funds to G.I. Bill profiteers, and William Valdes' determination to successfully carry out an efficient job placement program in military base closings are examples of the importance of individuals to a policy. Valdes and Martin Kriesberg, as have many others writing in the field of public administration, state that the members of the bureaucracy themselves provide a form of representation of the general public.

In brief, the pages that follow reveal:

- The degree and ways in which the public participates in Federal policy decisions, especially in the agencies.

- The challenge, excitement, complexity, and impact of the work of senior civil servants.

- The importance of well-trained, well-motivated, and ethical senior civil servants.

- That bureaucracy can work if it is staffed by can-do people.

- That barriers to effectiveness in big bureaucracy are substantial and complex, but they can be removed, overcome, or avoided by determination, resourcefulness, and understanding of the system.

- That dedicated stewardship of Federal activities under the constitutional, representative, and democratic dimensions of the American political system is understood by and characteristic of many Federal executives for whom the authors are prototypes.

Government Policy

All of the chapters which follow deal with policy primarily in relation to the particular subject matter discussed by each author. James Greenwood does more in that he entertainingly portrays what he regards as the fallacies of certain myths about policy, the current state of our knowledge about policy as he sees it, and proposes a systems view of the policy process. The reader who is interested in a more theoretical analysis of the policy process and some options as to the future study of the subject may wish to turn to Greenwood as a backdrop for other chapters.

The policy episodes presented cover a wide range of government activities, and while the drama of many of the events themselves is fascinating and informative, the primary purpose is to use these events to illustrate the role of individuals in the constitutional policy process. The writers present their personal observations and insights on the nature of the formation and execution of policy as they see it. They provide convincing testimony to the importance of civil servants to their government and the people.

Policy Subsystems

The chapters that follow inevitably describe various subsystems or "iron triangles;" namely, the interrelationships among an agency or bureau, corresponding Congressional committees, and the interest groups concerned with the policy area involved. Both Michael March and Rufus Miles present the interplay of forces in veterans benefits issues among the Veterans Administration, the then Bureau of the Budget, the White House, various Congressional committees charged with veterans matters, interest groups such as the American Legion, and various private sector groups interested in using veterans benefits for private enterprise profit. John Provan makes clear the interaction among the states, private contractors, truckers and other transportation groups, the Federal Highway Agency, the Office of Management and Budget, and Congressional committees. Martin Kriesberg points to the influence of farmers, grain dealers, the Departments of State, Commerce, and Agriculture, the United Nations Food and Agriculture Organization, and foreign countries in the formation of our policy on food aid for other nations.

James Greenwood and others describe the dangers inherent in special interest subsystems which threaten the cohesion of the government and society as a whole, and Rufus Miles portrays the initiative and fortitude often required on the part of staff and appointed and elected officials to put the public interest above special interest.

Shared Powers

The system of shared powers provided by the Constitution of the United States requires the participation of the three branches of government—Executive, Legislative, and Judicial—in the policy process. As is widely recognized, unless there is some kind of consensus or at least acquiescence among the major branches of government and strong interest groups, a stalemate results. It can even develop when two committees of the House of Representatives get into a fight over turf, as John Provan points out in the case of highway financing. He provides an example of the Congress, with some help from interest groups and highway agency staff, countermanding the Office of Management and Budget and presidential policy. Arriving at a consensus is not always easy or neat.

A perceived crisis is often necessary to create substantial movement forward, a crisis which impels the separate and differing interests to agree on a compromise policy and action. Taylor's chapter illustrates how World War II stimulated a dramatic production of ships that would have been impossible to consider a few years earlier and certainly would never have been funded in view of the strong isolationist and antiwar sentiment in the country. As Young points out, Sputnik I created a crisis in this country resulting in a policy emphasis on science education as well as on a crash space program, one of the objectives of which was to place a man on the moon and bring him back. Agreement of the public, the Congress, and the president on this policy and the amount of money required would probably have been impossible without the stimulus of the USSR space success. Following World War II, communist paranoia provided fertile ground for Senator Joseph McCarthy to scare us half to death with a fear of subversion. The resulting policy involved loyalty boards, wild and unfounded accusations, the accused being denied the specifics of charges and unable to face their accusers, and the lack of due process. It was a shameful aspect of our history and, as Greenwood points out, was very likely counterproductive.

Coordination of Programs

The authors describe not only cooperation between government branches and agencies, but also agency interaction with state and local governments. William Valdes discusses how several departments, state and local governments, and the Congress worked together in efforts to minimize the impact of military base closings by locating jobs for displaced employees and helping localities replace lost payroll and revenue. Edward Wenk struggled with the challenge of getting various agencies with programs related to the oceans to coordinate efforts and develop a national policy. One of the jobs of the Department of Agriculture as reported in Martin Kriesberg's chapter is to coordinate Federal and private sector interests. David Brown reports that William A. Jump was one of the first to use the budget as a policy coordinating process for his department and describes his selfless devotion to an effective Federal agricultural program as a mission of stewardship.

Career Civil Servants

The part played by career staff in the development of a consensus or a successful policy is evident in the pages that follow. Various authors describe the role of the bureaucracy and the bureaucrats, especially the career personnel, demonstrating that often such personnel are the major source of expertise, information, institutional memory with knowledge of past successes and failures, innovative ideas and suggestions, and the ability to deliver administrative results in accord with adopted policy. Senior career personnel in agencies with grant research funds took the lead in organizing the Science Information Exchange to provide information on research in progress. Miles, March, and Wenk, as career employees, pushed for new directions, and over time and with ingenuity, prevailed. Valdes dared to tell McNamara that the Department of Defense could guarantee an offer of a job to over 100,000 employees threatened by job loss due to base closings. He then organized an innovative program that delivered on the guarantee. Congressional staff, appointed officials in the Executive Branch, and private interest groups involved in highway transportation all depended upon John Provan's career staff in the highway agency.

Public-Private Sector Relationships

The interests of U.S. farmers and food processors are major components in the development of foreign food policy, along with diplomatic, military, and U.S. economic objectives in various countries. Public-private sector involvements are found in many programs: highway financing, space, vocational schools and universities which rely on Federal funds, and policy for the oceans. Battles involving the general public interest versus special private sector interests and the parts played by bureaucrats, appointed officials, and elected officials are described by March, Miles, Provan, Taylor, and Valdes.

Inspiring are the success stories of public-private sector cooperation such as the World War II shipbuilding program, the space program, and the Defense Electric Power Program. The farmers' use of the agricultural extension service and benefits from their own rural electric cooperatives financed by the Federal Government are also examples of public-private citizens combining efforts with dramatically successful results. The trust responsibility of the Federal Government for American Indian land and resources presents another government-citizen relationship.

Almost all of the examples point up a mixture of market, or private sector forces, and command, or government regulations and requirements, in setting and carrying out policy.

John Young's analysis of the production miracles of the nation's civilian space activity goes into more detail than other contributors about some of the critical administrative policy aspects of productive, private enterprise-government effort. Young stresses the importance of adequate in-house expertise to draw up clear specifications and to monitor performance. Taylor cites the private enterprise-government cooperation in the massive shipbuilding production in World War II. These efforts were arranged through contracts between government and industry.

Public-private sector cooperation through the contract route is productive. However, there are fast-buck artists interested only in private gain, not the general welfare. Competitive bidding for contracts is fraught with incentives to cheat through collusion, use of substandard materials, shoddy workmanship, and the "bid low and come out high through change orders" technique. Negotiated contracts may avoid some of the pitfalls of the bid process, but are also subject to abuse. This is a very difficult policy area. Government career personnel are the general public's primary protection.

The Challenge to Government

It is clear that the problems facing society and governments are varied, complex, and of vital importance to our democratic future. There is a strong inner fiber as indicated by Lowell Hattery in his comments at the end of the book and the chapters that follow leave no doubt on this score. Even though certain similarities may be discerned, so-called principles or generally applicable approaches may not always give helpful guides to solving problems that vary as much as indicated here. John Young points to the differences between the broad and multiple missions of the former Department of Health, Education, and Welfare (HEW) and the mission of the National Aeronautics and Space Administration (NASA), noting that some successful NASA policies in the administrative area did not fit and were not applicable to the HEW situation.

Most of our authors demonstrate that the need for an understanding of the general public interest, a dedication to serving the general interest, and innovative and persistent effort to pursue actions in furtherance of the public good are possible and necessary if our democratic society is to prosper, be economically competitive, and serve the people by providing maximum options for growth. There are constantly new challenges that need solutions and a McNamara's vision and fortitude in innovating policy to help provide solutions is valuable. McNamara posed the challenge to the people of the United States to take some responsibility for our fellow citizens when, through no fault of their own, their source of livelihood was cut off. With the current technological revolution, there is much structural unemployment and McNamara's vision of joint effort to find solutions has not had sufficient attention. This and other problems and tasks provide stimulating challenges for the future. Government and its career personnel can either be a part of the problem or a major factor in finding solutions. We know from the dedication and experience reported here by our contributors that career civil servants can be and are one of the keys to a successful governmental system.

Editorial Note: Michael S. March raises the question of "whether the machinery of the Presidency can work well enough to set and enforce national long-range spending priorities when confronted by powerful pressure groups." His explicit description of the actual workings of the legislative review process is one of the few in public administration literature and is based on his personal participation. This chapter is of major interest because it describes the pressures on various parts of our government by veterans organizations, particularly the American Legion, in shaping veterans pension policies, and also portrays the resultant working environment for a civil servant professional in a key institutional arm of the Presidency. Further, March has described the interaction and impact of able appointed and elected officials and of civil servants in shaping legislative clearance policies in the Executive Branch.

The relatively loose oversight of the potential impacts of proposed legislation by the Office of Legislative Review, especially provisions that would result in built-in budgetary growth, meant that unless conscientious civil servants or the Congress successfully raised questions regarding future costs, the legislative bills were not adequately evaluated. And Congress in the veterans area, says March, with few exceptions, worked hand-in-glove with the veterans groups. The result was a "piecemeal creep in uncontrollable programs." Remarkably, March was instrumental in securing creation of a Presidential Commission and through this route (March became its technical advisor) helped secure major changes in veterans pension laws. It was a rough life! But persistent and able staff work paid off with fairness to veterans and great savings to the taxpayers.

CHAPTER 1

LEGISLATIVE REVIEW AT THE BUREAU OF THE BUDGET: THE SHAPING OF VETERANS POLICIES IN THE 1950s

Michael S. March

This chapter deals with the role of a civil servant in the legislative policy-making process of the American Presidency. It describes some significant events in my career when I was a mid-level fiscal analyst in the U.S. Bureau of the Budget (BOB) analyzing veterans programs during the Truman and Eisenhower administrations. The views and interpretations presented are mine and do not necessarily represent those of any organization with which I have been connected.

Effective central review of legislative proposals at the Presidential level is necessary for sound national priorities and proper budgetary control. Legislation is a critical stage of resource allocation. Every Federal program must be authorized by substantive legislation before appropriations can be made. A large and growing part of total budget expenditures is mandated by the provisions of substantive laws for pension and other benefit programs.

The central issue in the case is whether the machinery of the Presidency can work well enough to set and enforce rational long-range spending priorities when confronted by powerful pressure groups. In this case the veterans organizations which wield power with the Congress and a recalcitrant clientele agency, the Veterans Administration, were the driving forces. The chapter also reveals the tensions between professionalism and politics in an institutional arm of the presidency and casts some light on the personal risk/reward implications of professional work in such a politically charged, high-policy setting.

To the outsider it might seem that, with its position near the apex of the Executive Branch and with the power of the Presidency to support it, the Bureau of the Budget could readily set and enforce sensible policies in the Executive Branch. Not so. A host of political, special interest, organizational, precedural, and human factors in the complex governmental system made (and still make) consistent, long-range and forward-looking policies extremely difficult to achieve.

As an anonymous civil servant in the BOB, this was my working climate as I tried to reform veterans policies which over more than 150 years had achieved the status of traditions and had become one of the biggest program categories in the U.S. budget. To enhance understanding of the situation, I sketch the Executive

Office setting and provide a candid look at the inner workings of the BOB as they applied to the setting of budgetary and legislative policies and priorities in the 1950s. Then I describe my experiences during the terms of Presidents Truman and Eisenhower when I tried to secure the enunciation of definitive, forward-looking Presidential policies on veterans benefits and then pressed for their application by Presidential action on specific veterans bills.

The Executive Office
Setting and Environment

The Bureau of the Budget

The Bureau of the Budget (BOB) was created by the Budget and Accounting Act of 1921 to assist the President in preparing and administering the national budget. In 1954, when the main drama of this case took place, it was the principal staff arm in the Executive Office of the President. It had been transferred from the Treasury in 1939 when the Executive Office of the President had been created pursuant to the recommendations of the President's Committee on Administrative Management (sometimes called the Brownlow Committee).[1] The 1937 report of the President's Committee had also led to a major reorganization of the agencies of the government into ten departments and three umbrella agencies. These organizational actions, with accompanying procedural improvements in budgetary and legislative coordination, were major steps toward strengthening the role of the President as policy maker and administrative manager of the Federal establishment.[2]

Management of the World War II effort, which at its peak took nearly 45 percent of the Gross National Product (GNP), had dictated rapid expansion of the BOB in the Executive Office. Although some retrenchment had occurred following VJ-Day in August 1945, the BOB in 1954 still remained a broadly staffed agency carrying out the many different types of functions essential to the conduct of a Presidency overseeing a government which was already the biggest business in the land.

The BOB in fiscal year 1954 was not a massive agency. It had a budget of $3.29 million which supported a staff of 421 people, of whom only the top four were politically appointed officials.[3] The 1956 budget document concisely described the substantive functions of the BOB as follows:

The Bureau assists the President in the discharge of his budgetary, management, and other executive responsibilities.
1. *Office of budget review.* - Budget instructions and procedures are

developed, review of agency estimates is coordinated, and the budget document is prepared.

2. *Office of legislative reference.* - Proposed legislation and agency reports on pending legislation, enrolled bills, and proposed Executive orders and proclamations are reviewed for the President.

3. *Office of management and organization.* - Programs and plans are developed for improved Government organization and procedures, and guidance is provided in the work of the Bureau to improve agency management and operations.

4. *Office of statistical standards.* - Proposed agency reporting plans and forms are reviewed, and the Government's statistical activities, coverage, and methods are coordinated and improved.

5. *Program divisions.* - Agency programs, budget requests, and management activities are examined, appropriations are apportioned, proposed changes in agency functions are studied, and agencies are assisted in the improvement of their administration.

Responsibility for this work with respect to particular agencies is divided among five divisions: (a) commerce and finance, (b) international, (c) labor and welfare, (d) military, and (e) resources and civil works.[4]

Other Major Executive Office Components

Within the Executive Office of the President (EOP), the BOB in fiscal 1954 interacted chiefly with the White House Office ($1.64 million budget and 246 personnel, not counting the Executive mansion); the relatively small Council of Economic Advisers, which was concerned with the objectives of the Employment Act of 1946; and the tiny President's Advisory Committee on Government Organization. In addition, the EOP contained a modestly staffed National Security Council and the Office of Defense Mobilization with a budget of $2.80 million and 313 positions.[5] In the EOP, only the BOB and the White House Office were significantly involved in this case.

The Inner Workings of BOB

With respect to substantive resource allocation policy, the BOB in the 1950s carried on its staff work through two principal sets of coordinating mechanisms which funneled information or completed staff products to the top.

Budget Review

Of the two, the *budget review* function was the most widely recognized. It was the principal function for which the BOB was created in 1921 and was the basis for the BOB's reknown. The annual budget is the best known product of this process. This process focused heavily on stewardship over authorized, ongoing programs.

The idea of a national budget system was justified even before President Taft's Commission on Economy and Efficiency in 1912 recommended establishment of a formal office to prepare the national budget on the grounds that it would be an instrument of "economy and efficiency." It was believed that the impacts of the system would improve the whole administrative organization and management of the government. General Charles G. Dawes, the BOB's first Budget Director, introduced the concept of economy and efficiency through business-like management and rigorous control into the conciousness and the procedures of the BOB. In his view this included review of existing policies, although formal, professionally staffed evaluation did not come until the introduction of the Planning-Programming-Budgeting System (PPBS) in the middle 1960s. "Economy" remained the primary thrust of the BOB during its fifty year existence and conversion to an Office of Management and Budget (OMB) in 1970 did not significantly lessen this drive. The Budget Circulars promulgated by General Dawes, especially Circular A-11 relating to budget preparation, have shaped U.S. Executive Branch methods budget ever since.[6] These circulars convey instructions to the various departments and agencies and form the basis for BOB work.

World War II demands had pushed the U.S. budget to over $92 billion in fiscal year 1945. President Truman first presided over sharp reductions in defense outlays, but built them up again for the Korean Conflict. "Economy" was the dominant thrust of the Eisenhower administration. Banker Joseph M. Dodge, the first Budget Director for President Eisenhower, severely cut back the last Truman administration budget so expenditures declined from $74 billion in fiscal year 1953 to slightly over $64 billion in fiscal year 1955 as a result of his economies and the end of the Korean Conflict.[7] In 1954, Budget Director Rowland R. Hughes was carrying on this philosophy with the assistance of Deputy Director Percival M. Brundage. As the budget document excerpt presented earlier shows, the budget preparation and execution function was coordinated by the Office of Budget Review.

Legislative Review

The second major BOB function having major resource allocation implications was *legislative clearance*, coordinated by the Office of Legislative Reference, which had 14 professional positions in 1954. This function does not generate a discrete document as the budget process does. However, the legislative reference activities of the BOB, and now those of the OMB, dealt with matters of great importance. By 1954 they affected the entire, vital stream of the Executive Branch's involvement in the legislative process, including the development and coordination of the President's legislative program and issuances such as Executive Orders and Presidential Proclamations. Legislative review operates at the front edge of new program and new policy development. It has exceptional potential for shaping the future of the government.

Many of the important outputs of the legislative clearance process are not visible to the public or to scholars of the public policy process as BOB products because they consist of unpublicized advice to the White House, or, if issued, appear in Presidential Messages on the State of the Union, the budget, or on special topics. They may even appear in program proposals or issuances or initiatives of Executive Branch agencies. For instance, BOB (and now OMB) advice to Congressional committees on pending legislation may be submitted directly in some instances, but it is predominantly conveyed in cryptic paragraphs included at the end of legislative reports by Federal departments and agencies. Direct testimony, legislative reports, and even occasional special studies, were submitted by the BOB to committees largely at their specific request. In rare instances, information was volunteered where the issue was deemed to require direct BOB advice, positive or adverse, in support of the "President's program." With the exception of appropriations, all substantive legislation was within the purview of this process. Much of it was affected, sometimes in detailed housekeeping matters, occasionally in major substantive respects, and sometimes adversely by benign neglect or lack of capacity. Yet, most of the workings and results of this vital and powerful policy-shaping process were cloaked in true bureaucratic anonymity.

The origins of the legislative review and clearance process were described by the BOB as follows in 1953:[8]

From the outset, since 1921, the Bureau of the Budget has exercised the function of examining for the President the relationship between his budgetary program and legislative proposals coming from the agencies of the Executive Branch. Originally confined to legislation that would have financial effects upon the Government, this central clearance by the Bureau was extended under the New Deal to all legislative proposals of such origin. The Bureau's work in this field falls into two broad categories—development of the legislative program of the President and clearance of legislation and Executive orders and proclamations.

In the development of the legislative program of the President, close working relations are maintained with White House staff. The determinations about specific items to be included in the legislative program are usually the product of joint action.

The legislative reference function rests implicitly rather than explicitly on the Budget and Accounting Act of 1921. [9] In 1953 this function (then performed by a "Division" of Legislative Reference) was described by the BOB as encompassing the following activities. [10]

> The division is charged with the analysis, review, and coordination of the views of the Federal agencies on proposed legislation, Congressional enactments, Executive orders and proclamations, and other formal papers and documents. Except on appropriation matters, the division also handles the Bureau's relations with Congress, including inquiries from individual Congressmen or from Congressional staffs. In addition to utilizing its own resources for legislative program review, liaison with the Senate and the House, legal counsel, and analysis of pending measures, the division makes use of the different specializations available in the Bureau.

> The division functions essentially as an undivided working group to bring about coordination of advice from the other divisions and the Executive Branch as a whole in order to indicate to other agencies as well as to committees of Congress the considered position of the President on matters of legislation.

The Executive Branch procedural "bible" for the legislative reference function in the 1950s was Circular No. A-19, entitled "Reports and Recommendations on Proposed and Pending Legislation" along with Circular No. A-9 on "Enrolled Bills." Two published hearings before the Congress in 1950 and in 1966 produced copies of BOB instructions to the agencies and elicited considerable information on how the BOB handled its legislative review and clearance activities. [11] Under those BOB instructions, the Office (originally the Division) of Legislative Reference served as the focal BOB unit which:

- Coordinated the views of Executive Branch agencies on enrolled bills and submitted its advice on them to the President.

- Coordinated and cleared agency reports, testimony, and agency proposed bills, and obtained the views of affected agencies, and advised the agencies and/or committees of the Congress on the relationship of the proposals to "the program of the President."

- Participated in the development of the President's legislative program, usually jointly with departments and agencies.

- Maintained liaison with the White House and with the committees of the Congress on legislative matters—and also coordinated BOB work on all legislative matters—except those pertaining to appropriations.

The BOB in 1954 also devoted significant resources to statistical coordination and to improvement of government organization and administration. However, these activities did not deal directly with spending priorities or levels as did the two key functions described above.

BOB Inner Working Arrangements

During my 28 years of service with BOB-OMB this agency was typically a two-decker organization, although the precise groupings and names of units changed from time to time. The bottom deck, where the bulk of *both* the budgetary review and the legislative review work was done, consisted of the "program divisions" which were structured vertically, with each division assigned groups of departments and agencies with related activities and maintaining day-to-day contact with those agencies. These divisions were typically subdivided into specialized units handling particular bureaus or groups of programs. The top deck consisted typically of "offices" which coordinated certain broad processes or functional activities horizontally across the whole BOB and the entire government.

The top-layer "offices" in charge of budget review and legislative review were both heavy users of the program divisions. Indeed, the bulk of the analysis and review on budgets and on bills or legislative proposals was farmed out by the coordinating offices to the program divisions. The recommendations from the staff in the divisions, oftentimes after considerable review within the division, flowed up to the top office for approval or disapproval and from there to the Director, the White House, or to the Congress, as the situation dictated.

There were, however, significant differences during my years in BOB between the internal processes for handling budget review and legislative review. The budget review process organized by the Office of Budget Review was typically marked by two rounds of systematic review involving the Budget Director and his chief policy assistants. One of these was the Spring Planning Preview of the coming budget which mostly focussed on major program issues and on overviews of likely budget totals broken by agencies and/or major functional categories. Some cross-cutting reviews were also held, for example, of public works programs. In the 1950s this process often ended in giving the agencies specific dollar budget targets to guide the preparation of their budgets. The second round was the Fall Budget Review at which the detailed budget submissions of the agencies for the coming year were reviewed for inclusion in the President's budget submission to the Congress.

Both rounds of budget review typically were conducted by the Director's Review, a committee headed by the Budget Director (historically the "President's man") or the Deputy Director, the political Assistant Directors, plus the career Assistant Directors in charge of the several offices. This board typically met with staff from the program divisions on division-by-division basis. Except for the consolidated budget outlook projections, the review "books" for these sessions were prepared by staff in the program divisions, sometimes with additional materials on organizational and administrative issues or on statistical issues from the other offices in charge of these matters. Proposed legislative issues, including cost data, were typically included by the divisions in their review books, but with the recognition, even in the Fall Review, that these items would be settled subsequently with the White House through the legislative clearance channel.

Budget review tended to be very pragmatic and quite negative, even arbitrary. Especially in the Fall Review, it basically revolved around the figures on costs and program levels. Since the focus was commonly on the next year, most of the decisions were confined to short-range time frames on what could he cut from next year's expenditures. Occasionally some program which had clearly outlived its perceived need came to an end. The "controllable" programs bore the brunt of th economizing through the budget review channel. The all-to-frequent end result of this process was that budgetarily "uncontrollable" programs in which the expenditures were mandated by basic statutes were not modified, although from time to time the need for doing something about them was discussed.

Moreover, the budget review process was commonly run agency-by-agency and program-by-program. Even though some cross-cutting reviews gradually emerged, this was not a process in which interprogram or interagency priorities were effectively addressed. On the whole, the overriding climate of budget review was one of "economy," a negative climate. This was especially true during the Eisenhower years when few programs prospered significantly except for national defense, social security, and the new Federal aid highway program. The last two were financed from earmarked taxes channeled into trust funds.

Procedurally, the program divisions were strongly in the flow of the budget preparation side of the process. They identified Spring Review issues, analyzed the agency submissions in detail, prepared the books for the Director's Review, were given the Director's decisions and fed the budget "marks" back to the agencies, analyzed any agency appeals, and received the budget "green sheets" from the agencies and reviewed and revised them for inclusion in the printed budget document(s). The Budget Director, staffed by the Office of Budget Review, tended to be the channel for interface with the White House and the

President on major budget actions. In the end, the annual President's budget document and its supporting volumes, if any, put together and summarized by the Office of the Budget Review, served as a concrete annual testament to the budget process as an organized, orderly institutional process. The Budget Message, which this Office put together from pieces drawn from all elements of the BOB, was the vehicle for Presidential policy, including brief discussion of the proposed legislation which involved dollars.

In contrast, the immensely important and more glamorous legislative reference process, despite the creation of a Division (later an Office) in the BOB in 1939 to head the function, operated in a less regularized, less institutional manner than the budget review process. This was true in the 1950s and indeed, with variations, was the general situation during my 28 years of association with the BOB-OMB. Successes there were, even occasionally great ones, but from the standpoint of consistent, even-handed, and far-sighted comprehensive priority-setting and careful long-range resource allocation, the performance of the legislative reference process did not always measure up to some of the admiring stories and articles about it.[12] A reasonably careful review using criteria of substantive effectiveness, as distinguished from political survival, would show some spotty results of this rough-and-ready process. Such an analysis would probably reveal that the legislative clearance process permitted enactment of large spending programs without adequate review and was susceptible to being overwhelmed by special interest or political pressures more than the budgetary review process. It would also probably reveal a deficiency in providing timely or sufficent warning to Presidents about huge and unwise commitments for expenditures under outmoded existing laws or proposed liberalizing amendments which seemed politically attractive but which would create serious budgetary boobytraps for the future.

Factors Affecting BOB Performance of Legislative Review

A number of reasons may help explain why the handling of BOB's legislative reference was a changeable and rough-and-ready process:

1. Statutory authority for legislative clearance by the BOB was not explicit and rested considerably on the exercise of the President's powers, unlike the clear and explicit authority in the 1921 statute for the budget review function. In the early years, agencies had bucked the legislative clearance process and Dawes had to back off from his initial broad effort. President Hoover had even signed clearances himself.[13] With its own charter a bit unfirm and its resulting dependency on the White House, BOB had to be careful in wielding legislative clearance muscle.

2. Presidential action on enrolled bills, Executive Orders and Presidential Proclamations, and the development of the President's program were White House actions heavily wrapped in Presidential political interest. Even the "clearance" of legislation involved liaison with the White House staff on critical issues in determining whether pending bills or new proposals were "in accord with the President's program," were "not in accord," were "not recommended for favorable consideration," were "no objection," etc. For these reasons, the Legislative Reference staff tended to deal directly with the White House or the Congressional committees, to exhibit a high degree of political flexibility, to adapt quickly to the political leadership of new administrations, and at times to be semi-independent of the regular BOB and to be reticent about the political guidelines from the White House.

3. Neustadt has described how the main White House contact point for Legislative Reference in successive early administrations was the attorney holding the position of Special Counsel to the President—Rosenman, Clifford, Shanley, etc.[14] This tended to take White House legislative guidance away from active concern about future budget costs, both in the White House and in the BOB. Budget considerations loomed much smaller in the new legislation area than they did in BOB budgetary review of ongoing programs.

4. Starting around 1947, the BOB legislative reference organization was drawn by the White House into applying its institutional role toward developing the *legislative program of the President*, a role which continued through the 1960s and 1970s with varying intensity. Neustadt has admiringly described the role of the BOB in helping to develop President Eisenhower's 65-item legislative program presented to the Congress early in 1954.[15] However, White House leaders of this activity were often engaged in creating an attractive political program consisting of new items, at times putting forward costly proposals which were good politics for the President but which they did not expect the Congress to enact. Deep involvement by the BOB in this role was significantly different from its stewardship over the ongoing budget, which for any given year was 90 percent or more predetermined by prior legislation. Oftentimes BOB staff in the program divisions who were engaged in both budgetary and legislative analysis sensed a BOB schizophrenia, tight signals on budgetary marks, a loose attitude toward the costs of the "iffy" or political items in the President's legislative program. Part of this attitude flowed from the reluctance of some Presidents to veto Congressional enactments. This was certainly true in the early Eisenhower years.

5. The legislative clearance process did not give adequate attention to the "fixed," longterm budget commitments that it was creating. Despite the large potential future budgetary implications of many legislative items in the 1950s such as veterans pensions and social security, the BOB Legislative Reference orientation, mirroring the common White House concern with the next election, was usually short-range. Budget staff who expressed long-range concerns were

often pooh-poohed or given a casual ear and disregarded. The main focus was on first year or, at best, 3- or 5-year costs. Likewise, there was little enthusiasm or effective, sustained, and organized support by Legislative Reference for legislative proposals to cut back ongoing programs which were questionable or to exercise White House political muscle on heading off low priority but costly program expansion bills. Such endeavors lacked political appeal and did not receive deep analysis in many instances.

6. In the middle 1950s, the era of analysis and evaluation had not arrived at BOB. The progran divisions were staffed with budget examiners, many of whom were political scientists. Program analysis competence in the BOB was scarce, limited to a few economists sprinkled around in the program divisions where they were transferred after the Fiscal Division was abolished in 1952. I was one of this limited group. Most BOB analysis tended to be of the "quick-and-dirty," curbstone variety during the 1950s. Staff resources of all kinds were scarce. There was little time for longer range projects. Moreover, in the legislative area, workload demands tended to be unpredictable and urgent, stemming frequently from Congressional timetables or actions. BOB could not plan its schedule here as it did in the budget review area. "Firefighting" drove out longer-term projects. The 5-day limit for BOB analysis of enrolled bills out of the President's 10-day allotment was short—and enrolled bills invariably came in large numbers at the end of Congress.

7. Intra-BOB processes relating to legislation reflected the BOB's lack of full control over these activities, and, even where control could have been greater, were commonly of a rough-and-ready, fire-engine company variety. Except for the partial inclusion of legislative items from a cost standpoint in the Director's Review on the budget, no systematic, regularized review process with the program divisions was organized by the Division or Office of Legislative Reference. Staff in the program divisions (or in other BOB offices) who had expertise in particular fields were assigned *ad hoc* the task of reviewing proposed bills or enrolled bills with the aid of the excellent historical files maintained by the BOB. However, when staff memos or proposed reports were forwarded from the program divisions to Legislative Reference, they were at times modified or alternate drafts prepared with *ad hoc* or no consultation with the originating staff. In contrast to the budgetary areas, program division staff clearly had a secondary, water-carrying role in legislative clearance. Feedback on attitudes or actions at the White House on major items was episodic or scanty.

8. The BOB's information on legislative developments in the Congress came from many sources, but was not always on top of critical developments. The BOB relied on agency legislative representatives, White House legislative staff, some direct contacts with committees, and on checking the *Congressional Record*, Congressional bills and reports, and reports in major newspapers such as the *New York Times* and the *Washington Post*. However, given that scores of

Congressional committees and subcommittees in the House and the Senate were working on thousands of bills and were issuing hundreds of reports, the BOB information system did not always produce timely or adequate information on the flow of legislative events and actions or the strategies behind them. The Congress could readily overwhelm and outflank an understaffed BOB in many areas outside the group of bills which were specific Presidential initiatives.

9. Finally, program division staff were faced with working simultaneously for two sets of coordinators, Budget Review and Legislative Reference, each with its urgent deadlines. The thin staff of BOB, "burned out" from one activity but confronted by an urgent deadline from another quarter, commonly reacted "same horses, new drivers." It was not surprising, therefore, that the Congress, with the aid of end-runs from clientele-oriented agencies, often overwhelmed the BOB and, in the end, the White House.

On the whole, the glamorous Legislative Reference Office, with its Presidential policy overtones, was a remarkable instrument for providing vital, indispensable professional services to the Presidents from the whole BOB staff. However, because of transitions between administrations and the resulting inexperience of new White House staff, the political nature of legislative policymaking, and less than perfect BOB organization of the process, the front door to the budget was frequently left more than a little ajar for unplanned, poorly conceived, and inadequately analyzed programs. Even the conservative, budget-cutting Eisenhower administration presented an inconsistent picture of cutting the ongoing budget deeply, but was compliant to the Congress on some costly expansionary legislation. Beyond question the Congress makes the national policies, but how they are made in areas where pressure groups are strong presents a major challenge to national budgetary priority-setting.

The Problem of Veterans Benefits

In the foregoing setting I was assigned, starting around 1946, to serve as the veterans programs analyst in the Fiscal Analysis Division of the BOB and continued in this role for some years after the Labor and Welfare Division acquired me in 1952. I was given this assignment after having served as the Fiscal Analysis Division's national defense analyst from the time of my entry into the BOB in early 1944 after my discharge from the U.S. Navy. Although I took on other assignments as the years progressed, I anonymously played a key role for nearly 20 years from my BOB position in shaping Executive Branch philosophy and policy on veterans programs. My most influential role in this area was in the 1950s. This was not, however, a role for which bureaucratic medals are awarded, because a good deal of "nay saying" was involved and neither the Veterans Administration (VA) nor its clientele organizations were particularly pleased with BOB review results.

Veterans Organizations as Pressure Groups

It is difficult to find an area of American national policy which has been as thoroughly dominated by well-organized and successful pressure groups as the field of veterans' pensions and other benefits. Military officers were agitating for benefits even during the Revolutionary War: "Every war has been followed by the establishment of a society of veterans to bring pressure for the creation of conduits from the Federal Treasury to the pockets of the veterans."[16]

The history of veterans pension, compensation, and other benefits is marked by the emergence of veterans organizations after each war. The secret Society of the Cincinnati was the most prominent of the Revolutionary War organizations which pressured the Congress. The Grand Army of the Republic (GAR), representing union soldiers of the Civil War, covertly allied with the Republican party, was immensely successful in procuring pensions. The Spanish American War Veterans (1898) obtained service pensions for its group. The post-World War I bonus and many other benefit liberalizations were led by the American Legion (1919) and other organizations such as the Veterans of Foreign Wars (1899), and the Disabled American Veterans (1920). The Veterans of World War I (1949) led an all out fight for a service pension for its group.[17]

World War II saw continuation and growth of the post-World War I organizations and creation of new ones such as the more moderate American Veterans of World War II and Korea (1947) and the citizen-oriented American Veterans Committee (1943). The same organizations embraced the Korean War veterans.[18]

Huge memberships running up to 3 million for the GAR and 2.7 million for the American Legion, coupled with their zealous focus on pushing through special pensions and related benefits, have made these organizations a powerful force in the politics of veterans benefits.[19]

The Impact of Veterans Programs on the Federal Government

Recurrent American involvement in wars, aggressive veterans organizations, and the easy compliance of the U.S. Government in enacting generous special benefits for veterans have made veterans expenditures a large item in the Federal budget ever since the founding of the Republic. Historical tabulations from Veterans Administration annual reports show that veterans outlays from the beginning of the U.S. through January 30, 1954 had totaled $88 billion, including $75 billion from general and special appropriations. In fiscal year 1954 alone, the total outlays ran $5.3 billion, including $4.3 billion from general tax funds. Prior to 1919 the U.S. had spent $5.8 billion, so it is clear that an enormous growth in veterans outlays had occurred after World War I with its 4.7 million servicemen.[20]

The literature on veterans benefits shows that large numbers of statutes have been enacted by the Congress to authorize, expand, and increase a widening array of veterans benefits. The works of Weber and Schmeckebier of the Brookings Institution, Glasson and Dillingham had chronicled the history of these programs through 1941.[21] The heavy emphasis on veterans non-service-connected pensions is evident in these works and in VA tabulations of statutes.[22]

The Revolutionary War had set a pattern for liberalization of veterans pensions. Initially compensation was for the service-disabled. Then came a "needs test" pension for veterans who were indigent. Later, liberalization of the eligibility requirements brought service pensions for all who had served some minimum period during the war, regardless of need or disability. This was then followed by pensions for the widows and children of such veterans. And throughout, rates of pensions would be periodically increased for the veterans and then for the dependents.[23]

This general pattern was followed for the War of 1812, the Mexican War, the Indian Wars, the Civil War, and the Spanish American War.[24] As the veterans organizations became better organized, the costs of benefits, mostly for nonservice-connected pensions, for the Civil War and the Spanish American War far exceeded the costs of fighting these conflicts. It appeared in the early 1950s that the same result would occur for the World War I group, even without a service pension.[25] Enactment of nonservice-connected pensions had become a costly tradition, regardless of the emergence of other social programs after 1935. Moreover, VA benefits on the whole were set by substantive legislation and hence were fixed commitments beyond regular appropriation control in the budget review process unless the laws were changed.

Changing National Circumstances
Affecting Veterans Pensions

I entered the veterans programs area about three years before the World War Veterans of World War I (the "Wonnies") were organized in 1949 to push for service pensions for their group in keeping with the traditional American treatment of veterans. That was 31 years after the end of their war and they were getting restive over the lack of a service pension.

One of my earliest and long-remembered bits of informal BOB indocrination on the problems of veterans legislation was by Rufus Miles, who at the time was head of the Estimates Division unit which handled the VA budget and was concerned about abuses of the G.I. Bill. He described the historic pattern of veterans pensions and the role of the American Legion. Then he pointed out how the enactment of a wide range of benefit programs for World War I veterans and of the G.I. Bill for the World War II group had drastically changed the treatment of veterans by giving them aid upon their discharge from service when they needed it most. But he suggested that it would be very difficult to change the traditional pattern of veterans' pensions. Instead the BOB ought to advocate creation of a Presidential Commission to review national policy in this area.

Before long Rufus Miles transferred to the Department of Health, Education and Welfare (HEW) to be the career Administrative Assistant Secretary. I continued in the BOB in a unit under I.M. Labovitz handling social welfare, social insurance, and veterans programs, first in the Fical Division and later in a new Labor and Welfare Division where Estimates and residual Fiscal Analysis staff were combined. Subsequently, Phillip "Sam" Hughes became my immediate superior in that Labor and Welfare Division unit. After he transferred to the office of Legislative Reference, Lawrence Wendrich became my boss. As an analyst largely concerned with veterans legislation and programs, one of my annual tasks was to draft the section of the President's Budget Message dealing with veterans programs.

Looking back, my assessment of U.S. veterans policies was shaped by a series of factors: knowledge of the World War II war effort and of military pay and retirement benefits previously gained as defense programs analyst; the ongoing job context in the cost-conscious BOB in which I participated in work on pensions and social security as well as veterans benefits; a growing awareness of the costs of veterans programs and the political pressures inherent in veterans legislation. I also recognized that there was a virtual absence of countervailing forces except for whatever a politically sensitive Presidency might generate. Contributing to this assessment were my own analytic tools from diverse fields—economics, statistics, and political science and public administration—plus a futures-oriented frame of mind.

By the beginning of the 1950s, I had identified a series of critical factors that deeply affected my view of veterans policies and which I used in evaluating veterans bills and shaping drafts of policy statements for inclusion in the Budget Message or other documents:

1. The immense increase in the U.S. veterans population due to 16.5 million World War II servicemen and, eventually, 5.3 million more from the Korean Conflict. The time could be foreseen when half or more of the entire population might consist of veterans and their dependents.

2. The huge potential future costs to U.S. taxpayers. If previous patterns of enacting service pensions were carried over to the World War I, World War II, and Korean Conflict veterans and their widows, the added costs to the U.S. Treasury over the years would run into several hundred billion dollars for the then existing veterans and their widows. The big immediate pressure point was the World War I group.

3. More constructive pay and benefits for servicemen while in service. In addition, more timely assistance after discharge through medical care, disability

compensation, and rehabilitation for the disabled, plus adjusted compensation and, for the World War II and Korean Conflict groups, readjustment assistance eligibility for all veterans in the form of education, training, and housing aid, etc.

4. The rapid development, starting in 1935, of general social insurance and welfare programs, particularly the more rapid maturation of social security by the enactment in 1950 of the so-called "new start" which provided general economic security programs for veterans and nonveterans alike. These programs increasingly met general needs not related to military service which had been filled for veterans in the preceeding century and a half by special veterans nonservice-connected pensions. In large respect, these developments were making veterans nonservice-connected pensions redundant.

5. The constructive major emphasis on adequate aid and compensation for the disabled and for the survivors of the service-deceased ex-servicemen, plus availability of readjustment assistance for all recent veterans upon discharge, appeared to permit a de-emphasis of the traditional pensions which had typically been provided many decades after service ended.

An Effort to Change Veterans Policy

How does an analyst try to change such traditional policies toward veterans? The answer is, gingerly and slowly by careful analysis and education of the policymakers. However, by virtue of my staff position as a BOB analyst who worked on parts of the Presidential Budget Messages, I had unusual access to influence and even initiate changes in policy. But in a cautious organization such as the BOB which consciously regarded itself as the institutional arm of the Presidency, there are many levels of concurrence on the Budget or Budget Messages and there were many people who could and would say no. From my mid-level position, my drafts had to secure acquiesence from (1) my Budget Examiner associates and my unit head, (2) the Division Director, (3) the Office of Budget Review (which edited the Budget Message), (4) the Office of Legislative Reference which carefully monitored the sections relating to legislation, and (5) the BOB Director's Office, which included the political Assistant Directors, the Deputy Director, and the Director—all sensitively policy oriented. Then the BOB Director had to secure clearance of the Budget Message from the White House, including the Special Counsel who presided over legislation and Presidential Messages. In this process many substantive suggestions and wording changes were received, so an institutional product emerged.

The process of policy change was further complicated by the fact that most policy statements were cleared with the affected agencies, in this case the VA. As I progressed in the BOB, I spent many Christmas seasons accompanying my Division Chief to meetings with agency and departmental officers and heads to secure Budget Message clearances in the areas in which I had prepared or coordinated division drafts.

Truman Budget Message Policy Statements

President Truman's Budget Messages for fiscal years 1948 and 1949 were still preoccupied in the veterans area with World War II readjustment benefits and touched very lightly on general veterans policies. The 1948 Message statement was largely a description of the various benefits, but it did state that "no new programs of assistance appear necessary."[26] In the 1949 Message (issued January 6, 1948), two gently phrased but germane facts appear: that the veterans population, counting 14.7 million World War II veterans, totaled 18.6 million so that veterans with their immediate dependents within a decade would constitute two-fifths of the total population. And that "many of our veterans have rights under more than one provision of Federal law and. . .veterans' benefits will remain a large part of the Federal Budget for many years to come."[27] In fiscal year 1947, expenditures for veterans benefits and services had been nearly $7.4 billion, or more than one-sixth of the entire General Fund Budget.

In the Budget Message for fiscal year 1950, I was able to secure inclusion of a comprehensive statement on veterans policy that enunciated priorities among the different types of veterans benefits. In addition, I also pointed out that the needs of veterans without service-incurred disabilities should take into account the benefits available under general social programs.[28]

The extent and scope of constructive measures to assist veterans of our earlier wars to return to useful civilian life were limited. Too often prior to World War I our country belatedly attempted to discharge its obligation to veterans merely by bestowing upon them pensions and gratuities. In contrast, survivors of World Wars I and II have received more timely and better hospital care, insurance benefits, vocational rehabilitation, compensation, and other benefits have been provided to disabled servicemen and to the dependents of the deceased. Servicemen of World War I received adjusted compensation while World War II veterans are receiving readjustment benefits to assist them in obtaining education, training, jobs, businesses, and homes. . . .

The program of veterans' services and benefits should reflect the fundamental fact that our primary long-run obligation is to dependents of veterans deceased from service causes and to veterans disabled in the service. . . .

The necessity for new and extended benefits for veterans without service disabilities should be judged, not solely from the standpoint of service in our Armed Forces, but in the light of existing social welfare programs available to all, veterans and non-veterans alike. In recent years, social-security protection, including unemployment and old-age survivors insurance and old-age assistance, has been made available to a large percentage of our general population. Prior to World War I the lack of our general benefits was, of course, one of the main reasons for the enactment of special benefits to veterans. At the present time, we seek to broaden and extend these social-security programs and to enact comprehensive national health and disability insurance programs for all our people, including veterans, who with their immediate families will soon constitute 40 percent of the population.

The President's 1951 Budget Message extended the description of veterans programs and elaborated on the philosophy from the prior year. It also pointed out that veterans and their dependents were already two-fifths of the total population, that proposals were pending in the Congress to increase greatly the special programs for veterans, and by way of policy stated: [29]

Almost 2,000,000 veterans with disabilities incurred in the service, and over 300,000 families of veterans deceased from service causes, are now being assisted under the veterans' programs. Our primary long-run obligations in providing veterans' benefits and services are to this group. We must give them timely help to surmount the economic and physical handicaps sustained as the result of military service and to assist them to assume the full responsibilities of civilian life. . . .

The remaining 17,000,000 veterans are practically all without service disabilities. The Government has made available liberal benefits to help all veterans of the two world wars make the transition from military to civilian life. The veterans of World War II, in particular, have received readjustment benefits to assist them in obtaining education, training, jobs, businesses, and homes. . . .

Veterans without service disabilities will continue to be eligible for liberal benefits under the permanent veterans' laws after the termination of temporary programs. At the same time, these veterans are eligible in many cases for benefits under the general social security programs of the Government. We now seek to improve and to broaden the general social security programs to provide protection against the economic hazards of old age, disability, illness, and unemployment. The social security proposals pending in the Congress apply to all the people, including veterans. . . .

I again urge that in considering new or additional aids for veterans without service disabilities, the Congress judge their necessity not merely from the standpoint of military service, but also on the basis of benefits under the general social security, health, and education programs available to all the people, including veterans. Our objective should be to make our social security system more comprehensive in coverage and more adequate, so that it will provide the basic protection needed by all citizens. We should provide through the veterans' programs only for the special and unique needs of veterans arising directly from military service.

The 1952 Budget Message (issued in January 1951 during the Korean Conflict while I was away on one year's mid-career study at the Littauer Graduate School in Harvard University) had a brief statement in the veterans section that the U.S. would have to maintain larger Armed Forces, and that in the future "nearly all the population may be veterans or the dependents of veterans." This assumption "requires a clear recognition that many of the needs of our veterans and their dependents can be met best through the general programs serving the whole population." Legislation directed to the problems of servicemen and their dependents "should provide only for those special and unique needs which arise directly from military service." [30]

I returned from Harvard in October 1951 to my prior position in the BOB with my "batteries recharged" and equipped with a broader understanding of public policy and its administration.

President Truman's 1953 Budget Message once more had a more extensive veterans section which conveyed a clear statement of priorities giving service-connected benefits (e.g., disability and death compensation) first place, housing and readjustment benefits second place, and largely discounting special veterans nonservice-connected benefits (e.g., pensions). [31]

In view of the large increase in the size of our Armed Forces since Korea, and the continued increase in expenditures for compensation and pensions, further large declines in veterans' outlays are unlikely. Our veteran population is increasing rapidly under the policy which requires all able-bodied young men coming of military age to serve their turn in the armed services. As our commitments to our growing number of veterans increase, we should constantly inquire into how we can best meet their needs and the needs of their dependents. In considering legislation affecting veterans, we must take into account the prevailing economic and military situation, the relation of veterans' programs to the whole range of Government programs, the availability of other Government services, and the lessons learned from experience.

The chief responsibility of the Government is to give medical care to veterans who have been injured in the service, to assist them to assume their place in society as productive and self-reliant citizens, and to given necessary aid to the families of veterans deceased or injured from service causes. We should also provide other de-mobilized servicemen with timely readjustment assistance on a sound basis.

The needs of veterans and their families not resulting directly from military service can best be met through the welfare programs serving the whole population. These programs have been expanded and improved in recent years. Only the special and unique needs of servicemen and their dependents arising directly from military service should be provided for in special veterans' programs.

Outgoing President Truman's "caretaker" Budget Message for fiscal year 1954 (issued January 9, 1953) stated that two main factors pointed toward increases in veterans costs: First, there were 19.8 million veterans and, if the Armed Forces continued at their current size, most of the people in the U.S. would eventually become veterans or dependents of veterans. Second, Congress had enacted over 500 laws extending and liberalizing veterans benefits in the preceeding 10 years. A concise statement of policy followed.[32]

I strongly support the policy of providing assistance to veterans particularly those injured in the service, in assuming their normal places in society. In considering new veterans' legislation, however, recognition should be given to the extensive development in recent years of general welfare programs, such as social security, which serve both veterans and nonveterans. There is overlapping at present between the two sets of programs which should be corrected.

President Eisenhower's 1955 Budget Message

Election of a President who had led the Allied Forces in Europe during World War II and was a five-star general presented a degree of uncertainty as to the future course of policy toward veterans demands. President Eisenhower, during his first two years did not veto a general veterans bill.

However, President Eisenhower in the 1955 Budget Message, his first (dated January 21, 1954) basically restated the veterans policies repeatedly outlined by President Truman:[33]

Since 1940 the number of veterans has risen nearly fivefold and it is still increasing rapidly as men are discharged from the Armed Forces. There are now more than 20 million veterans, who, with their families, constitute 40 percent of our people. Over 300 laws provide a variety of special benefits and services to this large segment of our population.

It is our firm obligation to help our veterans overcome the handicaps which they incurred in the service of the Nation so they can return to their normal civilian pursuits. We must first of all do what we can to ease the burdens of veterans disabled in service and the families of those who have died from service causes. This is our primary responsibility, and generous benefits to them are the core of our veterans' programs.

Secondly, we must make available readjustment aids through well-conceived and properly administered programs for those veterans discharged after service during national emergencies.

Finally, we must remember that the best way to help our millions of veterans is by making it possible for them to share fully in the economic and social gains of our country. This means assuring them adequate job opportunities. It also means assuring them, both during and after military service, of the same protection under the broad social-security program that is provided for nonveterans. Progress in achieving these objectives will lessen the need for pensions and other special benefits for the vast majority of veterans who, fortunately, did not incur disabilities during their service.

However, in the Message, the veterans section was moved up to be the second functional section, right after national defense as compared to being placed toward the end of the last Truman Messages along with "general government."

Our achievement of consistency in the policy line on veterans programs from the Truman to the Eisenhower administration was a major success for the institutional BOB. This was a tribute to Joseph M. Dodge, the first Eisenhower Budget Director, and to Roger W. Jones, the career Assistant Director in charge of the Office of Legislative Reference, who under Dodge had gained exceptional confidence in the White House. The benefits of his White House entree spilled over to the whole BOB policy process.[34]

The statements on veterans programs in the Truman and Eisenhower administrations were consistent with the public interest positions taken from time to time by earlier Presidents, Republican and Democratic.[35] The real question, however, remained: were these policies being implemented in the Executive Branch and in the Congress when it came to VA reports on pending bills and White House positions on enrolled bills? The truth was that there was a big gap between the general policy statements and action on specific bills.

Action to Implement Stated
Presidential Policies

Pressure Groups on the Offensive

The veterans organizations were not daunted by the budgetary policies enunciated in the Truman and Eisenhower Budget Messages. They had more than a century and a half of legislative successes marked by very few defeats. They viewed veterans programs as a tidy three-cornered game: the veterans organizations developed the policies, the House Committee on Veterans Affairs got them enacted into laws, and the VA cooperatively administered the resultant benefits. Presidents and their upstart tool, the BOB, were unwanted intruders into a nice, well-oiled process which in recent years has come to be called the *iron triangle*.

Notwithstanding the policy pronouncements by President Truman and in 1953 by President Eisenhower, the usual process of expanding and increasing veterans benefits continued in the 83rd Congress. In early 1953 and again in 1954, the Subcommittee on Compensation and Pension of the House Committee on Veterans Affairs held hearings on two large batches of bills.

The 1953 group of 24 bills on which hearings were held by the Subcommittee all concerned service-connected disability and dependents' compensation benefits.[36] The 1954 group consisted of 72 compensation and pension bills for veterans and their dependents, of which 3 concerned benefits for the Women's Army Auxiliary Corps, 28 were compensation bills, and 41 were pension bills, including a number of bills to authorize service pensions for World War I veterans.[37] In veterans programs, the term *compensation* is used to describe benefits for service-connected disability or death. *Pension* refers to payments to veterans or their dependents for causes not related to their military service, i.e., for nonservice-connected disability, lack of income, or old age, if there had been a period of service during a war.

The service-connected compensation bills proposed numerous changes to broaden eligibility for benefits and to increase rates: liberalize eligibility for statutory awards for conditions such as blindness; relax marriage criteria and the definition of widow; permit payment of compensation during active service; equalize wartime and peacetime rates; liberalize presumptions of service connection for TB, tropical diseases and sclerosis; raise basic disability rates by various percentages such as 20 or 25 percent; increase funeral benefits; increase statutory rates; prohibit termination of service-connected disability compensation after 10 years of payment; liberalize criteria for dependents benefits; increase dependents rates, including those for parents; liberalize eligibility for veterans of Mexican War, etc.

Likewise, the bills to liberalize eligibility for nonservice-connected pensions and to increase their rates took many forms: liberalize pension eligibility for World War II and Korean Conflict veterans and their dependents to accord with the World War I group; progressively reduce disability requirements with increasing age to enable veterans to qualify for a pension; increase disability and death pension rates; raise income limitations to qualify for pension; provide pensions for Medal of Honor winners or their widows; grant pensions to World War I group on same basis as for Spanish American War group, that is, a service pension; waive the income limitation for World War I veterans over age 70; provide benefits for certain Mexican border service veterans; increase pension rates for World War I veterans; liberalize marriage requirements; grant a pension of $100 a month for all World War I veterans over age 62; exclude life insurance payments from income limitation for pension; at age 60 grandfather total and permanent disability if it had been pensionable for 15 years; raise income limit for single veterans with dependent parents; pay a pension to totally and permanently disabled veterans regardless of length of service, etc.

In sum, these bills represented a classic operation of the well-known political process for incremental expansion and increase in VA compensation and pension benefits through cleverly designed exploitation of purported or actual inconsistencies, plus some efforts to hit policy home runs, such as to obtain a service pension for World War I veterans or get whopping rate increases through the Congress. The published hearings on these two sets of bills show active support from the veterans organizations such as the American Legion, AMVETS, Disabled American Veterans, Veterans of Foreign Wars, etc. Some 25 Congressmen also appeared in person to testify or made written statements in support of their particular bills.

The Executive Branch position was represented by the Veterans Administration. Its reports commonly discussed the technical aspects of the bills in relation to existing laws and the added costs, usually only for the next year. The VA reports were invariably in terms of VA-administered laws. No references to overlap of the VA pensions with Social Security and other HEW programs were included, nor were the broad perspectives on VA benefits as outlined in the Truman and Eisenhower Budget Messages reflected in the VA reports. All these reports had been cleared by the BOB. Neither the Office of Legislative Reference nor the Labor and Welfare Division had followed up in having the VA adopt the broadly based policy orientation then embodied for a number of years in the Budget Messages. Within the Labor and Welfare Division I did some of the reviews and other bills were analyzed by the Examiners or the unit head in my absence.

The VA reports dutifully stated in each case the BOB advice which had been given the VA. Review of the advice in these hearings shows no strong or very consistent Presidential position on either compensation or pension bills.

In both compensation and pension groups, a few bills were declared "not in accord with the program of the President," thereby raising the threat of a Presidential veto. In the compensation area, several statutory award and Mexican conflict bills plus a hefty rate increase bill costing $147 million the first year were declared "not in accord." In the pension program half a dozen costly bills to raise income limits, raise rates, or greatly liberalize pensions for World War II veterans were given "not in accord" advice. However, the most common BOB advice on both pension and compensation bills was that it "recommends against favorable consideration of this legislation by the committee." This is not particularly threatening advice. Moreover, for a number of bills in both the compensation and pension areas on which the VA reports were discernably or strongly negative, the BOB advice was merely that "there is no objection to the presentation of this unfavorable report." On a few other bills, noncommittal advice of "no objection to the submission of the report" was rendered; on a couple of other bills the advice was "no objection to submission of this favorable report"; on a few it was "strongly recommends against favorable consideration."

There were no discernible differences in BOB posture in 1953 and 1954. All in all, the BOB stance did not present a clearly drawn line on what legislation would be vetoed and what would be signed.

This lack of direction reflected the results of a piecemeal BOB clearance process in which different reports were cleared at different times without comprehensive, overall analysis. It also reflected the typical reluctance of the Office of Legislative Reference to take strong, negative positions in this highly politicized program field in which Presidents were typically reluctant to exercise their veto power. The House Veterans Affairs Committee did not solicit direct BOB reports or testimony on these bills, nor did the BOB volunteer such inputs during the hearings. On the whole, the legislative clearance record reveals the operation of a piecemeal bureaucratic process which seeks to get along with this key Committee which historically was very responsive to its particular pressure groups and typically had its way under both Republican and Democratic administrations.

In 1952 or 1953 I had proposed a significant new idea to my new unit head in the Labor and Welfare Division: that a sliding income scale be substituted for the "all or nothing" income limits for determining eligibility for nonservice-connected pensions for veterans starting with the World War I group. Under the sliding or graduated income scale, the VA pensions would have been inversely related to the amount of other income to provide a more effective test of need. This sensible solution was dismissed out-of-hand with the observation that the idea had been discussed before with the Veterans Affairs Committee and was not politically feasible. This idea remained one of my major objectives for the reform of veterans pensions but the ongoing process had provided no opportunity for its use.

The Congress Passes Two Veterans Bills[38]

The definitive Congressional action on veterans compensation and pensions which first crystallized out of the foregoing hearings was a new "clean" bill, H.R. 9020, in the 2nd session of the 83rd Congress. As introduced on May 5, 1954, and quickly reported on May 28, 1954, to the House, this bill provided general increases of 10 percent in both compensation and pensions, with some rates of limited applicability increased as much as 25 percent. The cost for the first year would have been $290 million. The VA report (included in H. Report 1685) stated that the BOB advised that the bill "was not in accord" with the President's program. This led to extensive White House-Congressional leadership discussions.[39] Of these I had only limited knowledge.

As a result of the Executive Branch remonstrances, H.R. 9020 was revised in the House to drop the increases in nonservice-connected pensions and to provide a general 5 percent increase in service-connected compensation, but with catch-up increases of 25 percent for dependent parents. The first year cost was estimated at $110 million for 2.34 million disabled veterans and dependents.

The revised H.R. 9020 was reported to the floor by the House Veterans Affairs Committee on May 28, 1954. It passed the House 399-0, with one member voting "present," on July 21, 1954. The Senate Finance Committee reported the bill on July 27, 1954. The hurry-up VA report of July 21, 1954, in the Senate Committee report on the revised bill stated that the BOB recommended against its favorable consideration by the Committee. The Senate passed the bill on August 11, 1954, without objection under suspension of the rules.[40]

While H.R. 9020 providing the revised compensation increases was making easy progress in the House, H.R. 9962 to provide pension increases was introduced in July 20, 1954, and reported by the House Committee on Veterans Affairs on July 28, 1954. It provided a 5 percent general increase in pension rates at a cost of $36 million the first year for 944,000 veterans and dependents. H.R. 9962 passed the House on August 4, 1954, by a margin of 399-0, with one member voting "present."

The VA's hurry-up report to the Senate Finance Committee of July 21, 1954, stated that the BOB recommended against favorable consideration of H.R. 9962—a rather weak position. Neither my records nor my memory serve to clarify whether I was involved in this clearance or was on vacation. This bill was also speedily reported by the Senate Finance Committee on August 6, 1954 (S. Rept. 2313), which adopted the earlier House report for the body of its own report.[41] It passed the Senate on August 12, 1954, without objection. However, in the House consideration of H.R. 9962, probably as a consequence of the White House discussions, Congressman Halleck on July 21, 1954, mentioned the need for a complete reappraisal and survey of the whole system and arrangement of payments to veterans.[42]

The BOB Establishes Its Position on the Enrolled Bills

The Congress had enacted two veterans bills costing $136 million for the first year which were not well-justified, but represented carefully calibrated political judgments on the Hill as to how much the Executive Branch would "buy." The bills represented the sort of piecemeal creep in uncontrollable programs which builds big budgets and creates anomalies in benefit programs over the years.

The action on these two enrolled bills was now in the Executive Branch's court. There the BOB had the first play through its legislative clearance process. In the BOB the Office of Legislative Reference assigned enrolled bills H.R. 9020 and H.R. 9962 to the Labor and Welfare Division whose chief was William D. Carey, one of the BOB's top career hands. In the Division it was routed to the unit handling veterans and social security programs, which then was headed by Lawrence Wendrich, a recent BOB arrival with congressional staff experience. As the program analyst in that unit, I received the files to do the paper work within the customary 5-day deadline for BOB action.

The Congress had passed both bills for 5 percent increases in benefits on a cost-of-living rationale, even though the consumer price index had only risen 1.9 percent since the previous round of increases in May 1952 for practically all pension and compensation rates.

The VA recommended that, in view of the circumstances involved in its enactment, H.R. 9020 be approved to grant the compensation increases. The cost of those increases would rise in future years to a peak of about 30 percent over the first year's cost.

The VA also indicated that it was unable to distinguish between the pension and compensation programs insofar as the effect of cost-of-living increases was concerned and recommended that H.R. 9962 also be approved by the President. This position failed to take into account the distinctions previously enunciated in the Presidential Budget Messages.

I agreed with the VA view on the compensation increases because the BOB's position had been that the service connected disability and dependency cases should be treated generously, even if, in this case, the increase was more than 2 1/2 times the cost of living increase since the last adjustments.

However, with respect to the pension increases, given the President's position as stated in the 1955 Budget Message, I believed that H.R. 9962 should not be approved for the following reasons:[43]

1. Nonservice-connected pensions are a gratuity in partial support of needy veterans, unlike disability compensation which is designed to replace income lost due to disabilities in service. Moreover, there was no objective information in the hearings on the extent of unmet needs on the part of the nonservice-connected pensioners.

2. BOB estimates were that because of projected large increases in the pension roll, the initial $36 million cost of the pension increases would triple by 1975 and quadruple by 1985 to $180 million per year. Although this information had been provided in the White House meetings to the Congressional leadership and the House Veterans Affairs Committee, there was no evidence that the general membership of either chamber had been apprised of these facts.

3. The cost-of-living index had increased only 1.9 percent since the previous increase. Moreover, since 1939, pension rates for veterans under age 65 had increased 110 percent and 150 percent for those over 65—thereby outrunning the consumer price index increase of 94 percent.

4. The large problem of growing overlaps between VA pensions and social security had not been considered by the committees of the Congress in developing this pension bill. Instead they treated VA pensions as if they were the sole assistance program and the general Social Security and public assistance programs of HEW did not exist.

On the basis of this reasoning, and in the absence of my unit head, I concluded that I would incorporate the essence of these points into a "memorandum of disapproval" on H.R. 9962 to try "up the line." I was in the midst of this task when the Assistant Director for Legislative Reference accompanied by my Division Chief came into my office to find out where the paperwork stood on the two enrolled bills. When I stated that I was drafting a proposed disapproval memorandum, the Assistant Director, usually a man of suave and even demeanor, became explosively angry. This shook me deeply, because this was a key official in my BOB world and a long-time supporter. His behavior was rather surprising because I had received the file only a day or two earlier and my BOB credibility was unusually high then because of recent yeoman work for the Director's office on termination of the Korean Conflict emergency and staff work relating to the President's Committee on Pension Policy for Federal Personnel. My Division Chief supported me by suggesting that I be given time to finish my work so they could both see what I would produce. I reasoned that the explosion may have occurred because commitments about approving the 5 percent pension increase might have been given in the White House discussions. Moreover, I knew that the Office of Legislative Reference was stretched thin under a flood of enrolled bills at the end of a Congress.

The memorandum to the President outlining my analysis and recommending the approval of the H.R. 9020 and the disapproval of H.R. 9962 along with a draft memorandum of disapproval went forward from the Division Office to the Office of Legislative Reference. The draft disapproval statement stated that the President was organizing "a thorough study. . .of the role of veterans pensions in our changing society and the relationship which they should bear to our general economic security programs." Congressman Halleck's earlier statement on the need for a study was mentioned in my supporting memorandum. After completion of the study by "the best and most impartial persons" which could be found, the President would review the situation relating to veterans benefits and make appropriate recommendations to the Congress.[44]

I do not know as I write this whether my staff product was revised by the Office of Legislation Reference or whether they perhaps wrote an alternate draft to go along with my disapproval draft. I had done my professional duty as I saw it and I had paid a certain price in an atmosphere of heavy pressure on the BOB under a flood of enrolled bills at the end of a Congress. The episode in my office was never mentioned to me subsequently by either of the other participants.

The President Acts

President Eisenhower issued a "signing statement" as he approved both bills, which became P.L. 695 and P.L. 698, 83rd Congress. He approved the compensation bill because it represented an attempt to compensate veterans for earning power loss attributable to injuries or death during service in our armed forces.

He approved the pension bill "solely for humanitarian purposes," but recognized that it perpetuated anomolies and inequities within the pension system itself and in relation to closely related government programs such as Social Security. He thereupon announced that he was ordering steps "to examine the entire structure, scope and philosophy of our veterans benefit laws in relation to each other and to other government programs."[45] (See Exhibit A for full statement).

The Presidential announcement of a full-dress study pleased me. There would be a sustained effort to sort out factually the tangle of veterans programs and laws which had grown up over many years of piecemeal legislation. Even more important, a mechanism was being created to set in motion countervailing forces to offset the one-sided pressure group process, at least for a time. There was hope for a more rational set of policies.

My records show that in the next several months I was deeply immersed in staff work relating to a Presidential Commission to study veterans benefits. The 1956 Budget Message by President Eisenhower (issued in January 1955) further elaborated on the need for the study. It also stated that he was going to appoint a Commission on Veterans Pensions to carry out the study. The budget included $300,000 for the work of the Commission in fiscal year 1956.[46]

Subsequent Outcomes

The following actions are beyond the scope of this paper, but significant results were achieved. General Omar N. Bradley was appointed Chairman of the Commission on March 5, 1955.[47] Immediate funding for the Commission during fiscal year 1955 was provided from special funds of the President. Major General (Ret.) E.M. ("Mike") Brannon was appointed Executive Director of the Commission. He soon sought me out and eventually obtained my loan from the BOB to serve as Technical Adviser to the Commission. In this capacity I planned and directed the day-to-day fact-finding and technical work of the research staff.

The Commission reported to the President and the Congress on April 23, 1956. Its main report contained 70 recommendations. This report was followed by 12 supporting staff reports.[48]

The Commission's recommendations regarding survivors' benefits helped lead to major improvements in the survivors' benefits system for military personnel and veterans.[49] Its findings that service-disabled veterans who had disabilities rated at 90 percent and 100 percent were undercompensated set a pattern in the Congress of increasing the rates for the 100 percenters which in time substantially increased their rates.

Most important of all, the Commission's recommendation for a graduated income scale system for veterans nonservice-connected pensions was embodied by the BOB and the VA in a legislative proposal enacted by the Congress in 1959.[50] This law adopted the Commission's concept that veterans with low incomes from other sources should receive the highest VA pension rates and that the pensions should be phased out step by step as other income was higher.[51] However, although the ongoing pension rates were not reduced in the short-run by the 1959 pension law, this law had the effect of firmly cementing the principle of pensions based on need into Congressional VA pension policy. As a consequence, neither the large World War I nor World War II groups of veterans have thus far been able to pressure through a service pension payable without regard to need for veterans without service disabilities, such as had been traditional for all other groups of veterans from the Revolutionary War through the Spanish American War. This has saved American taxpayers tens of billions of dollars.[52]

Even so, my goal of achieving adequate coordination between the growing Social Security benefits and VA nonservice connected pensions, to achieve reasonable consistency between Federal payments for such veterans and other Americans, has not been achieved. VA nonservice-connected pensions still provide large opportunities for legitimate budget economies because they are an extra layer of payments to veterans which is denied to non-veterans who have to live just on their Social Security pensions. Equitable coordination of U.S. pension programs still remains to be achieved.

Exhibit A

220 ¶ Statement by the President Upon Signing
Bills Increasing Payments to Veterans or Their
Dependents. *August 28, 1954*

I HAVE TODAY approved H.R. 9020 and H.R. 9962. Both of these Acts provide for an increase in payments to veterans or their dependents—in the one case, for service-connected disability or death compensation, and in the other for nonservice-connected disability pensions.

H.R. 9020 related to the rate of payments made to veterans or their dependents as a result of wounds, injuries, disabilities, or death incurred as the result of military service. It represents an attempt to compensate them for earning power whose loss is attributable to service in our armed forces. H.R. 9962, on the other hand, relates to the rate of pensions payable to veterans and to the dependents of veterans whose earning power was or is limited by reason of nonservice-connected disabilities; it is designed only to meet minimum economic need.

Since the time of the Revolutionary War, the American people have been determined to demonstrate their recognition of the sacrifices made by those who have served in our armed forces. I share this determination. I deeply believe in the principle of our disability compensation and pension laws. We must remember, too, the difference in the principles upon which these two systems are based. We must also remember their difference in purpose.

I have approved H.R. 9962 solely for humanitarian reasons, for I recognize that many of the individuals who will benefit from this increase are now living under circumstances of extreme hardship. Statistics also show, however, that many will receive this increase who need no additional assistance. In this respect H.R. 9962 is inconsistent with the principles of our pension system and tends to perpetuate inequities and anomalies which have risen not only within the pension system itself but also in its relation to closely related government programs.

Although additional benefits have been granted from time to time, our basic veteran laws have not changed materially in the last thirty years. We must also recognize the fact that, because of the inauguration and growth of closely related—and uncorrelated—Federal programs designed to provide assurances against want to all of our citizens, there are today many instances of uneven and inequitable benefits. Under the present system, for example, there are no means of taking into account the degree of a veteran's need—no relation between payments received under the veteran pension laws and payments received, for example, under our Old Age and Survivors Insurance system.

It is essential, therefore, that steps be taken to examine the entire structure, scope and philosophy of our veterans benefit laws in relation to each other and to other government programs. I am ordering such a study. On the basis of this study I shall recommend to the Congress such legislative action as will correlate our many programs and thus strengthen them. Such action will inevitably be in the interest not only of our 21 million veterans and their families, but of all 162 million Americans. In this endeavor, I am confident that this Administration will have the full support of all veterans and their organizations.

I should like it also understood that the Administration will continue to watch closely changes in economic conditions and, when warranted by reason of such changes, will seek appropriate adjustments in compensation and pension laws.

NOTE: As enacted, H.R. 9020 and H.R. 9962 are Public Laws 695 and 698, 83d Congress (68 Stat. 915, 961). The statement was released at Lowry Air Force Base, Denver, Colo.

Footnotes

1. Percival F. Brundage, *The Bureau of the Budget* (New York: Praeger Publishers, 1970), pp. 272 ff., laws and Executive Orders creating the BOB.

2. President's Committee on Administrative Management, *Report with Special Studies* (Washington, D.C.: Government Printing Office, 1937); Fritz Morstein Marx, ed., *Elements of Public Administration* (New York, Prentice-Hall Inc., 1946), pp. 22-25, and Fritz Morstein Marx, *The President. and His Staff Services* (Public Administrative Service, Publication No. 98, 1947). The PAS booklet deals with the linkage between the BOB and the World War II Office of Emergency Management. The Bureau of the Budget "Staff Orientation Manual" first issued in 1945 and revised in 1951, 1953, and 1958, contained considerable information on the original mission and the development of the BOB.

3. *The Budget of the United States Government for the Fiscal Year Ending June 30, 1956* (Washington, D.C.: Government Printing Office, 1955), p. 51 and *Appendix* pp. 20-21. There also might have been a few non-career subordinate "confidential" employees, but their policy role was not noticeable at the career staff level. The key point is that in the BOB the "office" and "division" chiefs were career professionals—but this does not mean that they were insensitive to the political climate.

Many personnel in the 1940s and 1950s had academic political science or public administration backgrounds and were well acquainted with survival in a milieu of pressure group politics.

4. *Ibid.*, p. 51.

5. *Ibid.*, pp. 19-24 of Appendix.

6. Charles G. Dawes, *The First Year of the Budget of the United States* (New York, Harper and Brothers, 1923).

7. Percival F. Brundage, *op. cit.*, p. 34.

8. Executive Office of the President, Bureau of the Budget, "Staff Orientation Manual," May 12, 1953, p. 45.

9. Regarding the statutory basis see testimony of F.J. Bailey, the first chief of the Division of Legislative Reference, in Hearings on *Investigation of Civilian Employment*, U.S. Congress, House of Representatives, Committee on the Civil Service, 78th Congress, 1st Session, Part 2, April 14-June 3, 1943, pp. 361-363. For further detail on early history see Richard E. Neustadt, "Presidency and Legislation: The Growth of Central Clearance," *The American Political Science Review*, Vol. XLVIII, No. 3 (September 1954), pp. 641-671.

10. BOB "Staff Orientation Manual," *op. cit.*, p. 26.

11. U.S. Congress, House of Representatives, House Select Committee of Lobbying Activities, *Legislative Activities of Executive Agencies*, Hearings, Part 10, 81st Congress, 2nd Session, March 30, May 5, July 26 and 28, 1950, pp. 3-6. Also U.S. Congress, House of Representatives, Committee on Agriculture, *Legislative Policy of the Bureau of the Budget,* Hearings before the Subcommittee on Conservation and Credit, 86th Congress, 2nd Session, July 11, 1966, pp. 2ff.

12. For example see Katherine Hammill, "This is a Bureaucrat," *Fortune*, Vol. 48, pp. 156 ff (November, 1953) which describes the outstanding achievements of a highly respected BOB head of Legislative Reference, Roger W. Jones. See also Richard E. Neustadt, "Presidency and Legislation: Planning the President's Program" *The American Political Science Review*, Vol. XLIX, No. 4, (December, 1955), pp. 988-1021, a knowledgeable piece describing the processes used in developing, or putting together, the legislative programs of Presidents Roosevelt, Truman, and Eisenhower. Neither of these pieces evaluates the substantive quality of the legislative programs, no matter how interesting the performances were.

13. See sources in footnote 9.

14. Richard E. Neustadt, in the two articles cited above.

15. Both the items in footnote 12 relate to this performance by the BOB.

16. V.O. Key, Jr., *Politics, Parties, and Pressure Groups* (New York: Thomas Y. Crowell Company, fifth edition, 1964), p. 106.

17. "Veterans," *Encylopedia of the Social Sciences* (New York: The MacMillan Company, 1934), vol. 15, pp. 243-247. See also William Pyrle Dillingham, *Federal Aid to Veterans*, 1917-1941, Gainesville, Florida, 1952.

18. *The World Almanac,* 1968 (New York: Newspaper Enterprise Association, Inc., 1967), pp. 33, 639 ff.

19. See V.O. Key, pp. 106-111. Key's figure of 3 million GAR members contrasts with other estimates of 2.2 million union soldiers participating in the conflict.

20. President's Commission on Veterans' Pensions, *Veterans' Benefits Administered by Departments and Agencies of the Federal Government, Digests of Laws and Basic Statistics*, Staff Report No. II, 84th Congress, 2nd Session, House Veterans Committee Print No. 262, June 26, 1956, p. 194.

21. William H. Glasson, *Federal Military Pensions in the United States* (New York: Oxford University Press, 1968); Gustavus A. Weber and Lawrence F. Schmeckebier, *The Veterans' Administration* (Washington, D.C.: The Brookings Institution, 1934); William Pyrle Dillingham, see footnote 17.

22. See for instance the successive documents entitled "Compensation and Pension to Veterans or Their Dependents—Analysis of Elements of Entitlement to and Rates of Compensation and Pension," e.g., House Veterans Committee Print No. 173, 82nd Congress, 2nd Session, August 1, 1952.

23. President's Commission on Veterans' Pensions. *The Historical Development of Veterans' Benefits in the United States*, Staff Report No. I, 84th Congress, 2nd Session, House Veterans' Committee Print No. 244, May 9, 1956, pp. 94-99.

24. *Ibid.*, pp. 99-105.

25. President's Commission on Veterans' Pensions, *Veterans' Benefits in the United States*, A Report to the President, 84th Congress, 2nd Session, House Veterans' Committee Print No. 235, April 23, 1956, pp. 112 ff. (The figures are in current dollars not constant dollars, but the comparisons are nevertheless startling.)

26. *The Budget of the United States Government for the Fiscal Year 1948*, p. M23.

27. *The Budget of the United States Government for the Fiscal Year 1949*, p. M21.

28. *The Budget of the United States Government for the Fiscal Year 1950*, pp. M27-28.

29. *The Budget of the United States Government for the Fiscal Year 1951*, pp. M35-M36.

30. *The Budget of the United States Government for the Fiscal Year 1952*, p. M57.

31. *The Budget of the United States Government for the Fiscal Year 1953*, pp. M67-M68.

32. *The Budget of the United States Government for the Fiscal Year 1954*, p. M48.

33. *The Budget of the United States Government for the Fiscal Year 1955*, pp. M50-M51.

34. See pieces by Hammill and Neustadt cited earlier.

35. For statements by Presidents Coolidge, Hoover, and F.D. Roosevelt see President's Commission on Veterans' Pensions, *Veterans' Non-Service-Connected Pensions*, Staff Report No. X, 84th Congress, 2nd Session, House Veterans' Committee Print No. 288, August 27, 1956, pp. 55-61.

36. U.S. Congress, House of Representatives, Committee on Veterans' Affairs, Subcommittee on Compensation and Pension, Hearings on *Bills Providing Benefits for Service-Connected Disabled Veterans and Their Dependents*, 83rd Congress, 1st Session, March 31, April 15 and 21, 1953, pp. 771-871.

37. U.S. Congress, House of Representatives, Committee on Veterans' Affairs, Subcommittee on Compensation and Pensions, Hearings on *Compensation and Pension Bills for Veterans and Their Dependents*, 83rd Congress, 2nd Session, March 31, April 1, 2 and 6, 1954, pp. 4499-4813.

38. For the legislative history of H.R. 9020 and H.R. 9962, 83rd Congress see *Congressional Record*, 83rd Congress, 2nd Session, December 2, 1954, p. D767 (Vol. 100, Part 14, Daily Digest).

39. My file memoranda of August 4, 1954 and August 20, 1954 relating to these bills.

40. House Report 1685, 83rd Congress, 2nd Session, July 21, 1954. Senate Report 1986, July 27, 1954. See *Congressional Record*, July 21, 1954, p. 11250 for revised 5 percent pension bill.

41. House Report 2560, 83rd Congress, 2nd Session, July 28, 1954. Senate Report 2313, August 6, 1954 (includes VA report).

42. *Congressional Record*, July 21, 1954, p. 11265.

43. Based on my draft file memorandum of August 20, 1954.

44. My file draft of disapproval statement accompanying my memorandum of August 20, 1954.

45. Dwight D. Eisenhower, *Public Papers of the Presidents of the United States*. (Washington, D.C.: U.S. Government Printing Office, 1954), No. 220, pp. 770-772.

46. *Ibid.*, Dwight D. Eisenhower, 1955, No. 17, p. 134.

47. *Ibid.*, Dwight D. Eisenhower, 1955, No. 51, pp. 320-322.

48. President's Commission on Veterans Pensions, *Veterans' Benefits in the United States*, A Report to the President, 84th Congress, 2nd Session, House Veterans' Committee Print No. 235, April 23, 1956. The 12 Staff Reports were issued in House Committee Prints Nos. 244, 262, 246, 261, 243, 260, 247, 281, 275, 286, 289, 291, 270, 288, 259, and 292 (some in several parts).

49. Public Law 84-881, Servicemen's and Veterans' Survivor Benefits Act, 84th Congress, 2nd Session, August 1, 1956.

50. Public Law 86-211, Veterans' Pension Act of 1959, 86th Congress, 1st Session, August 29, 1957.

51. For an analysis of the results of the action by Congress see Michael S. March, *Veterans' Benefits and General Social Welfare Benefits: A Study in Program Relationships*, Cambridge, Mass.: Harvard University, 1962 (an unpublished Ph.D. dissertation available from the Harvard Library), pp. 267-290.

52. For the budgetary consequences of a VA "service" pension for World War I and II veterans see the main report of the President's Commission on Veterans' Pensions, pp. 107-117.

Editorial Note: John D. Young writes about program and administrative policy related to one of the most dramatic government-private sector programs in U.S. history, the space program which put men on the moon and brought them back. The major challenge was how to integrate the previously ongoing programs of the National Advisory Committee for Aeronautics, the Operations Division of the Army Ballistic Missile Agency, and the Jet Propulsion Laboratory into a coordinated effort under the new National Aeronautics and Space Administration (NASA). Young cites six elements that contributed to NASA's success: continuity of leadership and concepts, evolving coherent roles for the members of general management, the muting of certain centrifugal forces, maintaining in-house technical capabilities joined to an effective procurement process, evolving concepts of program and project management, and changing things that did not work. Young believes that the two most important of the above factors were: the continuity of leadership and the maintenance of technical in-house capabilities necessary to effectively contract out most work to the private sector. Young later moved to the Department of Health, Education, and Welfare as Assistant Secretary, Comptroller, and compares the settings, concluding that the program and management policies that worked at NASA are, in most cases, not relevant to the management of most social programs.

CHAPTER 2

ORGANIZING THE NATION'S CIVILIAN SPACE CAPABILITIES: SELECTED REFLECTIONS

John D. Young

This chapter covers selected reflections on the organization and management of the National Aeronautics and Space Administration (NASA) during its formative years. The period covered runs from NASA's inception on October 1, 1958, through October 7, 1968, the date James E. Webb resigned as NASA's second Administrator. These reflections are based on the author's role with McKinsey and Company, a management consulting firm retained by NASA's first Administrator, Dr. T. Keith Glennan, to conduct several major organization and management studies of NASA in its formative years and the author's role as a member of the NASA staff from 1960 through 1965. In the latter role, the author served as Director of Management Analysis, Deputy Director of Administration and as Director of Administration.

Part I covers major historical and environmental forces and factors that influenced what NASA came to be. Part II covers the critical elements contributing to NASA's development of effective organizational and managerial arrangements. Part III will summarize the first two parts and make some overall judgements on the applicability of NASA's experience to other large scale public endeavors.

Part I

Historical and Environmental Factors

Historical Background[1]

The National Aeronautics and Space Administration was born out of fear, chagrin, and a perceived loss of national prestige. When the Russians orbited Sputnik I, the world's first artificial satellite, on October 4, 1957, the American public's perception of being number one in technology was shattered. Less than a month after Sputnik I, the Russians launched Sputnik II with a dog as a passenger. On December 6, 1957, this nation's first effort to launch an artificial satellite, Vanguard, blew up on the pad and fell over the blockhouse in a fiery cloud of flame and smoke. However, on January 31, 1958, America orbited its first satellite, Explorer. Its payload weighed 14 kilograms compared with Sputnik II's 500 kilograms. Explorer had been successfully launched by a combination of the Army Ballistics Missile Agency team headed by Dr. Wernher Von Braun and the Jet Propulsion Laboratory managed by the California Institute of Technology for the Army, and headed by Dr. William H. Pickering. Both of these groups were to become key building blocks in the National Aeronautics and Space Administration.

While these events were unfolding, a political consensus was growing in Washington that the country needed a vigorous space program. Competition had also been forming as to who would run the program. The major contenders were the Department of Defense and its three services, the National Advisory Committee for Aeronautics (NACA), a little known public agency, and to a lesser degree the Atomic Energy Commission. How this issue was resolved is an intriguing story in itself. However, this story is not critical to this particular set of reflections on the organization and management of NASA. The final decision was to create a new independent agency with a single administrator to be known as the National Aeronautics and Space Administration. NASA came into being on October 1, 1958. Three aspects of the creation of NASA are significant in terms of what later followed in the organization and management of the new space agency: the use of NACA as the initial building block; the broad, uncluttered responsibilities and authorities given NASA; and the enabling legislation's provision for relatively easy transfer to the new agency of space and aeronautical activities of other departments and agencies. A brief word or two on each of these should suffice to clarify for the reader what comes later.

The National Advisory Committee for Aeronautics was created on March 3, 1915, when President Woodrow Wilson signed into law a Navy appropriations bill with a rider setting up an independent Advisory Committee for Aeronautics. This committee had a unique structure. It was made up of twelve Presidentially appointed members, serving without pay. These were drawn from the military and scientific sides of the Federal Government and from the nation's scientific community. The Committee was charged with supervising and directing the scientific study of the problems of flight with a view to their practical solution. This the NACA did wisely and carefully. By the time of the creation of NASA, NACA had built up an internationally known reputation in aeronautical research and its practical applications. From the 1950s on, NACA had given more and more attention to missile research, while still not neglecting aeronautical research. NACA professionals contributed significantly to such advances as ablation as a means of controlling the intense heat generated by warheads and other bodies reentering the earth's atmosphere as well as such advances as the blunt-body shape as an effective design for bodies reentering the atmosphere.

In the process of conducting both space and aeronautical research, NACA had slowly and carefully built up research and test facilities at Langley Research Center and Wallops Flight Center, both in Virginia, Lewis Research Center at Cleveland Airport, Ames Research Center at Moffett Field in California, and the Flight Research Center at Edwards Air Force Base in California. At the inception of NASA on October 1, 1958, NACA became the initial nucleus of NASA with the 8,000 people, the above listed research and flight facilities worth $300 million, and an annual budget of $100 million.

The second major aspect of NASA's creation was the broad, uncluttered responsibilities and authorities NASA was given in the National Aeronautics and Space Act of 1958 (P.L. 85-568). This Act was signed by President Eisenhower on July 29, 1958—less than ten months after the launch of Sputnik I by the Russians on October 4, 1957. Key features of the Act in terms of their subsequent influence on the organization and management of NASA are:

1. A single agency head, an Administrator, reporting directly to the President of the United States—no multiple leadership such as the Atomic Energy Committee. The agency head was to be appointed by the President and confirmed by the Senate.[2]

2. Only one other political officer in addition to the Administrator—a deputy appointed in the same manner as the Administrator. This limitation on political appointees freed the two political heads of the new agency from significant problems of political maneuvering and patronage at the lower levels of NASA.

3. Only three broad responsibilities: to "plan, direct and conduct aeronautical and space activities;" to involve the scientific community in these activities, and to widely disseminate knowledge and information concerning aeronautical and space activities.

4. A wide variety of administrative and management authorities, such as making rules, hiring employees, acquiring property. From an organizational and managerial perspective, the most significant of these powers was the one giving the NASA Administrator authority to hire up to 260 persons at rates up to $19,000 ($21,000 in ten positions) without regard to the Classification Act of 1949. This flexibility became critical in terms of quickly staffing top positions. The Administrator was also authorized to hire new scientists and engineers at two grades above

those provided for by the General Schedule of the Classification Act of 1949.

In addition to these broad uncluttered responsibilities and authorities, the Space Act provided a relatively easy way to build up to the capabilities of the new agency by transferring space and aeronautical activities from other agencies without creating major political hassles. Two temporary sections of the Space Act gave the President a four year grant of power to transfer to NASA space-related functions of other agencies. If done before January 1, 1959, Congress only had to be informed. Subsequent transfers would be subject to a 60-day Congressional veto period. The Act also provided ninety days for the transition from NACA to NASA after the Act became law on July 29, 1958.

Thus by the actions taken prior to the inception of NASA on October 1, 1958, we find a situation where the new agency is provided with:

1. A strong nucleus of federal government in-house research and engineering capabilities in the form of the NACA nucleus.

2. A strong inheritance of effective noncompetitive working relationships with other federal departments and agencies, particularly the the Department of Defense and with private industry and, to some lesser degree, with the nation's universities.

3. A single head, the Administrator, reporting directly to the president with no necessity to negotiate the appointment of additional political officers except the Deputy Administrator.

4. Broad and uncluttered responsibilities with substantial leeway in their interpretation and implementation.

5. Broad authorities of an administrative nature, particularly in the personnel selection and appointment area.

6. Authority to easily move space and aeronautical activities from other departments and agencies to the new agency.

Major Environmental Factors

A most important area needing study for the large-scale endeavor relates to the role of the environment. Our thinking about large public and corporate enterprises is generally in terms of a structural entity. Managment doctrine, even of the most recent vintage, has to do largely with what should and should not be done within an organization. Attention is given to interaction between an organization and the outside world, but usually only in the sense that these impact—help, hinder, or complicate—the organization and the job it is trying to do. . . . The environmental is not something apart from the endeavor; it is not just something in which the endeavor operates and which it needs to adjust; it is an integral part of the endeavor itself. . . . The total job (managerial job) encompasses external as well as internal elements, and success is as dependent on effectiveness in the one as in the other.[3]

It was this conceptual framework, articulated mostly by James E. Webb, NASA's second Administrator, that brings into focus several elements of the NASA environment that played substantial interrelated and interacting roles in NASA's organization and management. Several environmental forces and factors affected NASA management.

1. The space environment is completely unrelenting in its treatment of the smallest human error. This had also been much the same in the aeronautical medium in which most of the NASA personnel had operated in the predecessor agencies. All the various pieces of technology employed in space research and development had to fit into each other down to the smallest detail. The medium of space and the technologies were no respectors of the foibles of human beings in their efforts to develop and run effectively complex organizations. This environmental imperative was ever present in the organization and management of NASA. The space environment and the technologies required to operate effectively in it were constant constraints on organizational and managerial arrangements that compromised one or both.

2. Another major environment force affecting the organization and management of NASA was the national and international scope of the program. NASA was given from the start two overarching goals

    (a) First, NASA was to explore space to increase man's scientific knowledge and to place in effect useful space applications, while simultaneously maintaining a preeminence in aeronautical research and applications. This required continual attention to both organizational and management processes (for example, resource allocation processes) that ensured that aeronautical research did not receive short rations in the effort to quickly build up the nation's space capabilities.

(b) Secondly, and equally important, the United States sought to regain its prestige as the world leader in science and technology. The myth of science for science's sake did not fit this goal. NASA was an instrument of national policy and posture. This meant that much of the time NASA's general management had to cope with the many facets presented by this particular overarching goal. It also meant specific internal organizational arrangements to support NASA leadership, the President, and other national leaders in implementing this role. Initially, in 1958, this was an Assistant to the Administrator for International Activities. By 1961 a full-fledged Office of International Programs had evolved.

3.   A third major environmental force shaping NASA's formative period was the Presidential nature of several of NASA's key objectives. From October 1958 through the November 1960 elections, NASA had Presidential support, but not Presidential objectives per se. It was with President Kennedy's May 25, 1961, address to a joint session of Congress that certain of NASA's objectives got tied to Presidential objectives—and likewise to Presidential politics. President Kennedy's recommendations to the Congress followed Soviet Cosmonaut Yuri Gagarin's orbit of the earth on April 12, 1961. Man was now in space. The administration's response was to land a man on the moon and return in the decade of the 1960s. Few remember that James E. Webb, NASA's second administrator, sold President Kennedy (with a major role by Vice-President Lyndon Johnson) on much more than just a lunar landing and return. The President's recommended program was aimed at advancing space research and development on a broad front with a new family of large boosters, communications and meterological satellites, scientific satellites, and exploration of the planets. Thus a vast program of work was conceived, supported and gotten underway that would set NASA's objectives for the next eight to ten years. All of these undertakings have long lead times and are very difficult to stop short of their becoming out and out failures.

4. The environmental factors discussed here created the necessity of carrying out the program in an open manner and mainly by civilians. This meant that extensive and ever-changing methods had to be developed to continually interpret what was going on and why. It will be recalled that NASA was given only three broad functions in the Space Act. Two of those gave NASA little choice but to operate in an open manner. NASA was to arrange for the participation of the scientific community in the conduct of aeronautical and space activities and to disseminate widely the information about it's aeronautical and space activities.

Thus it was that these four environmental factors shaped in major ways the organization and management of NASA. As Jim Webb pointed out:

> The environment is not something apart from the endeavor; it is not just something in which the endeavor operates and which it needs to adjust; it is an integral part of the endeavor itself.

No truer words were ever said when it came to describe the interlocking of a public agency and its environment. It was these factors, in the main, on which NASA developed, following President Kennedy's May 25, 1961, basic policy assumptions recommended to Congress to guide achievement of the accelerated civilian space program. Some of the most significant of these basic policy assumptions were:[4]

1. *Total utilization of NASA resources.* This meant that assignments to the various research and development centers that had been transferred to NASA from other departments and agencies must be effectively coordinated. This required specific policies and procedures to do just that. These were not to come easily.

2. *Primary reliance on industry in combination with competent in-house technical supervision.* This meant heavy reliance on the nation's industrial capacity, and in many cases creating industrial capability and capacity where it did not exist. For example, the welding of large aluminum fuel tanks for the new line of boosters required to go to the moon and return necessitated increased capacity.

3. *Marked increase in the interest and involvement of the world scientific community and in particular American universities' research capability to bear on NASA programs and problems.*

4. *Maximum coordination with the Department of Defense, particularly*

in the use of costly and unique facilities and capabilities. This had to be done while simultaneously trying to demonstrate to the world the mainly peaceful nature of the U.S. space exploration program.

5. *Continued attention to aeronautical research to support both military and civilian needs.*

6. *Continuation of the multipurpose nature of most of NASA's inherited research and development centers.* This policy was tied to another policy of making maximum use of NASA's available resources. But it was also tied to the idea of minimum disruption of ongoing organizations and their work. The objectives and the externally dictated pressure for timely achievement would not allow such a luxury. However, leaving the multipurpose centers pretty much as they were transferred to NASA was partially the cause for some of the difficulties in working out headquarters-center relationships which will be discussed later. The centers that NASA inherited handled a combination of two or more of the following functions: suppporting research, advanced technology, space flight projects, systems and subsystems development, and technical and managerial support. This policy meant that these arrangements were to be continued.

In concluding this first part of this chapter, it is fair to say that the framework for NASA's organization and management was determined by:

1. The historical inheritance such as the NACA nucleus of in-house research and engineering capabilities.

2. Enabling legislation in the Space Act that gave focus for the agency's endeavors, but with flexibility to pursue those endeavors in light of changing environmental conditions and other circumstances.

3. Environmental factors that required NASA continually to be part and parcel of the environment, both influenced by the environment and, in turn, influencing that same environment.

With this multifaceted framework in mind, we will turn in Part II to a discussion of specific aspects of NASA organization and management that in one way or another contributed significantly to NASA's success.

Part II

Some Key Elements of Organizational and Managerial Effectiveness

The specific elements of NASA's organizational and managerial arrangements that contributed to NASA's effectiveness are:

- Continuity of leadership and concepts
- Evolving and coherent roles for the members of general management
- The muting of certain centrifugal forces
- Maintaining in-house technical capabilities joined to an effective procurement process
- Evolving concepts of program and project management
- Changing things that did not work

Continuity of Leadership and Concepts

One of the major causes for inefficient and ineffective management of many Federal departments and agencies is the lack of continuity in top management. New leaders hardly get a feel for the key elements of the job before they are replaced by another set of political officers. Each leaves his or her own management concepts and approaches in various parts of the nervous system of the organization, these only to be superseded or banished by the next wave of new political management. In a large department such as the Department of Health and Human Services (HHS), turnover of special assistants and assistant secretarys is significant. For example, in HHS these changes are occurring more frequently than every two years. This is a disaster for efficient and effective management of these large complex enterprises.

NASA was not to suffer the same fate in its formative years. From October 1, 1958, through October 7, 1968, NASA was to have only two administrators: Dr. T. Keith Glennan from October 1, 1958, through January 20, 1961 (about twenty-eight months), and James E. Webb from February 14, 1961, through October 7, 1968 (approximately seven years).

Besides the continuity of NASA's leadership over time, there were two other fortuitous circumstances:

- the backgrounds and experiences of NASA's first two Administrators, and
- the continuity in major organizational and managerial concepts from the Glennan initial period through the transition to James E. Webb's tenure as Administrator.

Both Dr. T. Keith Glennan and James E. Webb had backgrounds and experiences that fitted them ideally to the times they served and the roles they played as Administrators. T. Keith Glennan had been President of Cleveland's Case Institute of Technology since 1947. He had made Case into one of the top engineering schools in the nation, held an electrical engineering degree from Yale, and had spent most of his pre-World War II career in the motion picture industry where he specialized in sound systems. During World War II he had a stint of public service as Head of the Navy's Underwater Sound Laboratories. From 1950 to 1952 he was a member of the Atomic Energy Commission. He was a member of various Federal scientific and engineering advisory groups as well as a member of various corporate boards of directors such as Standard Oil of Ohio. In summary, he understood the environments, problems, and capabilities of universities, Federal research and engineering organizations, and the private sector—all of major significance in the role as NASA's first Administrator.

James E. Webb, NASA's second Administrator, like Glennan, had an extensive background in both public and private life. He had a degree in education from the University of North Carolina and a law degree from George Washington University and was a member of the bar. From 1936 to 1943 he worked in several managerial capacities for the Sperry-Gyroscope Company. During World War II he served as a Major in Marine Corps aviation. From 1946 to 1949 he was Director of the U.S. Bureau of the Budget. From 1949 to 1952 he was Undersecretary of State. He had several private top managerial positions from 1952 through his appointment as NASA's second Administrator, including director and officer of Kerr-McGee Oil Industries, Inc., and director of McDonnell Aircraft Corp. He had wide-ranging and in-depth interest in public policy and managerial issues as evidenced by his active participation in a number of professional organizations such as the American Society for Public Administration, American Political Science Association, and the Society for the Advancement of Management. James Webb even to a greater degree than Glennan understood the environments, problems, and capabilities of universities, Federal departments and agencies, and the private sector. However, he did not have Glennan's experience in research and engineering. As a result, he was careful not to delve into the technical aspects of NASA's work to the extent that Glennan did.

A second fortuitous circumstance for NASA's formative years was a relative smooth transition from Glennan to Webb. There was no abrupt discontinuity between one Administrator and the next in terms of basic concepts and approaches. This occurred for several reasons. Principal among these was the continuity provided by Dr. Hugh L. Dryden, the Deputy Administrator, and without question the most respected member of NASA's professional staff. President Kennedy had not accepted Dr. Dryden's resignation. He became Acting Administrator during Glennan's leaving and Webb's succession as Administrator. Webb asked Dryden to stay on. He agreed. In addition, Webb asked Dr. Robert Seamans, who had been Associate Administrator (NASA's general manager for day-to-day operations) since September 1, 1960, to stay on in that position. In other words there was *no* staff turnover.

This is not to say that Webb did not begin to put his own indelible imprint on NASA's organizational and managerial arrangements. He did, particularly with the advent of the accelerated space program in May 1961. However, he started from the rather well articulated set of managerial arrangements that Glennan had put in place during NASA's first two years. A major example is the policy of expanding the use of university and private sector resources, at the same time maintaining sufficient in-house technical capabilities. These capabilities were critical to the effective developing of specifications and in supervising the execution of projects in industry. This capability was to be maintained in an adequately equipped laboratory environment engaged in sufficient in-house research and development to render state-of-the-art assistance to NASA's project management teams.

Evolving and Coherent Roles for General Management

It is important to have political continuity of leadership in an evolving agency such as NASA, but in addition, it is critical that there evolve effective working relationships among the members of a department's or agency's general management. In this area also NASA was well served. The arrangement that evolved was one that many close observers of NASA's early days thought could never work. To understand this we need to first explain how the arrangement came into being, how it evolved, and why it probably succeeded.

When Dr. Glennan became the first Administrator of NASA, he insisted that he and the Deputy Administrator, Dr. Dryden, needed a third member in NASA's top management group, "a general manager." This had been in keeping with his earlier experience as a member of the Atomic Energy Commission. The Commission was a multiheaded organization that had a general manager as the operating head of the Commission. Glennan's idea was opposed by both Dr. Dryden and the key headquarters staff who saw the general manager as a layer between themselves and the Administrator-Deputy Administrator. However, Glennan persisted and a general manager position called the Associate Administrator was created. As things evolved, Dr. Glennan spent more and more of his time on external relationships with the White House, elements of the Executive Office of the President such as the

Bureau of the Budget, and with Congress. He still did not neglect the myriad of activities of internal management and organization required to get the new agency on a sound footing, such as a system for approving and managing NASA's ever-growing numbers of development projects. Dr. Dryden spent considerable amounts of his time in relationships with the science and engineering committees. The new Associate Administrator, NASA's general manager, began to concentrate on the management of day-to-day technical issues and problems and on making the evolving organizational and managerial arrangements work.

This was the situation when James Webb became Administrator in February of 1961. As previously stated, he continued both Dr. Dryden and Dr. Seamans as Deputy Administrator and Associate Administrator respectively. Webb took the then existing situation and markedly strengthened and added to the roles of the three members of NASA's top management. The arrangement came to be known as "The Trinity." What Jim Webb set out to do, he did, and it worked eminently successfully. It gave NASA a coherent top management system in its critical formative years. In Jim Webb's own words:

> The three of us decided together that the basis of our relationship should be an understanding that we would hammer out the hard decisions together and that each would undertake those segments of responsibility for which he was best qualified. In effect, we formed an informal partnership within which all major policies and programs became our joint responsibility, but with the execution of each policy and program undertaken by just one of us. This meant that everyone in and out of the agency knew all three of us would be involved in all major decisions; that with policy established, the orders for its execution could be issued by any one of us; and that, while NASA had an Administrator as a single point of final decision, to the fullest extent possible we would act together. . . . When one of us found the burden of his work too heavy the others stepped forward to share it. . . . This way the three of us could participate directly (without an intervening layer of management) to ensure a continuing evaluation of the performance and growth potential of our senior staff.

Webb was particularly successful in adapting these concepts of top management on all large contracts amounting to $5 million or more:

> We expected these boards (source evaluation boards) to appear before us personally in a formal setting and make a full and complete presentation of (1) the method chosen to break down for evaluation

the contractor proposals, (2) the results achieved in the application of this method, and (3) the judgement of the board on each of the categories of the breakdown. The effect of this systematic approach to a continuous emphasis on the judgement factor has been that for five years, on innumerable occasions and for extended periods, the three senior officials of NASA have sat side by side and personally examined in detail, and tested by question and answer, the quality of the individual and collective contributions of these boards to major decisions affecting the area where ninety percent of our resources are expended. . . . We believe this constant and visible personal contact among NASA's three senior officials and the other responsible personnel involved in the hard problems and decisions in procurement provided a great deal of stimulation, motivation and innovation throughout the organization.[5]

This approach to top management of a rapidly evolving agency worked for several reasons. Principal among these, in my judgement, were: (1) tremendous good will each had for the other two and what they were trying to do together; (2) a driving desire to make things work; (3) experienced maturity and judgement; and (4) the supplementary nature of their outlooks, values, and capabilities. This "trinity" of Webb, Dryden, and Seamans was indeed a fortuitous, synergistic happening as far as NASA was concerned, truly a situation where the total results were far greater than the sum of the parts.

The Muting of Certain Centrifugal Forces

Much of what has been discussed so far makes NASA look somewhat like a utopia of great opportunities wisely organized and managed. Needless to say, there were substantial problems that were not neatly handled and put to rest. A major set of these were problems in the period 1960-1963 of ensuring that critical elements of NASA, both in the headquarters and in the newly transferred research and development centers, did not become so strong that they would become obstacles to bringing all of NASA's resources to bear in planning and carrying out a rapidly expanding multifaceted program of space exploration while simultaneously maintaining emphasis on aeronautical research. In other words, in the early years of NASA, there were several internal forces at play that tended at any given time to pull the new agency apart, or at a minimum in different and conflicting directions.

1. The fact that NASA was basically constructed on building blocks transferred to NASA from other departments and agencies caused some difficulty. In late 1963 16,000 of NASA's 34,000 employees had been acquired in this manner. All of these building blocks were made up of highly

professional personnel with significant space projects and aeronautical research already underway. They came to NASA with their own program and project ideas and their own ways of how best to do what they were already doing. Two of these projects were headed by internationally known figures. The Operations Division of the Army Ballistic Missile Agency was headed by Dr. Wernher von Braun. It was belatedly transferred to NASA in 1960 after the conclusion of a missions and roles argument in the Department of Defense. The Wernher von Braun group comprised 4,300 employees with a history extending back to Germany and the V-2 rockets of World War II. The other group was the Jet Propulsion Laboratory managed by the California Institute of Technology and headed by Dr. William H. Pickering. This group was transferred to NASA in 1959 with 2,400 employees. It was the Wernher von Braun and William Pickering groups that had successfully orbited the first American satellite. These two groups along with the 8,000 National Advisory Committee for Aeronautics personnel comprised the initial nucleus of NASA. Almost all of these personnel were in research centers located throughout the United States.

2. A very limited heardquarters capability was another divisive factor. Initially central personnel was comprised of approximately 200 employees from NACA with a reputation of effectively managing the NACA centers by maintaining a light rein, appropriate to NACA's research and development mission. Thus NASA started with very strong field components, all with their own way of doing things, and a rather limited headquarters capability which in the ensuing years had to be increased almost ten-fold to around 3,000. This had to be built by bringing personnel from numerous places and backgrounds. Consequently the headquarters never, in the period we are talking about, approached the cohesiveness that any of the major research and development centers possessed. NASA started at the headquarters level with very limited capabilities in program and policy development and integrating capabilities available to NASA's general management.

3. A third force that had a centrifugal pull on effective organization and management of NASA was the great emphasis placed on the lunar landing in the decade of the 1960s after President Kennedy's May 25, 1960, announcement. It had a tendency to dominate organizational and managerial decisions and processes to the detriment of other programs and projects such as aeronautical research, space sciences, and applications (such as communications and meteorological satellites).

4. The fourth divisive factor was the very limited depth of NASA's general management group. It consisted of only two political officers, the Administrator and the Deputy Administrator. The third member was created by Glennan. This was the Associate Administrator and NASA's general manager of day-to-day operations. This was indeed a very limited managerial

group in number to maintain general control of a rapidly expanding program of Presidential and national significance.

5.   A final force was a tendency of certain of the headquarters program officers, due to personalities and experience, to subordinate NASA's general management concerns. These centrifugal forces were clearly evident during Dr. Glennan's two years in office as NASA's first Administrator. However, it was not until announcement of President Kennedy's accelerated program that they dominated organizational and managerial concerns and decision making.

In terms of the steps that were taken to contain these forces, there is wide disagreement among key participants and observers as to why they were taken, how effective they were, and why some of the major steps had to be changed. This writer is no exception. My views are clearly influenced by the fact that much of the underlying analyses of the problems and alternative solutions were either done by closely related associates such as the Director of the Office of Administration, Al Seipert, or in several cases by me and my associates in the Management Analysis Division. Be that as it may, here are the steps that were taken to cope with these centrifugal forces and my observations on them:

- Changing the headquarters-center reporting relationships through both a process of centralizing relationships and then later decentralizing these same relationships.

- Creating program integrating machinery at the level of the general manager.

- Developing and implementing NASA-wide ways of carrying out key management processes such as resource allocation and appointment of key personnel.

- Attempting to develop and implement a concept of functional management throughout NASA.

- Limiting the amount of functional staff in areas such as procurement and personnel management in the program offices versus the staffs responsible to general management.

All of these steps were purposefully thought out and decisions explicitly made on each by the three members of general management. Most observers and many of the participants had a tendency to focus on one or the other steps and failed to see the steps as the integrated management system which it was intended to be and was. I will now explain these steps in somewhat more detail including some of their shortcomings that necessitated further changes.

(1) The Headquarters-Center Relationships Problem

Headquarters-center reporting relationships became a most controversial area due to the fact that a major part of what was done in 1961 was changed in 1963. Initially all of the centers reported to individual program officers in headquarters. These organizational arrangements are depicted in Figure 2-1. In a major reorganization in November 1961 these reporting relationships were changed. All centers reported to NASA's general manager, the Associate Administrator (see Figure 2-2). This was done for the following reasons:

(a) In recognition that most of NASA's centers were multi-purpose centers. Although each had a primary orientation (for example, the Jet Propulsion Laboratory in interplanetary spacecraft), most had an across-the-board capability that was important to maintain in terms of the then internal health of the centers. It was also critical to use these other than primary capabilities in getting NASA's many projects completed even though the leadership on a given project might not be in that particular center.

(b) Provided opportunities for the center directors to have an increased voice in day-to-day policy making and program decisions.

(c) And frankly, but not all that clearly stated, this arrangement tried to ensure that the centers gained a NASA-wide perspective and were not captured as the sole provinces of a given headquarters program director. In other words, it was to strengthen the role, influence, and control of NASA's new and evolving general management over NASA's basic operating elements, the centers.

This arrangement left the centers with two bosses in headquarters, the general manager and one or more headquarters program officers for which they worked on specific projects.

Initially, most of the center directors supported the idea of reporting to NASA general management. However, as the program rapidly expanded, particularly the manned space flight program (the lunar landing), the dual reporting relationships became difficult to maintain. In addition, the workload on the general management had become excessive. In 1963 the earlier decision was reversed and the centers again reported to a given headquarters program office. The resulting arrangement is depicted in Figure 2-3. However, by 1963 the headquarters program offices had been realigned with clear focus on NASA's major programs: manned space flight, space sciences and applications and advanced research and technology. This to some degree simplified the

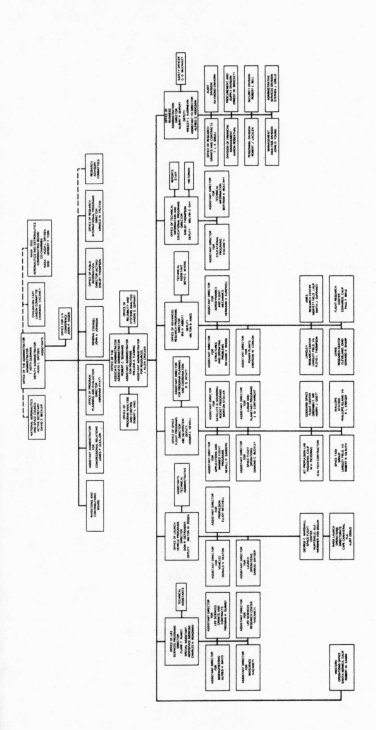

Figure 2-1. — NASA organization chart, 17 January 1961. (Source: Arnold S. Levine, *Managing NASA in the Apollo Era* (Washington D.C.: National Aeronautics and Space Administration, 1982) p. 32.

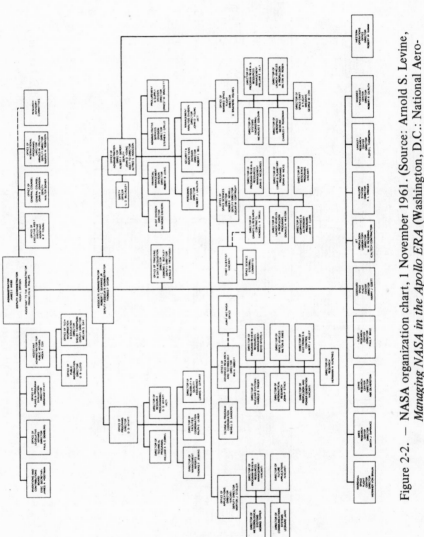

Figure 2-2. — NASA organization chart, 1 November 1961. (Source: Arnold S. Levine, *Managing NASA in the Apollo ERA* (Washington, D.C.: National Aeronautics and Space Administration, 1982), p. 37.

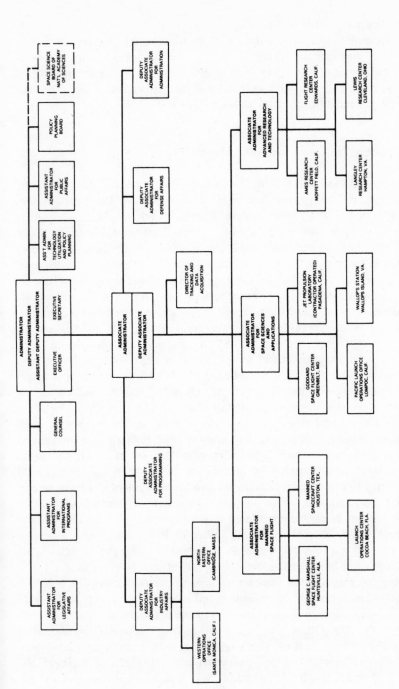

Figure 2-3. — NASA organization chart, 1 November 1963. (Source: Arnold S. Levine *Managing NASA in the Apollo Era* (Washington, D.C.: National Aeronautics and Space Administration, 1982), p. 44.

reinstated direct reporting relationship.

Some observers contend that the initial decision to have the centers report to the general manager was wrong. I do not, and neither does Jim Webb. It was critical at the time that it was done to mute some of the centrifugal forces that were at play. This was one way to achieve this. It is clear in my mind that it did make some signficant contribution to this end.

(2)   Creating Program Integrating Machinery

The reorganization of NASA in November 1961, in addition to having the centers report to the general manager, also realigned the headquarters program offices. Prior to this time, development of hardware such as engines and launch vehicles had been in one program office while space flight programs were in another. This caused conflicts between the program officers and increased the work of the general manager and his then very limited staff integrating capabilities. The 1961 reorganization solved this problem by setting up program offices that clearly focused on NASA's major programs: space science, manned space flight, applications and research and technology. Also, an Office of Tracking and Data Acquisition was established for agency-wide support in telemetry and automatic data processing. The realignment of the program offices served as a means of resolving conflicts and integrating hardware and flight programs short of NASA's general manager.

Another step taken to provide for an agency-wide focus on NASA's rapidly evolving programs was to create in June of 1961 the Office of Programs which reported to the general manager. This was to be a staff arm charged with resources programming; project review, approval and evaluation; management reporting and evaluation, and facilities coordination, all of which had to be closely related in order for NASA general management to be truly general management. Prior to this, these activities had been fragmented among several headquarters organizations. This was true particularly of budget preparation and execution not being closely related to program and project development and approval. Prior to creation of the Office of Programs, NASA's general manager just did not have the horses to be general manager and to check the ever growing power of the headquarters program offices. NASA was faced with the problem of fragmenting into several strong bureaus over which NASA general management would have limited influence in which the NASA-wide program concept might well have perished in the process.

The new Program Office with its key integrating responsibilities was to be staffed by some of the most capable engineering management personnel from the headquarters program offices, particularly the strongest of these offices, the Office of Space Flight Programs. It was absolutely necessary that this strengthening of general management staff capabilities be undertaken before the reorganization of November 1961 when all of the centers would report for the next two years to the general manager rather than to the various headquarters program offices.

(3)   Developing NASA Wide Management Processes

Critical to holding a rapidly growing organization together is the development, obtaining agreement on, and implementing of certain organizational wide processes such as: doing business with centers that do not report to a given headquarters program office; appointment of key personnel in both the headquarters and centers; and resource estimates and allocations of dollars, staffing levels and facilities. This is particularly critical in a situation where the program is expanding and changing at the same time, external environmental changes are taking place in such areas as Congressional support, and reorganizations are required to keep pace with these and other changing conditions.

In the formative days of NASA, we worked continuously and hard on these integrating processes. Often we courted disaster. For example, after the November 1961 reorganization, the budget process was close to being in complete disarray. In the perceptions of some it was. In the first two years of NASA's life, a formal project approval and management system did not exist. It was not until just before Glennan's leaving in 1961 that he was able to get a fix on all the projects that had been approved in NASA's first two years.

All this was less than neat and nice and a formal management manual system was never really achieved. Many observers point to this lack of the manual as a major failure. It was, per se, but almost always—sometimes just in the nick of time—the agency-wide processes such as project management were developed, approved by all major parties, and implemented. After some rough run in time, almost all of them worked in getting done what they were supposed to get done.

(4)   The Concept of Functional Management

Functional management by specialists in procurement, personnel management, and tracking/data acquisition was another concept used to maintain NASA as an integrated whole. Its success was mixed at best. The functional management concept was two-fold in its efforts to serve as an agency-wide integrating device. The functional staffs such as personnel and procurement which reported to the general manager were to serve as staff to all three members of general management and to ensure, agency-wide, that these specializations were being carried out effectively and efficiently. This arrangement truly left headquarters program officers and center directors with two bosses, the line officials they reported to and the various staff functional specialists. A similar system has worked successfully in such companies as American Airlines, U.S. Internal Revenue Service, and is a common organizational phenomenon in U.S. military organization.

In the NASA situation, functional management had limited success mainly because of the difficulty of accepting the "dual supervision" concept and because of the relative weaknesses and lack of coherence in the newly formed or expanded headquarters functional staff groups such as personnel management. The relative success varied markedly from one functional area to the other. For example, procurement was much more successful than personnel management.

In spite of the mixed reviews, functional management was only one of several organizational and managerial approaches used to keep NASA from succumbing to the early centrifugal forces that were at play.

(5) Limiting Types and Amounts of Personnel

Directly related, and often confused in NASA with functional management, was directly limiting the amount of functional staff both in the headquarters program offices and in the central staff units reporting to the general manager. The idea was very simple and straightforward. To keep the headquarters program offices from becoming semi-autonomous bureaus, the concept was to limit the functional staff in the program offices and make them depend on the specialist staffs reporting to general management. This would not only serve as another way of integrating the NASA headquarters, but also prevent—or at least limit—counterparting of specialists at two levels of the NASA headquarters. Counterparting, a widely observed phenomenon in large complex Federal departments and agencies such as Health and Human Resources, becomes very divisive, takes in lots of its own laundry and is terribly expensive. The NASA concept was to stop this counterparting—or at least stunt its growth. To this end we could prevent the consequent divisiveness of the two groups of specialists making work for each other, saving staff, and preventing dual, micromanagement of the NASA centers.

This effort to limit functional staff worked with limited success. The major reasons for this were the pressure to rapidly move ahead, particularly in the manned space flight area, the relative weaknesses in several elements of the staffs reporting to the general manager, and slowness in understanding and responding to the needs of the program offices.

In summary, I believe it is fair to say that in NASA's formative period, serious forces were at play that threatened NASA's long term effectiveness and efficiency. These were frankly recognized by NASA's general management, particularly Jim Webb, and several explicit actions were taken to curb these forces. For observers to look at each of these in isolation and to judge its success or failure as such misses the point. These actions were envisioned and developed as an interrelated series of managerial and organizational actions that in the large did achieve what they were supposed to do. Their overall objective was to maintain NASA and its programs as a generally integrated whole, not a lot of "little NASAs." These would have been picked off one by one as the national coherence on the NASA program began to break down in 1963 and later.

Maintaining In-house Technical Capabilities

If I were allowed a choice of only two elements related to NASA's effectiveness they would be the continuity of leadership provided by Glennan and Webb and the ability to maintain strong in-house technical capabilities. The maintenance of strong in-house capabilities was absolutely essential in NASA's ability to effectively contract out most of its work to the private sector, mainly American industry and universities.

In the main, the in-house technical capabilities came to NASA in the form of the basic building blocks that were transferred from other departments and agencies. They consisted initially of the field centers from NACA. These laboratories with their 8,000 personnel and advanced facilities made up this nation's principal governmental research capability in such areas as aerodynamics, propulsion, structures and materials research. Next transferred to NASA was California Institute of Technology's Jet Propulsion Laboratory with additional capabilities in propulsion, spacecraft technology, lunar and planetary sciences, and deep space tracking and data acquisition. In 1960, the President transferred to NASA Dr. Wernher von Braun and his Development Operations Division from the U.S. Army Ballistic Missile Agency. With this transfer came essential engineering strengths in launch vehicle design, development, assembly, test, and launch operations.

Therefore, at an early juncture NASA had the in-house technical capability to

- conceive of space flight development and research projects

- develop technical specifications for private contractors to follow, and

- supervise contractor efforts to ensure high reliability of systems, subsystems, and components in their early development stages.

The major policy decision that had to be faced early on was whether or not to expand this capability or to limit it to its then existing level. This decision in turn rested on the acceptance or rejection of the idea that in order to maintain effective in-house capability, this capability must be based in a laboratory environment and continuously assigned significant and challenging work. Glennan apparently never bought this concept, and by the imposition of tight personnel ceilings let the centers grow very little during his time. He did this to ensure that most of NASA work was contracted out.

James Webb, NASA's second Administrator, held views similar to Glennan's on the necessity of getting most of NASA's work done by private enterprise and the universities. However, he did endorse the concept of maintaining effective in-house technical capability by providing laboratory environment where challenging work was performed in-house by civil servants. During Webb's period of tenure, the in-house centers grew from their original strength of approximately 16,000 personnel to about 30,000. At one juncture NASA staff proposed that NASA grow to approximately 80,000 persons. Webb immediately squelched this idea and reaffirmed his policy of contracting out most of NASA's work while simultaneously maintaining a limited in-house capability somewhere around the 30,000 persons.

Many observers have been puzzled about the genesis of the decision to rely on private industry while maintaining sufficient in-house technical capability to effectively manage the majority of the work to be contracted out. In my view, this decision clearly evolved from the inheritance of in-house capability in the centers and the strong views held by the leadership of the centers that this was the only way to effectively do this kind of work. These two factors were supported by the rapidly growing program which made it almost impossible to build up in-house capabilities as fast as the programs' expansion required and the political element of maintaining the support for the programs by the aerospace industry by contracting out the majority of the work.

The in-house/out-of-house division of work as stated in various NASA policy pronouncements was broad enough to allow its application to the various centers in varying degrees. For example, the Wernher von Braun group at Huntsville was allowed to do much more in-house than other centers wanted to do or were allowed to do. However, this issue did create tension between Washington headquarters and the Huntsville group. But accommodations were continually made by both sides within a continually evolving set of policies.

Again let me say in summary, if I had only two choices in regard to elements of NASA effectiveness I would choose the continuity of agency leadership under Glennan and Webb and the decisions to maintain effective in-house technical capability. The other elements are all important, but these two were critical, in my judgement.

Arm in arm with decisions to maintain in-house technical capability while contracting out most of NASA's work was the necessity to develop an effective procurement process which effectively related these two basic concepts. This NASA was able to do by keeping the procurement process under study continuously and changing it in light of what these studies revealed. No attempt will be made here to lay this out in any detail, but merely to illustrate some of the key decisions that were made in this area. These included, among others:

1. Jim Webb's decision to involve all three members of general management in making decisions as a group on all procurements in excess of $5 million.

2. In March 1963 creating an Office of Industry Affairs with the transfer of NASA's Procurement Division from the Office of Administration where it was one of several functional divisions, to where it became the key element under a Deputy Associate Administrator. Thus procurement was given an organizational status equal to its growing importance to NASA's effective contracting out.

3. Moving from cost-plus-fixed-fee contracts where industry had little incentive to control costs to various forms of incentive contracts.

Evolving a System of Project Management

Closely related to contracting out from a solid base of in-house technical capability was the necessity to develop a system of program-project management. In this respect, Glennan took two important actions before he left office in January 1961. The first was to identify all ongoing projects and provide for their formal authorization by the Administrator. This exercise revealed all sorts of ways in which projects had been initiated, some with formal authorizations, others by mere word of mouth. This act by Glennan gave the incoming new Administrator a base from which to authorize additional projects.

Secondly, Glennan signed a NASA-wide instruction setting forth a formal system of planning and implementing programs and projects. It called for formal project development plans and listed the steps the projects would have to go through before finally being authorized by the Associate Administrator, NASA's general manager. From these early beginnings, NASA over the next five years developed an effective project management system. There were seven major elements of the system as it finally evolved:

1. Project management under a project manager in a NASA center where the in-house technical capability could be brought to bear as it was needed. The major exception to this was the lunar landing in which some key elements of project management were located in NASA headquarters.

2. Project management teams made up of both technical and administrative personnel in such areas as procurement, reporting directly to the project manager.

3. Project management control over financial and technical personnel even though these technical personnel were based in other discipline-based parts of the center, such as electronics and structures. NASA did not initially start this way. Initially a project manager's authority was limited in terms of resources and over the discipline-based personnel. This did not work and as a result soon evolved to a concept of a strong project management system.

4. Overall project management responsibility was placed in a lead center with policies and procedures to use the capabilities of other centers. These supporting capabilities were used in the development and supervision of contractors on various subsystems and components of projects.

5. A custom made training program for both technical and administrative project management personnel.

6. In 1965 the adoption of a phased project-procurement management system, among other steps, to gain better control over what was becoming project failures, slippages, and cost overruns. Phased project planning involves going step by step through advanced studies, program definition prototype design, flight hardware, and finally, operations. Each step in the sequence is to be completed and the results analyzed and incorporated into the next step before proceeding. The process can bring a project to termination or major revision at any step.

7. Clarifying the relative roles of headquarters program management and project management in the NASA centers. This had been an early sticky problem in relationships because several of the key headquarters program staff had come from the centers where doing things a certain way was a way of life. In general, the approach that evolved was to try

to limit the headquarters program staffs to approval of project development plans, schedules in terms of major procurement actions and technical milestones, and budget justifications and financial operating plans. In addition, the headquarters program staffs evaluated ongoing projects and approved changes which significantly altered objectives, schedules, and costs.

Changing Things That Did Not Work

The last element that will be discussed in relationship to NASA's effectiveness was its ability to stop doing and change things that did not work. This will be illustrated by two examples: the creation and later abolition of the headquarters Office of Life Sciences and the initial separation of launch vehicles from space flight programs in headquarters and their later combination.

(1) The Office of Life Sciences

In March of 1960, a major headquarters technical program office, Life Science Programs, was established as a direct result of the NASA Bioscience Advisory Committee. This Committee was established by NASA's first Administrator, Dr. Keith Glennan, and was composed of outside persons selected from the life sciences community. The Life Sciences Programs Office was responsible for aerospace medicine, bioscience and biotechnology, including human research.

Here is an example of where the concept of "organization by emphasis," that is, a separate organizational unit at the highest program level in an organization, did not work. The Life Science Programs Office found ever increasing problems of effectively relating the various elements that constituted the life sciences to the other NASA programs and projects of which they were an integral part in achieving any given mission. For example, there was difficulty in relating aerospace medicine to the various manned space flight projects Mercury, Gemini and Apollo.

In the summer of 1961 it was concluded that the life science concerns in achieving NASA's programs could be better achieved by relating these elements, from an organizational point of view, directly with the programs of which they were an integral part in mission achievement. As a result, on November 1, 1961, we officially abolished the Life Sciences Program Office and placed aerospace medicine in the Office of Manned Space Flight, bioscience in the Office of Space Sciences and biotechnology, including human research, in the Office of Advanced Research and Technology. These arrangements worked much more effectively, even though the life science community was most unhappy. But this eventually faded away.

(2) The Separation of Launch Vehicles and Spacecraft

In anticipation of the transfer of the von Braun team from the Army Ballistic Missile Agency, NASA created an Office of Launch Vehicle Programs in the fall of 1959. Two headquarters program offices had been responsible for the total technical program, one for advanced research and one for all space flight development. It made simple sense to NASA that this large but latecoming addition to NASA be assured equal understanding and attention to their requirements at headquarters. So NASA created a third program office for launch vehicles. This office was to concentrate attention on the important problems associated with the development of a "family" of launch vehicles to meet the range of needs imposed by future spacecraft and mission requirements. The development of the spacecraft themselves, and the scientific program for which they were being developed, continued to be the responsibility of a separate Space Flight Programs Office in the NASA headquarters.

So in effect what NASA did in anticipation of the transfer of another major building block was to separate at the highest program levels of NASA responsibilities for launch vehicles from spacecraft. This separated the most closely interrelated areas involved in achieving space flight missions. Needless to say, this caused severe problems of coordination at the NASA headquarters level and resulted in cumbersome and time-consuming committees and procedures. Once the von Braun team leadership and NASA headquarters learned how to do business with each other, it became more important to resolve the inherent weaknesses of separating at the top of the organization the vehicle aspects of a flight mission from the spacecraft which flies on such a vehicle. Problems of this sort, coupled with the need for giving special organizational emphasis to the manned lunar landing program, resulted in NASA's placing at the program office level responsibility for both launch vehicles and spacecraft in the fall of 1961.

The organizational lesson involved here is that organizational arrangements must be changed to meet the continually changing nature of the problems to be coped with at any given point in time. If agency leadership gets fixed preconceptions that any one organizational arrangement is permanently a good thing, it is not long before problems to be solved or end objectives to be achieved and organizational structure are at cross purposes with each other.

This particular example points up an additional lesson in organization. It is related to the problem of handling "tradeoffs." Any given organizational arrangement that is devised to meet a given problem or achieve a given objective carries with it certain advantages and disadvantages. Discerning management must find ways to inform itself of these advantages and disadvantages prior to making organizational decisions. Organizational decisions always involve accepting some disadvantages, as in the case of establishing a separate Launch Vehicle Program Office to provide a focus for evolving effective working relationships with the von Braun team upon its transfer to NASA.

Elements of Effectiveness: Summary Remarks

No observer, participant observer or otherwise, can, with any degree of assurance, choose, weigh, and rank the key elements of NASA's organizational and managerial arrangements in terms of their contribution to NASA's effectiveness. Yet, this is what has been attempted in this part of this chapter. Six elements were selected:

1. Continuity of leadership and concepts
2. Evolving and coherent roles for the members of general management
3. The muting of certain centrifugal forces
4. Maintaining in-house technical capabilities joined to an effective procurement process
5. Evolving concepts of program and project management
6. Changing things that did not work

Further, I made the judgement, that if I had only a choice of two of these elements, I would pick:

1. Continuity of leadership and concepts; and
2. Maintaining in-house technical capabilities joined to an effective procurement process.

If one has not already done so, one might certainly at this juncture raise the question of what criteria were used to define or establish "effectiveness." I do not believe the question of NASA's effectiveness through Jim Webb's resignation in October 1968—NASA's first ten years—requires an extensive answer.

From its beginning in October 1958 through October 1968, NASA was able to build and manage an organization that resulted in:

1. Apollo II astronauts Neil Armstrong and Edwin Aldrin landing on the moon on July 22, 1969, approximately eight months after Webb's resignation.

2. Successful completion of the several projects leading to the lunar landing and return, among them Mercury, Gemini, Ranger, and Surveyor.

3. Development of operational meterological satellites and their transfer to the National Oceanographic and Atmospheric Administration.

4. Development of operational communications satellites and the beginnings of a large commercial enterprise, COMSAT.

5. The beginning of an extensive and successful interplanetary exploration program, including an encounter with the planet Venus.

6. The maintenance of an extensive program in aeronautical research and in other areas of space research and technology.

These are the highlights that illustrate NASA's effectiveness in its first ten years. There were failures also. The most serious of these was the death of the three-man crew for NASA's first manned Apollo space flight. This occurred on January 27, 1967 when a flash fire swept through the Apollo 1 spacecraft on the launch pad at the Kennedy Space Center. Victims were Virgil Grissom, one of seven original Mercury astronauts, Edward H. White, and Roger B. Chaffee.

Part III

Some Summary Judgements

In addition to the above summary remarks on elements of effectiveness, the reader needs to recall certain historical and environmental factors that played significant parts in NASA's development. Major among these were:

1. NASA's inheritance of highly professional groups—elites if you will—to form its basic core.

2. A single leader reporting directly to the President of the United States.

3. Broad and uncluttered responsibilities with substantial leeway, initially, at least, in their interpretation and implementation.

4. Flexibility in administrative areas, in particular, selection and appointment of key personnel.

5. A limit of two on the number of political officers required.

Major among the environmental factors that influenced NASA and NASA in turn had to try to influence were:

1. The unfriendly, unforgiving, and demanding environment of space itself.

2. The national and international scope of the program.

3. The Presidential nature of several of NASA's objectives, which in turn placed NASA in an envelope of Presidential politics.

4. The necessity of carrying the program out in an open manner and mainly by civilians.

In turn, these environmental forces caused NASA to develop and implement a set of basic policies. Key among these were:

1. Total utilization of NASA's resources.

2. Primary reliance on industry and the universities tied to, and supervised by, highly professional, effective in-house capabilities.

3. Continuation of the multipurpose nature of most of NASA's inherited research and development centers.

Unfortunately for the United States, it is difficult to find similar public endeavors where the confluence of historical, environmental and organizational forces came together as effectively as they did in the case of NASA. You hear many say "if we can go to the moon why can't we do such and such?" Unless the key forces that made up the NASA situation can be created and brought into a synergistic relationship, the answer is a flat no, or at best a very limited application of NASA's experiences.

The great barriers to applying the lessons of NASA—sometimes referred to as "space age management"—was never so clearly driven home to me as by my experiences first as Assistant Secretary Comptroller of the Department of Health, Education, and Welfare (HEW) and later as Assistant Secretary for Management and Budget (1973-1978). Let me, in conclusion, highlight some of the key differences between NASA and HEW.

1. NASA had rather clear and tangible objectives, some of these tied to, and backed by, the President. Many of HEW's programs, particularly those in such areas as education, have multiple, and conflicting objectives that came out of the workings of the American pluralistic political process.

2. NASA had a continuity of leadership, two Administrators in its ten formative years. HEW Secretaries, their myriads of Special Assistants, and numerous Assistant Secretaries come and go on a frequency of about every two years—sometimes less, sometimes a little more. Each group brings its own concepts of management. They crank them into the nervous system of the organization. Then they go away and the next group goes through the same process, never quite understanding the ideas and residue of the previous group. As one Secretary of HEW remarked, "This department is run by the GS 15 career staff—not by political officers." The answer was simple. Who else?

3. NASA not only had a continuity of leadership, but there was a coherence among the three members of NASA's general management from the beginning as to their roles, their relationships among each other, and joint decision making in such crucial areas as selection of NASA's major contractors. Sometimes there has been a semblance of these characteristics in HEW's general management, but often this has not been the case. This is particularly likely to happen when the Secretary is not allowed to select his or her own Undersecretary. This builds in conflict at the very top of these large complex enterprises such as HEW.

4. NASA had only two political officers, the Administrator and the Deputy Administrator. Both Glennan and Webb picked Dr. Dryden as the Deputy Administrator. He had been the Director of Research of NASA's largest building block, the National Advisory Committee for Aeronautics. In HEW there are many political appointees in such positions as Regional Directors, Confidential Assistants to Assistant Secretaries and the like.

    The selection of these involves the Secretary, the Undersecretary, the White House, the National Democratic or Republican Committee, and most of all, the myriad of special interest groups. The result is lack of identification with HEW's top management, a great many mediocre selections, and in many visible cases, outright incompetence. This phenomenon has been particularly noticeable in the Carter-Reagan administrations.

5. NASA was built on a highly competent, professional core staff. It was an elite group. It was large enough to maintain much of its elite characteristics even when it had to be more than doubled in its size. HEW has some elements like NASA, such as the National Institutes of Health. But, it also has many disparate groups that are far removed from professional elite in training, experience, but most importantly, in attitudes and values.

6. NASA was impacted in only a limited manner compared to HEW by the "workings of the iron triangle." Here we are talking about the relationships among members of the bureaucracy, interest groups, and Congressional committee members/staff in influencing public policies and decisions. NASA was influenced by the aerospace industry, but that was limited. There were others, but their influences were also limited. HEW is influenced continually by interest groups, several of them built by law into the HEW decision-making process. Department management ignores them at their own peril. They consequently dominate much of HEW decision making, with inordinate amounts of time required to cope with their workings as part of the iron triangle.

7. NASA did not have to work to any appreciable extent with other parts of the Federal system of government, state and local governments. This is not the case of HEW. Many of its programs, such as Aid to Families of Dependent Children, by law, must be carried out by state and local governments. This adds immeasurably to the problem of designing and implementing an effective management control system.

8. In the main, NASA developed programs and projects which were to serve national objectives, that is, governmental objectives. These were limited in number. HEW has numerous programs, approximately 300 at one time, providing services to millions of individuals either directly or through other organizations. For example, Medicaid provides medical services to about 23 million participants annually with an expenditure of about $15 billion—about three times NASA's annual budget. This is done through the states who in turn get the services through health providers.

    These differences in program orientation and characteristics make them little amenable to most of the organizational and managerial arrangements employed effectively by NASA.

In conclusion, space age management remarkably fitted NASA's formative time and needs. Were that it were so that most, if not all, of this could be applied to other large scale, complex organizations such as HEW. Unfortunately it cannot be done.

Footnotes

1.   Historical background is based primarily on Frank W. Anderson, Jr., *Orders of Magnitude: A History of NACA and NASA 1915-1980* (Washington, D.C.: National Aeronautics and Space Administration, 1981). Anderson was a member of the Scientific and Technical Information Branch.

2.   The Space Act did provide for a Space Council composed of the President, Secretary of Defense, NASA Administrator, AEC Chairman and others. However, due to a combination of Executive Office of the President and NASA Administrator pressures the Council never interfered significantly with the clear reporting relationship between the NASA Administrator and the President of the United States.

3.   James E. Webb, *Space Age Management: The Large-Scale Approach* (New York: Columbia University, 1969), McKinsey Foundation Lecture Series, pp. 73-74.

4.   See NASA staff study, *Organizing To Achieve The Objectives of an Accelerated Civilian Space Program*, June 12, 1961, pp. 3-5.

5.   See James E. Webb, "Foreword" in Robert L. Rosholt, *An Administrative History of NASA 1958-1963* (Washington DC: National Aeronautics and Space Administration, 1966). Rosholt was a member of the Scientific and Technical Information Division.

Editorial Note: Rufus E. Miles focuses attention on the great costs and inefficiencies caused by lack of attention to how legislation will be administered. The exploitation of the G.I. Bill by slick entrepreneurs through perversion of the purposes of on-the-job training and the proliferation of profit-making educational institutions to take advantage of training funds for veterans were the result of not carefully thinking through how the bill could be implemented in such a way that the fast-buck artists could be contained.

The provision in 1962 of authority for payment of three Federal dollars for every state dollar to support social services that would help persons on welfare get off welfare and would help those who might end up on welfare except for the provision of such services was not carefully thought through and states stretched this subsidy far beyond the original intent of Congress.

Miles believes President Carter's welfare reform proposal would have been an administrative nightmare had it passed. Though the objectives were laudable, assumption of administrative responsibility by the Federal government would have been complex and have led to many interrelationship problems with other social services performed by the states.

One of the most stimulating aspects of Miles' paper is its clear portrayal of how civil servants, appointed officials, and members of Congress who are dedicated to the public good attempted to correct the deficiencies of the G.I. Bill and social service legislation. In the case of the proposed Carter welfare reform, Miles again took the initiative to raise questions about administrative feasibility. This is public service at its best.

CHAPTER 3

A COSTLY DEFICIENCY IN PUBLIC POLICY FORMULATION

Rufus E. Miles, Jr.

When new or revised social programs requiring large appropriations are initiated by the Federal Government, the factor that receives the least attention in relation to its importance is that of designing the programs so as to make possible—and even encourage—effective and efficient achievement of intended purposes. The main concerns of legislative designers are, to use Harold Lasswell's classic phrase, "Who gets what, when, and how." These are the political issues of the first order, and as such they inevitably receive foremost consideration, but this should not mean, as it commonly does, a very low level of attention to the need for administrative design to prevent abuse, encourage intelligent cost control, and maximize the effective use of appropriations. Unfortunately, most legislative designers in both the legislative and executive branches assume that any program that is strategically acceptable to the executive branch and politically acceptable to Congress can be effectively and efficiently administered. This assumption is without foundation and has produced some dire and expensive consequences. The political climate now seems congenial to altering this practice.

As I reflect on three decades of Federal service ending in 1965 and another decade and a half of occasional critiquing of government performance, this deficiency in public policy formulation stands out in my mind as especially glaring. Three cases, stimulated by unforgettable encounters with political reality, are adduced to illuminate this thesis. Others could readily be developed. The subject is worth a research project of substantial magnitude.

The first and longest case concerns a series of attempts to plug gaping holes left by the authors of the Servicemen's Readjustment Act of 1944, better known as the G.I. Bill of Rights. These errors of legislative design need never have occurred if appropriate attention had been given to problems of administration, including potentials for abuse, in the early stages. The second describes the manner in which grants to states for social services developed a billion dollar loophole, a loophole that in retrospect should have been plugged long before it became scandalous. And the third addresses one of the most difficult problems of legislative design imaginable—welfare reform. Out of these three cases, plus observation of others that seemed to teach similar lessons, I have deduced what I hope are some useful generalizations.

The Badly Flawed G.I. Bill

In November of 1942, President Franklin Roosevelt appointed a study group called The Armed Forces Committee on Post-war Educational Opportunities for Service Personnel, headed by a distinguished civilian businessman called into uniform, Brigadier General Frederick H. Osborn, Director of Special Services Division, Army Service Forces.[1] Two years earlier, Roosevelt had appointed Osborn to head a Committee on Selective Service, a role that he had discharged with distinction. In 1943, when Osborn's new Committee submitted its report, it also appeared to be a first-rate piece of work. The trouble was that, although the conceptual ideas were laudable, the Committee had given little consideration to the problems of administration. The failure to consider problems of administration led to scandalous results.

The main thrust of the educational part of the bill was to enable young veterans who had interrupted their education to bear the burden of war to resume their education at government expense. Most of the emphasis was on college education. High school graduates who had not started college, including many who had not even intended to go to college, were to be encouraged to reach a higher level of formal education than they had earlier visualized. But when the Committee got to discussing the matter, it was pointed out that there were many who either had no interest in further academic training or did not have the aptitude for it, or simply preferred some form of vocational skill training. For these, the Committee reasoned, there could be a parallel system of on-the-job training, modelled on apprenticeship training (they assumed), enabling veterans to enter as learners with learner rates of pay, and gradually increase their incomes as they learned on the job, whatever vocation they chose. The Committee provided, therefore, that such veterans should receive subsidies during the early stages of their working careers.

Based on this Committee's recommendations, President Roosevelt recommended to Congress and Congress enacted the educational components of the G.I. Bill of Rights, (officially, the Servicemen's Readjustment Act of 1944) entitling veterans of World War II to enter educational institutions of their choice and not only have their tuition paid by the government, but also to have Uncle Sam provide them with a so-called "subsistence allowance" to cover, at a modest level, the estimated cost of food and lodgings. In considering the bill in the Spring of 1944, while the Allies were preparing to invade the beaches of Normandy, the two committees of Congress that handled veterans affairs were operating in an atmosphere in which they felt that "nothing is too good for our boys." They paid little attention to the possibility of loopholes that would invite the waste of hundreds of millions or billions of dollars. They passed the bill overwhelmingly two weeks after D-Day.

Demobilization got into full swing shortly after the Japanese surrender on August 15, 1945. Two months later, President Truman appointed General Omar Bradley, fresh from his string of victories on the Western Front and one of the most illustrious soldiers of the war, to head the Veterans Administration (VA). Two administrative tasks of major magnitude were laid upon General Bradley's shoulders. One was to gear up for and administer the new G.I. Bill, and the other was to overhaul the antiquated and totally inadequate hospital system in which tens of thousands of veterans would seek recuperation, restoration of their broken bodies, and physical and vocational rehabilitation. He set about these tasks with typical vigor.

Shortly thereafter, on December 6, 1945, I returned from military leave to the Bureau of the Budget, and was promptly assigned, as a GS-13 budget examiner, to work on the budget of Veterans Administration, concentrating on the G.I. Bill. Within weeks, I began to sense that scandals were brewing that could cost the taxpayers hundreds of millions of dollars. Reports coming in from the four field offices of the Bureau of the Budget indicated that employers, in ever increasing numbers, were conniving with veterans to enroll them in alleged programs of on-the-job training that would enable them to qualify for subsistence allowances from the Veterans Administration. Substandard wages were paid to the veterans, but the wages plus the subsistence allowances brought them up to, or above, the normal wage level for the jobs they were performing. The so-called on-the-job training was perfunctory or nonexistent; it amounted to no more than the normal supervision and instruction that was given to any new employee.

On-the-job training was growing by leaps and bounds, doubling every two months, with the clear prospect of becoming a billion dollar enterprise of little benefit to the veterans. Employers were reaping a bonanza through the substandard wages. Armed with detailed reports, I went to see the Assistant Administrator of the Veterans Administration for Vocational Rehabilitation and Education and asked him what he proposed to do about the growing scandal. His answer rocked me back on my heels. The G.I. Bill, said the Assistant Administrator, had made it clear that the Veterans Administration should not inject itself into the determination as to what constituted adequate training. That was a state responsibility. The state accrediting agencies were charged, he said, with approving on-the-job training programs as well as institutional training, and his hands were tied. The scandal would be the responsibility of the state accrediting agencies, not the Veterans Administration.

It seemed hard to believe that a top official of the Veterans Administration could watch an enormous leakage of taxpayer's dollars going down the drain at an ever faster rate without deep concern and some sense of challenge to see that it was stopped. I urged the Assistant Administrator to discuss the matter with the VA General Counsel and with General Bradley and see whether they shared his view that the hands of the VA were tied. If they did, I said, then it was vital that the law be changed and changed quickly. It was the Assistant Administrator's turn to be amazed. He said it was not up to civil servants of his or my status to decide that a law should be changed: "If those above us who are policy officials, such as General Bradley or President Truman, think the law should be changed, all well and good, but it is not up to us to tell them what to do." That was the tenor of his reply. I left feeling thoroughly deflated.

My status was such that I could not go direct to General Bradley and discuss the issue with him. My immediate superior had just had a severe heart attack and was unavailable. His superior was preparing to retire and did not want to become involved. And the official at the third echelon above me, whom I felt intuitively would want to be helpful, was so overburdened that taking on further larger initiatives seemed out of the question. I decided on a new tack. Friends of mine in the Department of Labor where I used to work told me about Marine Corps General George B. Erskine who had recently been appointed by President Truman to a newly created position as Administrator of the Retraining and Re-employment Administration. They said that he had a beautiful big office but no clearcut mission and, without one, he was floundering. It occurred to me that General Erskine might be the key to a resolution of this difficult problem. More precisely, the key would be Clara Beyer, one of the few women in government holding a high executive post, that of Assistant Director of the Bureau of Labor Standards, and a very competent person, while General Erskine would become the emissary to General Bradley.

When I outlined my concerns to Clara Beyer, she was extremely helpful. We discussed how best to develop a set of standards for on-the-job training that might be issued by the Veterans Administration to all state accrediting agencies, assuming the VA concluded it was legal for them to issue such standards. The way to handle it, we agreed, was to have the Bureau of Labor Standards, in consultation and collaboration with the Office of Education, call a conference of selected state labor commissioners and state commissioners of education and hammer out a set of standards that the Labor Department might then recommend to General Bradley. With this plan well mapped out, Mrs. Beyer arranged an appointment for the two of us with General Erskine. He was most receptive.

By that time, I was getting some juicy cases that I could use as horrible examples. I remember one, especially. A bank in Kentucky had set up an "on-the-job training program" for its up-and-coming vice-president to train him to become the president. The vice-president was getting a full "subsistence allowance" while "in training." After I reeled off a string of these and reported to General Erskine my frustrating conversation with the VA Assistant Administrator, he was ready to pick up the telephone and ask for an appointment with General Bradley. But first he wanted to know how we proposed to solve the problem. Mrs. Beyer explained how the Bureau of Labor Standards could be helpful in convening a conference to develop a set of standards. That was all that was needed. General Erskine was on his way.

Even without consulting his general counsel as to whether the VA had the legal power to issue such standards, General Bradley immediately and enthusiastically accepted General Erskine's offer. In a matter of only a couple of weeks the conference was scheduled. Clara Beyer and I agreed that it would expedite matters if we were to develop ahead of time a draft of a set of standards that could be brought out at a propitious time in the meetings as a "preliminary discussion draft." Each of us developed such a draft, then merged the two, and we were ready for the conference. To our enormous pleasure, the preliminary draft ended up with only nit-picking changes. Shortly thereafter, it was dispatched by General Erskine to General Bradley.

The essence of the standards was simple. First, they required that the training programs be spelled out in detail—what was to be taught, how, and by whom. Second, the length of the training courses was to be related to the difficulty and complexity of the subject matter. No simple courses could be strung out over a long period of time, as was beginning to happen. Third, the progression of students was to be carefully recorded and if a student was not progressing at an acceptable rate, his subsistence allowance would not be continued. Fourth, a periodic wage progression was required, reflecting the progression of the veteran in the training, with a corresponding diminution in his subsistence allowance. With the completion of the course, the journeyman rate was to be paid. There had to be a reasonable prospect that each employer would continue to employ the veterans who satisfactorily completed their courses. This was to preclude the situation which was already beginning to show up where it was evident that employers intended to discharge their trainees at the end of their subsidized so-called training and hire others at substandard wages to replace them. Finally, a wage ceiling was to be set, above which the government would not provide "subsistence allowances" to working veterans. Obviously, this was to prevent vice-presidents of banks or any other businesses from pretending they were in need of wage supplementation.

When the standards were finished, they were promulgated on an advisory basis to the state accrediting agencies by the Department of Labor and the U.S. Office of Education early in April 1946, but they had little effect. Unfortunately, most of the state accrediting agencies had no money with which to hire people to see that these new standards were enforced, and many had little enforcement power anyway. Almost none had any experience with this new mode of training employees because the employers had had none either. Something more needed to be done.

Back at the Bureau of the Budget, I was getting support for my activities from Lee Martin, the Director of the Division of Estimates, and Paul Appleby, the Acting Director of the Bureau. I was impatient to see the Veterans Administration make up its mind whether it had the legal power to issue the new standards as regulations, or, if it did not, to seek an amendment to the law. I prepared a lengthy memorandum that was transmitted by Appleby to General Bradley, laying out the problem and urging legislative action if that is what it took. More than a month went by with no action. I heard by the grapevine that the VA general counsel had advised General Bradley that his power to issue the standards as regulations was dubious. To be on sound ground, said the general counsel, it would be necessary to get the standards enacted into law. Time was running short. Congress intended to adjourn *sine die* early in August and it was already early July. Was it conceivable that there was time left to get the law changed before Congress went home? Most people said no, but I thought it worth a try. I prepared a letter, signed on July 10, 1946, by Acting Director Appleby to General Bradley pointing out the probability—not merely the possibility—of hundreds of millions of wasted dollars if Congress went home without being asked to amend the law to prevent such a scandal. General Bradley may already have made up his mind to act before he received the letter. In any case, he directed his legislative staff to draft a bill incorporating the standards that had been promulgated by the Department of Labor and requesting authority to use VA funds to make grants to states to enable them to hire staffs in their accrediting agencies that could make site inspections.

One crucial decision remained for Bradley. Ever since the Veterans Administration had been set up, it had been customary to accord the major veterans organizations the courtesy of reviewing and commenting on proposed legislation since Congress was unlikely to pass legislation to which the veterans organizations were strongly opposed. In this case, however, time was of the essence and there was not more than a month left. Furthermore, Bradley had strong reason to believe that the American Legion would either oppose the bill outright or suggest changes that might emasculate the bill. The general decided that the public interest would be his sole guide. He determined to try to get Congress to pass the bill before adjournment.

On July 19, General Bradley wrote to Senator Walter George, Chairman of the Senate Finance Committee, and on July 22 he wrote a similar letter to Congressman John Rankin, Chairman of the House Committee on Veterans Affairs, enclosing the draft bill. In each letter he stressed that the number of veterans in the uncontrolled program had increased from 24,627 on January 1 to 228,523 on May 31, and quoted General Erskine as saying: "I can easily foresee a condition with over a million veterans involved in on-the-job training programs at an annual cost, for subsistence alone, of nearly a billion dollars a year." General Bradley urged immediate action on the amendments.

There is probably no case in modern legislative history where Congress acted with such rapidity on an important piece of legislation that did not involve a widely recognized national crisis. From the dispatch of General Bradley's recommendations on July 19, until the bill was passed by both houses and sent to President Truman on August 1, was just thirteen days. So great was the confidence of the Congress in General Bradley that they approved the modifications in law exactly as he requested them, and without hearings.

At this point the National Commander of the American Legion—John Stelle—a former lieutenant governor of Illinois—woke up to what had happened. He discovered that the so-called subsistence allowance of thousands of Legionnaires would be curtailed or eliminated and the possible future benefits of other veterans whom they hoped to recruit as Legionnaires would be terminated before they started. Telegrams poured in on President Truman urging him to veto the bill. Truman not only did not veto it, he was delighted with the performance of General Bradley. When it came to gut courage, these two men had a mutual admiration society.

Two months later, General Bradley was on a plane headed for San Francisco to give the main address to the national convention of the American Legion. He was going over his prepared speech as the plane came down in Denver for a stop. There he was handed a message informing him that National Commander Stelle had delivered an excoriating attack on General Bradley for his actions in recommending to Congress the enactment of strict standards for on-the-job training under the G.I. Bill. He accused Bradley of breaking faith with the American veteran. John Stelle had been a thorn in General Bradley's side for some time, but Bradley had contained himself. Stelle's public criticism of Bradley was too much for him to take. He decided to throw away his prepared speech and reply to Commander Stelle, over the head of Stelle to all Legionnaires and to the American people.

In just twelve minutes, General Bradley told Stelle, the Legion, and the American people what he thought of Stelle's behavior. The rapier-like quality of that speech revealed the character of a totally committed public servant:

> Forty-eight hours ago, while I was enroute to your national convention as guest of the American Legion, my host, your national commander, accused me of breaking faith with the American veteran. At the same time my host, your national commander, said, and I

quote: "I do not hold the General entirely responsible. The Veterans Administration is first a Government agency, and secondly, a veterans' agency."

My host, your national commander, was prompted in his attack by a law enacted by Congress. This law prevents a privileged minority of veterans from profiting unfairly by the G.I. Bill.

The American Constitution has guaranteed democratic government for all citizens of these United States. There is no agency of our American Government that dares place its special interests before the interests of this nation. The Veterans Administration *is* first an Agency of Government. It is thereafter an ally of the veteran. While I am Administrator of Veterans Affairs the Veterans Administration will do nothing to surrender the welfare of this nation to the special interests of any minority. The American veteran is first a citizen of these United States. He is thereafter a veteran.

By this action, General Bradley demonstrated that he was not only a distinguished and courageous soldier, but an equally outstanding and courageous public administrator. Unfortunately, it also became clear that never again could he repeat such a tour-de-force when other aspects of the G.I. Bill became conspicuous wastes of public funds. For even as General Bradley was giving a tongue-lashing to Legion Commander Stelle, he and we, in the Budget Bureau, knew only too well that other scandals were rising to haunt the Veterans Administration. These had to do with the perversion of the law by clever entrepreneurs and willing veterans who saw in it an opportunity to use it for leisure-time and avocational purposes. If these abuses were to be brought to a halt, it would be necessary for General Bradley to go about the matter in a very different way.

In the summer of the following year, 1947, not long before General Bradley was named by President Truman as the Chief of Staff of the Army, the new Budget Director, James E. Webb, who had taken a personal interest in the matter of correcting the flaws in the G.I. Bill, sent a letter to General Bradley asking him to make a thorough survey and report to Congress on a new set of perversions of the G.I. Bill. This time the problem concerned large amounts of money that were flowing into such so-called educational pursuits as weekend joy-riding by veterans, many of whom were experienced pilots, in small private aircraft. Such activities were never even imagined by the original lawmakers. General Bradley willingly accepted the challenge of such a study.

When the detailed report was finally completed several months later, the new administrator, Carl Gray, a reserve corps general in the transportation corps, was very unenthusiastic about accepting the role of gladiator with the American Legion that General Bradley had bravely endured (or perhaps even relished) a year earlier. Yet the facts indicated the clear need to ask Congress to change the law. Budget Director Webb decided to enlist President Truman in the effort to get Congressional support for such a change.

The Truman Budget Message of January, 1948, asserted that "The law [the Servicemen's Readjustment Act] is being used in some cases to provide training for avocational or leisure-time activities at high cost to the Government and without a commensurate benefit to veterans.... A re-examination of the basic purposes of the law and suitable modification of its provisions should result in substantial savings. . . ." This was followed a month later by a letter from Budget Director Webb to Edith Nourse Rogers, then Chairman of the House Committee on Veterans' Affairs, attaching a report that spelled out the abuses in some detail. A similar letter was sent to the Senate. The report emphasized that the original intent of the law was to enable any veteran who was under 25 when he entered the service, "whose education or training was impeded, delayed, interrupted, or interfered with by reason of his entry into the service," to continue his education at the expense of the U.S. government. When the act was amended in 1945, these provisions were stricken so as to enable any veteran to obtain the benefits of the act, but it unintentionally opened the door to leisure-time and avocational training.

According to the Budget Bureau report, flight training was costing the government $230 million annually for "tuition payments" for 118,300 veterans, nearly $2,000 per veteran, in contrast to $588 million for all other tuition payments for education and training in colleges and vocational schools for 1,741,245 veterans, an average of only $340 per veteran. It asserted that more than 90 percent of all flight training courses served no occupational purpose and had no appreciable value for national defense. As of the date of the report, the costs of such joy-riding were still growing.

Flight training was not the only target of the report. Social dancing courses, avocational music courses, "applied horsemanship" courses, and a variety of others were quickly developed to enable veterans with full-time employment to jump on the G.I. Bill bandwagon. The report ended by recommending that the law be amended to specify that education and training courses in schools other than elementary and secondary schools and institutions of higher learning must be pursued for the purpose of vocational or occupational advancement needed by the veteran.

It was the great good fortune of the nation and the Budget Bureau that when the report was received by Congresswoman Rogers, there happened to be a junior Congressman from Texas, Olin Teague, recently released from service with a distinguished war record. Teague was deeply disturbed to see the way the G.I. Bill was being manipulated by clever entrepreneurs and unconscionably used by his fellow veterans to get whatever they could out of "Uncle Sugar." Like General Bradley, he wanted veterans to be able to hold their heads up proudly, not become the object of derision. He made it his business to do everything in his power to see that President Truman's and Budget Director Webb's recommendations were carried out. Quickly, a close working relationship developed between Congressman "Tiger" Teague and the staff of the Budget Bureau, and a productive relationship it turned out to be.

Teague saw to it that the House hearings were so complete and devastating in their effect that not even the American Legion could gird itself for a strong fight against the amendments. The bill eventually passed the House without great difficulty. It would also have passed the Senate rather readily had it not been for the intervention of a prominent senator who had an influential supporter who was the owner of a flight school, one that converted itself into a string of flight schools to take advantage of the obvious opportunity for a bonanza. The senator could not bring himself to oppose the bill publicly; he could only stave off passage as long as feasible. Finally, the bill became law with telling effect. Flight training plummeted to a tiny fraction of what it had been; it was confined to genuinely vocational training. But many millions of dollars had gushed as from a slit artery before the hemorrhage was stopped.

One might reasonably suppose that after two such successful attempts to correct deficiencies in the G.I. Bill, it should have been in good shape. Not so. When on-the-job training began to be brought under control as a result of the new standards, another form of abuse began to mushroom. This time it was training that was alleged to be vocational in purpose and was conducted by newly formed, profit-making, so-called educational institutions. They offered courses in every conceivable subject and they strung their courses out over long periods of time in order to enable veterans to collect subsistence allowances as long as they were eligible. Some of the most popular courses were in photography, auto mechanics, upholstering, cooking, hairdressing, bartending, and radio repair.

A single case example, taken from a report dated February 9, 1950, submitted to the President by the Director of the Bureau of the Budget and by the President to Congress, illustrates the unintended permissiveness of the G.I. Bill that eventually showed up in the extensive waste of public funds:

Case #17

Enrolled at university for course in Applied Arts. Stopped 5 weeks later.

Five months later, enrolled for course in Voice Training and Lyric Acting. Stopped after 3 1/2 months.

Three months later, enrolled for Specialized Automotive Tune-up course. Interrupted 11 days later because of illness.

Two days later, enrolled in Voice course. Attended about 10 1/2 months.

Immediately applied for course in Business Administration (denied).

Three months later, applied for permission to take course in Chef Cooking.

Five days later, before application for Chef Cooking was processed, applied for 40 week course in Fountain Grill Operation.

After this veteran failed at his initial try in a genuine university, all his subsequent training was provided by profit-making institutions organized explicitly to take advantage of the G.I. Bill. The absurdity of a forty-week course in "Fountain Grill Operation" is self-evident; yet such courses were approved by the poorly staffed accrediting agencies in various states. By 1949, even General Gray was persuaded by such examples sent to him by the Bureau of the Budget that the situation was getting scandalous. With a nudge from the White House, initiated by the Bureau of the Budget, General Gray agreed to develop a joint report to the Congress that spelled out the nature of these abuses in great detail and asked Congress to change the law once more.

When the 1950 budget was submitted to Congress in January 1949, it was estimated that the cost of veterans education and training during fiscal year 1950 would be $1,993,000,000. For the 1951 budget, it was necessary to revise this 1950 estimate upward to $2,663,000,000, primarily due to an unexpectedly rapid increase in enrollment in vocational training of dubious value. Just one month later, the estimate was revised upward again by another $91,000,000 for the same reason. It was in this atmosphere that President Truman recommended to Congress (as his Budget Bureau had recommended to him) that the law be changed again to establish standards that would apply nationwide to all profit-making vocational schools. And again Congressman Teague became the leader of the Congressional effort to battle the amendments through the Congress. And again he was successful. Another monstrous wastage of tax dollars was brought under control.

Three success stories or one monumental failure of legislative design? At the time, I thought of it more as the former, but as the years went by and I had more opportunity for reflection and observation, I came to the conclusion that it should have been possible in the first place to assemble a group of persons among whom were several who had extensive experience in public administration and who had the wisdom to look at the legislative design with a knowledge of institutional capacities and an understanding of the need to establish intelligent protections against foreseeable avarice.

The matter lay quietly in my mind until I read a newspaper article in the fall of 1979 that described the abuses that had developed under the Vietnam Veterans Readjustment Act. Again, the Veterans Administration was having troubles of the same sort that it had in the late 1940s in respect to profit-making schools that would never have existed but for the opportunity to lure veterans to come in and take substandard courses of little or no long-term value. As far as I could determine, the experience of the 1940s was not properly recorded in either the Veterans Administration or the Office of Management and Budget, and certainly not in the House Veterans Affairs Committee. There was little, if any, institutional memory in any of these three places where the policies for veterans benefits were formulated. My conscience pricked me deeply. I had never taken the trouble to see to it that future generations of analysts and officials of the Bureau of the Budget and its successor, the Office of Management and Budget, would have ready access to the relevant experience of the late 1940s concerning the perversions of the G.I. Bill and the actions that were taken to correct them.

This is not an unusual failing. In fact, it has been more the rule than the exception within the mammoth Department of Health, Education and Welfare, and probably most other departments. There was one exception. Because of the way the Social Security Administration evolved, it did develop a good institutional memory for all significant policy decisions. Following enactment of the Social Security Act in 1935, the law was administered for eleven years by a three-person Social Security Board. For the first four years of its institutional life, it was an "independent agency," reporting directly to the President. When it was assimilated into the Federal Security Agency in 1939, it retained its form as a largely independent three-person Board. Regular meetings were held and the secretary of the Board made a careful record of all decisions and the discussion that led to them. When the three-member Board was replaced by a single commissioner in 1946, the Chairman of the former Board, Arthur Altmeyer, was converted into the Commissioner and he continued to serve in that position for another seven years. During all this time, the practice continued of carefully recording all policy decisions and the analysis that supported them. The habit became institutionalized and was continued by succeeding commissioners. But this was, as I say, a fortunate exception to a common failing. That failing was an aspect of my own tenure as the senior administrative official of the Department of Health, Education, and Welfare (HEW) for a dozen years (1953-65), about which I am most regretful.

With the rate of turnover of policy-making officials and even career officials that has prevailed in recent years, the necessity for a careful system of recording experience in a form useful to future officials is especially acute. Formerly, there used to be a considerable amount of "institutional memory" in the heads of those who were kept on from one administration to the next, but the trend has been steadily toward clean sweeps of top officials whenever there is a change of administration—and sometimes in the middle of them—so that fewer and fewer old hands are available to report to the new officialdom about the good and bad experiences of former administrations. Thus, the development of formal, written, and readily retrievable institutional memories is imperative.

In addition to these conclusions about the great importance of institutional memories, the following lessons seemed to emerge clearly and strongly from the experience with the G.I. Bill of Rights:

1. Any commission appointed to develop a new or revised social program involving income transfers should include experienced public administrators who have demonstrated they understand the dynamics of income transfer programs, including incentive structures and potentials for abuse. If a Federal-state program is contemplated, there should be members who understand the strengths and weaknesses of state and local governments and the mechanisms by which the Federal Government can effectively achieve acceptable standards of performance.

2. Multiple options should be developed by persons of differing institutional and ideological points of view.

3. Options should be compared by "gamesmen" and "gameswomen" skilled in microeconomics. Questions like this should be asked: What will be the incentives to the intended beneficiaries to get on the gravy train? What will be the incentives to entrepreneurs (both profit and non-profit) to use the beneficiaries as their pawns in a multi-million dollar game? By what means can these undesirable effects be minimized?

4. A two-part monitoring program should be established concurrently with the initiation of each substantial new program, involving the administering agency and the Government Accounting Office (GAO) so that at the first signs of any unanticipated perversions of the law, changes in law or regulation can be sought and achieved before the vested interests in the perversions become organized and influential.

The Open-Ended Gusher for Social Services

A second example of a major failure of both the initial design of legislation and the ensuing regulatory process occurred during the Kennedy, Johnson, and Nixon administrations. It concerned grants to states by the Department of Health, Education, and Welfare (HEW) for social services. Ultimately, in the summer of 1972, it became a national scandal before it was brought under control.

It began in 1961, the first year of President John F. Kennedy's administration. Abraham Ribicoff, Connecticut's governor and one of Kennedy's earliest and most ardent supporters, was named to head HEW, and Wilbur Cohen was the immediate choice of both of them to become the Assistant Secretary for Legislation. Ribicoff had developed a keen interest in welfare problems when he served as a municipal judge in Hartford for a dozen years, and Cohen had spent twenty years working on Social Security and welfare policies for the Social Security Administration (which became a part of HEW in 1953). The two of them very soon began thinking about how best to improve the nation's welfare program. Both were believers in seizing upon politically favorable opportunities to build upon existing programs rather than seeking to replace them with radically new systems.

Following this incrementalist approach, Ribicoff and Cohen, with full support from the White House, developed a number of important amendments to the Social Security Act affecting Aid to Dependent Children which was retitled Aid to Families with Dependent Children, a program of grants to states for the support of the very poor. Until then, none of the funds could be used for families where both parents were in the home. The presence of unemployed fathers made households ineligible for welfare, causing many such fathers to desert their families to enable the remaining members to become eligible for aid. A more callous policy would have been hard to devise. That, too, deserves a case study, but it is not the central focus of this analysis. The Ribicoff-Cohen package that ultimately became law went a long way toward correcting this glaring error in the law, but did not eliminate it entirely, since it only *offered* Federal matching funds to states that wished to provide aid for destitute, intact families. Most of the states of the north and west accepted the offer, but many of the states of the south and southwest did not; in those states the problem still exists. In several other respects, the Ribicoff-Cohen recommendations resulted in significant improvements in the welfare provisions of the Social Security Act.

One of the most inconspicuous of these provisions at the time was one that seemed to be a logical and wise adjunct to the improvements in the program of Aid to Families with Dependent Children (AFDC). It concerned the provision of various types of social services to members of poor families. The conventional wisdom of those days was that expert casework counseling could go far toward helping many dependent families find their way out of their cycle of dependency, and that it was almost self-evident that such counseling, supplemented by specific services found to be needed, would be an excellent social investment. Toward this end, Cohen developed, with the aid of an HEW lawyer, an amendment to the law that would encourage states to provide much more comprehensive social services than they had been providing. It offered the states a matching formula of three Federal dollars for each state dollar spent on services to welfare recipients, in contrast to a dollar for dollar matching in respect to general costs of administration, such as determining eligibility and writing checks. The Cohen proposal did not spell out what constituted authorized social services; this was to be left to regulations. Therein lay the beginning of the sad story.

At the time, I was the Administrative Assistant Secretary of HEW. Years later, after I had left the Department in 1965 and as I began to observe perversions of the new law, I wondered how I could have been so short-sighted as to have agreed to the formulation of such a vague bill. Of all people in HEW, I should have been the one who, on the basis of my earlier experience with the G.I. Bill of Rights debacle, should have realized the hazards of writing a law that created, in effect, open-ended appropriations without adequate specificity and safeguards. Like the G.I. Bill, the law created what were treated unnecessarily as legal entitlements that required Congress to appropriate whatever amount of money was needed to fulfill its part of the matching contract. I recalled no action on my part to get the HEW draft bill written so as to make very clear just what constituted the social services that were to be authorized, and I felt quite sure that I would have recalled it if I had put up a fight for appropriate specificity. Eventually, in 1974, two years after the situation became so bad that Congress simply had to rein in the runaway entitlements, Martha Derthick of the Brookings Institution did a careful research analysis of just what happened and wrote a superb case study of the way in which social service expenditures got completely out of control.[2] Her study partially, though not completely, assuaged my conscience. She discovered that the bill was written by a lawyer, Sidney Saperstein, at Cohen's direction, without involving, as had been customary in the previous eight years, the office of the Administrative Assistant Secretary. I am sure, in any event, that I could not have foreseen the magnitude of the administrative Pandora's box that the bill slowly but surely opened.

There were two other provisions that, coupled with the first, paved the way to the ultimate debacle. With encouragement from the Bureau of the Budget, Cohen and Saperstein drew the bill to authorize state welfare departments to make use of other agencies of state governments (vocational rehabilitation agencies, health agencies, and such other agencies as the Secretary determined to be appropriate), in providing needed social services to the poor. This was originally interpreted by the Bureau of Family Services to mean that other agencies should be enlisted in a cooperative effort to help the poor overcome their various barriers to employment and self-reliance. The intent was not that state welfare departments were supposed to start using Federal three-for-one dollars to pay other agencies for performing services that were part of their ongoing responsibility and were being financed from other sources, even if it meant some expansion of those services. Only later did that interpretation receive official Federal blessing.

The third element of the law that ultimately contributed greatly to the hemorrhage of Federal funds was the authorization to provide services not only to persons receiving welfare assistance, but also to persons who had previously received such assistance and the much vaguer group of those who, but for the provision of some form of constructive social service, seemed likely to become welfare claimants. At the time, all three provisions seemed to the authors both in the interest of the potential recipients and in the public interest, and they saw no serious hazards looming on the horizon. But they had not looked very hard.

From the enactment of the new law, the Public Welfare Amendments of 1962, until 1967, grants to states for social services increased quite moderately, increasing from $194 million in 1963 to $359 million in 1966 and dropping back to $282 million in 1967. Two events occurred in 1967 that were to lead to a much more rapid increase in expenditures for social services. The first was a reorganization of HEW that merged the Welfare Administration and the Vocational Rehabilitation Administration into a new organization called the Social and Rehabilitation Service (SRS). John Gardner, then Secretary of HEW, put Mary Switzer, the Administrator of the Vocational Rehabilitation Administration, in charge of the new SRS.

In the latter part of her 45 year period of Federal service, she had earned a reputation as a uniquely effective promoter of a program for the handicapped that proudly proclaimed that it made "taxpayers out of taxeaters." A much-quoted study purported to show that for every dollar spent on rehabilitation, ten dollars would eventually be returned to the Federal treasury in the form of the taxes paid by rehabilitated workers. The general theory of the merger and the appointment of Mary Switzer in her twilight years was that she would work the same magic on welfare clients as she had worked on victims of polio, auto accidents, industrial accidents, blindness, and so on. Without fully realizing how different the challenge was, Mary Switzer plunged in with typical zest. And one of the first things she wanted to do was to use the same general technique in reducing welfare dependency as was used throughout the country in rehabilitating the physically handicapped, that is, developing a full diagnosis as to what kinds of services were needed and then purchasing them by contract with nonprofit as well as public agencies. Another justification for the purchase of services from nonprofit agencies was to authorize the use of such agencies for the care of children of welfare mothers while the mothers were undergoing training to equip them for employment. Miss Switzer found that a small amendment to the law was needed to facilitate such purchases of service on behalf of welfare clients, as was authorized for the physically handicapped.

And so it was that the Welfare Amendments of 1967 included an inconspicuous provision that authorized state welfare agencies to contract with other public and nonprofit agencies to provide social services (again, not specified in the law) to recipients of public assistance, present or past, and to persons who, without such services, seemed likely to become welfare recipients. For some obscure reason, the 1967 amendment also dropped out the provision of the 1962 amendment that enabled the Secretary of HEW to prescribe and specify what constituted social services eligible for three-for-one matching. The burden of proof to demonstrate that the services did qualify shifted from the state to the Secretary of HEW to show that they did not. It seems certain that neither Mary Switzer nor Wilbur Cohen (who by then was Undersecretary of HEW, but still as actively concerned as ever with amendments to the Social Security Act) realized that when put together, the 1962 amendments and the 1967 amendments might open the door to massive manipulation of state financing. Numerous services that had traditionally been performed by the states, either without Federal matching or with matching at a much lower ratio could be charged to the "open-ended" appropriation for grants to states for the administration of public assistance (with three-for-one matching). But that is just what happened.

California led the way. Initially, California had seen the three-for-one matching ratio as a means of increasing the level of social services for welfare recipients of social services, and so used it. But when the 1967 amendment was enacted, California immediately perceived that it would be possible to use the law also to enlarge substantially the Federal financing of various of its ongoing programs that came under the rubric of social services. In 1967, Federal grants to California for social services and training amounted to $60 million; in 1968, $86 million, in 1969, $143 million; and in 1970, $205 million. California made no bones about its strategy: "to deploy (California's) existing expenditures in a way which will produce an optimum return of Federal dollars for a minimum amount of state and local dollars."[3]

In looking back on California's clever grantsmanship, one cannot help but wonder why it was that other states did not follow suit with great alacrity. Not until 1971 did Illinois perceive, or at least act upon the perception, that the open-ended Federal appropriation for social services was a potential gold mine that would enable them to obtain three-for-one matching to pay for a lot of activities previously regarded as outside the jurisdiction of the welfare department and which were financed either wholly or in major degree by state funds. This included parts of programs dealing with drug abuse, alcoholism, mental illness, mental retardation, and juvenile and adult corrections. Illinois was even more blatant about its efforts to use Federal grant monies to substitute for state dollars than California had been, driven by the desperation of rapidly rising welfare costs and the prospect of a severely unbalanced budget. Governor Ogilvie and his budget braintrusters spearheaded the effort to maximize the flow of Federal dollars from the social service grants spigot, basing his case on the California precedents. Ironically, the officials before whom he initially pleaded his case in HEW (before he pulled out all the stops and went to OMB, the White House, and Congress) were the very same officials who had been in power in California a few years earlier and had developed the scheme that Ogilvie now wished to follow—Undersecretary John Veneman and his assistant, Tom Joe, a super-expert at the science of grantsmanship. But Veneman and Joe were now working for President Nixon who strongly desired to hold down expenditures. Their ambivalence led to delaying tactics that eventually benefited Illinois but not the American taxpayers.

The Illinois case became embroiled in very high politics, carefully and dramatically described by Martha Derthick in her case study. As 1971 dragged into 1972 and both President Nixon and Governor Ogilvie, also a Republican, faced reelection, the financial plight of Illinois, always a key state in national elections, became an increasing concern of the White House, and then of Congress. With the help of other states, Senator Percy and the Illinois Congressional delegation pushed the idea of a rider on a tax reduction bill that would relieve the states of increases in welfare costs for one year. This alarmed Nixon and his budgeteers. Eventually, the White House and HEW Secretary Richardson agreed to approve most of the Illinois plan for grants for social services, bringing significant fiscal relief to the state. But by doing so, they opened a floodgate of prospective requests for additional funds.

By this time, all the states in the country had become aware of the bonanza that awaited them if they followed the lead of California and Illinois. In 1971, when the full implications of the Illinois plan became painfully evident, the Office of the Controller of HEW had worked hard to gain agreement on a ceiling on the appropriations for social service grants, but without success. Their proposal was to limit expenditures to 110 percent of the previous year's outlays, but this was objected to by all those that had not yet supped at the table of plenty. If any ceiling was to be imposed, it should not start from current levels of expenditure, said the latecomers, but from ground zero, with allocations made on some equitable basis. Perhaps the 110 percent formula galvanized them into action; perhaps it was all the publicity that the Illinois fracas was getting. In any event, in mid-July 1972, at a meeting of the governors, a list of all the state requests was totted up and it came to $4.7 billion, more than twice the amount that HEW had estimated it might reach. This sent shock waves around the country and sent a particularly strong message to Congress. The *New York Times,* the *Washington Post,* the *Wall Street Journal,* and various weekly news magazines highlighted the scandal immediately. Nine states had projected increases of more than 1,000 percent and Mississippi projected an increase of 42,118 percent—to a sum that was more than half of the state's budget.

Clearly, no such absurdity could be tolerated, especially during an election year. Congress quickly devised a formula that would close the open end of the appropriation and establish an allocation formula based on population. The ceiling on the appropriation was established at $2.5 billion, a figure that would allow an increase for most states, but would cut back on New York, which by this time had gotten on the gravy train too.

In her final chapter, Derthick begins by asserting, quite properly, that the first and main lesson to be learned by this debacle is: the Federal Executive Branch should formulate grant-in-aid regulations systematically and with due concern for the financial costs and other consequences; it should state them clearly and apply them equitably. The Executive Branch violated all these elemental principles in this case—and violated them flagrantly, to the point of farce.

Her case study is a careful documentation of the failures of the Executive Branch, especially the Department of Health, Education, and Welfare, to think carefully about what it wanted to achieve through both legislative channels and through the regulatory process that Congress delegated to HEW. The bumbling in the handling of the regulatory process receives particularly devastating illumination. The Secretary of HEW had control powers that he and his fragmented bureaucracy (that seemed constantly in a state of reorganization and confusion) simply failed to use. The HEW defense that the law made the appropriation totally open-ended and therefore uncontrollable simply did not hold water.

Ms. Derthick might well have given even heavier emphasis to the sins of omission of both the Congress and the Executive Branch in the formulation of the legislation, for both gave it short shrift and neither made any genuine attempt to consider what the problems and hazards might be of the broad grants of authority given in the 1962 and 1967 amendments. Neither branch of government performed its role with reasonable prudence and responsibility.

This case illustrates with unusual clarity the hazards of writing potentially expensive legislation with almost no specificity as to its purposes and limits. All was left to the Executive Branch, presumably to be spelled out in regulations. At no point were experienced administrators, skilled in understanding the operation of state governments, accompanied by clever "grantsmen" and "grantswomen" involved in designing appropriate limitations. As in the case of the G.I. Bill, what should have been done was to assemble a group composed equally of experienced and knowledgeable welfare administrators and budgeteers at state and local levels and some champion Monopoly players (or their equivalent, in terms of their ability to take maximum advantage of any given system) and ask them to develop a scenario to see if they can beat the system and obtain grants in substantial quantity, not pecadillos, for purposes that were not intended either by the Executive Branch policy officials or the Congress. If this approach had been applied at both stages of the process—at the stage of preparing the legislation and at the stage of writing the regulations—it should have obviated the whole mess, or certainly most of it.

As in the earlier case which dealt with the G.I. Bill, the second lesson that deserves emphasis is that once a grant program starts to balloon in size, it develops very rapidly a powerful political constituency. In that earlier case, few, if any, Congressmen would have been likely to vote for avocational flight training as an authorized form of benefit for veterans in the original bill, but by the time it was ultimately arrested because it had become a national scandal, the program had developed into a $100 million dollar industry with a powerful lobby. So it was with social services grants. It is imperative, therefore, to spot any evidences of the misuse of funds at a very early stage and move in rapidly to plug the loophole. By *misuse*, I do not mean illegal use. I mean the use of the funds in a manner that may be technically legal, but which was not given affirmative approval in either the legislative hearings or the regulatory process, and would probably have been prohibited if it had been considered. When loopholes are caught before they provide the livelihood of thousands of people, it is far easier to correct them than when such corrections engender a lot of human misery.

It is self-evident, too, that in any department responsible for the dispensing of large amounts of grant-in-aid money, the degree of care that is exercised to assure the expenditure of those funds for the purposes for which they are intended, and for no other, will depend in substantial degree on the attention that is paid to this element of administration by the secretary and his or her staff. And that will depend in no small degree upon the selection of key appointees by the President and the sailing orders he gives them.

Social service grants and their diversion did not constitute the only case involving billions of dollars that occurred in HEW during the 1960s and 1970s and from which the same general lessons can be drawn. The much larger case is that of Medicaid, enacted in 1965, for which $21 billion is requested in the 1983-84 budget. Space does not permit a discussion of it here, but to any person who is interested in pursuing that case in depth, there is another excellent case study by Robert and Rosemary Stevens entitled, *Welfare Medicine in America* (The Free Press, 1974). The problems are very different, but the high desirability of having had much clearer purposes at the outset of the law and of having had the draft legislation (and the regulations, too) reviewed with care by a variety of imaginative critics is no less evident.

Aid to Families with Dependent Children

In the history of Federal legislation, probably no challenge of legislative design has surpassed that of reforming the welfare system, especially when the proposal is to undertake a massive shift from state and local to Federal administration. Any plan for reforming the multibillion dollar program of Aid to Dependent Children—and there have been a number of proposals to do this—must face or perilously ignore the extraordinarily complex problems of feasibility, coordination with related programs, transition, and undependable cost estimates. In every case, the amount of attention given to problems of administration in writing the proposed legislation has been woefully inadequate in relation to their magnitude. One of the most useful examples of this was President Carter's welfare reform plan of 1977.

The Carter plan for reforming the nation's welfare mess, a program called Better Jobs and Income, (BJI), was almost certainly the most complex and extensive redesign of a group of governmentally operated social programs ever undertaken in the United States, and perhaps in the world. It deserved, therefore, great care in its planning. The Department of Defense normally spends about five years in the planning and development of a new weapons system and another five years in bringing it into full production and operation. The planners of the BJI program were given one hundred days by President Carter to develop a new program, later extended by another ninety days when the options presented were more expensive than expected. While it is not suggested that five years were needed for planning the BJI program, the 190-day crash plan resulted in such serious shortcomings that it was fortunate that it was not enacted.

President Carter gave the assignment to HEW Secretary Joseph Califano almost immediately after he was sworn in, right after Carter's inauguration. A complete package was to be presented in three months (by May 1, 1977), with the expectation that it would be sent to the Congress very shortly thereafter. To have any chance of accomplishing this, Califano had no choice but to make use of the staff that he inherited from the Republican Nixon-Ford administration that had worked on earlier versions of welfare reform. These were economists who were strongly influenced by the ideology of the Negative Income Tax. Califano also decided, at least as a public relations gesture, to give people all over the nation a chance to say what was wrong with the system and what ought to be done about it. A series of regional hearings was held and so many people wished to be heard that statements were usually limited to ten minutes. Understandably, most of those who testified directed their pleas toward some aspect of who gets what, when, and how, and nobody was given time or opportunity to analyze and comment on alternative options from an administrative standpoint.

Finding that the schedule was an impossibility, Califano requested an extension to early June. What he presented in June was a proposal that was significantly more expensive than was acceptable to President Carter. The group was sent back to HEW with instructions to pare it down but have it ready to send to Congress by August 1. Naturally, at such a White House discussion, there was no opportunity to probe the complex problems of administration. As in all such cases, it was assumed that whatever was decided upon could be effectively and efficiently administered, or at least that no administrative difficulties could be so great as to have a major influence on the choice among options. Such assumptions represent one of the most serious fallacies of governmental policy making.

President Carter announced the outlines of his new plan for welfare reform on August 6, 1977, but it was more than a month later, on September 12, that Secretaries Califano and Marshall (who, as Secretary of Labor, was the key official concerned with the jobs part of the program) presented the official proposal to Congress in the form of a 163-page bill. The bill was complicated to begin with and made still more difficult to comprehend by its legal jargon. As a new and simplified system to substitute for the existing welfare program, it seemed anything but simple. A special Subcommittee on Welfare Reform of the House Ways and Means Committee, chaired by Congressman James Corman of California, scheduled hearings almost immediately. Copies of the bill were fanned out to governors and welfare directors all over the country, with invitations to testify. The governors and welfare directors quickly asked their staffs to analyze the bill and tell them how much their state was likely to lose or gain by the new plan. Its fiscal impact was considered so important in comparison to all else that virtually no attention was given to the potential difficulties of administration. Many welfare directors who found that their states would be significantly benefited financially were not hesitant to endorse the bill and testify for it, even though it became apparent in their testimony that they had not carefully read the bill.

Congressman Corman's Subcommittee was even more unrealistic in its allocation of sufficient time for a thorough review of the bill than President Carter had been in setting his initial deadline for the development of the plan. The Subcommittee set a target deadline of the end of November, just over two months after the beginning of hearings, to complete its consideration of the bill, to be followed promptly by Subcommittee decisions and actions. The two-month period was to include hearings around the country as well as in

Washington. The Subcommittee met its self-imposed deadline. It was almost as if its members had come to the conclusion that anything would be better than the existing program, and if this new plan was what Jimmy Carter wanted, why not let him have it? After all, he would be the one who would get major credit or blame if it succeeded or failed.

With this kind of rush to complete action on the bill, it was impossible for the Subcommittee to give any time and attention to administrative issues. As in most pieces of legislation, the Congress does not have enough background in or understanding of problems of administration to bring about useful interrogation of witnesses about administrative feasibility, effectiveness, administrative costs, and the like. And the bigger and more complex the program, the less likely it is to pay appropriate attention to these problems.

Watching these events unfold from an Ivy League sanctuary (the Woodrow Wilson School of Princeton University), I became increasingly uncomfortable, realizing as each week went by how serious the implications might be if such a bill were to be enacted without any careful review of its administrative feasibility, costs, and other effects. Finally, I could bear it no longer and decided to undertake an analysis myself. I did so in two stages: first, a rapid review to serve as an alert to some of those who were working on the bill, and second, a longer, more careful analysis that was published as an Occasional Paper by the National Academy of Public Administration with the title, "The Carter Welfare Reform Plan: An Administrative Critique." In the preparation of this paper, I enlisted the advisory assistance of Robert Ball, Martha Derthick, Mitchell Ginsberg, Richard Nathan, and Harold Orlans, who encouraged me and suggested valuable and useful improvements. The monograph was published in January 1978, shortly after the Corman Subcommittee had reported its version of the bill to full Committee and before the full Committee began its consideration of the bill. The first two pages of the summary of the NAPA Occasional Paper give a useful overview of its conclusions:

Summary and General Conclusions

The Carter welfare reform plan seeks to accomplish a number of important objectives: (1) provide more jobs instead of welfare payments to unemployed people able to work, (2) provide a cash supplement for those who work but whose incomes are inadequate to support their families, (3) assure the provision of decent minimum payments to families and individuals who cannot work and should not be expected to work, (4) abolish the pressures toward family breakup, (5) remove existing disincentives to work (where multiple benefits add up to more than a principal wage earner could possibly earn) by making it more profitable to work than not to work, and (6) provide a larger earned income tax credit for low income people.

These objectives are basically sound and should be pursued vigorously. The appropriate questions are how best to achieve these goals, not whether they should be sought.

The "Better Jobs and Income" plan (BJI) would, if enacted as proposed, completely redesign the welfare system of the nation. Because of the magnitude and complexity of the undertaking, it deserves an extremely careful analysis of its administrative feasibility, a subject largely neglected in the development and early legislative reviews of the legislation. This analysis is directed primarily toward that subject.

A review of the cash assistance proposal leads to the following principal assessments of its administrative consequences:

Disadvantages of Federal Administration

The foremost administrative question is whether cash assistance should be Federally administered, wholly or partially. Should the Federal government determine eligibility and write the checks? This analysis concludes that it should not, even if some states would like to pass the job over to the Federal government. These are the reasons:

1. *Federal administration would proliferate the offices dealing with the poor, confuse them, and reduce the possibility of moving toward integrated access to social services for low income people.*
   Essential social services would continue to be provided by states, their subdivisions, and non-profit agencies: employment services, unemployment insurance, skill training under CETA and the public schools, vocational rehabilitation, housing assistance, day care, child welfare services, family planning, Medicaid, and others. Emergency financial assistance would also be provided by state and local public agencies. Increasing effort needs to be devoted to the coordination of these services through central intake and referral offices operated by the states and their subdivisions. A totally separate, federally operated set of offices dispensing cash might remove all contact between many persons who need help and the community services they need. Also, lines of

communication and responsibility between such Federal payment offices and other local offices providing jobs or cash (the employment service, CETA prime sponsors, and the local emergency needs offices), would become very confusing.

2. *Federal administration would cost much more than state operation.*
   Federal salaries, retirement and other fringe benefits are much higher than comparable state compensation—at least 30% higher than the median state when all costs are considered. Total Federal operation would require some 120,000 to 150,000 Federal employees.

3. *A Federally operated electronic data processing operation would be subject to numerous hazards and is not needed to minimize fraud.*
   A state operated system with incentives for efficient administration (a new and excellent proposal is part of the Carter plan), could achieve low levels of fraud and error and be less vulnerable to large-scale breakdowns.

4. *Transition to Federal operation would be disruptive, costly, and require three years or more to complete.*
   Transition costs would be extremely high and the existing system would deteriorate badly while the new one was being installed.

5. *A partly state and partly Federal operation would be an unstable and confusing arrangement and would probably drift toward Federal takeover.*
   Since total Federal operation has been adjudged to be undesirable, so, too would the hybrid, state-option system be. *States, therefore, should not be given the option of turning over the total operation to the Federal Government.*

Implications for the Legislative Process

Both the executive and legislative branches should recognize the necessity for the participation, at an early state in the development of any important piece of social legislation, of persons who are experienced and skilled in the implementation of laws of sufficient similarity to make comparisons useful. This applies to the departments originating such legislation, to the OMB, and to the Congressional committees reviewing the legislation. Within the Congress, a more formalized procedure drawing more heavily and explicitly on the GAO, with the assistance of the Congressional Research Service and the Congressional Budget Office, would give the legislative process some of the same discipline in respect to issues of administrative design of legislation as has been given to the budget process by the enactment of the Congressional Budget Act of 1974.

For a variety of reasons, the Better Jobs and Income plan failed of enactment in the 94th Congress and the Carter administration started all over again with an entirely new approach in the 95th Congress, an approach that seemed to take into account, either coincidentally or purposefully, some of the considerations laid out in my monograph. The failure of the bill in the 94th Congress had little or nothing to do with the administrative issues I raised; it was the "who gets what, when, and how" issues and the opposition of Senator Long, the powerful Chairman of the Senate Finance Committee, that assured its defeat.

Why were important issues of administrative feasibility and soundness given so little attention in the first version of the Carter Welfare Reform plan? There were at least three reasons. First, there was the matter of time pressure. President Carter did not understand the complexity of the problem and assumed that a good design could be worked out very rapidly. Good administrative design takes time, and redesigning a program that has worked badly is likely to take considerably more time than starting from scratch. When a reasonable amount of time is unavailable, the administrative issues get short shrift. Second, as mentioned above, the principal designers were persons who had earlier been activists committed to one or another modified version of the Negative Income Tax which, if enacted, would have been administered by the Federal Government. So great was the ideological attachment to the Negative Income Tax idea that administrative issues were always subordinated to the conviction that Federal administration was essential and that since both the Social Security program and the Internal Revenue Service (IRS) had generally good records of administration, there should be no reason why the Social Security Administration (or the IRS, or some other Federal organization) could not do at least as well in administering the new BJI program. And third, the new administration had no effective voice among its new appointees who understood both administration and the ramifications and complexities of the welfare system as it had evolved since the enactment of the Social Security Act in 1935.

The second reason, the residual impact of the Negative Income Tax mystique, is worth a bit of elaboration, since there is a very interesting account of its effect upon an earlier Secretary of HEW, Caspar Weinberger. It is contained in a case study prepared by Cynthia Horan of the Kennedy School of Government at Harvard, under the supervision of former HEW Assistant Secretary Laurence Lynn, Jr. (Case Study C95-77-199, 1977, titled "Caspar Weinberger and Welfare Reform"). It describes the internal staff discussions with Secretary Weinberger about what kind of welfare reform program the Ford administration should support and a tour de force performed by Milton Friedman. Here is an illuminating excerpt from that case study which relates to Milton Friedman's participation:

In late August (1974) Weinberger and Taft left on a diplomatic trip to the USSR. Palmer's staff began to develop in detail the reform options presented to the Secretary in the briefings. At Carlucci's request, a copy of Friedman's article, "The Case for a Negative Income Tax" was pouched to Weinberger in the Soviet Union, where he and Taft spent much time discussing welfare reform.

Carlucci (Under Secretary) recalled that he and Morrill (Assistant Secretary) were becoming concerned that the briefings were breaking down:

Bill and I were discussing the lack of progress that had been made in the last one or two briefing sessions. Bob Carleson had developed a tendency to interrupt the briefers at every sentence, and it was clear to me that this was even beginning to frustrate Cap. At this rate, it would take us forever to get through the issues we had to address. We were looking for some dramatic way of achieving a breakthrough. Bill had been in touch with Milton Friedman and his name came up. We both agreed that it might be desirable to have a session with Milton. Bill wondered if he should go out and see him, and one of us suggested it might be a good idea to get him into HEW for a briefing. Who actually said it, I don't recall, but we both thought we had hit on something good.

In any event the idea turned out to be the best one we had. Friedman was absolutely brilliant and covered in five minutes what it might have taken us months to cover.

To many of the participants, Friedman's appearance at this point was critical. (Weinberger already knew Friedman through their mutual friend and colleague George Schultz, then Secretary of the

Treasury, who had been a strong supporter of [The Family Assistance Plan] FAP and had consistently advocated overhaul of AFDC.) Palmer recalled the meeting as finally decimating the lure of Carleson's conservative arguments:

Friedman was someone that Weinberger knew and certainly respected and believed had similar viewpoints to his own. We had a session where Friedman came and met with the same set of actors who were in the briefing sessions. Basically Weinberger asked Friedman, "What do you think we ought to do?" And Friedman was extremely articulate and convincing about the negative income tax as differentiated from FAP. That, of course, was one of the options in the memo we were working on. My recollection is that Weinberger more or less made up his mind subsequent to that session. That is, he didn't really make up his mind on the basis of carefully studying the things that we prepared as much as on having been moved along, having gone through an evolution in his understanding of the issue.

Morrill remembered a combination of intellectual virtuosity and committed conservatism:

Friedman's contribution to all of this process was an important one—less to the ultimate persuasion of Cap than in dealing more with Cap's own underlying reservations in a couple of areas. Friedman literally not only moved Cap across some threshold but changed an attitude of acceptance of what was necessary into a very strong positive enthusiasm.

There were two issues with which Cap struggled the hardest. One was, could you do it with jobs? This was an issue where what we knew was not all that strong. The other issue was the work requirement. Cap kept saying, "I'd rather do welfare reform with a jobs route. How much can we do?" And what we had to tell him was, "We don't think you can do it without getting into a public service job program, and from everything we know you can't do that without running up the costs fairly substantially." And because we couldn't deal with those two points, he moved away from what was intrinsically his preferred ideological position. I think Friedman dealt with those issues pretty successfully by saying, "Look that's an interesting question, but it's just irrelevant—that is, politically, the work requirement had to be there but conceptually it was not the guts of the debate. Out of all that we kept coming back to the issue not as "welfare reform" but more nearly as "tax reform."

Paul O'Neill, Assistant OMB Director for Human Resource Programs, had kept in touch with Morrill and Carlucci on the welfare policy process, although he had not attended prior HEW briefings. O'Neill had also worked with Weinberger at OMB and had known the strong objections Weinberger had to FAP. He recalled the impressions Friedman made on the Secretary at the meeting. Friedman stressed that the negative income tax would abolish large bureaucracies, concentrate funds on the poorest and promote work through permitting recipients to retain portions of their earnings. He also answered Weinberger's concern that the negative income tax would become fiscally uncontrollable since the states would have no fiscal stake in it and thus would not serve as counterweights to inevitable political pressures for continually higher benefit rates. By integrating the tax and transfer system, Friedman pointed out, fiscal control over welfare spending would be augmented: any increase in breakeven level of income would simultaneously require an increase in tax exemption for tax purposes and this in turn would require higher taxes on higher incomes.[4]

Three weeks later on November 6, Secretary Weinberger sent a memo to the President, titled "Major Domestic Programs and Tax Reform," advocating the integration of the tax, welfare and domestic assistance programs along the general line of Friedman's Negative Income Tax (NIT) scheme. Neither President Nixon nor President Ford accepted Weinberger's recommendation, but the case study is a strong reenforcement of the generalization that *major decisions on policy tend to be made without much, if any, discussion of the administrative problems and implications. Ideological thinking often has strong influence on decisions, usually to the detriment of any cool analysis of administrative issues.*

Lessons from Welfare Reform

Most of the generalizations drawn from the two previous cases are also applicable to welfare reform, especially the need to take adequate time to give full consideration to the administrative problems involved. But there are two other generalizations to note.

1. *It is particularly important to examine with great care the claims of those who promise to solve the most deep-seated social problems with systems that are simple, clear, and economical to administer.* This brings to mind a saying of H.L. Mencken: "For every complex social problem, there is a solution that is neat, simple, and wrong." The negative income tax idea was like a supernova to economists—an explosion of light in the sky that seemed to reveal the possibility of

abolishing poverty by a system so elegantly simple as to be like a social science equivalent of $E=MC^2$. The magnetic power of that idea was so great among the economics fraternity, from Friedman to Galbraith, that it dominated the thought and action of would-be reformers of the welfare system for nearly two decades. But the more carefully and objectively experienced administrators looked into the matter, the more Mencken seemed to be right.

Friedman's negative income tax was supposed to abolish poverty at not too high a social cost while eliminating a huge bureaucracy at the state and local levels, adding only a very modest number of people to the staff of the Internal Revenue Service. It would not have abolished poverty; to do so, using his NIT formula would have cost enormous sums. And with the modifications that later disciples of the basic idea found to be necessary to make the scheme workable, it would have been expensive to administer and would have greatly increased the difficulties of coordination with social service programs. Simplistic proposals are often wrapped in very attractive packaging, but the contents need to be examined with the greatest of care.

2. *Experience with welfare reform proposals suggests the desirability of creating competitive teams of analysts within the Executive Branch to develop alternative plans and to critique each other's recommendations.* In respect to welfare reform, it would clearly have been useful to have one team working on a plan that would have undertaken to see how many of the objectives that were agreed upon could be achieved by substantially improving the existing Federal-state program while another team proceeded with its more radical proposal for federalizing cash payments to the needy. If the plan for major incremental improvement had been chosen in 1977, it seems highly likely that it would have been enacted, since there was a good deal of steam behind some form of welfare reform. No good alternative along these lines was presented to the policy makers. The administration finally came to the conclusion that the major incremental approach was the only one that was politically feasible, that of establishing basic minimum standards while retaining the Federal-state system.

Can the "Costly Deficiency" Be Partially Overcome?

These three examples of the failure of administrative design are illustrative of a much larger array of such cases that might have been adduced. The need for extreme care applies equally to programs that do not involve large income transfers to individuals or expensive services for their benefit. In some instances, Congress has written legislation that deliberately passed the buck to the Executive Branch to work out extremely perplexing administrative problems. And when that happened, a very heavy burden was placed on the Executive Branch to hold hearings and write regulations that would take account of numerous factors that were never given any consideration in the writing of the legislation. Examples of this Congressional propensity are the laws that required the withholding of Federal funds to institutions that did not offer equality of athletic opportunities and programs to women and men, required withholding of Federal funds to institutions and school systems that did not offer equal educational opportunity to the handicapped and did not *mainstream* (educating them in the same classes as the nonhandicapped wherever conceivably possible) such handicapped students, and required the withholding of funds for subsidy of urban mass transit systems that did not provide full access to mass transit by the physically handicapped. Writing regulations in these cases took two or more years, so complex were the issues raised by the general language of the legislation without consideration of its implications.

Is there any way to cure or ameliorate these bad legislative habits on the part of both the Executive Branch and Congress? It will not be easy, and it may not even be possible, but is is surely worth a try. Two general approaches occur to me. Earlier, I referred to the widespread failure within the Executive Branch to develop, systematically, an institutional memory of policy and program development that would be readily accessible to each new set of officials and was so designed as to make it easy to use it. Such institutional memories should exist in all departments and agencies, in all major components of departments, in the Office of Management and Budget, in the White House, in the Congressional Research Service, the Congressional Budget Office, and the General Accounting Office. A variety of systems should be developed for recording, filing, and retrieving information on the processes of analysis and policy formulation, and the successes, failures, and missed opportunities of each set of officials put in charge of an organization. No single system should be designed on high and imposed on the entire Executive Branch, but all agencies should be instructed by the President to develop systems that will leave to their successors a useful record of the lessons they think they learned from the rough and tumble of their years in office. High on the list of priorities should be a recording of what was done and not done in considering very carefully the administrative issues in respect to the design of most new legislation. This should be followed by some assessment of the successes and failures of the administrative design after the legislation was enacted.

Such an emphasis on the systematic development of an institutional memory at each important nexus of public policy formulation should open the way to fruitful interaction between the Federal government and academia, and between the state and local governments and academia. I am thinking particularly of the graduate schools of public affairs and public administration. Many of them make extensive use of case studies of public policy decision making as teaching tools and a number of them are deeply involved in the production of significant and useful case studies. While there might be some difference in emphasis in a case study produced for the use of a future Secretary of Defense, for example, and one that would have optimal pedagogical use for young students seeking a master's degree in public affairs or public policy or public administration, it seems highly probably that the same body of information could serve both purposes.

Why would it not be a good idea for the President's Management Improvement Council to take the leadership in exploring the possibilities of collaborative effort by the appropriate components of the Federal Government and a group of graduate schools of public affairs in developing, quite purposefully and systematically (but not singlemindedly), "institutional memories" for the key decision makers of government and for use as teaching materials for the graduate schools? Obviously, both the government and the graduate schools would have to be prepared to make a contribution in skilled professional personnel and the Federal Government would have to make a larger resource commitment to this purpose than the skimpy allocation it has made to this purpose to date.

A second approach that seems worthy of consideration is for the President to issue an Executive Order that would apply to all bills, whether initiated within the Executive Branch or in Congress, the annual cost of which is expected to exceed, let us say, $5 million. The order would direct that a careful analysis be made of each such piece of proposed legislation to determine just how the bill would be administered, how many people would be required to administer it, what its impact would be on state and local institutions and private businesses in terms of administrative burden, the advantages and disadvantages of contracting out significant portions of the administrative processes (as occurs in Medicare, for example), how the necessary coordination with other programs would be achieved, and, as one of the most important considerations, what the incentives and disincentives are that would affect the way in which the program would influence the institutional and individual behavior of those who would be the beneficiaries of the legislation. Not least, in respect to all legislation that is initiated within the Executive Branch, the analysis should show what options were considered in developing the legislation to achieve the specified purposes and the reasons for choosing the preferred option over those rejected.

Estimates of cost are already required in connection with new legislation and these include estimates of the number of administrative employees needed to implement new legislation. What I am suggesting goes well beyond the current requirement. It would involve a much more detailed description of the nature of the administrative problems anticipated and the manner in which these would be dealt with. Although there are obvious limits to the predictability of such problems, a general format could be developed that would require more specificity in spelling out what is expected to be done and how than is now the case.

Some will object that this will add more paper of questionable value to the mounds of it that have already resulted from such programs as Planning, Programming, Budgeting (PPB), Zero Base Budgeting, sunset laws (or their equivalent in the form of short-term authorization acts), and the like. To this I would respond that the trouble with most such programs is that they are nonselective. The key to success in the legislative field is to be selective, to avoid trying to review all programs and all issues, great and small, every year. One important secret of success that should no longer be secret is that it is possible to avoid making many mistakes if more attention is given to the administrative issues at the beginning. It is imperative to get the incentives straight from the outset so that it will be in the public interest for the beneficiaries and participants to behave as the law intends. In selecting targets of opportunity on which to concentrate, none is more important than the launching of a new piece of significant legislation. This would be a small burden compared to sweeping annual reviews like Zero Base Budgeting.

These two approaches would reinforce one another. The development of good institutional memories that would serve top policy officials well, that would be so organized as to make quickly accessible key information in reasonably accurate and usable form, would also stimulate extensive interest in and out of government in widening the policy options and in critiquing proposals before they are written into law. It would focus far more attention on the administrative and management components of the legislation and make it far clearer than has been customary in the past that every program must be administratively well designed from the beginning if it is to be successful. It is to be hoped that such an approach would not only encourage better beginnings, but direct much more attention to the revision of legislation that has not been generally rated as successful. This is often more difficult than starting right in the first place, but feasible, in many instances, if well conceived and well executed. We should not have to wait for national scandals to develop before correcting ill-conceived beginnings.

Footnotes

1. Named to serve with Osborn were Cortlandt C. Baughman, Director of Special Activities, Bureau of Naval Personnel, Rufus C. Harris, President of Tulane University, Dexter Keezer, Deputy Administrator, Office of Price Administration, Young B. Smith, Dean of Columbia Law School, and John W. Studebaker, U.S. Commissioner of Education.

2. Martha Derthick, *Uncontrollable Spending for Social Services Grants* (Washington, D.C.: Brookings, 1974).

3. "California Welfare: A Legislative Program for Reform," A Staff Report to the Assembly Committee on Social Welfare by the Assembly Office of Research and Staff of the Assembly Committee on Social Welfare (Sacramento: February 1969), processed, pp. 216-218. See Derthick, *op. cit.*, p. 32.

4. Friedman's article "The Case for a Negative Income Tax" concludes: "The cost of the payments is in one lump sum that can be calculated and that will be painfully obvious to every taxpayer. It will be obvious that every rise in the rate applied to negative taxable income raises the cost."

Editorial Note: From his vantage point in the U.S. Department of Agriculture (USDA), Martin Kriesberg has participated in the formulation of policies involving food and international organizational affairs. He describes from first-hand experience the policymaker's desire to strengthen farm prices, help needy countries, and be instrumental in development procedures involving foreign nations. Whether officials in the USDA are elected, appointed, or career civil servants has a bearing on their views and Kriesberg compares the different administrations in this respect. Much of his discussion concerns the World Food Conference held in 1974 and the U.N. Food and Agricultural Organization (FAO) Conference of 1979. He traces the increasing emphasis of developing countries on food security, but points to the often controlling factors of budgetary costs, commercial and price stability goals, and foreign policy emphasis. Kriesberg concludes that members of the career service working with appointed leaders in the various departments are representative of their various constituencies and reflect constituency interests in policy formation. He says "the Federal bureaucracy is indeed governance by the people for the people."

CHAPTER 4

FOOD AID AND FOREIGN POLICY: A CASE STUDY OF INTERAGENCY POLICY MAKING

Martin Kriesberg

NO GRAIN OF COMFORT FROM THE UNITED STATES was the headline of a tabloid published in Rome in connection with the World Food Conference of 1974. President Ford had not approved a cabled request for a larger food aid program from the U.S. delegation at the Conference. Secretary of Agriculture Butz led the delegation, but the request was largely the result of pressure from some U.S. Senators, principally the late Senator Humphrey, who felt that the United States should increase food aid to meet the needs of developing countries as urged by their representatives. Again, at the biennial Conference of the U.N. Food and Agriculture Organization meeting in November 1979, developing countries voiced concern about food aid during times of worldwide shortages. (There was no global shortage then, but serious shortfalls in Soviet and Indian harvests contributed to developing country anxiety.) This paper examines the U.S. policy during these two periods and how U.S. policy on food aid has evolved. The writer had direct knowledge of many of the events described as a result of his responsibilities in the Office of International Cooperation and Development, U.S. Department of Agriculture. The views expressed here are the writer's and not necessarily those of his agency or of USDA.

Food Aid at Issue During World Food Conference

The World Food Conference became an arena in which ideas of food aid, developed in periods of plenty, clashed with ideas generated by the new period of scarcity. The Conference, proposed by Secretary of State Kissinger at a United Nations meeting, was convened under U.N. auspices as a meeting of government representatives to deal primarily with the longer run problems of food production, distribution, and security. But delegations from many developing countries whose precarious domestic food situation had worsened as the result of drought sought increased food aid to meet their current needs. They became particularly apprehensive over the decline in U.S. grain stocks triggered by large Soviet purchases in 1972 and worsened by continuing poor harvests (including a shortfall in U.S. corn production in 1974).

Several hundred nongovernmental organizations were on the scene in Rome; a large proportion were engaged in missionary and charitable work around the world. They served as conduits for food aid received largely from the United States. For most, their *raison d'etre* was to carry on such works of charity; grants of food were a principal means of access to those they seek to help. They were concerned that a cut in U.S. donations would mean serious cutbacks in their own programs. Many publicists on international food and agriculture at the Conference joined forces with most of these charitable groups in urging more U.S. food aid and greater commitment toward multilateral food aid efforts.

The United States Delegation, prepared to address the long-term issues as announced by the Conference organizers, was distressed by these demands for more food aid to meet current needs. It sought to hold the position established in pre-Conference planning sessions by agencies of the Federal Government. That position, influenced by short grain supplies and high food prices, was to hold to relatively low tonnage levels of food aid, both bilateral and multilateral. Although led by Secretary Butz, the delegation included representatives from the Departments of State, Treasury, and Commerce, and a contingent from the U.S. Congress. While each agency saw the situation from the perspective of its own mission responsibilities, at the time there was consensus on the food aid position. However, differences arising out of partisan politics (Humphrey and Butz) and ideology (hunger issue organizations versus government guardians of the public purse) divided the delegation when it assembled in Rome.

The U.S. Department of Agriculture (USDA) recognized the precarious state of U.S. and world cereal stocks and wanted, insofar as possible, to maintain commitments to regular commercial customers and to those (like the Soviet Union and the Peoples Republic of China) who had recently been purchasing from U.S. suppliers. A significantly larger amount of commodities, set aside for grants and concessional sales to needy countries, might preempt supplies from commercial customers and push up prices for U.S. consumers.

Treasury was concerned with holding down U.S. consumer prices and the country's adverse balance of payments. It was reluctant to give food away which, if available to the domestic market, might help to hold down domestic prices or, if sold to foreign commercial customers, would earn more foreign exchange.

State was strongly committed to help selected new friends in the Middle East as well as those in the new detente and to maintain bilateral commitments to countries in South and Southeast Asia. New food aid pledges might undermine those already made.

Of course, had the 1974 grain harvests been as bountiful as anticipated before the poor summer rains and the early autumn frosts, decisions for these agencies would have been easier, as they had been in previous years and as they were during the middle 70s.

Shortly after the Conference, the Ford Administration drew up an options paper to consider costs and implications of alternative food aid program levels. A low option of $764 million would have met the foreign policy needs, but little would be left for other objectives of U.S. food aid programs. A middle option of $1,110 million would permit an earmarking of $612 million for aid to countries in which the U.S. had special political interests (principally Southeast Asia and the Middle East) and still leave a reasonable amount for critical food short countries like India and Bangladesh. A high option, set at $1,300 million, would ease the strain for all U.S. concerns.

Events shaped the decision. The President announced in January that he had approved a food aid program of $1,600 million!

Among the factors influencing the decision was a provision of the Foreign Assistance Act passed in December 1974 that for FY 1975 no more than 30 percent of "concessional food aid" could go to countries that were not among those hardest hit by the world food crisis. If this criteria were to control, the lower options would have left a level of food aid in support of foreign policy objectives significantly less than the Administration's estimated need. Several newspaper reports on the subject and church and charitable organizations continued to raise questions about the priorities in food aid allocations as between humanitarian and foreign policy objectives. These differences were debated in the Interagency Staff Committee meetings which included representatives of all the U.S. agencies concerned with the Food for Peace program, PL 480.[1] Then the Soviet Union and the Peoples Republic of China announced that they would not take delivery on a portion of their contracts to purchase grains from the United States. A total of 800,000 tons was involved. It began to appear that the supply situation at prevailing prices would not be as short as anticipated several months earlier. Grain prices softened. The way was clear for meeting both foreign policy and humanitarian objectives in full measure. Budget considerations bowed to the imperative of foreign policy commitments and to pressures from producers and the "hunger issues" groups.

Evolution of Food Aid Policies

The United States has spent over $30 billion in overseas food aid during the past 28 years. Throughout most of this time, the Food for Peace program was a convenient marriage of commerce and compassion. It added to the market for U.S. farm commodities, thus bolstering farm prices. It also fit in well with the American sense of compassion for those in need, the hungry in Asia, Africa, and Latin America. Commerce and compassion persist but do not wholly characterize the rather distinct eras within the 28-year history of PL 480.

A Time of Surplus Disposal and Market Development

In its early days, PL 480 served as a relief valve to help drain off some of the grain surpluses which imposed a heavy burden on U.S. farm programs. By the early 1960s, U.S. grain surpluses were running in excess of 30 million tons and were costing U.S. taxpayers billions of dollars in payments for farmers and for storage costs each year. So self-interest on the part of the taxpayer as well as producers lent significant support to the food aid effort. Moreover, as populations in developing countries became accustomed to relatively low cost wheat and bread, a continuing market was created in these countries. Burgeoning city populations turned to wheat rather than more traditional grains indigeneous to the country as they adopted Western patterns of living.

The India Drought and Food Aid for Development

In 1965-66, two years of drought brought India to the edge of widespread famine. U.S. food aid in unprecedented amounts—14 million tons of grain—went to her relief. Some thoughtful observers argued that the near disaster in India was in part induced by a food aid policy that encouraged recipient governments to avoid difficult domestic policies necessary to increase their own output of food. They argued that unless countries like India increased their self sufficiency in food, the United States (and the international community) would face mounting food aid needs which ultimately could not be met. Development oriented staffers at USDA such as Lester Brown and his counterparts at the U.S. Agency for International Development (AID) took this view and persuaded Secretary Freeman to follow this approach in negotiations with India's leaders.[2]

Assistant Secretary Jacobsen then took the lead in formulating new legislation enacted in 1966 which provided that concessional food sales should be tied to each recipient country's own efforts to improve agriculture. This was a major element in the reoriented food aid legislation.[3] Each food aid agreement contained provisions outlining specific self-help measures the country would carry out in exchange for the assistance. Under these provisions, development plans were required that assigned higher priority for agriculture in many of the recipient countries. An especially appealing aspect of the program was that the money generated by the sale of the commodities within the recipient country could be used to finance their agricultural development projects.

Foreign Policy Purposes to the Fore

The third change in food aid policy began about 1972. Food aid policy entered a new phase only partially because of new legislation. New economic confrontations between developing countries and the industrialized countries and the growing dependence of developing countries on imports of U.S. grains put into focus the possibilities of using food as an instrument of U.S. foreign policy. The war in Viet Nam demonstrated how food aid could provide essential economic support for governments in which the United States had special political and/or military interests.

In 1972, a major shortfall in Soviet grain production caused the USSR to come into the world market to buy grains on a commercial basis and the evolving detente led to purchases in unprecedented amounts from the United States: the Soviets purchased 25 percent of the total U.S. wheat crop. The United States facilitated the purchase by providing near term credits. At the same time, significant shortfalls in food production in South Asia and the Sahelian Zone of Africa once more claimed large amounts of food aid. U.S. grain stocks (and those in other exporting countries) were drawn down precipitously. Grains became scarce on the world market for the first time since 1966. With the worldwide shortage in food supplies in 1973, market forces pushed up grain prices and major exporting countries were faced with the prospect of selecting the countries to whom they would sell.

A second traumatic event shook the United States and the world in October 1973 when the governments of the Organization of Petroleum Exporting Countries (OPEC) used their control over another commodity—oil—as a political and economic weapon. Exports were embargoed to some countries; quantum increases in prices were decreed for all. It suddenly became clear that a small group of countries controlling a major share of a commodity that other countries needed to import could exact a steep price, not only in coin, but in foreign policy orientation.

World production of grains failed again in 1974 to achieve levels adequate to satisfy current demand and to rebuild stocks. Many developing countries, including India, Pakistan, and Bangladesh, were caught in an economic vise. Larger imports of higher priced fuel and food strained their foreign exchange to the limit. Grain exporting countries found themselves in a position to profit from their strategic control over vital commodities. As the world's largest exporter of grains, the United States found the situation conducive to having food aid serve its foreign policy objectives.

Seeking to bolster the government in South Viet Nam, the United States sent a major portion of its total food aid there—about 25 percent during 1973 and 1974—to provide food for rural populations drawn to the city for security reasons and to help finance government operations. South Korea also received large amounts of food aid—some 16 percent. This was substantially more than its economic condition alone would warrant. Pursuing Mideast peace efforts, the United States also reestablished in 1974 large concessional sales of food to Egypt, and to Syria as well (and to a lesser extent, Israel and Jordan).

Factors Influencing Current U.S. Policies

World events and changes in administrations in the late 1970s again pushed humanitarian and development considerations to the forefront in food aid policies. New legislation as well as administrative arrangements underscored this emphasis. But food as an instrument of foreign policy was not forgotten then, nor by the Administration that came into power in 1980.

New Legislation in 1975 and in 1977-78

Experiences in the allocations of food aid in the early 70s under President Nixon led to new legislative mandates on the Executive. Recognizing the needs of the low-income food deficit countries for greater assurance of food aid, the International Development and Food Assistance Act of 1975 (which amended the prevailing PL 480 measures) provided that 75 percent of Title I (embodying the basic concessional sales provisions) be directed to countries with annual per capita GNP of $300 or less. The legislation further set minimum tonnage levels of 1.2 million tons of food assistance under Title II (embodying provisions for food aid as grants through national and international agencies which distributed the food). These provisions clearly made food aid an instrument for humanitarian and development purposes. It limited its uses for market development and for U.S. foreign policy purposes (although these might well be served by the humanitarian and development goals).

Continuing to write stronger humanitarian and development objectives for U.S. food aid, the Congress further altered the legislation in 1977. The 75 percent of Title I food assistance would go to developing countries meeting the World Bank's criteria for concessional loans ($550 per capita in 1976 dollars). A human rights qualification was added. The legislation also established a new

Title III which provides that revenues generated by recipient governments from Title I sales could be used for development projects and thereby be counted toward repayment. (This is a provision similar to the self-help intent of PL 480 legislation in the late '60s.) Emphasizing humanitarian considerations, the legislation also provided that priority be given to malnourished children and people in the poorest regions of recipient countries.

New Administrative Arrangements

With the new Administration of President Carter, there was widespread agreement on the objectives that Congress had set: assistant secretaries responsible for implementing the new PL 480 measures at State, AID, Treasury, and the USDA were in basic agreement with the new emphasis and the underlying reasons for it. At the Department of Agriculture, for example, the Assistant Secretary for International Affairs and Commodity Programs, Dr. Dale Hathaway,[4] was, before his appointment, an academic widely known for his concern with world food problems and developing country needs. His outlook was in contrast to several of his immediate predecessors who were linked with large grain trading companies (before and after serving in USDA). Hathaway accepted the findings of studies which projected continuing and growing food problems of low-income, food deficit countries which made the earlier concerns for surplus disposal obsolete. His counterpart at Treasury, Fred Bergsten, who was at Brookings prior to his appointment as Assistant Secretary, reflected a similar change from his predecessors in that post. The two were thus prepared to work together with counterparts at State and AID, as well as within the policy framework of the new legislation to which they had contributed prior to their appointment.

In response to often-heard criticisms on the lack of coordination among U.S. agencies concerned with foreign food aid and taking into account the new policy emphasis, President Carter put into place new interagency bodies. To coordinate the overall foreign assistance activities of the Federal Government, he established a new coordinating mechanism, the Development Coordinating Committee (DCC) under the chairmanship of the AID Administrator. Under the DCC, a Subcommittee on Food Aid was created, chaired by USDA, to develop policy and coordinate programs and budgets for all food assistance purposes—for development, humanitarian, foreign policy, and market development. A food Working Group, also chaired by USDA and including State, Treasury, AID, and OMB, was also established under the Subcommittee to replace the Interagency Staff Committee that had reviewed and coordinated PL 480 programs at the operating level for two decades. A Title II Subcommittee was continued, chaired by AID, and included USDA and

OMB. It reviewed and recommended approval of country programs to the Working Group.

The dynamics of discussions within the DCC Food Aid Subcommittee and its Working Group, reflected the hierarchy of the agencies and the individuals involved. In recent years, the USDA chairman has been an individual with AID and development experience. There has been substantial agreement on policy and programs between USDA and AID. Ranged on another side in the discussions, there have been representatives of the State Department, Treasury Department, and the Office of Budget and Management (OMB). Often these agencies have been concerned with the budgetary impact of programs; State and OMB have also been outspoken for U.S. foreign policy objectives. While membership in the DCC Subcommittee is nominally at the subcabinet level, in practice, representatives are senior officers from each of the operating bureaus concerned. There has been a tendency for spokesmen of State and OMB to intimate that they speak for the President and thereby add weight to considerations of foreign policy and budgetary restraint.[5]

A report issued by the General Accounting Office (GAO) in October 1979 criticized the layering of reviews and decision-making bodies. Focusing on Title II, with its emphasis on grant and development aid, the report recommends that AID or its new umbrella organization, the International Development and Cooperation Administration, (IDCA) have primary responsibility for Title II programs. Not unexpectedly, the USDA saw a need for considering all PL 480 titles together and indeed, for viewing all concessional commodity programs as being interrelated. In a more comprehensive study on food aid prepared for the Secretary of Agriculture, and published in May 1978, USDA had also expressed a similar concern for coordination, but the DCC and its Subcommittees were viewed as largely meeting the needs for coordination. The report leaned toward larger USDA responsibilities.

There is more understanding and agreement now than in previous years on the multiple purposes served by U.S. foreign food assistance. Purposes of surplus disposal and market development in the early 80s were seen as less important, even within the Department of Agriculture,[6] until the large buildup of grain stocks held by the U.S. in 1981 and 1982 occurred. Reserve stocks had been seen as less of a burden on the market than as a means, in concert with other countries, to provide some stability in world supplies and hence some moderation in prices. Responsibility to the international community, to concessional as well as commercial importers, is widely accepted by public and private agriculture officials. In 1979 this change was underscored when the U.S. announced its willingness to participate in a new international Food Aid Convention (an agreement among major wheat

Theodore Lownik Library
Illinois Benedictine College
Lisle, Illinois 60532

exporters to provide a portion of their grain on concessional or grant basis to needy developing countries). Previously, the United States and other major wheat exporters maintained that it was necessary to link a Food Aid Convention to a new International Wheat Agreement, that is, make food aid a factor in wheat agreements which were essentially concerned with commercial trade. The reason for the linkage was to have all exporting countries share in the *food aid burden* as well as the *commercial trade.*

There has been a significant decline in the size of food aid programs relative to commercial commodity sales during the years since the mid-1960s, so USDA staffers no longer see food aid as critical to maintaining high levels of commodity exports. In 1965, PL 480 programs had a value of $1,570 million compared to $6,100 million of total agricultural exports, i.e. 26 percent. In 1968, PL 480 sales fell to $1,279 million and total exports rose to $6,400 million. PL 480 then accounted for 20 percent. But in 1973 and thereafter, the relative importance of PL 480 programs fell more sharply. In 1973, the year of a world food crisis, PL 480 sales dropped to 7 percent of total agricultural exports by the United States as the price as well as the volume of grain exports rose rapidly, reaching $12,902 million. That trend had continued. From 1974 through 1978, PL 480 sales have been 4-5 percent of total exports and in 1980-81 will probably fall to 3 percent as commercial sales reach $40 billion.[7]

At the same time, there has been a congruence in U.S. foreign policy objectives and in U.S. disbursements of food for humanitarian and development purposes. When the Congress mandated that 75 percent of PL 480 food should go to the lowest income countries, it was a reaction to President Nixon's use of food aid for foreign policy purposes in Viet Nam and several other countries. Now a large allocation of food aid to Egypt as part of the general peace effort in the Middle East is consistent with humanitarian and development objectives, since Egypt is included in United Nations and World Bank lists of very poor, food-deficit countries.

Despite broad agreement on policies and objectives for food aid during 1978 and 1979, there remain the skirmishes over turf and territory. Each agency concerned with food aid has a lengthy history of battles won and lost in the process of resolving differences, and agency officials seem to take up their agency's banner when they enter on duty. When a former AID official transferred to USDA in 1978, he became one of the most ardent supporters of his new agency's cause. One of the arrangements worked out between USDA and AID is that each Agency alternates in leading the U.S. Delegation to the semiannual meetings in Rome of the Committee on Food Aid Policies and Programs. But when a new State Department appointee as Minister-Counselor to the food organizations headquartered in Rome asserted his authority to lead one such delegation, AID and USDA closed ranks and successfully argued that their "agreement" of the past ten years controlled delegation leadership!

Food Aid and Food
Security—1979 Conferences

Secretary Bergland and Undersecretary Hathaway led U.S. Delegations to
two important meetings in the second half of 1979: the 5th Ministerial
meeting of the World Food Council in Ottawa and the 20th biennial
Conference of FAO in Rome. Food aid issues were important items on the
agenda in both meetings and they had been preceded by a spring meeting of
the Committee on Food Aid Policies and Programs and another meeting of an
FAO Committee on Food Security.

The two earlier meetings, under FAO auspices, were held at staff levels and
no new policies were enunciated by the United States. Treasury and OMB, and
also State, continued to press for restraining budgets of international
organizations and programs. USDA was rethinking policies following a
breakdown in negotiations with principal wheat exporting countries in which
an effort was made to link a new international wheat agreement with a shared
responsibility for food aid.[8] By the end of the summer, mounting grain stocks
in the United States pointed to the need for earmarking larger quantities of
wheat for food aid and away from commercial marketings. The way was clear
for Secretary Bergland to make his statement at the World Food Council
meeting in Ottawa conveying U.S. concerns about world hunger and indicating
a modification in U.S. policy on food aid.

In his statements at the two world meetings, first at the World Food
Council and then at the FAO Conference, Secretary Bergland took pains to
explain how U.S. farm policy was contributing to world food security. He said,
in part, that the United States had built up large farmer-held reserve stocks of
grain to provide price and supply stability and the means to satisfy
commitments for commercial customers (including huge new sales to the
USSR announced in the fall of 1979) as well as food aid claimants. His
statements reaffirmed generous U.S. food aid commitments:

> We also support—and have pledged 4.47 million metric tons of the
> annual 10 million ton total as a Food Aid Convention to meet
> emergency needs.

He indicated that the United States would pursue a policy of sustained high
production. He also made the point that experience had shown that the
productive and dependable U.S. farmers were an essential element in world
food security:

> Our reserve—backed by the productive ability of the American

farmer—will allow us to meet our massive commercial demand without endangering our humanitarian commitments.

The Secretary's statements were as well received in Midwest America as in the forums of the world organizations.

Some developing countries, nonetheless, were anxious. There were probably several reasons why these countries couched their concern for food aid in terms of the broader issue of food security:

• Increasingly, food aid, both bilateral and multilateral, was focusing on the most needy 25-35 countries and U.S. bilateral food aid seemed principally directed to relatively few friendly nations. Many other developing countries who could not qualify for food aid sought to make a claim for assistance on food security grounds.

• Food security emcompassed a range of other issues in the relationship between developed and developing countries, including larger resource transfers, trade adjustments to favor developing country earnings, and more assistance to increase production and food self sufficiency in developing countries.

• The United States and most other donor countries had largely acceded to the food aid targets urged by the developing countries. Some of these countries may have felt that new, larger goals were needed to maintain the momentum toward a new international economic order which would be more favorable to the less developed countries. Apparently, the form of food aid established by the United States (like the form of foreign assistance since the '60s) is no longer in line with relationships now sought by some developing countries like Mexico, Venezuela, Libya, and Algeria. Countries like these openly argue for a new international economic order in which more of the world's wealth would go to them and other developing countries, not as an act of charity, but by right and in restitution for years of exploitation.

Secretary Bergland's statements clearly indicated that the United States would not be drawn into this kind of debate in the context of food aid policies and programs. For the most part, U.S. policy makers and staffers have seen the country's program of food aid as generous and helpful in relations between the United States and the developing countries. Demands for a new international economic order would be dealt with elsewhere. On this there is general agreement among staffers in the interagency bodies. [9]

128   Federal Public Policy

Both in 1979 and in 1974, U.S. Presidents faced the prospect that the
dollars appropriated for food aid would be inadequate for all food aid
objectives because once again the price of grain had risen following disclosure
of serious shortfalls in Soviet production. In October 1979, the Soviets had
come to the United States to request substantially larger purchases than had
been anticipated.[10] Harvests had not been good in several African countries
and in India, and it was uncertain how much additional grain they would need
after drawing down their reserve stocks to compensate for a poor year.
Undersecretary Hathaway, who was principally involved in the USSR
negotiations, indicated to the press then that U.S. grain reserves held by
farmers and by the government were ample to meet Soviet needs and food aid
commitments, and hence should have little affect on consumer prices in the
United States. Indeed, there were ample supplies; as prices rose, farmers
released significant portions of their stocks accumulated against government
loans and a price rise was moderated.

Again, the United States was faced with the question of priorities in food
aid allocations. The food aid agreement with Egypt provided for specific
tonnage in food grains and as the market price per ton went up the amount of
dollars appropriated for overall food aid would buy less commodities for other
needy countries. To meet the problem, Secretary Bergland sought a
supplemental appropriation. The Congress, hoping to hold down inflation and
particularly food prices, was reluctant to provide more funding, and the
requested $96.7 million was not acted upon promptly. Congress planned to
review the request further when its sessions resumed in January 1980. A USDA
press release of December 31, 1979, noted that some revisions in PL 480
country allocations (before Congressional action on the new supplemental
requests) had been made: additional funding was allocated to Egypt to meet
commodity commitments there and new but small commitments were made to
Nicaragua to help shore up the new government there. Hence, the importance
of food aid within the framework of U.S. foreign policy considerations was
again underscored. Still, the need of countries like Cambodia (Kampuchea)
and persistent food assistance needs in countries of Sahel Africa continued to
pose dilemmas of priorities.

Again, events altered the environment for U.S. decision makers. Early in
January the USSR moved military forces into Afghanistan and President
Carter responded by invalidating the increased grain sales for 1980 delivery
(the 17 million tons over the 8 million tons in long-term U.S. commitments).
The availability of U.S. grain for food aid was thus drastically changed; the
President, Secretary Bergland, and Congressional leaders from farm states,
along with their constituents began to explore ways of maintaining grain
prices. Proposals were heard for increasing the food aid program and the full
supplementary budget request seemed likely to pass.

Reflections on the Process of Policy Making

Policies and the Process of Implementing
Them Are Constantly Evolving

There is a tendency to perceive legislation as the culmination or final product in a lengthy policymaking process. More often, it is a transitory statement of policy reflecting a temporary consensus among bureaucratic and political interests involved. A piece of legislation and the process for implementing it are provisional, the result of a complex of forces and the interaction of many individuals and their best judgements at a given time. The U.S. foreign food aid program first became embodied in legislation in 1954; it has been amended in some degree almost every year since then (although significant changes did not occur until 1966-67 and then again in 1975 and 1978). As we have noted, some of the amendments have shifted the basic orientation of the program. The amounts of money and commodities to be used have changed every year. While the same agencies and bureaus have been involved during the past 28 years, the individuals concerned change every few years and each imparts his or her interpretation of the intent of Congress and the President (and their individual preferences in food aid purposes).

Legislation changes to reflect new elements in the external situation as well as shifts in the political consensus. In the case of food aid, the reality of supply and demand and the needs of food deficit countries impel reappraisals of existent policies. The amount of food crops harvested in the United States and in other exporting countries, and the amount harvested in principal low-income importing countries such as Bangladesh, Indonesia, Egypt, as well as the amount harvested in "swing" countries like the USSR (where grain harvests vary substantially from year to year)—all affect supply availabilities for food aid and the cost to the U.S. budget. Hence there is need for annual appraisals of food aid needs, costs, and the impact on the national budget. Moreover, there has been continuing pressure among church and charitable groups within the United States and governments of needy countries to insulate food aid from political considerations and changes in market conditions. This study notes that these forces converged to effect a development and humanitarian orientation in the food aid legislation during the second half of the 1970s.

External reports and studies also influence the policy and program views of Executive (and Congressional) staffs. There have been many analyses of how the food aid program is managed in Washington and within recipient countries and the impact of food aid on policies and production in recipient countries. These studies are by objective groups in academic institutions, the General Accounting Office (GAO), and other government agencies, as well as by special interest groups. The findings and recommendations of these studies provide new insights for all the concerned agencies and are part of the environment in which policy decisions and program changes are made. Congressional staff and bureau staffs are continually seeking to bring about program changes and improvements.

Policies are Often Designed to Meet Past Problems Rather than Current Realities

Food aid legislation in 1975 was, in part, a reaction to the high priority that had been accorded Viet Nam under the Nixon Administration, but that situation had largely passed when the legislation became operational. The 1978 legislation establishing a new Title III to give more development emphasis to food aid was enacted when many recipient countries were already giving their food and agriculture sector high priority because of rising prices and supply uncertainties. It is not clear whether provisions of Title III will make a significant difference.

One reason that legislation deals with past problems is that there is a time lag between the emergence of a problem and the awareness of it among many Congressmen and their concerned constituents. In presenting the PL 480 program and justifying annual budgets, it is often simpler and easier if the proposals are treated as newly designed to meet problems that Congressmen may be newly aware of. Also, it is difficult to gain political support to meet problems that *may* arise or are not yet critical. Senator Moynihan, writing of his tenure as U.S. Representative to the United Nations, notes how U.S. policy continued to reflect stereotyped views about the U.N. long after the growth of developing-country membership had radically changed the nature of the U.N. General Assembly.[11] Charles Yost, writing about his experiences in the same post some years earlier similarly observed the lag in U.S. perceptions of the USSR and China inhibited changes that would have made U.S. policies more in keeping with realities respecting those two governments.[12]

Federal Programs are Developed by Consensus Among Concerned Agencies Reflecting their Constituencies

Federal bureaucracies, no less than the Congress, reflect constituencies as they participate in shaping national policy. As noted in this study, the USDA and Treasury, as well as State and AID, felt it necessary to speak for their respective missions and constituencies. On several occasions, as USDA staffers sought to reflect the view on food aid as an element in foreign development strategies (essentially taking into account the known views of AID), former USDA Assistant Secretary Bell would comment that USDA needed only to be concerned with representing and reflecting its constituency (the farm and commodity interests) since we could count on the other agencies to reflect other points of view.

Interagency bodies become forums that seek accommodation and consensus, recognizing the legitimacy of the various missions represented. Of course some of the interagency differences, expressed in terms of program policies, may really reflect postures favoring an agency's role, constituency pressure, or merely turf sought or guarded. Where the staff level individuals in interagency groups cannot agree, one or more will escalate the issue to an Assistant Secretary or higher to gain leverage or to deal with the problem from a policy (often translated as political) level. Assistant Secretaries also recognize the need for accommodation and reckon that a concession made on one issue provides a claim against another agency at some future time.

Chance Factors Influence Policies in Ways Difficult to Anticipate

Events in other countries such as abnormal weather and military engagements may lead to food shortages and influence food aid requirements. Weather affects the size of harvests in most growing areas of the world (drought during growing periods and heavy rains during planting and harvesting periods reduce production) and give rise to larger import requirements. Military actions which keep farmers from the fields, interfering with plantings or harvestings, or drive rural workers into the relative security of cities, can similarly impel larger food aid imports. For example, during 1979-80 there was a large increase in the number of refugees fleeing from countries such as Cambodia and Afghanistan to neighboring countries to avoid warfare and repression at home. Food aid needed to be provided to makeshift camps in the countries to which these people fled, that is, Thailand and Pakistan, which did not have food to spare. U.S. policymakers seek to be responsive to these unanticipated needs whether for humanitarian or foreign policy considerations.

Sometimes, personal characteristics or personal interactions among the involved policymakers give unexpected turns of policy or unanticipated agreements. The new development orientation of the 1978 legislations was largely the result of efforts by young Congressional staffers serving under (former) Senator Clark and (the late) Senator Humphrey. Several of these staffers moved to the Executive agencies after the Carter Administration came to office. They reflected broad agreement on the new development orientation for food aid. But because of their deep concern, they engaged in long debates on the new Title III provisions among themselves in the interagency working group meetings. This, in turn, contributed to resistance among a few "older hands" who had seen a similar emphasis come and go during the earlier food crisis of the mid-'60s. The old hands sought to avoid the delays and frustrations involved in trying to win country agreements acceptable to all concerned within the United States and within governments of recipient countries over what constitutes adequate development uses of PL 480 commodities.

Foreign policy and budgetary objectives have often prevailed over other considerations in food aid policies. Thus, despite changes in the PL 480 putting greater emphasis on food aid for development, events since 1973 suggest that highest priority is given to foreign policy considerations.[13] This is evidenced by decisions made by the Presidents and their cabinet officers as well as the workings of interagency staff groups. Under the Nixon and Ford Administrations, the two countries receiving most concessional food assistance were South Viet Nam, with about 25 percent of the total during the years 1973-74, and Korea, with about 16 percent. With the termination of the war and the U.S. pullout from Viet Nam, food assistance from the United States stopped. President Carter has used food aid extensively to further the accommodation between Israel and Egypt. Egypt received almost 20 percent of U.S. food aid during recent years as part of a package to further the accords reached at Camp David.

However, once foreign policy objectives were assured (the Egyptian agreement on food aid provided for tonnage levels rather than dollars so it was insulated against rising prices), budget constraints were an overriding consideration in setting overall food aid goals. It was not until President Carter had embargoed sales of grains to the USSR in January 1980 and the Federal Government had already taken on the cost of withholding a portion of the grain from commercial markets that the way was cleared for the Administration and the Congress to agree on a supplemental appropriation to maintain overall food aid levels despite higher grain prices.

Some participants, by virtue of their positions in the policy making process or their personal forcefulness can have a special influence on policy outcomes. A Congressman, speaking as chairman of an important committee, can push his policy views onto the bureaucracy from secretaries to assistant secretaries to staff, even when they recognize that he neither speaks for his whole committee nor for the Congress. An Assistant Secretary of State, having felt the anger of one Committee Chairman, directed his staff on the Interagency Food Aid Committee to make the concern voiced by the Congressman about food aid shipments to one country as the principal consideration in international food aid pledges. This was in order to avoid further confrontation with the irate Congressman.

Within the Interagency Food Aid Committee, the Department of State and the OMB exercise clout by implying they speak for the "President's policy." Since all Cabinet officers are similarly spokesmen for the administration, their staff representatives might just as validly make that claim. But the relationship between the agencies and their representatives is such that State and OMB views are given special weight.

Reflecting further on the process of policy making, I conclude that there is more honest searching for the national interest and there is more weighing and balancing of cost and benefits in reaching conclusions than the public perceives. Moreover, there is a sensitivity to the many constituencies that make up this vast land and usually a genuine willingness by the bureaucracy to involve the various interest groups in decision making. The process of policy making may at times seem slow and layered, but withal it produces rational, reasonable policies for the nation. And staffers at all levels of the bureaucracy are continually seeking new insights to better the formulation and implementation of policies for which they are responsible. The Federal bureaucracy is indeed governance by the people for the people.

Note: This case study was written during the winter of 1979-80, while the events described were current. The paper was reviewed again in the fall of 1983 for publication. Although a new Administration has come into office during the intervening years, giving important new directions to foreign and domestic policies, the process of policymaking on food aid described in the case study is essentially valid still.

Footnotes

1. Agricultural Trade Development and Assistance Act of 1954, as amended, P.L. 480, 83rd Congress.
2. See Lyndon B. Johnson, *The Vantage Point* (New York: Holt, Rinehart and Winston, 1971), chapter 10.
3. During the previous several years, Secretary Freeman sought simple extensions of the legislation in order to avoid controversy with other agencies and (hopefully) with Congressional Committees. But in hearings on the extension, it became clear that the Executive was not united behind the USDA request, and the forces of State and AID contributed to Congressional rewriting of the legislation to serve foreign policy considerations more than it had previously. For further analysis of this period, see Peter A. Toma, *The Politics of Food for Peace* (Tucson: University of Arizona Press, 1967).
4. Dr. Hathaway was later designated Under Secretary for International Affairs and Commodity Programs.

5. During the years covered by this paper, the writer personally knew the agency principals involved and periodically participated in the interagency working groups on food aid and development.

6. In 1982 and 1983 considerations of surplus disposals and market development were seen again as important in USDA and the agricultural community.

7. But, in the face of mounting dairy surpluses, in 1982, USDA was able to win agreement among the agencies concerned, to add $50 million in contributions to the UN/FAO World Food Program, specifically for dairy commodities. The increase was encouraged by the foreign aid and development group in the bureaucracy (including the writer) on humanitarian grounds as well, and for strengthening the U.S. image in that respect.

8. The principal purpose of the new wheat agreement that was being negotiated was to establish economic provisions, including levels of reserve stocks, in order to make trade in wheat more orderly and prices more stable.

9. The writer was an active participant in shaping statements by several Secretaries of Agriculture when they spoke at international forums such as the FAO Conference and the World Food Council Ministerial meetings.

10. According to the consultation of October 3, 1979, the USSR could purchase up to 25 million tons of grain or 17 million tons over the 8 million provided under a 5-year agreement negotiated in 1975. The agreement required further U.S. Government consultation when purchases would exceed the 8 million tons.

11. Daniel P. Moynihan, *A Dangerous Place* (Boston: Little, Brown and Co., 1978).

12. Charles Yost, *The Conduct and Misconduct of Foreign Affairs* (New York: Random House, 1972).

13. In this paper, "food aid" has referred to concessional sales or grants under PL 480 to assist developing countries. But in times of serious shortfalls in Soviet grain harvests, sales at market prices and commercial terms are also helpful. And in 1980 when President Carter embargoed grain sales to the USSR, there was doubt that other sources could make up the amount of grains the Soviets sought to import for maintaining livestock herds and consumer demands. Hence, U.S. action was clearly intended to use food as an instrument of foreign policy. The situation during the 70s was different from that which George Kennan reports during the 50s when he served in the foreign service and found domestic politics and policies controlling foreign policy actions. See George Kennan, *Memoirs* (Boston: Atlantic, Little, Brown, 1972), Vol. 2, 1950-1963.

Editorial Note: James W. Greenwood has written a thought-provoking analysis of the myths of policymaking in his discussion of the free enterprise system, the role of reason, and his division of reality into parts for intensive study. The former myth that only Congress makes policy is entertainingly analyzed. Greenwood then proceeds to propose a systems view of the policy process which he believes is a more valid description of the interactions that actually occur than most current views. Greenwood states "that a great deal more has been written about public policymaking than is actually known, and a great deal more is known than is actually true." Most policy writing uses anecdotal or case study approaches (including this book) and the development of a science of policymaking lies in the future. The most immediate practical objective is to gain an understanding of the nature of policy and the actual systemic operation of the policymaking process. Special interest subsystems, Greenwood feels, are threatening the system as a whole as well as the public interest. Examples presented include: the Federal loyalty program of the 1950s, the pricing policy for state-controlled liquor stores in Pennsylvania, postal service provision of coin operated copying machines for the public, location of a field office, impact of patronage upon appointment of a Director of the Federal Mediation and Conciliation Service, and Cyrus S. Ching's preventive mediation policy.

CHAPTER 5

REFLECTIONS ON THE SYSTEMIC NATURE OF POLICY

James W. Greenwood, Jr.

The writer has been an avid observer of, and sometimes participant in, the public policy-making process for more than forty years. During this time he has served in a number of local, state, and Federal Government agencies, as well as in an international organization and private enterprise. He has served at various levels of the administrative hierarchy from low to high, in agencies with a single head and in agencies with tripartite (board) leadership, and in both staff and line positions. His experience covers the entire continuum of policy-making activities, from initiating, drafting, establishing, and promulgating policies to executing, administering, and modifying policies. He has been the victim of policies that were claimed to be equitable, but seemed to him iniquitous; he has made or enforced policies that seemed to him to be equitable, but were sometimes alleged by others to be iniquitous. (The role of perspective in the policy-making process will become apparent in the discussion that follows.) Throughout his career, the writer has, in addition to fulfilling his other roles, tried to maintain the role of observer with a minimum of bias, but with what degree of success, the reader may judge from what follows.

The basic aim of this paper is to identify and challenge some of the traditional beliefs, opinions, and dogmas in the mythology of public policy making. The approach is essentially personal, informal, and anecdotal. Myths have distinct values in all our pursuits; we probably could not operate without them. But from time to time we need to challenge their continued validity and reexamine their current utility.

Three motifs pervade this discussion: the inherently systemic (but unsystematic) nature of public policy making, its twofold mythological burden, and its essential irrationality. Until recently, writers on the subject of the governmental policy-making process have rarely recognized its systemic nature, yet this is probably its most signal characteristic. It is highly interactive: policies, procedures, people, and politics continuously interact in sometimes tortuous, sometimes daedalian ways, in this never-ending, highly complex process. It exhibits both equifinality and multifinality; that is, many different courses of action may lead to the same or similar results and any given course of action may lead to any of a wide variety of results. The variety of inputs of policy making has a continuing and noticeable effect on both the further outputs and the process itself. No given policy is ever final. Even though the words and the formulae may remain the same, the words undergo changes in meaning and our understanding of the terms and formulae change over time. All policies are subject to continuing and inevitable modification and eventual demise.

The twofold mythological burden of policy making consists in its heritage of primeval, ancient, and medieval custom, and its mythopoeic tendencies. One of the primary functions of myth throughout the tenure of human existence has been to serve as a warrant for traditional rites and customs. Events on earth have conventionally been justified by mythic accounts of analogous events in the abode of the reigning tutelary deities. In the course of time, as these rites and customs became embodied in the canon, common, or statutory law, they became policies. This formal designation, however, did not change their basic prescriptive or regulatory character. In addition to this passive role as the beneficiary of the doctrinal myths of the past, policy making has itself, over the years, acquired a more active role as a myth-generating agent and has built up an aura of myth about its own activities and nature.

Despite the efforts of some writers to impose their own views of a basic pattern on what they find exhibited in the process, it is fundamentally unsystematic. Just as research scientists do not follow the scientific method in their work, so policy makers do not normally follow any predetermined pattern of policy making. Such patterns are imposed on the phenomena a posteriori.

Perspective of the Writer

Long ago, an astute observer of the political scene, Henry Taylor, warned against the dangers of treating politics metaphysically.[1] Although the study of politics has gained respectability and some measure of recognition as a separate discipline since the 1830s, the struggle to gain release from the shackles of abstruse philosophical thought continues. One effort in this direction was the proposal about midway in this century for the development of a policy science, envisioned as a form of interdisciplinary cooperation for the solution of political problems.[2] More than a quarter of a century later, progress toward such a goal on the academic front seems to have been slight, the impact on the practical art imperceptible. Why does the process of policy formation seem so staunchly to resist scientific examination? Why do policymakers seem so impervious to suggestions for improving the process? The following random observations and reflections of a former bureaucrat address these questions, among others, but do not presume to offer any specific degree of scientific validity (whatever that may be). They simply represent one person's perspective on some vital aspects of the political scene, this writer ignoring Taylor's advice, even as he himself did.

Early Impressions

This writer acquired a worm's-eye view of the public policy-making process in his first position in the public service, that of Liquor Store Clerk for the Pennsylvania Liquor Control Board. The Board was established during the administration of then Governor Gifford Pinchot, a renowned conservationist and a political conservative. Pinchot's conservatism extended well beyond the environmental aspects of life, but the so-called Prohibition Amendment was in the process of being repealed and he recognized the inevitable. A number of states with conservative governments or conservative citizenry were planning to operate state-owned liquor stores as a means of controlling the commerce in alcoholic beverages, and with the ultimate and ulterior motive of tempering the expected high level of consumption, Pinchot joined the parade. As a further means of discouraging excessive consumption, he emboldened the Board (which he had appointed) to initially establish relatively high prices. When the price list was made public, prior to the January 1934 opening of the stores, the outcry from the press and public was immediate and unmistakable. The Board, recognizing the traditional relationship between discretion and valor, quickly retreated, reduced some prices, and added to the list a number of less expensive brands. Unmollified, the public continued to complain about high prices. Then, with sales booming, the Board and the administration began to realize the revenue possibilities; they had a gold mine on their hands. Here was a truly exceptional opportunity to boost state revenues relatively painlessly. The Board began to stock still more inexpensive brands, among them a particularly potent beverage called *Sweepstakes*, selling for one dollar a fifth of a gallon (a popular size in the premetric age). Sweepstakes became an immediate best seller, the distillery hardly able to keep up with the demand. It must have been aged in the bottle at least two hours before reaching the store shelves. On the label of this puissant potation was the pictorial representation of a horse race with only half of the lead horse showing. To express their appreciation for Pinchot's capitulation to public opinion, the customers promptly and affectionately dubbed this picture of half a horse "Pinchot's Portrait" and asked for the bottle by that name. Such are the rewards of a political endeavor and the vagaries of public opinion.

In this simple example, we may observe a variety of characteristics of the systemic nature of the process. The complexity is illustrated by the variety of forces operating within it: reformers, politicians, customers, distributors, salesmen, retail dispensers, distillers, communications media, and the general public, all interacting in multifarious ways. The effect of feedback illustrates the cybernetic operation of the process, while its multifinality may be seen in the transmogrification of a device intended to promote temperance into a felicitous means of raising revenue, an entirely serendipitous effect. Any political science analysts who could find any degree of rationality in the process would be likely candidates for analysis themselves.

My second position in the public service, Assistant Fiscal Accounting Clerk in a regional office of the U.S. Soil Conservation Service, was an opportunity to observe some of the effects of failure to secure coordination of policies in the internal administration of interagency programs. In the early days of the New Deal administration, the Department of the Army administered one of the so-called relief programs, that of providing work training for young, unemployed males by the Civilian Conservation Corps (CCC). The Soil Conservation Service (SCS) utilized the services of some of the members of the CCC in a number of soil conservation demonstration projects intended to persuade American farmers of the economic advantages of certain practices such as contour furrowing to avoid soil erosion. To finance these activities, the SCS received allocations of funds from those originally appropriated to the Department of the Army. Disbursement of the funds, however, continued to be made by the Army Finance officers rather than the Treasury Department. Naturally, the Army Finance office requirements for certification and payment of disbursement vouchers were different from those of the Treasury Department which disbursed all other SCS funds.

The subtleties of these differences of fiscal policy, for unknown reasons, never fully permeated the fiscal offices of the SCS. When this writer arrived on the scene at the SCS regional office, the difficulties arising from these policy differences were reaching the critical point. The SCS regional office had been certifying vouchers for payment by the Army Finance office for over a year. The payees (suppliers to the SCS demanding payment for services rendered) were complaining about not being paid. These complaints were shuttled back and forth between the SCS regional office and the Army Finance Office. Finally, the SCS regional office dispatched a representative to the Army Finance Office in another city to investigate the difficulties. He discovered that the vouchers certified for payment did not meet the procedural requirements of Army Finance Office policy. The solution of the local Army Finance Officer to this difficulty had been to reserve a large table on which were piled the vouchers certified for payment by the SCS regional office. He apparently thought or hoped that the difficulty would outlast his tour of duty. The writer spent the better part of his first year of service in the SCS trying to resolve the accounting problems resulting from this snarl.

These early experiences convinced me of the significance of the *execution and administrative stages* of the policy-making process and alerted me to the need for close observation of the process in all its stages and ramifications as I pursued my further career in the public service. Some of the results of these observations are recounted here.

Myths of Policymaking

The allusion above to the aura of myth enshrouding the subject of policy making requires but slight elaboration. Galbraith refers to certain myths of the free enterprise system such as market control of prices and the separation of enterprise from the state.[3] This writer would suggest that the so-called free enterprise system was eliminated with the advent of the species homo sapiens, if not before. After that, freedom of enterprise was simply a matter of degree. Even in the species of homo antedating homo sapiens, there existed some sort of organization, however loose, and inherent in organization is some sort of constraint. From then on, the limitations on free enterprise never disappeared, although they may have varied considerably in degree and form (taboos, "thou shalt nots," laws, regulations, taxes, and so forth). Through it all we hear the cries of the entrepreneur protesting the trammels of government and deploring public policy that interferes with making an honest living. The cries have not been without avail. During all this time, the influences of private enterprise and the state on each other have fluctuated in varying degress from time to time and from place to place, with first one and then the other in the ascendancy. Their relative ascendancy has, of course, significantly influenced the public policy-making process and the resulting policies.

Another myth, which for long appeared to deceive the classical economists, has also clouded the view of political scientists: the alleged predominant role of reason in the behavior of the so-called average citizen or the general public. Ancient, but apropos, is the New Deal era story of the midwestern farmer who, when questioned about his intentions in the then-upcoming presidential election in which Franklin D. Roosevelt was running for an unprecedented fourth term, responded that of course he would vote Republican. When asked why, the farmer answered candidly that he had voted Republican in the previous three presidential elections and he had never had it so good. The myth of the predominant role of reason nevertheless apparently continues to maintain its hold among the proponents of a policy science.

Analogous to the myth of the predominant role of reason in the policy-making process is the widely held view that the human mind, especially among scientists, tends to divide reality into parts for intensive study; that is, that human beings are inherently analytical in their efforts to acquire understanding of their environment. This view is disputed by the Gestalt psychologists. Its validity is seriously questioned by the adherents of general systems theory and others inclined to holistic ways of thinking, including, for example, devotees of certain oriental philosophies. The schism continues unabated. The approach or perspective varies according to the object or event being observed, the mood or bent of mind of the observer at the time, or the particular purpose of the observer.

Perhaps not yet attaining to the status of myth, but maintaining wide prevalence among students of policy making is the tendency to equate the policy-making process with the decision-making process.[4] This view derives support from the two myths identified immediately above concerning the predominant role of reason and the ubiquity of the analytical approach. This writer rejects these views: the reasons will become apparent in what follows.

The myth that only the Legislature makes policy and that the Executive and the Administrative Branch carry it out was quite prevalent in the latter part of the nineteenth and the early twentieth centuries.[5] The view was still quite evident in many of the opinions and decisions of the Supreme Court on early New Deal policies and programs. It continues to influence some policy makers today. Witness the Congressional furor over some policies and decisions of the Food and Drug Administration (cyclamates, saccharin) and of the Federal Trade Commission (undertakers, advertising for lawyers and physicians). Representative Elliot Levitas (Ga.) is quoted as complaining that "the unelected Commissioners of the FTC issue rules that have the same force as an Act of Congress."[6] He wants to know who should make the laws in this country, the elected Congress or unelected bureaucrats. He might be surprised by the answers of some of his own constituents, the beneficiaries of those regulations.

This particular myth has an ancient lineage and may be traced back through Locke to Justinian, but it is only one of two conflicting strands of thought with which the writers of the Constitution wrestled. Hamilton, during the administration of Washington, espoused the more practical view, recognizing the impossibility of having Congress make all policy decisions. Jefferson endorsed the classical view in theory, but ignored it in practice (witness the Louisiana Purchase and many other actions that some students of political history judge to have exceeded the presidential powers). Lincoln apparently never had any doubts on the subject, or at least gave little evidence of such. Wilson appeared to agree with the classical view in his early writings, but changed his views even before assuming the presidency. The administrations of Theodore Roosevelt, Woodrow Wilson, and Franklin D. Roosevelt effectively disposed of the myth for all practical purposes. Only a few diehards still try to maintain it, but then some people still believe the earth is flat.

In summary, this writer believes that contrary to a number of widely held myths, there is not now and never has been a truly free enterprise system. The economic and political systems of any given society significantly influence each other, with public policy constituting the direct or indirect issue. Public policy is not determined solely by a rational process, is not the product of analytical thinking, and is not to be confused or equated with the decision-making process. The Legislature is not the sole source of public policy and if the students of public policy making will rid their minds of this antique furniture, they might be able to develop a clearer understanding of the public policy-making process than now prevails. As a substitute for the rationalistic, analytical, decision-making approach to the study of public policy making, this writer suggests a systems approach.

The Systems View

The term *systems approach* has become, in the past thirty years, a much used and abused appellation applied to a variety of techniques and technologies for the study of a range of subjects. Whoever uses the term, therefore, bears a certain onus of explication. For the investigation and study of organic systems at every level of organization, from the single cell to that of human society as a whole, this writer suggests the appropriateness of an approach similar to that espoused by many general systems theorists such as James G. Miller.[7] In this approach, living systems (including human beings, groups, organizations, societies) are viewed as hierarchically organized, complex structures that individually process various forms of matter and energy (including information) and interact with each other and other elements of their environments in a complex, cybernetic manner. As Miller demonstrates, at least in a preliminary fashion, his living systems theory would provide a useful framework for the study of the public policy-making process.

There are a few recognizable difficulties in the suggested approach. First, for most purposes, the systems dealt with must be viewed as black boxes; that is, we may observe the system inputs and outputs, but the internal processing may be only deduced. It cannot be observed directly. Secondly, there is danger of arriving at oversimplified conclusions logically derived from the model, but not necessarily applicable to reality. Thirdly, there is the danger of excessive reliance on the model, to the exclusion of, or even in the face of, contrary evidence from other sources. The solution is to use multiple models. Finally, there is always the difficulty of accounting for the role of perspective and the related danger of equating multiple subjectivity with objectivity. Human perception and observations are notably subject to the influence of individual perspective.

There is one further difficulty in the study of any social or political process:

the constancy of change. In their everyday lives, human beings in society tend to focus on the relatively stable elements in their lives. They readily perceive the regularity, the continuity, the general reliability of objects and patterns of events and tend to ignore the ineluctability of change, the inherent unpredictability of events, the continuing evolution of social processes. This paradox of apparent stability in the midst of constant change is a significant factor in the process of public policy making.

Despite these difficulties, this writer believes that viewing public policy making as a dynamic, cybernetic process taking place in a complex, hierarchical structure has significant advantages for the study of the process. The hierarchical structure is the society or nation-state as a whole, with its numerous, continually interacting subsystems, consisting of governmental and nongovernmental organizations and formally organized and unorganized groups as well as over 200 million individuals. The individuals and the groups and organizations (because they are composed of individuals) must be viewed for the most part as black boxes, systems whose internal processing is not available to direct observation. The process involves the input, throughput, output, and feedback of energy primarily in the form of information. It appears to be an ideal subject for the systems approach.[8]

Policymaking: Science v. Art

Even a brief bibliographic survey gives one the distinct impression that a great deal more has been written about public policy making than is actually known and a great deal more is known than is actually true. (Of course, the subject of public policy making is not unique in this respect; the condition appears to be endemic in the social sciences.) The literature of political science and public administration, as well as that of political history, is replete with anecdotal reports on the formulation of a particular governmental policy or on the policy-making process in a particular milieu.[9] Some of these reports were written by individuals who were privy to, or participants in, the processes they describe; some were written by academic observers of the policy-making process, usually on a postpartum or even a postmortem basis. For the most part, these accounts are impressionistic, retrospective, historical-descriptive reports of the series of events and the cast of participants fulfilling limited roles over a limited period of time. Some are primarily legal or legislative histories, some are primarily of the executive or administrative aspects of policy making. Many are normative, containing recommendations for reform of one or more aspects of policy making. Many others are more concerned with the substantive content of a given policy than with the process of policy making itself. Few, if any, of these accounts would measure up to what Nagel terms controlled inquiry (the social scientists' counterpart of the physical scientists' controlled experimentation).[10] They more nearly accord with what physical scientists call naturalistic observation.

Many, if not all of these reports are in the form of (or equivalent to) case studies; few, if any, are theoretically based. Conducted by different persons for different reasons at different times over a wide span of years, they are, understandably, not directed at providing a body of comparative data and are, therefore, of little if any value as a basis for formulating generalizations or testing hypotheses. Other study methods generally applied in political science (such as quantitative analyses, polls, survey techniques, model building, simulation) have apparently not been broadly utilized for the study of the policy-making process. Serious observers of the policy-making process deplore this dearth of significant, comprehensive, empirical, theoretically grounded, scientific studies.

Some of these observers attempt to compensate for this lack of scientific knowledge by providing introspective analyses of the policy-making process and, in many instances, numerous recommendations for its improvement. The policy makers themselves have reacted to such proposals with typical Olympian indifference or obliviousness. While distrust of intellectuals is pandemic in our society, this peccancy seems to be particularly virulent among policy makers (both governmental and entrepreneurial) so as to be almost an occupational disease. Perhaps it is an essential element in the inherent hubris of policy makers at the higher levels. They tend to have an instinctive aversion to theory and theoretical approaches to their art. In 1933, the President's Research Committee on Social Trends recognized the problem with pellucid, if painful, clarity when it observed in its report that it did not wish to exaggerate the role of intelligence in social direction, nor to underestimate the important parts played by tradition, habit, unintelligence, inertia, indifference, emotions or the raw will to power in its various forms.[11]

Even a cursory review, however, of the number and nature of existing social, economic, political, and ecological crises should be enough to convince the most complacent policy maker that the rate of improvement in the process has not noticeably accelerated in this century. The suffering citizens may still justifiably complain, with Bobby Burns, "The best laid schemes o' mice and men gang aft agley."

The proponents of a policy science, nevertheless, believe the means are at hand to remedy this situation. One of these proponents, Yehezkel Dror, suggested that there is a significant gap between the ways in which policy is made and the available knowledge on how policies can best be made.[12] This writer would suggest (1) that not only does Dror overestimate the available knowledge of how policies can best be made, but (2) that the difficulty is really more fundamental. Dror's basic thesis should be recast to read that there is a significant gap between (1) the ways in which policy is made and (2) the available knowledge of the ways in which policy is made. The available knowledge of how policy is actually made is extremely casual, is unevenly distributed, particularly among policy makers themselves, and is heavily overlaid with myth, misunderstanding, and wishful thinking. As indicated above, even professional observers of the policy-making scene lack comprehensive, systematic knowledge of the process. The study of policy making continues to be characterized by the accumulation of random data, by desultory methodologies and, most significantly, by the absence of a theoretical framework.

Despite the weaknesses in both the process and the study of the process, the policy scientists believe that they can develop a policy science that will significantly improve the quality of public policy making and its product. A more cautionary approach might be more appropriate. Before embarking on any grandiose scheme for improving the process (see, e.g., Dror, Chapter V),[13] a firmer foundation of knowledge of how the process is actually operating should be established. Without such a foundation, policy scientists, policy makers, and others would have some difficulty in determining whether any proposed changes constituted real improvements. The measure of progress requires the prior establishment of some kind of benchmark. As of this writing, there is no such benchmark and no indication that one is being developed.

In summary, a policy science or a science of policy making is still in the future. In the meantime, we may lay the groundwork for such a science by trying to gain as thorough an understanding as possible of the nature of policy and the actual systemic operation of the policy-making process. Some suggestions for developing such an understanding follow.

Scope of the Discussion

For the purposes of this discussion, the terms *policy* and *policy making* are used in their broadest sense. A policy is any type of guide or decision rule intended to influence the future behavior of one or more individuals or groups. A public policy is one officially adopted by the responsible government or government agency. Policy making is the process, formal or informal, of determining what the policy shall be. In this view, the distinction between a public policy and other types of guidelines for future conduct such as laws, rules, regulations, and procedures is not rigorously precise, but is a matter of perspective. Whether a given statement in whatever form is a policy depends on one's point of view. The boundaries are vague. One man's mete is another man's postern.

Policy, of course, need not be explicitly stated in writing; indeed, it need not be stated in writing at all. In some instances, it may be implied only, or even conveyed by other signals (facial or bodily gestures, colors, or a variety of other symbols). Many instructions that may serve as policy are given orally. Further, certain practices or customs consistently followed for a sufficient length of time acquire the status of policies without ever being stated at all, orally or in writing. This type of development of policies corresponds to the evolution of common law. The behavior of an individual or an organization may serve as policy and an organization's heritage of common knowledge may constitute a policy. Even certain attitudes such as discrimination on account of race or sex may be observed as policies, just as forceful in their effects as the most rigidly enforced statute.

Thus, both the sources of policy and the forms it may take are many and varied; it originates, in one form or another, at points along the means-end continuum of political activity and among the several levels of the governmental hierarchy. It may range from the informal to the formal, from the unstated to the explicitly stated or legislatively enacted, from the concrete to the abstract, from the amorphous to the most graphically delineated, and from the substantive to the procedural. Whatever the source or form, the one certainty about policy is its inevitability; even when it is unstated, all concerned may infer its existence and its substance. The existence and inevitability of policies derive from two fundamental beliefs of human beings: (1) that life is essentially repetitive in nature in that events and situations tend to recur with sufficient frequency to make worthwhile having a pattern of behavior or body of precedent available for dealing with them efficiently, and (2) that human beings, with forethought, can influence or control such recurrences. In the language of systems theory, a policy is a means of reducing entropy, that is, of improving organizational relationships and effectiveness.

Assuming that reduction of entropy is one of the aims of well intentioned top management, the conclusion automatically follows that to be effective, policy making should be rational and systematic. It should be logical, orderly, and give full consideration to its systemic effects as well as its feasibility and desirability. Insofar as policy making fails to meet these standards, it is likely to fail in achieving its goal of reducing entropy. That it sometimes does fail is evident from the record and from the present plight of our society. Some of the reasons for this failure will be explored below. Here we are concerned solely with the policy-making process per se.

Several other significant characteristics of the policy-making process are worth noting. First, it is a cyclical (cybernetic) process; information from the execution and administration of policy feeds back into the system to modify the further application of the policy on a continuing, self-reflexive basis. In fact, the very process of applying a given policy is an integral part of the policy-making process. Secondly, policy making is not the exclusive province of any one branch or level of government. Each of the three branches (Executive, Legislative, Judicial) at all levels (Federal, state, local) of government provides information required in the policy-making process to others; each branch and level utilizes information from the other branches and levels in its own policy-making activities. In addition, all branches and levels receive inputs from various interest groups and the general public. Further, information flows up, down, and across the levels of each organizational hierarchy to serve as a basis for the policy making that takes place in that hierarchy. Policy making is, therefore, a function of the system as a whole, not of any one component.

In policy making, the number of alternatives seriously considered is frequently limited (for example, in voting at polls or in legislatures, the choice is usually limited to either yes or no). The reasons are many and varied. The need or demand for action may be urgent, leaving insufficient time for consideration of more than a few readily identifiable alternatives; or current knowledge of the situation and of potential developments may be inadequate, thus restricting identification of more than a few alternatives; or information about potential effects of certain alternatives may be lacking, thus deterring their consideration; or current modeling techniques may be amenable to predicting the effects of only certain alternatives.

Finally, the policy-making process rarely follows a rational course. Rather, it involves both rational and irrational elements at every stage. (Witness the present political struggles over the issues of abortion and equal rights for women.) The process is extremely complex, highly dynamic, self-reflexive, aggregative, adaptive, continuing, and mutable. It includes a variety of subprocesses such as metapolicy making (making policy about the policy-making process itself), basic policy making, and numerous orders of subpolicy making at subordinate levels of the hierarchy. It involves a wide variety of contributors, all of uncertain motivation, ranging from the most devious and selfserving to the most direct and altruistic. While the public policy-making process is presumably always aimed at the public good (the public interest), it is actually an interwoven mesh of uncertain interests and influences, including: power struggles; conflicting political, social, economic, ethnic, and religious views; normative judgements; avowed and unavowed aims.

From the above discussion, one may readily conclude that the terms *policy* and *policy making* are words of art, not scientific terms. Public policy is a multiform expression of the intent of the government to control or influence the future behavior of certain government officials and employees, and certain citizens, groups, organizations, and other entities. From the management point of view, it is a means of reducing entropy in one or more governmental organizations and one or more portions of the related society. From a broader perspective, it is an intervention in the social system presumably aimed at the long-range benefit of that system and its components. Public policy making is a dynamic, cybernetic, systemic process of inordinate complexity, with an indeterminable number of participants. For the student of public policy making, each participant constitutes a black box system with uncertain motivations and unascertainable cognitive and affective processes. The number, nature, and effects of the interrelationships of the participants, their actions, interactions, and mutual influences are, for the most part, likewise indeterminable. This inordinately complex process is the subject matter of policy science.

At the level of the individual participant, decision theory may yield some insights. At other levels, we may have to call upon other disciplines for aid in understanding the policy-making process. The policy scientists suggest the need for an integration of philosophy, history, and a number of scientific disciplines to provide such understanding. The level and objectives of the particular study should determine which disciplines are needed.

Critical Factors in Public Policy Making

Some politicians tend to overemphasize the role of public opinion in policy making and, in the process, may underestimate or even fail to recognize the effective components of political behavior and other critical factors. This failure to give adequate consideration to all of the critical factors may well account for many of the imperfections and unfortunate consequences of public policy making.

One of the most bizarre examples of such a failure was the infamous Federal Loyalty-Security Program of the 1950s.[14] The innocent victims were legion and there would seem to be little point to adding to the list at this time, but this writer's personal experience points up the failure on the part of several participants to consider certain critical factors. In addition, it sheds some light as well on the roles of several internal transducers in the making of public policy.

The program evolved slowly over a period of years, but was finally formalized by President Truman in March 1947 (Executive Order 9835).[15] an action he later confessed that he regretted having taken, although at the time it seemed like the best way to head off efforts by some members of Congress to impose an even more stringent and perhaps unworkable program on the Executive Branch. About one year later, the President issued a directive establishing the confidential status of employee loyalty-security records in the Federal civil service.

In the meantime, this writer had been appointed first a member and later chairman of the agency Loyalty Board for the Federal Mediation and Conciliation Service (FMCS). Subsequently, in two successive years (1952 and 1953), while this writer was serving as Associate Director of FMCS, a member of the House Appropriations Committee raised questions about the loyalty of a certain, unnamed mediator in FMCS. The Director and I tried desperately in the 1952 appropriation hearings to satisfy the Congressman without violating the terms of the Presidential Directive of March 13, 1948, concerning confidentiality of loyalty records, but to no avail.

In preparation for the 1953 hearings, the new Director of the Service conferred with White House officials (under a new Administration, that of President Eisenhower) and at their suggestion, I conferred with the Attorney General, the principal architect of the Eisenhower version of the Loyalty-Security Program. The instructions from the White House and the Attorney General were to be cooperative, but not to violate the terms of the Presidential Directive on confidentiality which had been reaffirmed by the new President. The Congressman, however, was persistent and would not be placated. The Director and I were caught in the middle but were unable to secure any further guidance or relief from either the White House or the Attorney General.

Several years later, as a direct result of this conflict of interests, I was requested to resign from a position in another agency of the Federal Government, not because of any question of my loyalty or security, but because I had become a "controversial figure." Thus, I became unsuitable for Federal employment for having firmly adhered to a Presidential Directive and the oral instructions from the highest sources in the Administration.

From the time of the issuance of the 1947 Executive Order, the loyalty program was in a continuing state of revision and reformulation. The personal incident cited above was by no means unique in its adverse effects on individuals and on genuinely loyal employees. Appropriations Committee hearings for practically all departments and agencies became hunting grounds for Representatives and Senators of all suasions and multifarious motivations who felt impelled to save the nation from Communists and communist sympathizers who might be trying to infiltrate the Federal Government. The fever spread to state and local governments too. Most of these legislators evinced little regard for protecting the innocent or for preserving the traditional rights of the individual; each vied with the others to demonstrate beyond all doubt his super patriotism. Such an atmosphere provides a fertile breeding ground for the irrational elements in public policy making. Practically every Appropriations Act carried some special provision on the subject; numerous bills were introduced in both the Senate and House every session, each aimed in the eyes of its author at tightening or improving the efficacy of the Loyalty Program. A study by this writer (1960) lists ten significant laws on the subject between 1947 and 1955 in addition to the provisions in Appropriations Acts.[16] The number of bills introduced outnumbered the enactments by several orders of magnitude.

Meanwhile, a number of lawsuits brought the courts into the process, which initially necessitated greater care on the part of the government in the application of the program to individual employees. Later, the decision of the Supreme Court in Cole v. Young had the effect of practically inverting the basic purpose of the program while in effect retaining it.[17] The decision resulted in the anomalous situation that incumbents in nonsensitive positions had no statutory rights to a hearing or review of their cases, while the incumbents of sensitive positions did have such rights guaranteed by statute. Thus, the net cumulative effect of Legislative, Executive, and Judicial action up to 1956 was to produce a policy under which the occupant of a sensitive position had a greater procedural protection in tenure than the occupant of a nonsensitive position. This result was certainly contrary to that originally intended, which was to facilitate the process of separating from the service employees whose continued employment posed a threat to the national security.

Conceived in hysteria, born in fear, raised in confusion, the Federal Loyalty-Security Program, after a premature senility, died in ignominy, having accomplished next to nothing but the bringing of embarrassment and misery to thousands of innocent victims. Shakespeare warned us long ago not to cry Havoc!, when we should hunt with but lesser warrant. In retrospect, at least, one may see that the basic objectives of the program could have been accomplished certainly more economically and efficiently, probably more effectively, and with much greater regard for the fundamental civil rights of those most directly affected with the established machinery for personnel administration and without the elaborate superstructure of security officers and loyalty boards. Perhaps, if there is another occasion requiring such measures, the nation may succeed in achieving a higher level of civility.

However bizarre it may have been, the Federal Loyalty-Security Program clearly illustrates the dynamic and cybernetic nature of the policy-making process. Even when operating in its most nearly rational manner, the process does not culminate in a single, definitive, fixed policy. The policy-making process and its output continue to evolve over time. The very process of administering the policy contributes to its further evolution by filling in the interstices and by feeding back information on its effectiveness, strengths, weaknesses, and the needs for further revision. Legislative committees, through the several means of administrative oversight and continuing challenges of administrative decisions, observe for themselves the effectiveness of the policy and the need for its revision. Courts, exercising their reserve power, provide input and feedback through judicial decisions on legal challenges to the policy or its administration. Every policy, therefore, is in, or subject to, a continuing state of flux or evolution. The administration of a policy is normally sensitive to this continuing flow of information and itself evolves accordingly, sometimes obviating the need for formal policy revisions, or at least, for legislative action.

The Federal Loyalty-Security Program also illustrates more clearly than most policy-making efforts the role of irrational factors in the process. It vividly demonstrates the fact that policy making is by no means a linear, logical, orderly, rational human activity. The affective elements in the process probably reached an apogee in this particular effort. The wave of hysteria that hit the legislature, the irresponsible demagoguery, the haste to take political advantage of a factitious issue, were all sufficient to quiet, at least for a time, even the few more sober, more judicious individuals in that body. Some apparently feared to appear unpatriotic; some probably hoped the whole affair would die down and blow away in time. But not until the fever had almost run its course did the sequestered solons regain sufficient self-control to call a halt to the ludicrous legislative performance.

Another example of irrationality in policy making on a somewhat less momentous level of political and social significance occurred a few years ago. The Postal Service had installed coin-operated copying machines in the lobbies of certain post offices and branches where there seemed to be a demand for such service. Some business people viewed this action as a further intrusion by the Postal Service into the legitimate domain of private enterprise and protested long and loudly; they also enlisted the support of Congressmen. Finally, succumbing to this double assault, the Postal Service announced withdrawal of the machines, and some were actually removed. The postal patrons who had been using the machines and many others who presumably thought they might need them sometime then protested even more loudly to the Postal Service and to their Congressional representatives. Caught in this cross fire, the Postal Service, apparently desiring to avoid having its policy fixed in legislation, quietly restored the machines and the issue lapsed into dormancy.

In originally installing the copying machines, the Postal Service failed to consider the interests and potential reaction of the private enterprise organizations that were already providing a similar service. In summarily withdrawing the machines, it failed to consider the interests and convenience of those members of the public who had become accustomed to the ready accessibility of the machines. In both instances, it neglected to give consideration to the critical factors in its policy making and to the systems effects of its actions.

Sometimes this type of easy capitulation to popular clamor leads some individual citizens to fail to discriminate between their power as individuals and the power of the citizenry as a whole. We may find symptoms of this type of confusion also in such campaigns as those of the self-appointed protectors of the snail darter, or of public morals, or of the opponents of nuclear missiles, or of nuclear electric generating plants. Members of Congress are also subject to this type of delusion, mistaking their own power for that of the Congress as a whole, at least on certain issues such as the Loyalty-Security Program described above. Pursued to its extreme, this type of delusion leads to megalomania, as in the instance of the list-waving Senator who was finally brought to heel by his own excesses and a fearless Yankee lawyer by the name of Joseph N. Welch.

Two much less extreme and relatively minor examples of this tendency occurred during this writer's tenure with the Federal Mediation and Conciliation Service (FMCS). In the first incident, the FMCS was planning the establishment in Seattle of a new regional office as part of a general reorganization and decentralization of authority and operations. The entire staff of the regional office would total about ten or twelve persons: mediators, clerks, secretaries, and a regional director. Wherever it might be located, the operation would have miniscule economic impact. We in the FMCS, however, failed to anticipate the political reactions. The then two Senators from Oregon saw the decision as sufficiently important to call on the Director in person to try to persuade him of the greater desirability of establishing that regional office in Portland instead of Seattle. They saw the Director's plan as part of a general policy of the national administration favoring the state of Washington over the state of Oregon, and they were bent on changing it. They indicated the likely displeasure of the Congress and its Appropriations Committees over the continued pursuit of such a policy. The Director correctly diagnosed this as an empty threat and reaffirmed his decision.

The second incident was inherently less significant but had much more unfortunate consequences for FMCS. It involved a New Jersey Senator and his misreading of the established custom of so-called senatorial courtesy in the clearance of Presidential appointments. In accordance with that custom, the President would ordinarily seek advance approval of the Senator of his own political party on the appointment to an administrative post of any person from that Senator's state. At the time, a nomination for a new director of FMCS was pending before the Senate. The nominee happened to be from New Jersey. In this instance, the Senator from New Jersey attempted to establish as a condition of his approval of the nomination an agreement with the nominee that the Director would clear with the Senator the appointment of every mediator, not just the ones from his state. (Mediators at the time usually entered FMCS at grade GS-9 or GS-11, ordinarily not a high enough level to attract Congressional interest as a source of political patronage. The jobs were, however, exempt from civil service rating and perhaps looked like an opportunity for exploitation of patronage.) The nominee for director declared himself opposed in principle to the Senator's demand and firmly in support of the policy established by the preceding director of making appointments solely on the basis of merit. As a result of the impasse, President Eisenhower finally withdrew the nomination at the request of the nominee and submitted the name of someone from another state. A Pyrrhic victory, as it turned out; FMCS won the battle over patronage, but suffered a severe loss in the quality of its leadership.

The reader may detect faulty thinking on the part of several participants in this process. This sort of faulty thinking tends to overlook the interdependence of all the components of the policy-making and political processes. Every participant is, in fact, dependent, in one way or another, on every other participant; all are mutually involved in the policy-making process and the political process, albeit with varying degrees of activity and varying degrees of effect. But, in principle at least, every participant has a right to be heard and every voter has an equal voice in the outcome. Thus, in the final analysis, the policy-making process should present a comprehensive image of the political process, with due consideration for the values, interests, views and demands of all participants, regardless of their apparent irrationality.

Unfortunately, this ideal is frequently ignored and the legitimate input of many elements of the policy is disregarded by tightly knit coalitions of private interests who are able to prevail over the general interest; for example, in the taxing of income from petroleum production, in the appropriation of funds for the Army Corps of Engineers and the Bureau of Reclamation, in the provision of farm subsidies for tobacco growers, and in the provision of loan guarantees to defense contractors. In these and many other areas of policy making, a tendency develops for an easy liaison to arise among a particular interest group, the administrator of a given program, and the Congressional Appropriations Subcommittee with jurisdiction over the program. The situation stimulates recall of Lasswell's observation that, in the political process, distribution depends on myth and violence (or on faith and brigandage) as well as bargaining.[18] The outstanding successes of a few of these unholy coalitions may lead us to overlook the ubiquity of the tendency. There is a natural gravitation of interests at work throughout the political process. Every legislator, executive, and administrator seeks to develop a support system for his or her particular special interest; these officials find such support among other government officials and the outside groups with related interests. They provide each other such comfort and support as is in their power in a cyclical feedback system and, in the process, tend to forget the larger values involved in the political system as a whole, as well as the lesser, interacting values and interests of other citizens in the subsystem they are controlling. This tendency is receiving wider recognition among the electorate as indicated by the recent increase in the number and degree of activity of political action committees and the proliferation of special interest groups campaigning for specific causes.

While this increasing interest in political affairs has its healthful aspects, it has at least one unfortunate consequence. It tends to fragment the political system, with the result that legislators are elected and administrators are appointed to an increasing extent, because of their endorsement of, or support for, special interests instead of for their broader concern for the public interest. In the words of the systems analyst, there is a trend toward suboptimization; that is, toward improving the effectiveness of subsystems at the expense of, or without regard for, the consequent effects on the system as a whole.

An example of this kind of suboptimization can be found in the Federal welfare programs. The increasing emphasis on and appropriations for categorical grant-in-aid programs (old-age assistance, aid to the blind, aid to dependent children) resulted in decreased emphasis on and decreased funds for the nongrant programs of the several states for general public assistance. The systems effects of these suboptimizing efforts were overlooked or ignored.

A similar tendency existed for a while in the field of Federal support for medical research. The number of constituent Institutes at the National Institutes of Health (NIH) and the amount of appropriations to each Institute for categorical grants increased from year to year with minimum support for research in the health delivery system. This imbalance was finally recognized, however, and steps were taken to rectify it.

The Techniques of Policy Making

Fortunately again, however, the difficulties that affect the process of formulating policy on the large and important issues facing society are not characteristic of the entire process. We seldom read of the ordinary, routine operation of the process within the political system in which policy-making activity takes place. The newsworthy items are the occasional blatant failures or amusing blunders, muddles, and fiascoes, not the regular, successful, apparently humdrum completion of responsible and effective policy making. The ordinary citizen tends to take this process for granted, but it is neither simple nor automatic.

For the most part, the policy-making process operates smoothly and routinely on a basis of consensus; only the occasional controversial issue upsets the normal routine. Political organizations generally aim to take account of, if not to accomodate, the expressed interests of all citizens. They do this by making the issues sufficiently general as to arouse the least amount of controversy and by attempting to synthesize the various views so as to allow a consensus to develop. In the course of securing a consensus, they gradually reduce the number of alternative choices until a decision is reached. This is normally a time-consuming business, but to the legislator, politician, or bureaucrat at the apex of the particular policy-making process, who, after all, is primarily interested in survival, it seems to be a necessary procedure. There are, however, some dangers. What appears to be consensus may result, not from positive interest, but from apathy. The adoption of the Eighteenth Amendment to the Constitution may be an example. A real consensus develops from positive conflict and reconciliation of views.

Franklin D. Roosevelt used the technique of deliberately cultivating conflict among the members of his Cabinet. He would maintain an Olympian aloofness until all the arguments had been advanced, then he would make a decision. That decision then became a "consensus." Sometimes, however, he would allow the conflict to continue to simmer after the decision had been made just to keep the concerned administrators alert and effective. This technique was particularly noticeable in the unceasing and open warfare between Hopkins and Ickes over the relative merits of their respective programs, the Work Projects Administration and the Public Works Administration. Ickes wanted to stimulate the economy through expansive public works projects on the theory that the benefits would trickle down through the creation of jobs for the unemployed. Hopkins was impatient with this slow approach. He insisted on more direct action with more immediate results, employing large numbers of persons on projects that were worthwhile, but labor intensive, thus offering more jobs to more people faster.

Left to their own devices, Cabinet members and other high officials generally refrain from a formal or scientific approach to policy making, preferring a more pragmatic course of action. Applying the insights and perspectives gained through experience, or relying on their own intuitive judgement, they normally make policy indirectly on a case-by-case basis, resulting in administrative decisions that cumulatively develop into an unstated, informal policy. Fully aware of the dearth of information needed for informed decision, conscious of the multiplicity of constraints under which they operate, and recognizing the limited number of practicable alternatives available to them, these policy makers tend to move as cautiously as if they were advancing through a mine field. Contrary to the beliefs of some theorists,[19] however, this so-called pragmatic approach is not exactly the same as that of the theoretical "disjointed incrementalism" which started out as a description and ended up as a prescription. The pragmatic approach of the real policy makers is much less formal, less directed, much more desultory, arbitrary, and unplanned. In one sense, the actual approach is not so much a technique of policy making as an effort to avoid policy making. Nevertheless, policy inevitably evolves in the process.

Another way of seeking to avoid policy making is through the expedient of delay. Sometimes the responsible officials will delay in the hope that the need for a policy will pass, or that someone else will make the crucial decisions, or that the current controversy will die down, thereby eliminating the need for action. The Food and Drug Administration and some other regulatory agencies frequently resort to this device. The usual reason given is that more information or further investigation and experimentation is needed. The infamous Thalidomide incident is perhaps the most flagitious example.

The regulatory agencies are not, however, the only participants in the policy-making process guilty of such tactics. Other agencies in the Executive Branch as well as the Legislative and Judicial Branches at all levels of government resort to such remedies for the lack of omniscience. Referring matters to presidential commissions, advisory committees, study panels, legislative investigating committees, special hearing masters, and referees is standard practice.

Frequently, however, the elected official's intuitive judgement about what the general public expects or will accept in the way of a policy on any given topic is just as valid as the expert's advice on the subject; further, it is probably equally or even more important in establishing the applicable policy.

Such tactics are sometimes used also as a means of dodging responsibility as well as stalling for time. In arriving at unpopular decisions on Social Security policy, Congress frequently calls on advisory commissions for recommendations. At this writing, however, an instance of this practice appears to have backfired. A Presidential Commission appointed by President Reagan, or at least the Chairman and several members of the Commission, insisted that they cannot provide advice on the future financing of the Social Security program until the President and the Speaker of the House of Representatives reach a compromise agreement on what particular advice they are prepared to accept. Here we have the interesting, if paradoxical, situation of the appointed advisers asking for guidance on what advice they should provide. Undoubtedly this has happened before; advisory commissions and committees have probably been told in advance many times what advice they should give, but in the memory of this writer, this is the first time the Chairman and members of an advisory commission have publicly announced a desire, indeed, a need for such guidance. The obvious question is why appoint such a commission in the first place if it must return to the policy makers themselves for guidance on what to say. In a world of accelerating technological advance, legislative bodies find increasing need to call upon outside experts and a variety of consultants, advisors, commissions, and study panels. As the problems of a modern society become more and more complex and sophisticated, legislators find that the most profound political wisdom and the greatest political skills are increasingly inadequate to enable them to deal competently with the controversial issues with which they are daily confronted. This trend toward great complexity of policy issues tends to accentuate the dependence of the legislature on the administrative branch, where the technological expertise is supposed to exist. One evidence of this tendency may be found in the extremely close liaison that has developed between the concerned subcommittees of the Congressional Appropriations Committees and the personnel of the National Institutes of Health, or between the concerned subcommittees and the Army Corps of Engineers, or between the concerned subcommittees and the Maritime Commission.[20] Other examples may be found in other agencies with high levels of technological expertise.

Occasionally, one may find instances in which the policy maker resorts to expert advice to support a decision already made, but not yet announced. The policy maker is convinced of the propriety and rectitude of the proposed policy, but needs technical advice, assistance, or support in squaring it with existing laws or policies of a higher order, or with prevailing public opinion. Such momentous decisions as Jefferson's Louisiana Purchase, Lincoln's Emancipation Proclamation, or Roosevelt's Lend-Lease policy were of this type. On a much lower order of significance but of a basically similar nature were a number of policies of the National War Labor Board (NWLB) during World War II. Faced with an already consummated agreement of labor and management representatives on the need for specific wage adjustments, the public representatives found it necessary to resort to tortured interpretations of the wage stabilization regulations (aimed at containing inflation) in order to develop a policy that would maintain industrial peace, thereby avoiding interruptions of vital war production. Some of the exercises in logic would have warmed the cockles of the heart of a medieval scholastic.

Frequently, the policies thus evolved by the NWLB were so finespun that any one of them would not support more than the one case for which it was designed. This pragmatic, case-by-case approach to policy obviated the necessity for making major adjustments in the wage stabilization regulations and avoided any disastrous breakthroughs in the government's anti-inflationary policies, yet succeeded in maintaining a reasonable level of equilibrium in labor-management relations and relative peace on the industrial front.

The NWLB was not, or course, the originator of this strategy of policy making, nor was it the only agency to adopt the strategy, either during or since World War II. The strategy is typical of policy makers in positions of responsibility who find themselves constrained by higher level policies or laws with which they may or may not agree and in circumstances over which they have no control, with limited access to necessary information and with no clear conception of the public interest or popular wants. They find themselves in a dynamic, systemic process, strongly influenced by the cumulative burden of prior policy making, with inadequate resources for keeping current with the new demands for new policies or revisions of old policies. The flow of events is fast, multichanneled, and continually shifting. Needed information is spotty and of questionable validity and reliability. The flow is unsteady. Communication channels are wide open, free-flowing from special interests; irregular or clogged from other sources. Thus, feedback is undependable. Staff resources for analysis and interpretation are usually inadequate; staff resources for forecasting are usually meager and methodology deficient. In such circumstances, policy making tends to be halting, uncertain, discontinuous, even disjunctive.

This general approach to policy making is widely practiced throughout the Federal Government as well as in governments at other levels and in private enterprise. Admittedly, it is roughly equivalent to what Lindblom has characterized as "disjointed incrementalism," at least in superficial appearance, and this writer has no serious objection to such a characterization so long as the reader or student of policy making bears in mind that the practice preceded the label. No policy maker consciously practices "disjointed incrementalism." The description is what Reichenbach calls an "ideal reconstruction." Much the same may be said of many other attempts to apply broad-brush labels to what is essentially a stochastic, irrational process (rational decision making, Etzioni's "mixed scanning" method.[21], etc.). Only the occasional, high-level policy with broad implications and deep public interest receives any treatment even approximating the formal, rational approach.

Theoretically, under the applicable provision of the Constitution, the Congress exercises control over both policy formulation and policy execution through the "power of the purse," that is, its constitutional authority to control expenditures from the Federal Treasury through Appropriation Acts. On rare occasions, however, the Executive Branch may circumvent the will of Congress by using the President's emergency funds to implement a pet policy or program. Thomas Jefferson, Abraham Lincoln, and Franklin D. Roosevelt were adept at this type of maneuver.

The same tactic may also be employed by agency heads in their dealing with the Executive Office or with Congress. During the early days of World War II, the Administrator of the Office of Price Administration (OPA) established a small planning staff in his immediate office. The Bureau of the Budget, acting in the name of the President, but probably without his specific knowledge or sanction, disallowed funds for this staff in the President's budget. The OPA, however, was growing so fast and had sufficient funds and sufficient leeway in the use of those funds that the amount disallowed was relatively insignificant. Accordingly, the Administrator simply shifted funds and retained his planning staff. Each year for the duration of the agency, the Bureau of the Budget would disallow the funds for the special staff, but each year the Administrator held on to the staff and included the item in his new budget. The Bureau of the Budget maintained its policy of control, the Administrator held on to his staff, and all were satisfied until the end of the war and the beginning of the liquidation of the OPA.

Role of the Leader

Occasionally, a particularly strong-willed administrator or a politically powerful individual in an administrative post may resist these efforts at intervention by the Congress or executive control agencies. Harold Ickes was such a type; his diaries are replete with specific examples. Such resistance, however, is an extreme example of the influence of personality factors in the policy-making process. Any detailed analysis would show the effect on policy making of such factors as the economic security of the individual (his or her financial independence), political power (possession of a loyal and extensive constituency), personal prestige (reputation and public support), knowledge and political acumen, and self-confidence. Persons lacking most or all of these characteristics are likely to be relatively less effective in the policy-making role as well as in other aspects of top level management.

One such policy maker was appointed to the Service several months before I resigned as Associate Director. Prior to his appointment, a number of significant improvements had been made in the policies and administration of Federal Mediation, and Conciliation Service (FMCS): decentralization of authority and responsibility with a resulting increased responsiveness to the needs of its clients, upgrading of qualification standards and salaries of mediators, initiation of the preventive mediation program, and so on. Consequently, after the new Director had been in office for about thirty days, this writer asked him if he had had sufficient opportunity to become acquainted with the established policies of FMCS and whether he wished to make any changes. The new Director's response was yes, he wanted this writer to issue immediately a directive to the effect that everyone in FMCS should practice greater economy in the use of communications services, to wit, not to use the telephone when a letter would serve, not to use airmail when regular mail would serve. This momentous policy was probably his only positive contribution to the guidance of FMCS during his entire tenure as Director. This individual was an obvious adherent of the dictum propounded by Heinz von Foerster as the "First Law," to the effect that the more profound the problem that is ignored, the greater are the chances for fame and success.

Fortunately, there exist a number of institutional safeguards that tend to minimize the deleterious effects of such individuals on the agencies on which they are imposed. The official whose policy making and administrative practices vary too greatly from the established or generally accepted norms for the agency tends to attract adverse attention from the public, from the higher level officials, and from the Congress. He or she loses first the respect, then the loyalty of the members of his or her own agency. Finally, sooner or later, the official is dismissed or quietly departs under pressure. Organizational equilibrium is restored, at least for a time, with the appointment of a new leader. This phenomenon is evidence of the systemic nature of the policy-making process and of the entire political process; one cannot make only one change in any system.

No official is free to indulge his or her own fancies in the realm of policy making. To be sure, there is a certain amount of latitude, but only within the constraints imposed by the particular organization and its larger environment. To be effective, the policy maker must steer a course among a complex, interacting and often conflicting set of values, goals, interests, and needs whose relative degrees of influence and hierarchical order are not always entirely clear. These demands sometimes becloud the basic goals of the organization, sometimes overriding them. The desire for mere survival frequently becomes paramount for the individual and for the organization.

Occasionally, there comes an individual who can rise above the conflicting demands, above the drive for mere survival and point the organization in a new direction, set higher goals, and initiate new policies. In contrast to the general run of policy makers who strive primarily to avoid creating disturbances or controversies, whose aim is to maintain the system in a state of dynamic equilibrium, this rare individual aims to establish a new equilibrium, on a higher level of performance. I had the good fortune to work with one such leader, Cyrus S. Ching, the first Director of the Federal Mediation and Conciliation Service (FMCS).

The FMCS is a relatively small and little-known agency, but it performs a vital function in helping to maintain labor-management peace and, thereby, continued industrial production. It rarely receives attention in the daily headlines. Mediators seldom have their pictures or even their names in the news, preferring to maintain a low profile, keeping the focus of attention on the labor and management representatives who are responsible for collective bargaining. Thus, the general public has little appreciation of the important role of FMCS, but the representatives of labor and management who utilize the services of the mediators are well aware of the crucial role FMCS plays in the industrial life of the nation.

Ching (a naturalized U.S. citizen, born in Canada of Scotch-Welsh ancestry) used to claim that he was one-third Scotch and two-thirds soda. He was a physical giant of a man, six feet, seven inches tall (he used to say five feet, nineteen inches), weighing over three hundred pounds, and gentle as a lamb, with a handshake that would not bruise a rosebud. Ching came to this country as a youth to work as a motorman on a Boston trolley car. That job did not last long. Ching said the company promoted him to management because he was so tall he could not see out the front of the trolley car. He became interested in labor relations and rose through the ranks, eventually becoming director of public and labor relations for the U.S. Rubber Company. Recognizing his abilities, Presidents Roosevelt and Truman appointed him to several high-level government positions in the war agencies during and following World War II. Then in 1947, he became the first Director of the newly established FMCS (actually a statutory reestablishment of the old U.S. Conciliation Service in the Department of Labor). In the meantime, Ching had acquired a deep understanding of human nature, especially of the interests of the working man, and a nationwide reputation for fairness in his dealings with labor unions. Of course, his long career in management had provided him with an appreciation of management's point of view also.

With the benefits of that broad perspective, Ching realized that the long range contribution of FMCS to the maintenance of peaceful labor-management relations could not lie solely in the firefighting approach of settling disputes as they arose. On the contrary, the number of labor-management disputes was likely to increase faster than FMCS could acquire qualified personnel to cope with them. Instead, a way must be found to head off such disputes before they arose, to establish a climate of sound labor-management relations in which any differences could be resolved peacefully without resort to strikes or lockouts. Here and there throughout FMCS, a few old-timers among the staff of mediators had been following such an approach in a limited way on a strictly local basis and as a personal method of operation. Their tactics and techniques were strictly intuitive and highly individualized. There was no FMCS policy on the subject, no attempt to develop a rational methodology. Ching found the underlying philosophy of this approach consonant with his views of the agency's basic goals. In formal and informal meetings of labor and management leaders across the country, he found general acceptance of the idea. Corresponding to the analogy of dispute settlement as firefighting, the new approach was compared to fire prevention. The term *preventive mediation* was not entirely new, but with Ching it was given a new emphasis and adopted as a formal policy of FMCS.

Ching was clearly responsible for establishing the policy, yet never did clearly state what he intended by it. He left those details to members of his staff. A master of face-to-face communication, he seldom indulged in written exposition of his ideas or oral statements of policy. Although his oral communication was highly effective, a transcript would appear utterly unintelligible. He was at his best in appearances before Congressional Appropriations Committees, most of whose members showed him great deference. But his effectiveness lay not so much in what he said as in the messages conveyed by facial expressions and bodily gestures, often used as substitutes for words, phrases, or even whole sentences. What he left unsaid was often as important as what he actually uttered. As a result, when his staff was afforded an opportunity to review and edit a transcript of his testimony prior to publication of the *Hearings*, they were faced with the hopeless task of converting odd words and phrases into complete sentences conveying his meaning for the record. He did not hold the written word in complete contempt, but his attitude certainly bordered on that view. Rarely did he modify even one word of a written statement prepared by his staff and submitted for his approval or signature; in fact, there is some doubt that he even read most of them. Apparently he had confidence in his staff.

In its initial formulation, Ching's preventive mediation policy amounted to little more than an expression of the basic philosophy of FMCS. Henceforth, the agency would place increased emphasis on working with the parties to improve the climate of labor-management relations in individual plants, in communities, and on a nationwide basis so as to prevent or avoid the occurrence of labor-management disputes at time of contract negotiation or grievances arising during the contract period. Those mediators who had been engaging in such practices were encouraged to continue and extend their efforts in this direction. Other mediators were encouraged to initiate similar practices. Regional directors were asked to stimulate intramural discussions of preventive mediation at regional staff meetings, to prepare written reports of such efforts, to promote interchange of ideas among themselves and among the mediators so as to develop and improve the techniques of preventive mediation.

At the national level, the Director appointed a committee of mediators to develop means of promoting the policy within FMCS and acceptance of the policy among the FMCS clientele, that is, representatives of labor and management. In these and other ways, the policy began to become more specific, more concrete. Mediators were requested to file formal, written reports on their personal preventive mediation efforts and the more significant reports were circulated throughout the agency in the monthly FMCS newsletter.

Not all mediators, however, were either intellectually or psychologically prepared for this new direction. Most of the members of the mediation staff were former officials of local labor unions, carried over into the FMCS from the former Conciliation Service in the Department of Labor. They were neither educationally nor emotionally prepared to appreciate the significance of the new philosophy. Their personal experiences in the rough and tumble of labor-management relations of an earlier day tended to disincline them to an optimistic view of ever successfully preventing labor-management disputes. They considered any contract settlement without a prolonged strike a major accomplishment. Among management representatives, the old Conciliation Service had a reputation for a strong labor bias, due in part to its location within the Department of Labor and in part to the predominantly labor union background of the mediators. The reputation was not entirely unearned, but was probably exaggerated.

Nevertheless, Ching saw that a deciding factor in the success of the new policy of preventive mediation would be the general acceptability of the mediators to both labor and management. There was a critical need for revising the reputation of mediators, for removing the suspicion (deserved or undeserved) of a labor bias. At the same time, FMCS could not afford to embark on any wholesale replacement of mediators without risking widespread labor-management unrest throughout the nation. To accomplish his purpose while minimizing the risk, Ching adopted a new recruitment policy with higher qualifying standards for new mediators. No mediators were fired, but all replacements and mediators hired to fill new positions had to meet the new standards.

These two policies (preventive mediation and higher-level recruiting standards) together with Ching's personal prestige served to establish the FMCS on a new and higher level of acceptability and effectiveness in the labor-management community. Ching rescued an organization that had been in disrepute with the Congress, the Executive Office, and a major portion of its clientele. Subsequently, the fortunes of the agency have wavered depending on the leadership qualities of the current director, but the two policies have survived and the net effectiveness of FMCS has significantly improved. The preventive mediation program has undergone some name changes and the techniques are now more sophisticated, but the basic policy is essentially the same. In the words of one Regional Director, "mediators should have a continuing relationship with the parties to provide whatever services are necessary as a neutral to help them make their collective bargaining relationship effective."[22] He sees preventive mediation not as a separate task from the mediation of contract disputes, but as part of that continuing relationship with the parties.

This is a striking demonstration of the validity of the observation by James MacGregor Burns to the effect that policy makers who keep the wants and purposes of the great public in mind as representing the most compelling claim can and do produce real change.[23] The FMCS was fortunate in having as its first Director a man who could and did provide that kind of perspective, and the resulting changes were real and significant.

Incidentally, here may be noted in passing that while the preventive mediation policy had only very general sanction in legislation, once initiated, it did receive budgetary and political support from the Executive Office and the Congresses. Both branches quickly recognized the potential for long-range advantages, although no cost-benefit studies were ever done (initially or since). More important to the long-range success of the policy, however, has been the support received by FMCS from the parties it serves directly, the representatives of labor and management. Here one may observe the potential power of a policy-making official in his or her authority and responsibility for clarifying and making more specific the goals established for an agency by the Congress. One may also observe the systemic effects of two relatively simple policies in their indirect effects on the morale of the personnel of FMCS, on the relationships of the agency with its clientele and the Executive and Legislative Branches, and on the reputation of the agency generally, in addition to its direct impact on the nature of the work and responsibilities of the mediators.

Summary and Conclusions

The systems view of policy making sees it as a function, not of any one or more components, but of the political system as a whole. As such, it rarely follows a completely rational course; rather, it involves an indeterminate mix of rational, extrarational, and irrational forces operating at all levels of the hierarchy of the political system in a complex, highly dynamic, cybernetic flux. The active participants in the process, all of uncertain motivation, enter into the process in varying degrees at different times, depending in part on an incompletely known variety of other factors.

The aim of the policy-making process is to produce guidelines that will serve to reduce entropy in the social system by controlling or influencing the future behavior of certain government officials and employees in their performance of their assigned duties, and of certain citizens, groups, organizations, or other entities in their social, economic, political, or other relationships. The role of any individual participant in policy making is roughly analogous to the decision-making process, but is much more complex and, because the number of participants is so great and so indeterminate, the complexity of the process is compounded by the number and nature of their interrelationships. As a result, the policy-making process as a whole cannot be adequately represented by any model of the decision-making process.

The methods of policy making are many and varied; they may include any of the means by which the process of government is conducted. They range from the lowest level of individual decisions on implementation up through the prescription of methods and procedures to higher levels of strategy and eventually to ultimate goals, norms, and values. At the lower levels of policy making, the participants generally have an instrumental orientation; they are concerned with implementing one policy or a narrow range of policies on a case-by-case basis. In the process, they succeed, intentionally or unintentionally, in modifying the policy to some extent; in other words, they are, themselves, making policy. At successively higher levels of the policy-making hierarchy, the participants are concerned with an even broader range of policies. At the top levels, the participants are concerned primarily with the setting of goals consonant with the prevailing norms and values of the society; they are concerned with the implementation only in terms of general oversight to ensure conformance with the established policies. Among the levels, of course, there is a continuing, multidirectional flow of information and feedback and a continuing interaction among all participants.

All of this activity takes place in the context of all the economic, political, and social forces and influences operating in the society as a whole. These forces range from explicit to covert, from altruistic to selfish. They include all the ideologies currently prevailing in the country as well as the individual personalities, motivations, and attitudes of the policy makers themselves.

While the myth of the separation of policy making and administration continues in the popular mind, and even perhaps, in the minds of some policy makers, the fact is that policy making takes place at all levels and in all branches of the governmental hierarchy, from the individual citizen (voter) on up. The distinction may be made conceptually, but on the whole, the process of policy making blends imperceptibly into administration in the actual governmental and political processes. But if, as Brooks Adams observed, administration is the highest faculty of the human mind,[24] there would appear to be little cause for concern, particularly with the system of checks and balances operating in this nation.

Footnotes

1. Henry Taylor, *The Statesmen* (New York: Mentor Books, 1958). (Originally published, 1836).
2. D. Lerner and H. D. Lasswell, eds., *The Policy Sciences* (Stanford, Calif.: Stanford University Press, 1951).
3. J. Kenneth Galbraith, *The New Industrial State*, 3d ed. rev. (Boston: Houghton Mifflin, 1978).
4. David Braybrooke and Charles E. Lindblom, *A Strategy of Decision* (New York: Free Press, 1970), p. 249.
5. See, e.g., Frank J. Goodnow, *Politics and Administration* (New York: Macmillan, 1900); C. E. Merriam, *Primary Elections* (Chicago: University of Chicago Press, 1908); Woodrow Wilson, *Public Papers*, authorized edition, Ray Stannard Baker and William E. Dodd, eds. (New York: Harper, 1925-1927), 6 v. in 3.
6. *Family Weekly*, November 18, 1972, p. 2.
7. James G. Miller, *Living Systems* (New York: McGraw-Hill, 1978).
8. For further elucidation of the systems approach, see: Greenwood and Greenwood, *Systems Thinking for Managers*, forthcoming.
9. See Julian Feldman and Hershel E. Kanter, "Organizational Decision Making", in James G. March, ed., *Handbook of Organizations* (Chicago: Rand McNally, 1965), pp. 614-649; William C. Mitchell, "Systems Analysis: Political Systems", *International Encyclopedia of Social Sciences* (New York: Macmillan and

Free Press. 1968), v. 15, pp. 473-478; and Donald W. Taylor, "Decision Making and Problem Solving" in James G. March, ed., *Handbook of Organizations* (Chicago: Rand McNally, 1965).

10. Ernest Nagel, *The Structure of Science* (New York: Harcourt Brace and World, 1961).

11. President's Research Committee on Social Trends, *Report* (Washington, D.C.: U.S. Government Printing Office, 1933).

12. Yehezkel Dror, *Public Policy Making Re-examined* (San Francisco: Chandler, 1968).

13. *Ibid.,* ch. V.

14. James W. Greenwood, *Judicial Review of the Federal Loyalty-Security Program* (Unpublished Thesis, on file at The American University, Washington, D.C., 1960). Includes extensive bibliography.

15. Executive Order 9835, March 21, 1947. 12 F.R. 1935.

16. Greenwood (1960, *op. cit.*).

17. 351 U.S. 536 (1956).

18. Harold D. Lasswell, *Politics: Who Gets What, When, How* (New York: Peter Smith, 1950. (originally McGraw-Hill, 1936).

19. See, e.g., Braybrooke and Lindblom, *op. cit.*

20. J. Leiper Freeman, *The Political Process* (New York: Doubleday, 1955). Presents interesting case study.

21. Amital Etzioni, *The Active Society* (New York: Free Press, 1968).

22. Personal communication, November 21, 1979.

23. James MacGregor Burns, *Leadership* (New York: Harper and Row, 1978).

24. Henry Brooks Adams' evaluation of administration is a paraphrase from an uncited quotation contained in Paul H. Appleby, *Policy and Administration* (University, Ala: University of Alabama Press, 1949), p. 51.

Editorial Note: David S. Brown presents a glimpse of the values, operating methods, and policies of William Ashby Jump, one of the "deans" of practical public administration in the Federal Government. In presenting the panorama of Jump's journey from an assistant messenger to his assignment as director of the Office of Budget and Finance in the Department of Agriculture, Brown portrays Jump's personal modesty, tact, keen mind, capacity for hard work, and appreciation of the role of Congress in administration. His policies, related to both line and staff, reflected his great integrity. Jump contributed to the development of the budgetary process as a policy tool and his relationships with politically appointed secretaries of agriculture and elected representatives remained the same for both Republicans and Democrats. He believed civil servants were to execute the politically determined policies of the Congress and appointed officials and he was highly successful at carrying out his duties to the satisfaction of his political superiors. At a time when the politicization of high-level administrative positions seemed to be the trend, Jump's performance and reputation stand out as an example of a productive interface between the permanent civil service staff and the political side of our government.

CHAPTER 6

WILLIAM ASHBY JUMP: PIONEER IN PROFESSIONAL PUBLIC ADMINISTRATION*

David S. Brown

William Ashby Jump, for many years Director of Finance and Budget Officer of the United States Department of Agriculture, adviser and confidant of Secretaries of Agriculture, has been described as the first of the great, modern governmental controllers. Even so, this does not really do justice to the contributions of this remarkable public servant to the Department of Agriculture in particular and to American public administration in general.

Many of those who knew him and worked closely with him have retired and others have died, but his legend nearly 35 years after his own death still lives on. There is, for example, the W.A. Jump Foundation which each year selects one or two outstanding young men and women in the Federal service for meritorious commendation and a special award. There are also the Jump-McKillop lectures, held from time to time in the Department in honor of two of its most illustrious members, both of whom died in their prime.

Autographed pictures with suitable personal messages have hung in various departmental offices. My own occupies a place of honor at George Washington University. A plaque containing his picture and statements of commendation is in the Office of Budget and Program Analysis conference room at the Department of Agriculture.

Jump was a gifted, loyal, dedicated and highly professional public servant whose retirement for medical reasons in 1948 after 42 years with the agency was marked with letters of appreciation from President Truman who had known him as a Senator, Secretary Charles F. Brannan, and a number of members of Congress. In those 42 years, beginning in a part-time position in 1907, he had served eleven secretaries of agriculture and two war food

*© 1981 by David S. Brown.

administrators of varying political faiths and served them well.

He was a man of rare understanding of the American political and administrative systems, with a still rarer skill—the ability to make them work. He was a man of generally conservative beliefs and mien, but he was also a person who believed strongly in the desirability of change. He was an innovator but he was also immensely practical. Although he had little formal education, he looked to the universities as a major source of manpower for the increasingly complex tasks with which government is faced. Louis Brownlow, the Chairman of President Roosevelt's Commission on Administrative Management and himself one of the more illustrious names in the profession, called him an "elder statesman of public administration."

President Truman wrote to him on his retirement:

> You have become a symbol of such a high standard of public service that we cannot think of your retirement as ending your career. Your example of selfless effort to improve public administration has blazed a wide and clear trail which is already being followed by many of your associates and will be followed by many others for a long time.
>
> You carry with you the good wishes of your co-workers. It is a privilege and pleasure to extend to you the thanks of the government which you have served through more than four decades with such self sacrificing devotion and fidelity.[1]

Judge Marvin Jones, Chief Judge of the U.S. Court of Claims, and an Agriculture Committee member, later its Chairman during his years in the House of Representatives said of him:

> He was a man of unusually good judgment. He learned over a long period of years the needs and the mechanics of the operation of the Department of Agriculture. Then, what is far more important, beyond the fringe of known facts he understood the philosophy behind the mechanics and knew how to get at the spirit of the law and its outstanding purpose, and to give effect to what was intended to be the purpose of the legislation.[2]

One of his assistant budget directors and himself a long-time civil servant, Richard Maycock, spoke of his relationships with Congress:

> He built his reputation on the Hill by being honest, dependable and reliable. If Mr. Jump said a thing was so, it was so. He never tried to gain an unfair advantage. He was loyal to the Department and

supported the budget submitted, but wanted decisions made on the basis of consideration of all the facts. He had faith that the people's representatives would, by and large, make their decisions in the best interests of the people and the nation as a whole.[3]

Another of his associates, Professor Robert Walker of Stanford University, in one of the more definitive articles written about him, said of his contribution to governmental budgeting:

He played a major role in creating the modern view of the budget and of the budget official in governmental administration. In some twenty-six years as budget officer of the Department of Agriculture he had a key part in giving substance to the broad idea of executive budgeting embodied in the Budget and Accounting Act of 1921. Consciously and skillfully he participated in, and often led, the movement to transform the federal budget from an accountant's workbook to a policy-oriented allocation of financial resources among public programs. He stated many times, publicly and in personal conversation, that the budget was basically a "plan of work." The phrase has become commonplace, but it was not when he first began using it.[4]

This, in part at least, was what Wilfred McNeil, the first Assistant Secretary of Defense (Controller), meant in describing Jump to me in a personal conversation as "the first of the modern government controllers." Jump would probably have been surprised and flattered by the comment had he known of it, but McNeil was very much on the mark.

My Own Relations With W.A. Jump

I worked closely with W.A. Jump for a year in 1940 in the enviable role of personal assistant and then later in 1941 and 1942 as a part of his Office of Budget and Finance. I have always felt that I got my job with him through a combination of circumstances, one of which was that I was just finishing three and a half years of graduate study at the Maxwell School of Citizenship and Public Affairs at Syracuse University. Jump had had a close association with the School's Dean, William E. Mosher, over several years and had been invited there on several occasions to meet with students and to speak. But the other reason, possibly no less important, was that for two months in 1936, I had been a messenger in Works Progress Administration (WPA) headquarters in Washington. Jump liked those who were willing to start at the bottom.

He had, in fact, begun his own governmental service as an assistant messenger and so had Harry Nelson, one of his top assistants who participated with him in hiring me. I had been certified to the personnel office of the agency from a Civil Service Commission register and had come to Washington to investigate the opportunities this offered. A friend steered me to the office of the Director of Finance. Jump was not unaware of the inroads an aggressive personnel director was making at the time in areas he felt directly related to his own responsibilities. The combination of factors led to a job offer. My first six months of training consisted of occupying a desk in his own office and helping him as well as I could as his assistant.

During this period, we developed a personal relationship which included Mrs. Jump and his two sons who were within a year or two of my own age. Later, when I moved to his management analysis division, it was agreed that he would make materials and time available to me for a doctoral dissertation I was planning on the development within the Agriculture Department of the current system of preparing and administering the budget. World War II, however, intervened and the project was shelved. I could have returned to the agency after the war in 1946 but decided that my major interests lay elsewhere than in financial administration and, having served in the Navy's Air Arm as a carrier pilot, joined the staff of the Civil Aeronautics Administration instead.

This was with Jump's advice and encouragement. We talked several times about it, and while he welcomed me back and offered me a job, I know that he felt that my interests and talent lay in other areas. I was a bit disturbed about it at the time, but he was simply following in my own case the policy I had seen him follow with others—people I knew he regretted losing—and finally accepted it at face value. I received the autographed picture of him at his bedside a week or two before he died. The message it contained was prophetic with respect to the academic career I eventually followed.

Jump and the Budgetary Process

As indicated, Jump's career began modestly enough with a part-time job in the Bureau of Animal Industry when he was sixteen. He had not yet finished high school but earned his diploma by going to school between times and at night, and later took a variety of law courses. His father had died when he was nine and Jump's income, tiny though it was, was needed to help the family.

Later he was promoted from messenger to clerk and still later to administrative officer in Animal Industry. In 1919 he became assistant to the Director of Information which position presumably brought him to the attention of those in the Secretary's Office. In 1921, with the new Republican administration in office, a new Secretary, Henry C. Wallace, the father of

Henry A. Wallace, the man Jump served the longest, invited him to become his private secretary and still later his administrative assistant.

The Budget and Accounting Act was passed in 1921 and each department for the first time was required to have a budget officer. Jump was named for the Department of Agriculture. He held the position for the next 27 years. In 1924, he became, in addition, Assistant Director of Personnel and Business Administration and continued these multiple roles until 1934, when the Office of Budget and Finance (now, after a number of name changes, the Office of Budget and Program Analysis) was established. This gave him a new title, Director of Finance, to add to that of Budget Officer.

Actually, the two positions effectively complemented each other. With his budget officer role, he acquired a number of legislatively mandated powers having to do with the preparation and submission of the budget. While many others, of course, participated in the process, he was in a sense the "navigation officer" (as he liked to describe himself) who in point of fact planned and guided the agency's budgetary relationships with Congress. In doing so, he gradually built up the reputation that was to serve him and the Department so well with Committee Chairmen, Members of Congress, and their staffs.

As Director of Finance, Jump was responsible directly to the Secretary. Under the authority of this office, Jump began to develop the controllership concepts that contributed so much to the administration of the budget and to his own reputation as a financial manager.

The introduction of the budget idea to the Federal system had been greeted by no means with unalloyed enthusiasm by those to whom it applied. Departmental officials over the years had depended on their own relationships with members of Congress to get the funds they wanted and needed. Now, the process was being systematized—with the agreement both of Congress and the President—and the Budget Officer had suddenly become a key figure in getting the act together.

Many administrators during those early days of the Budget Act regarded the process as an invitation to get what they could under it. (Many still do.) Jump, however, believed that his role as budget officer and representative of the Secretary was one of insuring that the money voted to the Department of Agriculture be used for the purposes for which it was originally intended. The budget, as a plan of action and a method of programming work, was the instrument by which agreement had been reached between Legislative and Executive Branches. This meant that he was as greatly concerned with the execution of the budget as with its preparation. The creation of the position of Director of Finance reinforced and amplified this view.

Jump once summed up for an academic audience the development of the modern budgetary system:

Lets look at what has happened in twenty-five years! In that period the Budget has not ceased to be a fiscal document, but it has ceased to be just a fiscal document. It has become a great economic, social, and policy instrumentality of government in the broadest, most dynamic, and significant sense. In part at least this has come about by reason of the particular way in which we practice democracy in America—and in this we even differ from some of the other democracies. Under our procedure, the Federal Budget has become the vehicle by which the executive presents to the legislative body not only the expenditure, or fiscal plans, but also the proposed program of work of the Government of the United States for the ensuing year. . . . It is a big thought. It means that the Budget process is the means by which our Congress not only discharges its guardianship of the public purse in America, by determining how much may come out of that purse, but in practice it means that our Congress, at the same time, determines precisely what the program of work will be, after its consideration and evaluation of the proposals submitted in the Executive Budget.[5]

If the budget itself had faced opposition from those in the bureaus who preferred the greater freedom of the old system, this new role which Secretary Wallace and his associates had created to keep the vast new programs under some form of surveillance and control faced even more. In the hands of a lesser man, perhaps it would not have succeeded at all.

The Department of Agriculture was the first of the nonmilitary agencies to produce a billion dollar budget, a startling figure in its day though hardly notable in later times. This, due in large part to crop supports and commodity loans, was of sufficient size to give Jump and the Agriculture Department special status among Federal agencies. It also caused considerable concern lest money thus authorized be spent improperly.

Gradually, and over a period of time, Jump began to construct the elements of a modern system of controllership. At first he had to rely primarily on his own efforts, abetted by those of an assistant director with an accounting background. With his sensitivity to the policy concerns of those with whom he was intimately involved—and this included the Congressional Committees— Jump tried to keep track of major developments within the Department of Agriculture while W. R. Fuchs, his assistant, made sure that what was being done was legal.

This led, among other things, to a system called the Uniform Projects System (UPS) which provided a centralized file of descriptions of bureau work programs to aid in coordination and control of the Department's many programs. Among other things, it sought to indicate "the objectives or functional concepts of each activity rather than rely solely upon the bare bones of expenditure detail."

Even with the Uniform Projects System, however, Jump knew that the information he was getting was not enough, and this in turn led to the appointment of four staff assistants whose purpose was to know in detail what was happening in the various agricultural programs. From such a base, the financial management/controllership idea evolved so that the secretary and others on his staff could know in detail what was being done in the Department of Agriculture's various bureaus.

Jump as Staff Officer

The title of Director of Finance made Jump one of the highest ranking staff officers within the Department. As such, he became a close and trusted advisor to several Secretaries not only in financial management where he achieved some of his greatest influence, but in other areas as well. During the period of the Henry Agard Wallace secretaryship, which extended from the early thirties until 1941 when Wallace became Vice-President, it was often said that for practical purposes the Department was run by the trinity of Paul Appleby, then Undersecretary, Dr. Milton Eisenhower, Director of Information and Land-Use Coordinator, and Jump. It may well have been so. Wallace himself was an indifferent administrator who, it was revealed years later, sometimes fell asleep at meetings. Because he trusted his three associates so fully, much of the management of the Department was undoubtedly left to them. Wallace's interests were reform-motivated and political.

Professor Walker, who as an Assistant Director of Finance during most of the World War II period, notes the differences between the two positions Jump held, and in doing so, provides some useful insight with respect to his influence within the Department:

> Jump had a clear conception of the role of the staff officer which helps explain his great success in that role under many successive Secretaries of Agriculture. Thus he distinguished constantly and effectively between the separate, but often confused, roles of financial adviser to the Secretary, on the one hand, and custodian of certain specific legal powers as departmental budget officer under the Budget and Accounting Act, on the other.

> In the first capacity, he was always the staff officer—advising, counseling, advocating on the Secretary's behalf, and implementing his decisions as the occasion required. Here he was scrupulous in speaking, or writing, always in the name of the Secretary. "The

Secretary has asked me to advise you that. . .." was the typical form of expression in such cases, and he was extremely careful always to sign documents issued in his staff capacity as "Director of Finance," a departmentally-created position and title.

When, however, he was carrying out his responsibilities for budget preparation or fiscal control under the Budget and Accounting Act, which set forth legal powers and responsibilities for budget officers, he signed the documents as "Budget Officer." He was fully aware that these were binding directives on the agencies of the department in his own name. This careful separation of his authority to issue directives on technical financial matters and his staff role, where he never presumed to act as though he had line authority, was a major contribution—at least to the education of those who worked with him. Civilian administration seldom achieves such clarity.[6]

Legislative-Executive Relationships

The American governmental system, popular beliefs to the contrary, is not an easy one to understand and even more difficult to operate. This, perhaps, is why so few countries have sought to adopt it. It may be a tribute to American persistence and ingenuity that it has lasted so long and, on the whole, has been so successful.

I have always felt that W.A. Jump was one of those who understood it best. My period of training under his tutelage was one of the most valuable a future academician could have. The success over time of his relationships with the many participants in the process is evidence of the correctness of this understanding.

How well Jump managed with Congress is now legend. Rarely has a departmental executive enjoyed such high esteem in both branches of government. One of those who testified most strongly in his support was Representative Clarence Cannon, a Missouri Democrat who for years was a member of the House Appropriations Committee and at the end of his career, its Chairman. Cannon was not an easy person to work with. His demeanor was sour, often surly, and he had once been involved in a public fist fight with another member, but he was a power in the House of Representatives. He forewent his usual contumaciousness, however, to praise Jump on a number of occasions. I quote the following:

I know I express the opinion of every member of this committee when I say that Mr. Jump is one of the most valuable members of the department with whom we come in contact. . . . We have the greatest confidence in and regard for him.[7]

Judge Jones, quoted above, had this to say:

I heard during my twenty-odd years of service in the House, time and time again, the statement that, "I believe what Bill Jump tells me." I have heard him quoted time and time again. I have heard it said up there on numerous occasions that it didn't make any difference whether your question was favorable or unfavorable—if you asked it of Bill Jump he would give you an honest answer. I also heard the statement innumerable times, "When he tells us anything, we rely on it, and we will give Bill Jump anything he wants." They did that almost literally.[8]

Cannon and Jones were Democrats but Everett Dirksen, a Republican, expressed on many occasions a similar confidence. Dirksen, incidentally, was a man whom Jump correctly foresaw as having deep-seated political ambitions which underlay much of everything he did. These, Jump suggested to me privately, might even include presidential hopes as well. Dirksen later became a Senator from Illinois, the Republican leader in the Senate, and still later a hopeful vice-presidential candidate.

The keystone to Jump's understanding of Congress was what Sir Geoffrey Vickers might call his appreciation of the role of the Legislative Branch. This is summarized in a letter Jump wrote to Representative Cannon, dated a week before his own death. In it, he said:

I have found that Congress is generally strong and generally sound, and working upon a final discovery in the best public interest of a solution of the great pending questions of the day. Their success in finding these solutions, when you consider the enormous ramifications of current times when things legislative have grown and moved away from simplicity and assumed overwhelming complexity, is truly remarkable. The Congress is so much better than the American people believe it to be that it is a shame that this disparity between fact and theory prevails. It is the public itself that is the loser in its inability to grasp the significance of Congress in the whole scheme of economics, continuation of liberty and proper execution of a number of the most important constitutional requirements under our American system. My thirty years before Congress has led me to believe that there is not a single thing of such fundamental importance as for the people to grasp fully their great dependence on the legislative system.[9]

He was well aware that there were members of Congress who were serving interests with which neither he nor the leadership of the department agreed, but he did not begrudge them their right to do so, nor to ask those challenging questions of himself or other departmental witnesses in committee hearings. Much of what was asked, he felt, came from an earnest desire to learn more of what was being done rather than to obstruct or embarrass. Professor Walker reports that a draft of a review of a text on the Federal budgetary process, which he felt also to be not well understood, contained the following:

> I am personally aware of the fact that questions which Members of Congress raise about budget estimates come not from managing or devising on the part of members of the program agencies to have such questions raised so that they can get their wishes on the record, but they arise because tax-paying American citizens have exercised their right to make *their* questions, wishes and reactions known to their Congressmen who in turn examine budgets with techniques of their own that over the years I have found to be highly competent and effective. . . . I believe the country will be in a sorry state when the desire of legislative bodies to probe into judgments about budgets is dependent to that degree upon how bureau heads feel.[10]

We are indebted to Professor Lynn W. Eley, another of the several young men who left the Department of Agriculture Office of Budget and Finance to join university faculties, for a summary of the guidelines which Jump developed for departmental witnesses appearing before Congress. These provide testimony to the relationships he sought. Witnesses, he advised, should:

1. Lay necessary groundwork before discussing detailed program and financial requirements. . . .
2. Take the lead in discussing difficult questions and in presenting explanations. Facts should come out of witnesses—not have to be dragged out of them.
3. Emphasize programs and projects so as not to infringe on the Committee's time, but always be prepared to answer questions on operating detail.
4. Talk in terms of facts and figures, measurable units, and the workload data, where appropriate. . . .
5. Answer all questions directly—come to the point.[11]

Not only was Jump most perspicacious with respect to the preparation and presentation of the budget to Congress, but he was also greatly sensitive to the points of view of individual members. He believed, as Judge Jones has reminded us, that "administrators should not try to find a way around the provisions of an Act, but earnestly try to find the intentions of the Congress in passing the Act." I have personally witnessed his reading and rereading of the text of various hearings as well as the legislation itself in order to discover the intent behind it. He was reluctant, however, to go back to a committee or to an individual member for guidance, believing that the separation of powers between the Legislative and Executive Branches was not well served by such a device, yet he was quite willing to discuss with legislators, as occasion required it, the administrative problems being encountered with the legislation they had enacted. A Senator whom he felt to be unusually sensitive to the administrative process was Carl Hayden of Arizona. Invariably Hayden was helpful, but Jump was careful not to "strain" such relationships.

He spent many hours reviewing and correcting the transcripts of the various hearings before which he and other Department of Agriculture witnesses appeared. If such hearings are in executive session, and sometimes even when they are public, they ordinarily go through a laundering process before being released as "verbatims" of what transpired. Members have the privilege of revising their remarks, and if the witnesses are friendly ones, the committee staff is likely to accord this privilege to them also. Jump was in such a category, and used the occasion to make sure that the statements were factually correct, clearly made, and consistent with departmental and administration policy.

He was one of the few persons in recent years to have his salary raised by Congress, and while he expressed his opposition to its doing so and was probably embarrassed by it all, he would not have been human if he did not also appreciate it. A classification study undertaken by the Civil Service Commission rejected a departmental request that his position be reclassified upward. Members of Congress learned of this and on their own initiative set his salary figure at $8500 (this was in the late '30s) which was what had been requested "as long as the present incumbent shall be in the position." The Civil Service Commission got the word, and the reclassification was shortly afterwards granted.

In several respects, Jump felt closer to some of the committees of Congress than he did to the Bureau of the Budget, the President's budgetary arm. The philosophy behind the executive budget is that no request can be made by an Executive Branch agency without the approval of the President. The budget, perforce, is his budget; it is the President who shall say what is part of his program and what is not, and the Bureau of the Budget (now the Office of Management and Budget) speaks for him. This makes much sense, but it also introduces a new administrative level to the process and at times, if the Bureau of the Budget is so-minded, can undercut the relationship between a secretary and the president. Jump was greatly sensitive to the implications of this situation.

Moreover, he suspected that a number of bright and aggressive young men at the Bureau of the Budget were, by virtue of their mastery of the process, intruding into the domain of the operating departments. This was not his idea of what a true staff role should be. It was one which time and again he avoided within the Department of Agriculture itself at the risk of weakening his own function.

If he felt that what the Department wanted or needed was consistent with presidential policy, he would sometimes find a way around the cumbersome procedure which getting Bureau approval often involved. I was privy to one such incident and the notes I made reveal Jump's maneuvering. It involved the possibility of Bang's disease, a highly infectious disease of cattle, being present in other domestic animals as well. Believing this to be the case, the Bureau of Animal Industry sought authority to use funds already voted to explore the matter. Jump hit upon the stratagem of suggesting that a member of the committee raise this question of the Bureau's witnesses. He broached the matter to Representative Cannon who later did just that. Because departmental witnesses are required to answer questions put to them, the Bureau chief could now do so, speculating as the Congressman's leading question had suggested that there should be a study of this matter. It was subsequently authorized.

Although Jump's relationships with members of Congress were ordinarily harmonious, there were exceptions. These were probably bound to occur in view of the differences in function that the two political parties represented. I was privy to the after-effects of one of the more serious breaches between the two parties. At the time of the Agriculture appropriation hearings, it had become apparent within the Department that there would probably be need for a supplemental appropriation to make good the emerging deficiency in agricultural parity payments. In fact, such a request was already before the Bureau of the Budget, but the Bureau of the Budget and the President had yet to act upon it.

In testimony before Congress, no question was raised by members concerning this possibility nor was any information volunteered by the Department's witnesses, including, most prominently, its Budget Officer. Members were therefore left with the impression that existing funds were adequate. When the deficiency was finally revealed in a supplemental request, the members of the Appropriations Committee appeared shocked and took their hostility out upon both Jump and the head of the Agricultural Adjustment Administration. My own notes of the occasion reveal that "the full wrath of the Committee was substantially 'toned down' in the editing of the transcript of the hearings" but enough remained to make clear the

Committee's feeling that it had been misled.[12]

It did little good for Jump to explain the relationship between the Department of Agriculture and the Bureau of the Budget, an agency traditionally held in low esteem by most committees of Congress. "The Committee is somewhat disappointed," Chairman Cannon made clear, "to find that it is not as close to your confidence as the Bureau of the Budget. We are, to put it very mildly, surprised that we were not given this information." "May I suggest, Mr. Jump," he went on, "that in the future the committee takes the position that it should be apprised of all matters of which the Department is cognizant of this character, and especially one of such serious import as this is, and the committee believes that the Department fails to discharge its full duty in not giving us this information at the time." Jump said in response, "I think that we understand that, and it is helpful for us to understand that from you, because we are in something of a delicate position with respect to such matters until we have cleared them with the Budget Bureau.[13]

I talked with Jump later about this. The point was still a sore one, but he was able to laugh a little in retrospect, albeit a bit painfully. If the situation recurred, he said, he would have no alternative but to follow the same course unless the White House or the Budget Bureau permitted him (a highly unlikely event) to do otherwise. His attitude was *c'est la guerre*. These are the situations one sometimes faces, and, as in war, there is bound to be bloodshed.

Despite the respect he had for Congress, Jump was well aware that for a variety of reasons, Congress as an institution and legislators as individuals had much too little appreciation of the problems of administering the laws which they had so important a role in creating. Often, as Eley reminds us, Jump felt that Congress infringed on the prerogatives of the Executive Branch. He did what he could to see that this did not happen, or if it did, that there were remedies available.

Eley's observations on the subject are worth recording here:

His respect for Congress was counterbalanced to some extent by his feeling that too often Congress infringed upon and harassed the executive branch in the administration of programs. In his own case he had had many difficulties in administration which had arisen from legislative limitations and requirements that undoubtedly would not have existed if a spirit of mutual respect and cooperation had been carefully nurtured between the legislative and executive branches. But the solution to this distressing situation was held to be two-fold. First, the legislative branch must be made "to realize more and more that in our complex times it will be necessary for Congress' own sake in preventing the frustration of its transcendent function, to concern itself with the policy, substance, and other larger, rather than detailed aspects of the issues dealt with legislatively". Secondly, the executive branch must strive on its part "to develop and assure the widest possible appreciation by government personnel, all across the board, of the importance of the highest form of governmental ethics in relation to legislative intent and, on the operational side, a quality of public administration which is so well recognized that Congress will feel, and be, fully justified in performing its function at a high legislative and policy level".[14]

The Jump Style

In addition to the role he played in legislative-executive relations, Jump was also, as previously noted, a member of the secretary's staff and an administrator. While the Office of Budget and Finance probably never exceeded 100 persons at any one time, he was responsible for managing its affairs. It is doubtful that it required over a quarter of his time, but his success in a number of important activities was in part at least the result of his performance as a manager.

There is no question that Jump deserves well the distinction acquired during his last decade of service when he became nationally known among public administration professionals as the model of the great staff officer. The fact is, of course, that he achieved such a reputation within the department years earlier.

Reputations of this kind are not acquired overnight. It is difficult to say how or when Jump might have developed the style that was to make him very much an indispensable man to the eight secretaries of Agriculture whom he served as Budget Officer. He was a man of strong views and great integrity, but he believed that it was the responsibility of others—particularly those politically chosen—to make policy, and his job to help them with it. This assistance consisted in making available to them the alternatives, with which they were likely to be faced, given their objectives. I have heard Jump on many occasions give his own point of view, but usually only when he was specifically asked to do so. Even so, it was often couched in phrases such as "I am inclined to think" and "perhaps I am putting too much emphasis on this," if only as a reminder to his listeners that he did not wish to unduly influence the decision they would have to make. I did not sit with him, of course, in his meetings with the secretary, but I was privy a number of times to those with Appleby (Under Secretary), Eisenhower (the Assistant Secretary), and many bureau chiefs.

His memory was monumental. Not only was he able to recite the positions which various members of Congress could be expected to take, but he was able to recall the experience over many years which the Department of Agriculture, and sometimes other departments, had had with similar undertakings.

It was undoubtedly wise for him to have cushioned his remarks as I have indicated. His reputation by 1940 both within the Department of Agriculture and outside was such that it carried far greater weight than that of those who filled other staff positions, even those at operational levels. It is interesting to note that only a handful of people within the Department or outside spoke of him in familiar terms or used the nickname Bill. Almost universally, he was known as *Mr.* Jump, even by his assistant directors. This applied even when he was being discussed *in absentia* in the security of one's office or in private gatherings. While it is common practice in articles of this sort to use the last name only as I have done here, I find myself still thinking of him as I have thought of no other person with whom I have worked in nearly 50 years, with the *Mr.* as a prefix. Eley, in fact, refers to him in this fashion throughout the article I have quoted.

Walker remembers that Jump prefaced many of the instructions he passed on to bureau people with a phrase such as "the Secretary has asked me to advise you. . . ." My own view is that, whether spoken or not, it was so clearly implied as to leave no doubt that this was what the secretary had, in fact, decided. The part that Jump might have had in such a decision could be left to speculation. Walker reports an incident where a bureau chief, defending strongly the prerogatives of his office, refused to accept the decision Jump conveyed. His remarks were loud and offensive. Jump gathered up the papers he had brought with him, flushed angrily, said in effect that you have no choice, and left the room. The meeting was over.[15]

I was privy to a similar incident when the Chief of the Forest Service objected strongly to voluntary budget cuts which had been suggested in lieu of a proposed statutory 5 percent cut across the board and became personal in his remarks. Jump took off his glasses deliberately, turned to the man, and said in a few well chosen words that over many years he had established a reputation for reasonableness and integrity and he would permit no such comments now. This drew an immediate apology, which I remember thinking as much overdone as the man's earlier remarks had been uncalled for. Jump reminded him that he had the right of appeal to the secretary but, in view of the study that had already been given the matter, doubted that it would avail him a great deal. After the man had left the room, Jump turned to me with a smile, brushing off the incident as that of a person with strong feelings and a quickness of temper. I saw the two of them together a number of times after that. The incident appeared to have been forgotten.

Walker, in his article which appeared four years after Jump's death, attempted to determine in what he called an "administrative biography" the characteristics of the good staff man. Of those characteristics which Walker found to be the major source of Jump's "operating effectiveness," he noted "self-imposed demand for absolute reliability," extreme tact, which included "a great sensitivity to the effects of both the written and the spoken word on other people," a large degree of tolerance for points of view which may have differed from his own, and an enormous capacity for work.[16]

Walker's observations are very much on target. Jump's concern for establishing a reputation for reliability and integrity was the overwhelming passion of his life. He tried always to determine the true facts of a situation and when he found that he or others were in error, went to great lengths to make sure that the impression previously left was corrected. He was deeply concerned that what was said had face validity. Not only must the Department of Agriculture be in the right, but it must appear so as well. Farther along there will be reference made to his appearance on a matter of personal privilege before a House subcommittee to refute charges made against him. That he was successful in all of this, even where members (as in the case of Dirksen) had great doubts about many of the agricultural programs, is evidence of his standing with Congress.

His tactfulness was considerable. It was abetted by a degree of self-effacement which if it did not come naturally, fitted easily into the character he cultivated. Walker, who worked more closely with him over a longer period of time than I did, thinks its origins proceeded from a boyhood in which someone with his substantial mental capacities could not fail to have understood the deprivation that he suffered. As his influence grew, however, he surely must have realized his own great gifts and capabilities. The letters he sent from his deathbed to a variety of persons seem to reinforce this view, although their style, as with much of what he wrote, was humble and appreciative. Jump's manner was indeed always on the modest side, as was his appearance. He sometimes seemed to go out of his way to downgrade himself, perhaps in keeping with the idea current in the late thirties that staff people should possess, in Brownlow's words, a "passion for anonymity." Over the years, Jump was a background performer who seemed almost embarrassed to be center stage, and yet he was often there.

His considerateness was expressed in a variety of ways. He found it greatly difficult, for example, to tell some of those he was associated with that they were not doing what he believed needed to be done, and even when the issue had to be faced, his associates sometimes came away from the meeting with a view quite different from what he had wanted to convey. He could be blunt at times, as has been indicated elsewhere, but this usually only upon proper provocation. His concern for the feelings of others tempered much of what he did.

There were people in the Office of Budget and Finance whom I knew no longer had his confidence. I urged him to encourage them to leave, which they probably would have done. Some had opportunities elsewhere but felt a sense of loyalty to him and as a result stayed on. He was reluctant to face the issue, and there matters would usually stand until the person in question was passed over for promotion, finally realized what was happening, and then left on his own. When asked to give references, Jump spoke frankly of the person's strengths and weaknesses. Because of his reputation, and also his willingness to point up strengths rather than highlight deficiencies, a poor performer sometimes did better than he or she deserved.

His tolerance of the views of others was also notable. My own discussions with him revealed a native conservatism which at times seemed to be considerably at odds with some of the social programs which Wallace and his liberal associates were undertaking. We occasionally discussed the New Deal philosophy; there is no question in my mind that he had doubts concerning major elements of it. His boyhood and youth were spent, one should not forget, in what were at that time, two quite conservative southern cities, Baltimore and Washington.

Whatever Jump's private doubts concerning the widespread changes that were taking place in the New Deal programs, these, as with his religious beliefs, were private; and as long as his personal integrity was not at issue, his responsibility as he saw it was to serve his political chiefs. His belief in democratic ways of life and political patterns outweighed almost all else.

He disliked conflict, as Walker has observed, but not so fully that he was willing to sacrifice those other values he felt so important. He has been described as having a "hardheaded realism in bureaucratic maneuvering." Not only was Jump sensitive to the prerogatives of the Department of Agriculture, as noted in his associations with the Bureau of the Budget, but to his own office as well. As someone concerned with the financial well-being of the agency, he had a right—indeed, a duty—to inquire into any matters where the use of money was involved. That he exercised both judgment and restraint in doing so did not detract from his performance of his assigned function. I recall in particular a requirement having to do with published material issued by the Department. For oversight purposes, his office received copies of all issuances, ranging from advice on how to treat the boll weevil to ways of gelding rabbits. (More animals than I suspect most city-dwellers realize are gelded, and there are many ways of doing so.) A small part of my job was to retrieve from the volume of publications received anything which treated subjects of possible concern to a director of finance. Only occasionally did these retrievals result in more than an inquiry on Jump's part, probably more as a reminder to those operationally minded that what they produced was of concern to the secretary's office and in particular to the finance director. After several months of unparalleled good relations with Congress, Roosevelt is reputed to have asked his staff assistant, Judge Rosenman, to find him a "little bill that I can veto to show them I still have the power to do so." Jump may have been following some of the same philosophy.

Of his willingness to defend his own turf, Walker says of him:

> [If] any proposed administrative action threatened the powers or status of the Office of Budget and Finance, Jump was the master of bureaucratic protectionism. Drafts of Secretary's memorandums relating to the distribution of functions in the department were carefully drafted or scrutinized (as the case might be) with an eye to their effect on B&F. If the effect were to detract, careful modifications were made, informal discussions were had with members of the Secretary's immediate staff, and, if necessary, the threat of an open battle with the encroaching office (usually another staff office) was hinted. The basic criterion of B&F jurisdiction in such cases was the relation of the activity involved to budgeting, fiscal control, the Bureau of the Budget, or the appropriations committees. This led to the inclusion of management studies and the clearance of legislative reports—both paralleling functions of the Bureau of the Budget—and to departmental control of purchasing and travel in order to protect the budget dollar. Jump was particularly solicitous of these related, but sometimes questioned, budgetary functions when any reorganization was under consideration. [17]

As to work habits, if Jump were being described today, he would be labelled a workaholic. His devotion to his job resulted in his putting a priority on it that frequently left his family playing a secondary role. A bulging briefcase was his daily homebound companion. That he worked on the papers it contained was evidenced by the handwritten notes that he produced the following morning. He complained of not doing enough personal reading, which undoubtedly was true, but this was hardly possible in view of the official regimen he accepted for himself.

Budgetary hearings usually take place at the behest of committee chairmen and departmental witnesses are always expected to conform. Frequently, it was necessary for Jump to postpone personal vacation plans because legislative business intervened. If he was pained by decisions of this kind, he did not complain about them. If Mrs. Jump, a patient and considerate woman, had personal opinions on all of this, the two of them kept them to themselves. I have heard him remark on a number of occasions that "this will probably not make Nellie very happy" but she appeared to have accepted, as did he, their fate. I do not think he was trying to be an "indispensable man"—he was often given to saying that there were none such—but the pattern of work he and others accepted and the secretary's own habits virtually made him so.

There was little criticism of the boss by those who worked with him. Indeed, to have criticized him would have seemed *lese majesty*. Nevertheless, there was an awareness not only on the part of a number around him that he at times seemed unwilling to make decisions that needed to be made, but also that he was unwilling to delegate to others as fully as he should have. This was undoubtedly one of the reasons a number of people left him for jobs elsewhere. He was well aware of some of the problems this caused him, but excused himself on the ground that those to whom he might have delegated were not as sensitive to the problems they faced as the situation required.

As with many gifted people, he was acutely aware of the shortcomings of others, and while personally tolerant of them, he could not bring himself to give many of his subordinates the freedom that their development might have demanded. Also, as is characteristic of many who work with large sums of money, his actions were on the cautious side and this applied to promotions as well. A job in his office was always worth a grade or two higher elsewhere. Those in other bureaus and departments valued the training received at Budget and Finance and were willing to pay for it. There is no doubt that this, along with his failure to grant others the freedom of action which their jobs required, deprived him of talent he both wanted and needed. Walker tells us that during his last years, he modified this policy somewhat, but habits are habits and he continued in an avuncular way to keep an eye on almost everything that was happening.

Even though a newcomer to government, I found it difficult in the period I was closest to him to understand his reluctance to make decisions on issues which I thought were necessary. By putting before him in writing matters that I thought needed action, I had some influence on his work patterns. He readily saw through my stratagems, of course, and joked about them. He would sometimes explain that he wanted to think about the matter a while longer. Sometimes also, he would plead for more time to "see what will happen." He would sometimes say "I know that this is one of my weaknesses, and I know you know, but you must remember that I have been doing this for quite a while, and find it difficult to change my ways." But then he would add, in an almost kittenish way: "You keep on doing what you are doing. I need someone to remind me that I ought to do better." I tried for several months, but by the end of my period of training, I concluded I was not cut out for the type of staff service so acutely practiced by my mentor.

Habits can be catching. I acquired, of course, some from him. Jump's method of amending a letter or document someone else had produced was to insert in a small and neat hand various qualifying remarks which were written on the margins or at top or bottom and occasionally on the other side but joined by a penned line to the sentence they modified. I find I now use much the same approach. He was wordy and his sentences long and involved, but the words he chose were easy to understand and when he was finished, the paper usually said what he wanted it to say. Noting the difficulty he often had in achieving the right nuance, I developed a file of key ideas to save the trouble of composing each anew. The idea was a good one, but never worked very well. He revised his own revisions, and when I mentioned it to him, he said he was aware both of what he was doing as well as what I was doing, but had not really been satisfied by the wording originally achieved.

His Interest in Academia

Although earlier I have attributed my joining the Director's office in part to my earlier experience as a messenger and in part to the fact I was a graduate of a prestigious school of public administration, I am sure that the latter was the more important. Jump was one of the few administrators of his time who truly believed in the importance of the professionalization of the public service. At any time during his last years at the Department of Agriculture, one could find graduates of Chicago, Harvard, Syracuse, Cincinnati, American, Stanford, and elsewhere on his payroll.

He took an active interest in the Department of Agriculture Graduate School, sitting on various boards and committees as appointed. He regularly shared the teaching of a class in Federal budgeting at the Graduate School, and was an adjunct professor at American University. From time to time he was also invited to become a visiting lecturer at various universities, chief among which was Syracuse University's Maxwell School of Public Affairs and Administration. It was the practice at Maxwell to invite two or three notable practitioners a year to meet in seminars with students, to give lectures, and to counsel those who intended to enter the Federal service. Jump enjoyed such visits and often spent considerable time in preparing for them. In recognition of his services to the Agriculture Graduate School, a series of lectures took place annually which were known as the Jump-McKillop lectures, honoring him and another departmental official who had also met an untimely death.

Jump's university appearances caused some personal distress. A member of the secretary's staff who had earlier been fired, or at least encouraged to resign, believed that Jump was responsible for what had happened and wrote letters to various persons and agencies, including committees of Congress to claim that as the Director of Finance, he was receiving compensation from private sources while being paid by government. The extension of remarks of a member of Congress in the *Congressional Record*, quoting from one of these letters, resulted in a carefully prepared explanation of all of his professional activities of this kind. In it, he confessed to attending sessions and participating in roundtables at the American Political Science Association and the newly formed American Society for Public Administration at "no expense to the Government." He also admitted to working with the Committee on Public Administration of the Social Science Research Council and engaging in a few other similar meetings. Jump felt strongly that he was the victim of a vendetta and requested an appearance before the Committee to clear his name. In his appearance there, he also declared his personal philosophy about governmental-university relationships:

It seems to me that activity of this type, which brings together people in the Federal service and the State and local public services and people who teach and conduct research in public administration and political science is a good thing for all of us. It helps to break down the barriers that cause misunderstandings that are unfortunate at a time when so many problems of government involve the full cooperation of both Federal people and local officials. . . .

Another encouraging thing is the vital and very practical interest the educational institutions of the country are taking in the improvement of our administrative processes. This is shown by the increasing research and publications dealing with problems of public administration and by the number of highgrade young men and women who are taking civil-service examinations for administrative work. . . .

Anything we can do that causes the very ablest type of young men and women to consider public-service careers and train definitely for such work will help tremendously in the future operation of public services. I do not feel defensive at all about the matters I have been relating. All of them go to the point of trying to improve the competency of administrative processes that are our everyday concern; in my case, the Budget process.[18]

At the conclusion, Chairman Cannon made it clear that he believed the letters he and others received were the work of a crank and that "we have the greatest confidence in and regard for [Mr. Jump] and, for that reason, we include his statement in the hearing in order to make it a matter of record." This happened in 1941. The letters continued, however, and Jump, in his usual fashion, went to great lengths to insure that whatever he did was above reproach.

A Philosophy of Administration

Jump's philosophy of administration was lived more fully than it was written. As an active administrator, there was little occasion for putting down on paper the credo that he so scrupulously tried to follow. One can reconstruct it from a variety of sources as this chapter has tried to do, but recognize at the same time that one can only touch upon its major elements.

His letter of resignation, a long one, written while he suffered the great pain of his final terminal illness of cancer does, however, capture some of its more salient points. In this, written to Secretary of Agriculture Brannan, he comments on his feelings for the Department which for 42 of his 59 years had been his life and his home:

> Not a week passes, even after all these years, that I am not stimulated by some new and fresh evidence of the spirit of true public service and that is the strong foundation of the Department of Agriculture. Somehow, and in some way, the fact that from the beginning the Department has existed for the sole purpose of making life in America a better, richer and fuller experience, has resulted in an honest, vigorous and intensely realistic public service concept on the part of the staff of the Department, high and low, that is truly remarkable. This makes the Department a most stimulating and inspiring place in which to work. A member of the Department of Agriculture does not have the feeling that he is just helping to turn the wheels that make a large organization work; he feels he is a partner in a great enterprise. That has been my experience for 42 years.[19]

The Department of Agriculture, he felt, had achieved such a position by a combination of circumstances in which four elements predominated. These he listed as:

1. The impact of research on the character of the Department.

2. The practice of maintaining the closest possible contact with the people themselves and their elected representatives in Congress in determining what constitutes sound policy and program at any given time.

3. The collaborative and cooperative process.

4. The democratic process in internal administration.[20]

The last two points deserve greater amplification.

Of the collaborative and cooperative processes in which the Department was involved, Jump emphasized the "connectionalism" between the Department and the land-grant colleges and other state agricultural departments and institutions, farm organizations, the farmer committee systems, cooperatives, agricultural credit agencies, industry and trade groups, and Congressional committees which, in his words, "has developed a philosophy of collaboration and cooperation that has made an imprint on the Department and its methods of thought and action that is unique in government." My own observations over the years, although made in a far less definitive way than his, support this point. As to his choice of the word "connectionalism," he writes: "I know about the word 'nexus' but it's too simple a word to do justice to agricultural organization in the U.S."

His comments on "the democratic process" in administration are of particular interest because they were made at a time when the term was rarely used in this context. Indeed, it has been only in the decade of the seventies that there has been any real concern for the practice of the democratic processes so strongly embraced in our political institutions in either large-scale government or industry. Jump wrote:

Arising, I believe, out of some of the factors mentioned above the Department is distinctive in its practice of collaboration and cooperation in the development of policies and methods of internal administration and operation. This contributes tremendously to making the Department a wonderful place in which to work. I do not know of any place in the world where an arbitrary or unsound administrative policy or practice has less chance of survival than in the Department of Agriculture.[21]

This, as previously indicated, was Jump's final testament. A month and a half later he was dead. It is probably as clear a statement as could have been written of what he believed and what he tried to practice. The deep truths that it contains and his life's work illustrates, I believe, why his name is still remembered more than 35 years after his death.

Footnotes

1. Letter, Harry S. Truman, President, to W.A. Jump, Esq., Dec. 21, 1948. Reprinted in *Public Administration Review*, Vol. IX, No. 1, (Winter 1949).
2. Marvin Jones, Chief Judge, U.S. Court of Claims, "The Contribution of Bill Jump to Good Legislative-Executive Relations," in *Legislative-Executive Relationships in the Government of the United States*: a series of lectures, United States Department of Agriculture Graduate School, 1954, p. 1.

4. Robert A. Walker, "William A. Jump: The Staff Officer as a Personality," in *Public Administration Review*, Autumn 1954, pp. 233-246.

5. From a transcript of extemporaneous remarks made by W.A. Jump and quoted by Walker, *op. cit.*

6. Walker, *op. cit.*, p. 235.

7. Taken from *Hearings* before the Subcommittee of the Committee on Appropriations, House of Representatives, Seventy-Seventh Congress, First Session on the Agriculture Department Appropriations Bill for 1942, Part 1.

8. Marvin Jones, *op. cit.*, p. 1.

9. Marvin Jones, *op. cit.*, p. 3.

10. Walker, *op. cit.*, p. 236.

11. Lynn W. Eley, "William A. Jump—Budgeteer and Administrative Philosopher," in *Personnel Administration*, Vol. 17, No. 6 (Nov. 1954), p. 22.

12. From personal notes made by the author, 1941.

13. From *Hearings* before the Appropriations Committee. House of Representatives, on the Agriculture Appropriation Bill, 1940.

14. Eley, *op. cit.*, p. 22.

15. Walker, *op. cit.*, pp. 239-240.

16. Walker, *op. cit.*, pp. 238-241.

17. Walker, *op. cit.*, p. 241.

18. *Hearings* before the Subcommittee on Appropriations, House of Representatives, 1942, *op. cit,*

19. William A. Jump, letter to Charles F. Brannan, Secretary of Agriculture, Nov. 30, 1948, reprinted in *Public Administration Review* Vol. IX, No. 1, (Winter 1949).

20. *Ibid.*

21. *Ibid.*

Editorial Note: Edward Wenk, Jr. describes the development of a Federal policy relating the oceans to national purpose. Unlike most other such policies this was not initiated by the major economic beneficiaries of the sea, the fishing and maritime industries, nor by the seaboard towns largely dependent on the sea, but by the scientific community seeking a broader research program. Existing activity relating to the sea was divided among many agencies, each with its own parochial interests. However there was a growing realization of the importance of the sea as a result of oceanographic research, new technology, world populations outracing food supplies, concern over toxic waste in the sea, and interest in using the sea as a peaceful international arena. Stimulated by the National Academy of Sciences, Congress took the lead through Chairman Warren G. Magnuson of the Senate Commerce Committee and Chairman Herbert C. Bonner of the House Marine and Fisheries Committee. The two houses had different ideas, Magnuson proposing a cabinet level Marine Council chaired by the Vice President and the House proposing a national advisory commission on oceanography. Finally in 1966 a bill combining the two approaches was passed and it included a broad policy goal of relating ocean activities to economic, social, and political objectives. Thus was launched a policy of cross-department coordination unique in the annals of public administration.

Vice President Humphrey as chairman of the cabinet level council and Edward Wenk as staff director made the process work by tying projects to presidential interests, skillful chairmanship of action-forcing meetings, and competent staff work. Wenk continually struggled with departmental special interests and divergent views of the Office of Management and Budget (OMB). Important results were the Sea Grant Program, and policies such as coastal zone management, ban of nuclear weapons on the seabed, international cooperation in ocean exploration and promotion of ocean technology. The Food From the Sea Program did not do so well. Lacking strong economic interest group support, the council became inactive shortly after the change in national leadership in 1970.

CHAPTER 7

OCEANS AND NATIONAL PURPOSE

Edward Wenk, Jr.

Preface

In 1966, for the first time in American history, we adopted a policy relating the oceans to national purposes. The event was both an end and a beginning. It culminated a period of seven years during which the U.S. Congress wrestled with the paradox that the United States, which had been founded and developed as a maritime nation, had been recklessly neglecting the sea. It was also the beginning of an experiment in public administration where almost for the first time, policy planning apparatus to assist the President was put in the hands of the Vice President, with the collaboration of members of the Cabinet and heads of other independent agencies who had major statutory responsibilities dealing with the sea.

During this period I held four advisory posts in the Executive and Legislative Branches that dealt with these issues, the last as staff director for the Vice President's Council. From these vantage points, it was possible both to observe and to engage in the artistic processes of governance. This first-hand account is an attempt to describe what happened and to identify key actors and their interactions. The interval covered is roughly 1959 through 1970. That period has been followed by a decade of academic affiliations during which there was opportunity to sort out otherwise chaotic and confused events of the past. Put another way, the period of direct involvement was like being in the eye of a storm where it was difficult to know from which direction the wind was blowing. With the recent scholarly and meditative environment, there has been an attempt to comprehend political meteorology.

This account thus ends in an attempt to dissect and diagnose the public process so as to identify and evaluate those key features which not only drove and modulated the events of the time, but whose dynamics may furnish general lessons for the future.

This case study of marine affairs, however, had certain unique features. For one thing, the awakening in 1966 did not occur easily, spontaneously, or even visibly. No new scientific discovery shook the world, nor did any natural catastrophe threaten it. The security of no nation was significantly menaced by the maritime power of another. No underwater Sputnik triggered a frantic U.S. response as followed the 1957 space surprise of the Soviet Union. No powerful vested interest or constituency clamored for action. Indeed, a cliche was spawned that proved a marvelous symbol of endemic political lethargy: "The fish don't vote."

With neither palpable threat nor effective lobby, analysts would probably agree that for anything at all to happen was remarkable. Yet, to impart momentum amidst such apathy meant bending events, persuading people, moulding new understandings, and generating new institutions. So it is not surprising that progress was escorted by conflicts—conflicts in goals, in motivations, in priorities, and in power.

Out of that process, however, emerged a cabinet-level Council chaired by the Vice President whose track record of recommendations to the President, favorable critiques by disinterested outside observers and now, thirteen years after the Council's demise, a resurgence of advocacy for its reestablishment, all suggest that in some measure it met the hopes and expectations of its creators. In today's world of disaffection with government performance such a situation is so unusual as to earn careful examination.

Background

By way of background, it is necessary to sketch three different settings. The first concerns the stake which this nation, and in fact every nation, has in the sea. The second concerns ocean-related institutions and their complexity, variety, functional connections, and performance. The third setting concerns the political stage, particularly in the U.S. Congress, upon which the issue was first exposed and where a series of wandering and wavering congressional initiatives finally converged in 1966 with the enactment of unprecedented marine legislation.

As to the marine setting, all the human inhabitants of this planet reside on continental islands embedded in a vast ocean, and most of human activity has been conspicuously affected by a pervasive marine environment. While the role of the oceans in the destiny of nations and the processes of civilization can never be isolated from the remainder of the geopolitical theater, only recently has there been a marked transition from random maritime exploration and uncritical resource exploitation to a thoughtful appraisal of policy and development of a strategy to meet wide-ranging connections to societal goals.

Five unrelated circumstances set the stage for change. First, scientific oceanography generated a deeper comprehension of what is in and under the sea. From systematic observations over about one hundred years, a great deal was learned about the waters, their motions and contents, about the pockets of oil and gas buried under the seabed, and the mineral-rich, potato-shaped nodules resting on the floor itself. Tens of thousands of different species of animal and plant life have been observed and, of course, many serve as food for human consumption.

Next, technology was ripening to overcome the hostile and strenuous environment that had previously thwarted attempts to work in and under the sea. Much of this spun off from defense innovation or space exploration, such as deep-diving submersibles, radio-linked buoys, satellite observation platforms, precise navigation systems, and sensitive instruments.

Thirdly, world populations were outracing their food supply, their energy and mineral resources, and their sea coasts for both industrial development and recreation, and so the oceans attracted interest as a relatively untapped wilderness.

Fourthly, as these populations grew, they concentrated more and more along the sea coast. That coastal band, where not only the land meets the sea but where people meet the sea, became a source of conflict among many users as well as the unwitting disposal site for toxic industrial and municipal waste.

And finally, as international tensions persisted, the oceans were perceived as a new arena for both peaceful cooperation and for competition.

All of these circumstances stimulated a new level of interest in the potential of the sea. Fishery production could readily double in ten years and with the aid of aquaculture increase by a factor of four. Extraction of offshore oil and gas was expected to increase fivefold by the year 2000. Worldwide shipping was expected to increase perhaps by a factor of four and offshore platforms were being considered as sites for nuclear power generation, for supertanker terminals, or for metropolitan jetports.

At the same time, the oceans were being considered to meet humanitarian concerns. Inexpensive fish protein might counter a large fraction of worldwide nutritional deficiency. Ports and harbors that so often became the festering origins of urban decay could be rehabilitated as a start toward massive renovation of cities. Expanded sea shore recreation could be made more widely available and this natural legacy, if better protected from pollution and development, might serve future generations.

In the world community, there was recognition that public order might be enhanced by placing portions of the sea off limits to weapons of mass destruction, that international arrangements might insure that living resources are harvested equitably while maintaining abundance, that mineral resources could be extracted from the deep ocean beyond territorial limits of all nations so as to benefit developing as well as advanced countries, and finally, that as a common heritage of mankind, the marine environment could be employed as a rehearsal ground for international comity.

This apparent promise was, nevertheless, misleading; the total involvement of the United States was in truth thinly spread. As measured by funding for research, for example, less than 3 percent of the R&D budget was being devoted to marine activities, roughly half of what was being spent in the field of astronomy! Yet, the status of scientific oceanography was primitive. Maps were crude, geological samples inadequate, and fisheries statistics based on fish that were actually caught, not those uncaught. Of the millions of square miles of seabed beyond the shallows, man had directly seen but a hundred.

Diversity of Maritime Interests

In recognizing inherent human curiosity about the world around us and the desire to explore, we would expect the scientific community to serve as a springboard for a more concerted and sustained attack on the sea. It did. Sixty-three universities engaged in oceanographic research. Folk song and fantasy would also have action in the hands of sailors and fishermen. But as the plot unfolds, a more pragmatic appraisal reveals a cast of entrepreneurs, industrialists, lawyers, bankers, naval strategists, bureaucrats, diplomats, and politicians.

To begin with, in the U.S. government there were 29 bureaus and 11 departments and agencies involved; plus 33 subcommittees in the Congress and 30 states bordering the Great Lakes and our sea coasts. Beyond purely domestic institutions there were then 112 nations fronting the sea and more than 55 international organizations, both governmental and nongovernmental, dealing with ocean affairs. In the commercial sector there were chemical, mineral, oil, fishing, shipping, ship building, dredging, construction and recreational industries as well as the high technology sector and banking. Marine unions were concerned with ship manning and cargo handling. And the general public had interests in recreation and environmental conservancy. This inventory of different clientele and their interest in the oceans reveals severe fragmentation, different motivations, and sharp diversity in style. America alone lacked a coherent set of goals, priorities, strategies and government apparatus by which to turn the oceans to our national interest. The challenge, of course, was how to manage such diversity.

Involvement with the sea by the Federal Government extends back to the very origins of the country, in the founding of the colonies and in their dependence upon a long maritime umbilical cord to Europe for the transport of supplies. Of necessity seeking foreign exchange to nurture its economic independence, a fledgling government fostered a merchant marine, a fishing and whaling fleet that pressed its goods and services on overseas customers. The sea became primarily of interest to private traders. Nevertheless, the government afforded protection on the high seas against acts of piracy, and early on assumed the cost of hydrographic surveying and preparation of navigation charts. Indeed, the first marine related agency, the Coast Survey, was created in 1807. The Federal role grew at random with a succession of separate legislative assignments. The catalog of functions and agency responsibilities as of 1970 was wide and thinly spread. Table 7-1 reveals the taxonomy of that Federal involvement.

New Initiatives

Until 1966, however, the full implications of marine activities spread throughout government lacked any influential locus of responsibility. There was, and in fact still is, no department of the oceans. Moreover, ocean related missions were usually buried at the third echelon within individual departments and agencies or even lower. With few exceptions, special interest clientele were quiet and ineffective; and indeed, most of the marine industries, fishing and shipping in particular, were sick. Neither cared much about research, at least not enough to promote it strenuously. All they were interested in was governmental assistance.

It is interesting that the first and most effective lobby for calling attention to our anomalous maritime neglect was the scientific community. Its concerns about the woefully inadequate ships, laboratories, and support for scientific investigations led to three separate studies under auspices of the National Academy of Sciences. The first, in 1927, spawned endowments from private foundations to assist Scripps Institution of Oceanography, Woods Hole Oceanographic Institution, and the University of Washington. These fiscal hormones were temporarily reinforced during World War II by massive investments of the Navy in research related to submarine warfare. At the end of the war, however, even this activity declined and a second study was undertaken in 1949 by the National Academy of Sciences. It fizzled. The third initiative to increase attention to the problem and hopefully tickle funds from the Federal treasury was begun at the Academy in 1956 through a coalition of outside scientists with senior officials in a number of Federal agencies. That study was hatched on February 15, 1959, with a report entitled *Oceanography 1960-70*. Five general and twenty specific recommendations emerged, all essentially in support of accelerated Federal funding for marine research. There was, however, little mention of legal, economic, and political implications of the ocean policies, or of the tapestry of capital investment, technology, organization, and management necessary to realize these benefits. It was as though the scientific knowledge alone would catalyze the necessary endeavors. Put another way, oceanographers who prepared the report

            Federal Public Policy

Table 7-1

Federal Marine Science Activities, 1966-70

Agency	Mission
Department of State..............	Participation in international organizations; support of international fisheries commissions; international marine policies.
Agency for International Development.	Foreign assistance and food resources for developing nations.
Department of Defense........... (Navy; Advanced Research Projects Agency; Army Corps of Engineers.)	All phases of oceanography relating to national security; naval technology; statutory civilian responsibilities: Great Lakes, river, harbor, coastal, and ocean charting and forecasting; Great Lakes, river, harbor, and coastal development, restoration, and preservation.
Department of the Interior........:... (Geological Survey; Federal Water Pollution Control Administration; Bureau of Commercial Fisheries; Bureau of Sport Fisheries and Wildlife; Bureau of Mines; Bureau of Land Management; National Park Service; Bureau of Outdoor Recreation; Office of Saline Water; Office of Marine Resources.)	Management, conservation, and development of marine natural resources; lead responsibility for coastal zone management planning and research;ᵃ measurement and enforcement of water quality standards; acquisition, preservation, and development of coastal areas; identification and development of technology for evaluation of mineral resources; identification of sources and interrelationships for supply of fresh water.
Department of Commerce......... (Environmental Science Services Administration; Maritime Administration.)	Lead responsibility for air/sea interaction program and marine environmental prediction program;ᵃ tsunami and hurricane warning; charting and mapping of coastal and deep-ocean waters; research on ship design, shipbuilding, and ship operations; marine transportation and port systems.
Department of Health, Education, and Welfare. (Public Health Service; Office of Education; Food and Drug Administration.)	Human health, healthfulness of food, biomedical research, and support of education.
Department of Transportation...... (Coast Guard; Office of the Secretary.)	Safety and protection of life and property in port and at sea; delineation and prediction of ice masses; navigation aids; oceanographic and meteorological observations; transport systems analysis and planning.
Atomic Energy Commission........	Radioactivity in the marine environment; development of marine nuclear technology.
National Aeronautics and Space Administration.	Feasibility, design, and engineering of spacecraft and sensors for ocean observations.
National Science Foundation.......	Basic and academic oceanography; lead responsibility for Arctic research and the International Decade of Ocean Exploration;ᵃ facilities support; Sea Grant colleges and programs.
Smithsonian Institution...........	Identification, acquisition, classification, and ecology of marine organisms; investigations of the geophysical factors of oceanic environment.
National Council on Marine Resources and Engineering Development.	Assist the President in planning, development of policy and coordination of federal marine science activities.

ᵃ Lead agency designation involves federal leadership for stimulating the exchange of ideas with other interested agencies; planning in terms of the identification of goals with the advice and assistance of other agencies; and negotiating interagency support required for the achievement of goals in these areas—goals to be achieved through multiple, coherent activity of the interested agencies—funding gaps, where possible. No transfer of any agency's statutory responsibilities is involved.

Source: MSA, 4th report (1970), pp. 2-3. Also, Edward Wenk, Jr., *The Politics of the Ocean* (Seattle: University of Washington Press, 1972), p. 46.

essentially urged intensified study of the sea, but as though the earth were itself uninhabited.

The obvious target for this advocacy was the newly founded Office of the Assistant to the President for Science and Technology. That post of science adviser had been created shortly before in the aftermath of the 1957 Soviet space surprise and it was clear that major decisions were being made not only by the science adviser, but also by the associated apparatus of an influential President's Science Advisory Committee. Ironically, the National Academy of Sciences report on oceanography was turned aside. Among the reasons lay a long history within the scientific community of a pecking order that found high-energy physics at the top and oceanography at the bottom.

Congressional Involvement

The chairman and members of the National Academy of Sciences committee, however, were not to be denied. In anticipation of that potentially closed door, they had already taken the precaution of mounting a set of new relationships with individual members and committees of Congress that potentially had jurisdiction over the field of oceanography, but which up until then was the province of none. In the Senate, the mentor was the Commerce Committee Chairman Warren G. Magnuson. In the House of Representatives, it was the Merchant Marine and Fisheries Committee Chairman Herbert C. Bonner. In the House, however, a jurisdictional wrangle quickly developed. Riding the surfboard of momentum imparted by the swiftly growing space program, the newly created Science and Astronautics Committee made a vigorous but soon aborted move to use its science mandate to encompass oceanography as well. In any event, here was a new and attractive theme for the Congress, still basking in an era when "science was good for you," when the enthusiasm of the American people and its political reflection were catalyzed by a race with the Soviets.

Part of this race was simply in the spirit of an animated competition, but part of it was serious business. There had been a swift translation of technological superiority in space to an equivalent technological superiority in all fields of science and engineering, and in turn such capabilities were equated to military muscle. There was a widespread concern that the U.S. be first in *all* fields of science, more because of what was not known than what might have been documented as a rationale for such leadership. There was simply a fundamental anxiety that no one could be sure how leadership in any field of science might be turned to military advantage. Thus, an implicit policy concerning science and technology emerged that with Federal assistance, the U.S. should forge ahead in all. Quite naturally, the Congress jumped on this marine equivalent of a bandwagon with a flurry of legislation more symbolic than substantive. The Executive Branch under President Eisenhower was unmoved.

However, shortly after taking office in 1961, President John F. Kennedy did assert his interests in strengthening our marine research capabilities with a conspicuous budgetary add-on. This immediately led to a reinforcement of our small and feeble fleet of oceanographic research ships and laboratories and provided a base of scientific capabilities for marine research from which we benefit today. That thrust was short-lived, however, and by 1962 the Congress was again taking an initiative. This time it moved from the notion of simply playing catch-up with the Russians to a new set of concerns. First, Congress wanted some assurance that fiscal support for the field that had been reignited in 1961 would be sustained. More than that, however, it took note of the large number of different Federal agencies, some 23 in all running off in perhaps as many directions, and hammered away at the waste and duplication. Old as was that political issue, it rang with some authenticity here because indeed the coordinating apparatus that had been created in the early 1960s, an Interagency Committee on Oceanography reporting to the Federal Council for Science and Technology, was not believed sufficiently powerful to work at a policy rather than simply a program level.

One attempt to rivet attention on this issue succeeded in both houses by assigning leadership and coordinating authority to the director of the newly created Office of Science and Technology (OST) in the Executive Office of the President. That measure passed at the very end of the 87th Congress but was pocket vetoed by President Kennedy. While no public statement clarified the rejection, objections could be pieced together from other evidence. To give OST supervision over line agencies violated the principle that no machinery should be interposed between department heads and the President. Secondly, a special staff position in the Office of Science and Technology was considered an unwanted precedent that could proliferate for other fields. But thirdly, such an organizational structure—with the medium as message— would have given oceanography a priority to which the Kennedy administration was not disposed.

Rebuffed, stubborn members of the House opened fire immediately after the 88th Congress convened, pushing a revised measure to which the President's Science Adviser had written an endorsement. That measure was reported out favorably by the Merchant Marine and Fisheries Committee and passed the full House, but no action was taken by the Senate. Its Commerce Committee chairman was busy with other higher priority affairs and perhaps embittered that the bill was entirely a product of the House.

It was while this House bill languished in the Senate that Warren Magnuson introduced S.2990 to create a National Oceanographic Council. It would establish a policy planning and coordinating body at cabinet level in the

Executive Office of the President, chaired by the Vice President. Such a council had been created for space affairs when the National Aeronautics and Space Administration (NASA) was established in 1958, but had failed to gain respect for vigor or operational success. Nevertheless, Senator Magnuson took the view that only at that higher level of leadership and authority could the President gain the effective coordination necessary not only to establish coherence in policy across the government, but also a discipline of cooperation at the program level, which at lower echelons had proved unstable.

The House of Representatives, however, was less enthusiastic about this institutional innovation. They were well aware of the Space Council failure. They were also heavily plagued by lobbying from the Navy against the creation of any coordinating instrument as potentially powerful as this one might be and which might kibitz in Navy affairs that up until then had been immune. When the House failed to find any alternative, Congressman Paul Rogers proposed a presidential commission to study the problem. There was great suspicion, however, that such commissions are often simply delaying actions, and so at first this notion gained little support. The House, nonetheless, managed to attract interest to its proposal from the aerospace industry which at that time was beginning to feel the sting of slowdown in appropriations for the already massive space program. Neither bill gained impetus from any outside constituency, so that the 88th Congress adjourned without any legislative initiation.

With the 89th, Magnuson reintroduced the Council measure as S.944. Now, however, Magnuson was serious. With three days of hearings, sufficient testimony was collected from carefully selected advocates to assure passage. Witnesses recited the unfulfilled promise of the sea and government officials stumbled sufficiently over questions of coordination as to verify the unevenness and uncertainty of commitment. Indeed, testimony from President Johnson's Science Adviser, Donald Hornig, was particularly damning when he had to admit that the Federal Council had recently chosen not even to endorse feeble Interagency Committee on Oceanography (ICO) proposals. Senator Magnuson, however, did not bring his bill out of Committee. He was awaiting House action to see in what direction they might move so as not to undergo the embarrassment he had before when the House ungraciously dumped his initiatives in the 87th Congress.

The House's strategy was revealed on June 15, 1965, with reintroduction of Roger's bill to establish a presidentially appointed National Commission on Oceanography. Now Senator Magnuson acted, reporting his measure out of Committee, no longer entitled the National Oceanographic Act, but a far more mature initiative entitled the Marine Resources and Engineering Development Act. This change was more than cosmetic. For one thing, it reflected maturation from the earlier days of knee-jerk reactions to the Soviets and compulsions to flog waste and duplication. It contained a statement of national purpose that linked the oceans to our broader interests. It recognized that only the President of the United States could be bandmaster with an orchestra composed of the different agency instruments, and so he was given the unambiguous responsibility for setting goals, directions, strategies, and priorities. The Vice President, however, was charged with writing the music.

By late 1965, both Houses had reported out their different bills, but it was clear that they disagreed on fundamental principles. An ugly impasse emerged from behind closed conference committee doors where conferees from both Houses were attempting to work out a compromise. The Senate felt that the issue had been studied to death and that the time had come for action, rather than for yet further study by a commission. The House, on the other hand, was skeptical of the Council, partly because the Space Council model had such a checkered record of performance. The House also responded to a quiet lobby against the Council bill then being mounted in the Executive Office by the Bureau of the Budget and OST. Word was leaked by these presidential advisors that there was high likelihood of presidential veto. In recalling the setback of 1963, the House did not want to face yet another crushing failure by supporting the Senate's proposal. Those Executive Office components, incidentally, had always been assiduously opposed to new staff offices for the President, perhaps jealous of dilution of their authority or worried over another source of pressure on the budget by special interests camping within the presidential establishment itself.

The two Houses had invested considerable time and effort in their respective bills and the desire for reporting out some kind of legislation finally overcame the deadlock. On June 2, 1966, the final bill amalgamating Council and Commission language was reported out by both houses and sent to the President. Signature or veto? No one knew. But quietly, on June 17th, the President signed the Marine Resources and Engineering Development Act (PL 89-454) into law.

Implementing a New Ocean Mandate

This still left unanswered how seriously would the President support implementation. History was full of legislated apparatus for the President which he could choose to ignore. On the other hand, he could follow the letter of the law in appointing a Council, but then bypass its spirit by letting it wilt.

To an anxiously waiting oceanographic community came the answer with the commissioning of the Environmental Science Services Administration (ESSA) *Oceanographer*, on July 13th. President Johnson made a powerful statement: he emphasized freedom of the seas as a policy plank that was to be one of the major springboards for subsequent action. Then he dissolved uncertainties as to the fate of the Council by calling on that unit to get going immediately, even to bring in initial recommendations by January.

As to the mandate, PL89-454, in its declaration of policy, section II, stated *what* should be done: the assignment of leadership to the President in sections IV and VII asserted *who* should carry out its provisions and sections III and VI authorized creation of an interim National Council on Marine Resources and Engineering Development, chaired by the Vice President *to advise and assist*. Section V authorized appointment of a public advisory *commission*, particularly to recommend long-term organizational structure.

Until then, Vice President Hubert H. Humphrey had watched these developments quietly on the sidelines. (By a strange coincidence it had been Senator Humphrey who was the first member of either House of Congress to take note of the National Academy of Sciences report released in 1959 and to urge response of the Congress.) He was well aware of a delicate relationship between a President and his Vice President, so that any move by Humphrey to lobby for the Council or even to request its activation after enactment might have been interpreted as a self-serving grab for even a tiny morsel of independent political power. A Marine Council, however, was so intriguing that with the explicit signals from President Johnson, Humphrey went into full gear.

His first move was to recruit a full-time, presidentially appointed executive secretary that was provided for in the legislation. In the course of head hunting, my name had come to his attention as a person experienced both in ocean engineering and in science policy. Indeed, I had met Humphrey briefly when advising him from my perch in the Legislative Reference Service. He was also aware of my role there in advising both Houses on legislation, and my prior responsibilities on President Kennedy's staff for ocean research policies. His recommendation to President Johnson was approved overnight and announced by the White House on August 13th. On August 17th, the Council met for the first time.

The oceanographic press, serving a frustrated marine industry, gushed with enthusiasm. The *New York Times* took solemn note of the happening, while *Science*, serving the technical community, astringently observed that "at the moment the long-range outlook on the make-up and management of the national oceanography program is still hazy."

Starting a New Agency:
Basic Strategies and Concepts

Notwithstanding the clear and forceful language of the legislative mandate, the direction of the Council, its style, and its tactics were still to emerge. In short, even though Humphrey had received the Council's ignition key, the legislation provided only a rough blueprint for a car, plus reams of standard administrative regulations. The garage held no chassis, wheels, or engine, much less gas in the tank. We were thus faced with the challenge of institution building.

Given that unusual opportunity, I insisted that Humphrey and I meet privately for a sufficiently long interval so that we could develop some basic concepts for the structure and for the policies and strategies that would characterize the Council's action. Our conversations began on the dilemmas of our nation and of human society, with intrinsically no attention to the maritime content. Only secondly did we explore ways and means to deal with such problems whose solutions could be facilitated by more effective use of the oceans. We discussed the potential of the sea to mitigate world hunger and to provide fuel and minerals. We considered the increasing pollution and abuse of the coastal zone, the decay of the waterfront, the hazards of turning the seabed into yet another arena for nuclear armament, and the festering conflicts among nations competing for common property resources. The first decision we made was that the agenda of the Council in generating proposals for the President would be set by the national and global issues rather than within the parochial limits of ocean science.

Both of us had intimate knowledge of the impediments, strife, and false starts of any government agency, of the constraints, warfare, and bureaucratic games arising from legitimate competition for power. We were especially aware of the energies required to assist the President in the coordination of the operating programs of the agencies because we would ultimately have to carry out whatever policies would be generated by the Council.

A second decision was thus made that the Council should assume an activist style, not simply umpiring interagency conflict, but genuinely engaging in integrated initiatives.

By law, the Council had two components. One was a nine-man policy board composed of cabinet officers and heads of agencies, chaired by the Vice President. The other was the staff Secretariat. Our third decision was that the Secretariat should both develop policy recommendations for Council action and also follow through after Council or Presidential approval by threading programs over, under, around and through the maze of bureaucratic impediments that always seem invented to test the energies of an advocate, if not the merits of a program itself.

We recognized, however, that the President was the fundamental locus of decision making in marine affairs, not only because of the explicit language of the act, but because of the realities of government operation. This meant tuning Council antennae onto the policy goals and indeed the mood of the Johnson Administration to which the sea could genuinely contribute. We were aware of a coolness to funding for science as a whole, of inflation that was generating shivers through the economy, of issues over Vietnam and civil unrest that captured press and citizen attention. In this regard, we tried to keep marine affairs in a reasonable perspective, that the sea was not at the top of the nation's wish list. At the same time, we recognized that the intent of the legislation was that it should not remain at the bottom.

Within this complex array of goals, of governmental and institutional behavior, of a diversity of participants, we tacitly adopted five unifying themes. First, science and technology were to be key ingredients for effective use of the sea. Secondly, the Federal Government would have to expand its fiscal support for research and exploration. Third, as with land resources, private enterprise would continue to undertake marine resource development, but in some sort of improved public/private partnership. Fourth, geographically differentiated problems of managing inshore marine environment would require state and local participation. And fifth, in view of the explicit statement of national policy to use the sea for the benefit of *all* men, and considering the inherent international character of both the sea and of its study, a multinational approach was considered essential.

Council Tactics

After dealing with these strategic considerations, Vice President Humphrey and I then examined tactics to orchestrate the bureaucracy so as to pull together disparate agency competencies. Thus, in keeping with the legislative instructions, the Council would have to:

1) Identify unmet national needs and technological opportunities to which the oceans should be directed, especially considering gaps in programs that cross agency lines.

2) Recommend priorities to the president and identify impediments to progress with strategies for their circumvention.

3) Develop techniques by which the objectives and programs of one agency would not inadvertently conflict with equally valid but independent activities of another.

4) Coordinate programs that were of concern to many agencies, but which were likely to be overlooked as being of low priority in each.

5) Attempt to match appropriate resources of the Federal government to mutually agreed upon goals.

6) Install techniques of evaluation so as to eliminate marginal activities.

7) Take note of the richness of technological activities that required consideration of social, economic, legal and political impacts as well as scientific, identifying potential alternatives and criteria for choice.

This was an ambitious charter, even more so because of the melancholy history of interagency mechanisms. Vice President Humphrey and I were stimulated by the challenge and had an objective that the Council would be more than simply the sum of the parts.

Start-up Problems

When a new agency is created, its presidentially appointed steward has the irksome housekeeping chores of putting together the authorized machinery while at the same time outside clientele expect it to be functioning as though it had been in business for a decade. I was thus faced with generating a Council agenda at the same time it was necessary to put together the institution itself. This meant going back to Congress for specific appropriations, recruiting staff, finding office space, introducing measures of security for classified material and for fiscal accounting, building various networks of communications within the government at a cabinet level and within the government at the level of experts, in addition to similar networks to interests outside of government, to the universities conducting oceanography, and to the various industrial participants in maritime affairs.

The Council professional staff numbered 25-30. We endeavored to pick other brains, however, through contract studies that had been providentially authorized in the legislation and by advisory committees of outsiders. As well, we also established a committee infrastructure whereby the special tasks of the Council could be generated. This internal structure, incidentally, provided the base in an articulated hierarchy of units for the generation of policy concepts, for their fleshing out in operational terms, and for ultimately the drafting of proposals that were to go from the Council to the President.

Thus began a marine affairs transition. The anticipation of such maturity grew out of the shift in title of the authorizing legislation itself as it underwent metamorphosis in the Congress from a national oceanographic act to one focused on marine resources and engineering development. That transition was marked by a mandate to the Council to deal with ends as well as means, the ends being concerns about a more peaceful world community, famine, ill health, a better quality of life and economic growth. Thus, a traditional research activity that had been narrowly oriented toward simply describing phenomena of the sea was broadened to embrace a constellation of activities involving economic, social, and political considerations.

At this point we recognized a role for the Marine Council as being a maritime presence in the White House. What this meant was that to compensate for the absence of crisis and muscular constituency, there would be a locus of analysis close to the president to identify unmet needs and opportunities whereby the potential of the seas could be linked to social policy.

First, however, the Council endeavored to upgrade the priority for marine affairs. There were two operational choices. We could have stapled together existing programs and aspirations of the agencies and supported expansion in all. Or we could have refurbished meritorious rejects from earlier unsuccessful budget sorties. On the other hand, we could scan priority national needs and seek marine related programs for these targets, thus using rifles rather than shotguns. The Secretariat chose the latter approach. Throughout the life of the Council, there was an annual search for such policy guidelines that were characterized as "initiatives."

Initiatives were first generated in the Secretariat itself. They were then fed to two bodies simultaneously. Outside consultants representing a wide range of technical and industrial interests estimated relative priorities on *what* we should do. Another group of consultations was with the inhouse Council committees where each prospect was explored and expanded, especially on the question of *how* to do it.

These Council committees, established at the assistant secretary or bureau chief level, massaged the issues and working drafts of proposals were generated. As each item successfully passed screens of review of both the outside and inside groups, it was then submitted to the Council in the plenary session, then sent to the President.

Council Sessions: Humphrey Leadership

Each Council meeting was a carefully planned action-forcing scenario, with a script and stellar cast. The central plot was to transact business over bureaucratic counterplots manifested as constant bickering by recalcitrant players against the chairman's determination to make decisions effectively and harmoniously. My role was to ferret out the issues deserving attention at such a policy level, to fashion the agenda, prepare the advance papers, and make recommendations for action. All were run through the Vice President himself before a Council meeting so that he would have the benefit of homework and the Secretariat the benefit of his counsel. In preparing, incidentally, we meticulously tried to list all the known facts, background, and options because to have done otherwise would have eroded integrity of the office. We thus ran an honest, nonmanipulative game, but it was definitely not a neutral one, since we studiously avoided low impact compromise that characterized so many interagency bodies in the past.

These Council-level meetings were convened almost monthly, and supporting documentation circulated to Council members eight to ten days before a session, along with an aide-memoire that indicated specifically what action would be sought. Council members assumed correctly that the proposed recommendations reflected views of the Secretariat, but Humphrey was always careful to guard his own position so as not to inadvertently stir a conflict. Agencies very often came to these meetings with some opacity in their own views, hoping in some cases to spring surprises. The fact that during a meeting all agencies had to lay their different cards on the table for a public vote brought out differences, and of course the Council meeting was intended as a legitimate process to reconcile them. From time to time, this proved a painful discipline.

Humphrey endeavored to be even-handed, but his style was not simply to preside. When he received the presession briefing on ramifications, desirable outcomes, and disparate agency views, he considered the potential obstacles and countermeasures. At the meetings where the diverting rhetoric of participants might have tripped a less able chairman, Humphrey was quick, intuitive, and sure-footed. Attendance by Council members or their alternates at a high policy level was excellent, partly the result of personal invitations from Humphrey, partly because of the sense of collegiate effort that elicited willing participation.

At the sessions, dialogues were spontaneous. After Humphrey opened with his own paraphrasing of prepared material, he asked for my precis of the issue, then discussion. Participants having a direct interest in the issue were called upon to comment in efforts to prevent obfuscation and obstruction. He was always fair and considerate, but if there was a visible or suspected fence-straddling, his humorous probings soon brought out various points for resolution. Among other things, the Vice President endeavored repeatedly to raise each Cabinet member's perspective to presidential-level considerations, at least temporarily subordinating normal parochial concerns.

As a Council session neared a point of decision, the Vice President would phrase the decision and ask for dissenters to make their views known. This immobilized those who had reservations on the basis of narrow self-interest rather than logic, and the die was cast. Occasionally an issue paper proved inadequate and would be withdrawn to the kitchen for further cooking. Occasionally candor elicited a deadlock, in which event action was deferred until the next meeting, during which interval the Secretariat was expected to work with both parties to seek agreement.

The most unpleasant moments came when a Council member's position was contrary to what his subordinate had asserted or been persuaded to adopt at a preparatory session in lower level Council committees. Although a subordinate's principal was not committed at that time, it was usually assumed he had been consulted and tacitly approved. The uneasy suspicion emerged, however, that the earlier position had not been overturned, simply that the subordinate had chosen to defer a candid disclosure at the lower level sessions when he felt he could not hold his own in the hope that his principal would be more stubborn.

Minutes of these meetings were taken verbatim, from which a precis was prepared, circulated, and adopted as a formal memorandum of understanding. They were generally honored.

Decisions as Advice to the President

Once a decision was made, the next step was for the Vice President to transmit it to the President, either singly or once a year when a package of such initiatives were assembled in an annual report that was required by the legislation to be submitted each year by the President to the Congress.

From time to time these items that went up to the President were rejected, weakened, or switched in priority. The reasons usually were budgetary, wherein the Director of the Bureau of the Budget (BOB) in his access to the President would undermine the work of the Council. Attempts were always made to head off that contingency by having BOB representatives present as observers at Council sessions, but they played a peculiar game of silence, neither endorsing nor opposing moves, thus leaving open their options to intersect the Humphrey initiative at a later and more private time. On those occasions when this countervailing action became known, I usually acted on behalf of the Vice President to argue the case directly with the Budget Director; I probably won some change in his position half the time. Thus, over the years of Council life, a whole sequence of new initiatives entered the policy stream that for the first time in history became a matter of presidential-level authority to link the oceans to our national interests. Indeed, during the life of the Council from 1966 to 1970, some 65 such items were generated within the Council apparatus and approved by the President.

Translated into political terms, the question of how important the oceans are to the nation depended critically on how important President Johnson believed them to be. Of all the officers of government, the President had by far the greatest power to define the nation's agenda, to synthesize divergent interests, and to make available public resources to accomplish necessary programs. He is, of course, the systems manager of the bureaucracy, attempting to enforce coherence to fractured internal machinery and to deal with issues on the basis of their importance in the long as well as short-term national interest rather than simply on the basis of reflex response to vocal lobbies. As said before, we in the Council were realists in observing that even in our wildest flight of fancy, no one would have pegged the oceans at the top of the President's priority list; the question, however, was not how high ocean affairs might be, but whether they were on his list at all. Thus, we searched feverishly for opportunities that would appeal to President Johnson because of their consistency with *his* broader goals. For example, the President had said, "Next to the pursuit of peace, the greatest challenge to the human family is the race between food supply and population increase." This provided leverage to an initiative to use the sea in attacking worldwide protein malnutrition. We knew he was interested in the problem of the cities, and so we argued that urban development does not end at the water's edge; we searched for marine solutions in coastal management and pollution abatement. International cooperation in space had been one of Johnson's proudest achievements in 1958 when he took leadership in drafting the Space Act. It had a marine analog. And indeed that became one of our more vigorous initiatives throughout the life of the Council.

By January 1967, five months after the Council was activated, it had sown the seeds that President Johnson blessed, then fertilized with funding. This included major new initiatives in a food-from-the-sea policy to accelerate development of chemical processes whereby pure protein for nutritional reinforcement could be extracted from fish. We called attention to the need for coastal management. We helped ignite the Sea Grant Program, which for the first time provided a broader concept of university activities that took into account the economic and social aspects of marine activities and the need to develop linkages between government, academia, and industry. We initiated a new program to bring modern techniques into the management of oceanographic data, to improve the prediction of sea state, to accelerate mineral surveys on the seabed, to highlight the need for technology to operate in the deeper reaches of the ocean, and finally, to call attention to the Arctic as a much overlooked area of national interest, requiring not only research in natural sciences, but also the social sciences.

Key Role of the Annual Report

These internal decisions and plans, the successes and the failures of the Council were generally shielded from public view until the distilled results were released in an annual report by the President. As required by the basic legislation, such a report was to contain a description of government-wide programs with funding and activities across the government delineated by purpose as well as by agency, an evaluation of such programs in terms of statutory objectives, the rationale for new Federal initiatives, and recommendations for new legislation.

The product was somewhat unusual. Its chapters were organized according to major uses of the sea rather than by agency cognizance. It was prepared by Council staff instead of by the agencies themselves, which on prior occasions had merely resulted in stapling together of sectorial and selfserving statements. It was analytical in identifying issues and candid in underscoring unsolved problems.

The drafting of such reports constituted one of the most strenuous activities undertaken by the Secretariat. The outline of the report was developed by the staff, determining the scope and theme and stemming from the Council's prior agenda. Copies were then circulated to outside consultants for review of technical accuracy and then to some 16 agencies for comment and clearance. This latter process often became a test of wills. Almost all the agencies replied with the admonition "the report is too long, but you didn't say enough about us." They would then submit parochial details that they insisted we use, many of which of course collided with those from sister agencies. Our ground rules were to correct errors of fact, but to utilize prose only if it were appropriate to the quality of a presidential statement. Our primary Indian wrestling match, however, was with the Bureau of the Budget. They would pool remarks of a dozen or so subject specialists who were examiners for all the agencies encompassed by the Council, then demand their adoption. In the main, the Bureau of the Budget wanted to reduce the commitment of the President, either in terms of funds or future programs or by blurring policy directives. In their view, that would generate a protective stance. Mine, on the other hand, was to state clearly what had been developed by the Council and acted upon by the President. So the Bureau of the Budget and the Council staff walked down the same road as members of the President's family, but rather than hand-in-hand, we ended up jabbing each other in the ribs, each believing sincerely he was serving the President the best.

Those reports, incidentally, have subsequently been regarded as classics. Because of the breadth of material encompassed, they served as information conduits to the government itself, providing clues as to what each agency was doing that otherwise was usually hidden from view. Outsiders also were able to glean both the priorities and the substance of the government programs: scientists, industrial executives, officers of state government and interested parties abroad, and finally, of course, the press.

Quite apart from the identification of ocean priorities in these annual reports, the same material appeared in one place or another in the President's budget. Additionally, certain of these programs were highlighted in special messages: Food from the Sea, for example, in the message on foreign aid and new legislation for coastal management in the message on the environment.

Council Accomplishments

In the Johnson-Humphrey administration, Council proposals that gained presidential endorsement included the launching of an International Decade of Ocean Exploration, the drafting of a treaty that would provide for seabed arms control, the establishment of a framework to update the legal regime for the deep ocean floor, acceleration of technologies making use of satellite and buoy observation networks, and a new focus of attention on the Great Lakes, especially on its problems of pollution.

In retrospect, virtually all of these initiatives paid off. The International Decade of Ocean Exploration was mentioned in the State of the Union message and conducted, albeit at a disappointing budgetary level, from 1970 to 1979. Concern over the conflict in uses of the coastline and of its abuse ultimately resulted in legislation passed in 1972 providing for strong initiatives by the individual states to fulfill their responsibilities of stewardship. A treaty barring weapons of mass destruction from the seabed was signed by the U.S. and the Soviet Union and ratified in 1971. The Sea Grant Program, which got off to a fitful start in 1967, matured to one of the most respected of the government's subventions for multidisciplinary research. Restoration of the Great Lakes was begun.

Some of the Council initiatives, however, never made the President's hit parade. Ironically, these concerned accelerated engineering standards for offshore oil development, port development, and safety of marine transportation. All of those have subsequently earned policy attention. In addition there were some failures. The Food from the Sea Program that was launched not only with Presidential blessings, but Vice Presidential exuberance, staggered and ultimately collapsed when the line agencies having implementing responsibilities failed, not in support, but in competence. And our attempts to assist the fishing industry were frustrated by the fragmentation associated with different fisheries, different policies demanded by these constituencies, and by a weakness within the government of a fisheries agency that was never able to break through the maze of individual state policies which frustrated the generation of a unified approach.

Albeit temporary, the Council apparatus was continued for the first two years under the Nixon-Agnew administration. Indeed, continuity of the Council was preserved by the unexpected invitation by President Nixon for the Council's staff director, myself, to continue in a new administration of a different party. It was thus possible during that first year to maintain an agenda that included most of the important items of unfinished business left over from his predecessor. There was, however, one major difference after the transition which was a decisive factor in undermining the Council's effectiveness, and finally, its life. That was the difference in Council leadership. Agnew was no Humphrey.

Early in the Nixon administration, Vice President Agnew seemed to enjoy the prospects of Council life. Because of his origins in the coastal state of Maryland, I had hoped that this field would prove attractive. Moreover, the Council's importance to the President was sharply accentuated when, soon after inauguration, an oil well five and a half miles out in the Santa Barbara Channel blew out violently, spewing oil over the beaches and bringing with it political repercussions reaching into the White House. It was the Council that was called upon to monitor a contingency plan for containing such spills that the Council had itself initiated a year before in the aftermath of the Torrey Canyon incident in southern England.

The problem with Vice President Agnew, however was twofold. First, he was inept in presiding over a cabinet-level meeting. At the May 23, 1969, session, apprehension grew as we recognized that a number of the issues on the agenda were likely to be met with objections from some of the Council members. Unfortunately, the Vice President failed to do his homework so that at the meeting the agenda deteriorated, controversy arose, and before long it was clear that the Vice President was in a panic over his loss of control of the discussion.

Subsequently, I was asked by the Vice President to prepare a scenario for all future Council meetings so that the outcome would be known in advance and he would be able to prepare remarks and rebuttal to those of any recalcitrant cabinet officers. Otherwise, he said, he would not preside. That demand was impracticable and perverted the decision process. Moreover, trying to write a script for any cabinet officer with a guarantee he would follow it was beyond anyone's capabilities. The Vice President then refused to convene the Council as a whole in plenary session. Rather, he asked me to form a subcabinet group to carry out the functions of the cabinet at the level of assistant or undersecretary. This lower level Committee for Policy Review, created in the aftermath of the May 23rd debacle, was an effective instrument, but clearly no match for the higher-level body intended by the legislation. In October, a number of items of unfinished business from the Johnson administration were worked through that Committee for Policy Review and emerged in a special announcement of a five-point program on October 19th. By then, however, I recognized that the Council apparatus would be only a pale image of its former self and that the President and his immediate advisers had their minds on other issues, largely the politics of preparing for the 1972 election. It was at that time that I resigned, effective January 31, 1970.

The Council Demise and
The Loss in Marine Initiatives

The Council continued another year, but was terminated in 1971 without again registering any new initiatives for the Nixon administration. No further annual reports were released. The Presidential agenda had one last maritime gasp.

In 1970, President Nixon accepted recommendations of the public advisory Commission, created under the Marine Resources and Engineering Development Act of 1966, to consolidate activities into a new National Oceanic and Atmospheric Administration (NOAA). With its establishment came recommendations from within NOAA that it be given government-wide policy leadership for all ocean affairs, thus making unnecessary the continuation of the Council in performing that function. The Congress had been the primary supporter of the Council and now, with the House of Representatives as well as the Senate publicly expressing satisfaction over past Council performance, quietly accepted its demise because they had come to recognize the Council's loss in momentum and leadership. They were not, however, sanguine about NOAA being able to pick up these policy planning and coordinating responsibilities. Indeed, their perception proved correct. In retrospect, it is somewhat difficult to understand how leadership in NOAA could have been so naive as to believe that it would be in a position to coordinate activities of sister agencies over so wide an area. But secondly, it was short-sighted to assume that, operating from a second-level echelon within the Department of Commerce where it was situated, it could have the same continuous and powerful impact on Presidential decisions as did the Council residing in the Executive Office of the President.

Soon after the loss of the Council, however, members of the scientific community, industry, and the Congress began to see the nation's marine program wilt. As evidence of that loss in visibility, only two major statements have been made by presidents in the 1971-79 interval. Not surprisingly, drums began to beat for some renewed activity. One proposal was to form a Department of Oceans and Environment. This was later shoehorned into the concept of a Department of Natural Resources and Environment with which President Carter toyed for a year or so, but later abandoned. During this entire interval and subsequently have come repeated calls that the Marine Council be reinstituted.

Evaluation

In retrospect, it is of interest to review what happened and why over the life of the Council, at least from 1966 to 1970, to glean what lessons we can from that performance. In such an analysis, we have to recognize the importance of the setting. For one thing, by 1966, the enthusiasm for unqualified support of science had vanished, both in the Executive and Legislative Branches. There was thus no longer the momentum that had propelled support for all fields of science and technology from 1958-1964 in the aftermath of the Soviet space shot. Secondly, there was a steady drain of funds into the Vietnam conflict which made each successive budget cycle more and more excruciating. Third, the locus of decision making for a wide range of issues became more sharply targeted directly at the White House. At the same time, as far as marine affairs are concerned, neither before nor during the life of the Council was there ever a powerful lobby that could sustain the political energy of most government programs, not only in their inception but in their continued budgetary support.

Nevertheless, during this interval it is very clear that a number of unprecedented policies were generated and accepted by a president. Moreover, a sharp increase in funding for marine affairs resulted from these Council initiatives, largely, incidentally, in the civilian agencies dealing with the sea. The Marine Council thus counteracted deficiencies in advocacy and in the normal budget process balanced parochial departmentalism with a systems approach. It may be said to have succeeded because it matched maritime solutions to broad social goals. It tried to anticipate impediments to policy development through better planning and to assist all participants in thinking collectively through the use of such devices as the annual report. In its operation, the Council was fully aware that all of its activities depended upon a strong base of science and engineering, but it was as concerned with software as hardware, with the blending of economics, law, public administration, foreign affairs, resources management and environmental management into what otherwise might have been a purely technical business.

Apart from devotees to oceanography, outside observers deemed the Council a success. Said William D. Carey, former Assistant Director of the Bureau of the Budget:

> To balance the books, let me say that I have a very different estimate of the Council on Marine Resources and Engineering Development. This body, too, is an interagency committee which advises the President. What is different is that the Council was created by an act of Congress for a fixed time period, its chairman is the Vice President of the United States, its executive secretary is a Presidential appointee, and its money comes through a direct appropriation. While, even so, this Council might have been mere window dressing, in fact it has been a very lively body. When Vice President Humphrey had the chairmanship, he never failed to show up. He ran the meetings as though he were presiding over a working committee of the Congress. Before each meeting, the individual

members of the Council received pointed notes from the Vice President suggesting that he would be disappointed not to see them, and there was a remarkable attendance record. The Marine Council did not hesitate to advise the President; in fact, I have reason to believe that he received somewhat more advice than he cared for. It comes down to saying that this interagency body was an outstanding success story. Was it because of Mr. Humphrey, or because its executive secretary held a Presidential commission, or because it had a time-limited lease on life, or because oceanography is an important subject, or because an appropriations hearing lay around the corner—or did all these factors have a bearing on the results?[1]

With the advantage of insights from first-hand operation and a decade of an objective and scholarly approach to policy planning and design, the following criteria seemed to be paramount:

1) The legislative mandate for the social management of marine technology was clear, unambiguous, and relevant.

2) The Congress during this interval continued to shepherd implementation of its legislation and was a comfortable partner with the Council in achieving its goals through legitimate channels of direct communication with members of Congress between the Council chairman and Council secretary.

3) The staff machinery to energize the operation, albeit small, was highly effective, not only because of its expertise and imagination in developing initiatives to the President, but also because of its sophistication in understanding how the government works and how important were the network of communications within the bureaucracy and to outsiders, any of whom could, and some did, attempt to sabotage its efforts.

4) Lastly, however, and perhaps most important, is the recognition that must be given to the devotion, the talent, and the enthusiasm of the first Council chairman, Vice President Hubert H. Humphrey. The fact that he was designated chairman of the Council showed clear legislative foresight in that he is the only officer in the government, aside from the President himself, who can preside over multiagency activities and seek a unity in purpose and in tactics that otherwise is usually left to the individual missions and whims of the separate agencies. Moreover, he was willing to turn the matter of coordination into a viable task. He was, indeed, an "Assistant President."

For many years scholars have derided the processes of coordination. Said one observer, "Interagency committees, as a general institutional class, have no admirers and few defenders." Former Secretary of Defense Robert Lovett said that "such committees blanket the executive branch so as to give it embalmed atmosphere. Committees composed of rather lonely, melancholy men, who have been assigned a responsibility but not authority to make decisions, tend to seek their own kind. They thereupon coagulate into a sort of glutinous mass." Others have condemned committees as "organs of bureaucratic espionage." Nevertheless, in an environment of departmentalism, coordinating bodies must operate to gain consensus through mediation and persuasion rather than executive fiat. The Vice President clearly had the will, the stamina, and the competence to stimulate a sense of community and suppress parochial interests and to be assisted in this approach by a systemic rather than sectoral approach.[2]

Footnotes

1. U.S. Congress, House, *Presidential Advisory Committees, Hearings* before the Committee on Government Operations, 91st Congress, 2nd Sess., March 1970.

2. More details can be found in Edward Wenk, Jr., *The Politics of the Ocean* (Seattle: University of Washington Press, 1972).

Editorial Note: John R. Provan describes the almost inadvertent application of the trust fund concept to Federal highway funding in 1956, the growth in annual financing through the fund, the pressure to share funds for other transportation purposes such as transit, the development of opposition to the trust fund concept, and the final victory of trust fund advocates although the funding objectives were broadened and made more flexible. In this process, Provan clearly indicates that senior level bureaucrats often serve two masters, the Executive and the Congress, and have to keep their skirts clean with both. Although turf is very important to Congressional committees and a battle over turf brought the 1955 funding effort to a dead end, the net result in the House was the dominance of the Public Works Committee over the Appropriations Committee in the reality of determining appropriations—the authorization figure by Public Works dictating the appropriation figure in Appropriation Acts. The 1955 administration proposal of a highway corporation with authority to issue bonds for raising revenue was largely ignored by the Congress and highway interest groups, illustrating the limitation on all policy actors of the requirement to obtain a workable compromise. It is also clear that not much detailed thought was given to the administrative aspects of the policy adopted in 1956, witness the different interpretations in the 1970s of the 1956 Byrd Amendment concerning apportionment of authorized funds to projects.

CHAPTER 8

THE HIGHWAY TRUST FUND: ITS BIRTH, GROWTH AND SURVIVAL

John R. Provan

Introduction

About the Author

The invitation to contribute a chapter for this book cited as a theme "the policy decision process in the United States Government through the observations of experienced, senior participants."

I had no trouble fitting the "senior" description, having recently retired after 36 years' service in the Federal Government. As for "experience," I was very fortunate to have served for more than 25 of those years at senior levels in various agencies, usually in direct contact with and in support of political appointees. These assignments included Federal Civil Defense Administration, Second Hoover Commission, Department of Defense, Bureau of the Budget, Veterans Administration, Federal Aviation Agency (later "Administration" in the Department of Transportation) and the Federal Highway Administration (FHWA).

The Policy Decision Process

Reflecting back through those exciting and professionally rewarding years, it was abundantly clear that there is no such thing as "*the* policy decision process" in the United States Government.

Most obvious is the fact that there is a wide range in the levels of policy, from relatively minor bureaucratic interpretations and administrative actions to major United States Government policy decisions pronounced in landmark legislation. An example of the former type was the distribution of Federal aid highway "discretionary" funds (usually impounded "obligation authority") among the states which was executed by my office in FHWA. In election years, policy decisions on the method of distribution and allocation announcements, while administrative and not legislative, could well be made in the White House.

In quieter times (and with smaller amounts) I would make the distribution based on program considerations, keeping my political boss advised. Any heat from the disappointed could then be directed to an "overzealous bureaucrat" rather than to political motivation.

The creation and the survival of the Highway Trust Fund (the latter occurring during my tenure in FHWA) fall at the other end of the spectrum of policy development—major decisions arrived at through the legislative route. Using the highway term "route" is misleading, implying single repetitive paths clearly marked between two points. A better term would be "maze," with only the ultimate passage by Congress and signature by the President being fixed, with the origin and trail actually taken influenced by a multitude of everchanging forces and environments. A further distinction from a wellmarked route is the existence of frequent gaps in the recorded trail that the policy development did follow.

First, let us review briefly the traditional and, in part, constitutional process for enactment of a major piece of legislation. The President submits a message to Congress containing the proposed legislation along with such justification and explanation as is deemed necessary. The report is referred to appropriate committees and an "administration bill" is introduced, usually by a member of the President's party and frequently cited as "by request" (of the President). The Constitution requires that "All bills for raising revenue shall originate in the House of Representatives, but the Senate may propose or concur with amendments as on other bills."[1] Such a money bill would, therefore, be considered first in the House and before the Committee on Ways and Means (or a Subcommittee thereof). The Committee holds hearings on the administration bill and related bills and reports out a "marked up" bill to the full House. Debate and amending takes place on the floor and the House passes its "House Resolution." The Senate Committee (Committee on Finance for money bills, or again, a Subcommittee) holds its hearings on the House Resolution and any companion bills introduced directly in the Senate. The Senate's normal process is basically the same as the House.

After passage in both chambers, House- and Senate-appointed conferees work out differences in the two bills, report back to their respective chambers for (hopefully) acceptance, and final passage. The "enrolled" bill then goes to the President for signature.

So much for rules and tradition. Let us now move on to the birth and survival of the Highway Trust Fund.

Everyone Wants Good Roads

The Clay Committee Report

The "begin here" of the Trust Fund maze was the Clay Committee report,

A Ten-Year National Highway Program: A Report to the President in January of 1955. The report was produced by a President's Advisory Committee chaired by Lucius D. Clay. It made a very strong case for a significant acceleration of the highway construction program and a considerable increase in Federal financial aid. It recommended a one-time authorization in ten annual increments to fund 90 percent (proposed Federal share) of the estimated cost to complete the interstate system (total cost at that time estimated to be $27 billion). It further recommended that the Federal assistance for the remainder of the Federal aid highway program should remain at the then current rate of about $500 million a year (this "constant" grew to over $800 million by passage of the 1956 Act).

We come now to the proposal in the Clay Committee report that is the trail we will follow. The report recommended the establishment of a Federal Government Corporation authorized to issue bonds to finance the recommended Federal aid highway program, including completion of the interstate system under the 10-year authorizations. It avoided recommending dedicated user taxes but did project the gasoline taxes then in effect, plus proposed increases, through the interstate construction period to show that revenues going into the general fund would be roughly equal to the level of highway expenditures recommended in the report. There was the implication that there would be some conscious correlation between user taxes and appropriations for bond principal and interest payments, but no legal "linkage" of dedicated funds.

The process moved traditionally forward. The President, on February 22, 1955, submitted his "Message from the President of the United States Relative to a National Highway Program" along with recommended implementing legislation to both Houses of Congress.[2] In the House, the "administration bill" proposing the corporation (HR 4260) was introduced and referred to the Committee on Public Works on the same day. As will be seen later the misreferral of this money bill (the corporation and tax proposal portions of the bill) was a factor in the ultimate fate of the highway legislation that year.

House Hearings on the Corporation Proposal

Twenty-six days of hearings were held by the Public Works Committee. They did not begin until April 18, 1955, and continued until July 12. We won't try to summarize all of the testimony (over 1300 pages) but the following highlights indicate the tenor and provide a basis for comparison with the situation during the Highway Trust Fund survival fight twenty years later.

As for the witnesses from the Executive Branch, the Secretary of Commerce (Sinclair Weeks with officials from the Bureau of Public Roads) and Secretary of Treasury (George M. Humphrey, described by some as the "strong man" of the administration) put their full weight behind the proposed legislation. The staffs in both Departments provided supportive (as best as can be determined) testimony and "technical support" (sometimes a euphemism for backdoor lobbying). The Bureau of the Budget had some reservations (traditionally against government corporations, trust funds, or similar end runs to the appropriation, general fund, and debt control processes) but sent a "good soldier" letter to the Committee.[3] The Committee Chairman had specifically asked for Bureau of the Budget comments. An Assistant Director replied:

> In his highway message of February 22, 1955 to the Congress, the President emphasized that the Federal Government should give top priority to completion of the National System of Interstate Highways. With respect to financing he recommended planned use of increasing revenues from present gas and diesel oil taxes, augmented in limited instances by tolls.

> Since the above principles are embodied in HR 4260 and 4261, I am authorized to advise you that enactment of either bill would be in accord with the program of the President.[3]

Some support, since it merely says the President is asking for what the President wants! They had, however, won an important issue in the trenches with the Clay Committee and the President—no "dedicated revenues."

The testimony of interest groups who appeared before the House Public Works Committee confirmed Secretary Humphrey's observation that "everyone wants good roads—more and better roads."[4] There were a few who wanted the Federal Government out of or severely limited in the highway construction and highway standards business such as the Private Truck Council and the American Farm Bureau Federation. Obviously, both these organizations were very strongly in favor of improved roads with government support, but were concerned about the intrusion of the Federal Government into such things as land acquisition for highways via eminent domain, regulation of truck design and weights, "excessive" fuel taxes on trucks and farm vehicles, and redistribution of revenues among the states. They evidenced more confidence, comfort (and control?) in dealing with the state governments. The Association of American Railroads stated "there is no question in our minds about the need for good roads. Our concern is with sources and methods of their financing. As the essential guiding principle, highways should be financed on the basis of adequate and properly scaled user charges, so as not to disrupt the functioning of the Nation's entire system of transportation."[5] Even the Wilderness Society witness assured the Committee that "we of the

Wilderness Society and our cooperators in the many other conservatory organizations and agencies are in no sense in opposition to the development of adequate roads in the United States."[6] His reservation was that "within the areas. . .zoned for preservation we seek. . .protection." The American Transit Association's statement dealt entirely with discrimination between the railroad and transit in Federal reimbursement for removal or relocation of railroad facilities required by highway construction, but not of transit facilities.

The dark cloud in this sunny sky appeared not over the need for highways, but over our primary focus, the method of financing. On May 17, 1955, the Comptroller General, Joseph Campbell, appeared before the Committee. His testimony and the questions and answers that followed took less than 15 minutes, but his opposition was loud and clear. The corporation proposal has "the effect of obscuring the financial facts of the Government's debt position" and "Congress would, to some degree, lose its control over the program."[7] As he put it, he had been in the job "only since December" (five months before he appeared), but he was rapidly becoming a power to be reckoned with in Executive/Legislative relationships. He had already testified in opposition to the corporation proposal before the Senate Public Works Committee (his first appearance before Congress since his appointment).

Treasury Secretary Humphrey was not fazed by this position. In fact he stated very frankly before the House Public Works Committee that one of the reasons he favored the corporation proposal was that "it does not interfere with the long term objective of reducing Federal expenditures and reducing general taxes,"[8] a familiar refrain.

Jurisdictional Problem

According to some who participated in the House deliberations, a national policy on an agreed-upon acceleration of the Federal aid highway program was doomed to failure in the first session of this 84th Congress because of the committee jurisdiction fight in the House. As indicated earlier, the entire administration proposal including the corporation and tax portion, clearly a money bill, was referred to the Public Works Committee. It extended the olive branch to the Ways and Means Committee by offering the latter seats at the Public Works Committee hearing with all the rights and procedures of full committee members, *except voting*. At one point, according to an eye witness, representatives of the Ways and Means Committee stood in the doorway of the Public Works hearing room and a shouting match took place over the protocol to be followed. The hearing record, however, was cleaned up nicely. (Committees exercise considerable latitude in editing their transcripts.)

The Chairman of the House Public Works Committee on June 28 introduced a new bill in the House with increased taxes but without the corporation, saying, "While we were holding hearings on that [corporation bill], the Senate took action and disposed of that plan by a majority vote. We knew it was impossible for this committee to go into conference with the Senate [with the corporation proposal]."[9] He set aside two days (July 11 and 12) for the financing section of HR 7072 which provided for increased taxes, and the bill was reported out as HR 7474, a "clean bill" on July 21. Debate was held on July 26 and 27. The administration bill substitute motion was rejected and then HR 7474 itself was soundly defeated. Highway legislation died for the first session of the 84th Congress.

Illustrative of the heat generated by the Committee jurisdictional squabble were the words of Congressman Earl Wilson on the House floor regarding the Public Works Committee:

> . . .they want to grab the power over, and the control over, the biggest public works program that has ever been submitted to this Congress. Now, is the Congress going to delegate to the Public Works Committee the authority to levy taxes, which belongs to the Committee on Ways and Means? Are they going to delegate to this committee the power to appropriate funds, which power belongs to the Committee on Appropriations, and such other power as they will need to usurp from other legislative committees to operate this program? Folks, it is time you stopped, you looked, and you listened.[10]

And they did.

Action in the Senate

What had transpired in the Senate while the House was mired down on jurisdiction? The Subcommittee of Public Roads (under the Committee on Public Works) began hearings on February 21, 1955, well ahead of the House. (So much for rules and tradition.) They already had S 1048 before them, introduced on February 11, which provided for continuation of the traditional Federal aid highway authorizations at levels estimated to be fundable within the then current tax structure.

On the second day of hearings, the administration bill on the corporation was also before the same Committee as S 1160. On March 28, S 1973 which combined the two was introduced and referred to Public Works. Hearings were held in February, March, and April with many of the same witnesses as would later appear before the House Committee, including the Comptroller General with his objections. He had a strong ally in Senator Harry F. Byrd who appeared as a witness before the Public Works Committee. He was Chairman of the Committee on Finance under whose jurisdiction the financing portion of the bill would usually fall, but he did not raise the jurisdictional issue (on the record, although the Public Works Committee action that followed would indicate he had communicated off the record). S 1048 was reported out from the Committee with five year authorizations including a beefed-up interstate program. No additional taxes were proposed. The Committee report stated "we recognize that revenue measures are not within the jurisdiction of the Committee on Public Works. It is hoped that the appropriate congressional committees will give this matter early considera- tion."[11]

The administration bill with the corporation was dropped by the wayside. Floor debate began May 23. The Senate minority leader dutifully proposed substitutions of the administration bill on the floor which were defeated 60 to 31. S 1048 was passed on May 25. The later House debacle made the passage of S 1048 irrelevant. As indicated above, it did result in the House Ways and Means Committee Chairman switch from the corporation proposal to an increase in nondedicated user taxes, which got nowhere.

Relevance of the 1955 Experience

At the close of the First Session of the 84th Congress, nothing remained of Federal aid highway authorizations or financing but a trail of records and legislative debris. The term *trust fund* had not even been used in policy deliberations. The dedication of highway taxes for highway purposes (mechanics undetermined) was discussed but quickly dismissed. In fact, Congressman Hale Boggs (who was on the Ways and Means Committee but sitting in on the Public Works Committee hearings somewhat under protest) stated "I have my doubt about the legality of it."[12]

If our subject is the Highway Trust Fund, what is to be gained from having gone through the 1955 debacle? The principal reason is that the climate for Federal aid to highways in which the Trust Fund proposal emerged and was enacted is more adequately illustrated in the hearings and debate in 1955. Everybody was on board the "more and better roads" bandwagon. They just hadn't figured out how to hitch up the horses, that is, the dollars to pay for them. The record in 1956 added little to this background and, as will be seen, provided practically no substantiation of or reaction to the Trust Fund proposal itself. This provides an interesting comparison to the environment awaiting the Trust Fund as it fought for survival twenty years later. But also of interest to the student of government is what can happen to a major policy proposal submitted to Congress by the Executive Branch, sometime for all the wrong reasons. It was obvious early on that the corporation proposal was going to die. It is easy to surmise, however, that had the finance portion of the administration bill been handled by the House Ways and Means Committee in the traditional manner, a companion tax measure to provide increased revenues would have emerged. These funds probably would have continued to go into the general fund. If this had occurred, who knows when or if the Highway Trust Fund would have ever been created.

Creation of the Highway Trust Fund

Congress Takes the Lead

In the second session everything *in Congress* went "by the book." The House acted first, introducing one highway program bill with authorizations (HR 8836) and one financing bill (HR 9075). Each was referred to the appropriate committee (Public Works and Ways and Means, respectively). The jurisdictional lesson learned in 1955 was clearly in evidence. The trail we follow is HR 9075, which provided for increased taxes estimated to support the level and timing of the companion authorization bill, but still no dedication of taxes to a Trust Fund.

But where were the President's Message and the administration bill? Both bills introduced were the product of committee staffs and individual Congressmen. Technical support had been provided by the bureaucracy, principally in the Departments of Treasury and Commerce (Bureau of Public Roads). Many tables of data and backup information attributed to the two agencies were cited and discussed in committee hearings.

Again the principal administration witnesses were the Secretaries of Treasury and Commerce, with supporting staff. They appeared before the House Ways and Means Committee. This time they took the position of providing technical support to the Committee, carefully avoiding specific endorsement of the tax rates or the balance among the various taxes in the Congressionally drafted bills. Treasury Secretary Humphrey stated "As I understand it, the President's program is dead [and now] I'm definitely in favor of the pay-as-you-spend program."[13] Secretary Weeks similarly endorsed the principle of pay-as-you-spend and also avoided endorsement of any specifics in HR 9075.

The Trust Fund Emerges

It is during Secretary Humphrey's testimony that the Trust Fund emerges on the record. Following are excerpts from the dialogue that took place between the Secretary and Congressman John W. Byrnes after the latter pressed Humphrey for specific ideas on tying taxes to highway use:

Byrnes: "You would suggest that we can take and dedicate all
           future revenues from present gas tax and present diesel
           tax and then dedicate exclusively to this highway
           purpose also any new taxes raised?"
Humphrey: "That is right."
Byrnes: "Now do you have any procedures to accomplish this
           dedication?"
Humphrey: "I would suggest this, Mr. Byrnes, that we follow a
           practice similar to the practice that is followed for Social
           Security."[14]

So there it is! The Trust Fund concept recommended by the Secretary of
Treasury. He went on to describe in more detail how Treasury could operate
such a Trust Fund, that is, basically as it now does under legislation that
emerged from these hearings. Was this dialogue spontaneous or prearranged?
According to one active participant in the passage of the 1956 highway
legislation, the Trust Fund as an idea whose time had come was broached in
the Secretary of Treasury's limousine, but not by the Secretary. The scuttlebutt
at the time had the Staff Director for the Ways and Means Committee and a
Department of Treasury Assistant Secretary sharing the borrowed limousine
after another frustrating meeting in search of some way of assuring concerned
Congressmen that the Federal aid to highways would not get out of control
and eat into already inadequate general funds. By the time of the hearing, the
idea of using such a fund had been fleshed out to their bosses. The fact that
Congressman Byrnes who triggered the Trust Fund dialogue was from the
President's party (Republican) would add weight to the supposition that, as
frequently is done, the friendly questions were arranged. There are probably
many inside and outside Congress who may lay claim to being the father of the
Highway Trust Fund (assuming it is being looked upon with favor at the time).
In actual fact, the idea of such a fund for financing Federal aid to highways had
surfaced periodically in preceding years. On at least one occasion (1953),
similar bills were introduced by Congressman John C. Kluczynski (HR 3637)
and Senator Warren G. Magnuson (S 216) providing for a Highway Trust
Fund, but they went nowhere. Let us accept, at least for illustrative purposes,
that the successful conception giving birth to this major government policy
took place between two subordinates in a government limousine.

But back on the trail of the Trust Fund. No further discussion or testimony
on this funding concept took place in open hearings except that Mayor Charles
P. Taft from Cincinnati stated several days after Humphrey's testimony that
"The money raised should certainly be placed in a trust fund readily
identifiable, and not mixed up on budget balancing."[15]

Then, on March 19, the Ways and Means Committee's House Report 1899 reported out HR 9075 as revised, citing that "Section 9 establishes a highway trust fund."[16] In *Supplemental Views*, the Republican members of the Ways and Means Committee claimed "We recommended and the committee accepted, the establishment of a highway trust fund." In the interim, intense drafting effort had taken place among House staffs and staffs of agencies in the Executive Branch. The latter were principally in Treasury Department with the highway bureaucracy kept at arms length since the bill was aimed at keeping them reined in. This is interesting to recall when reviewing the survival fight twenty years later when most of those out to kill or severely restrict the Highway Trust Fund saw their mission as reversing a great coup of the highway bureaucracy and its allied highway lobby some twenty years earlier.

The Trust Fund Sails Through Congress

HR 9075, after coming out of the Ways and Means Committee, was referred to the House Public Works Committee who now knew better than to mess around with something rightly the province of Ways and Means. They merely merged it with their authorization bill and on April 21 referred HR 10660, which contained Title I, the Federal-Aid Highway Act of 1956, and Title II, the Highway Revenue Act of 1956, to the House. Floor debate began on April 26 and HR 10660 passed the House on April 27 on a recorded vote of 388 to 19. Quite a difference from 1955. The debate was on such matters as the Davis Bacon Act (labor rates), utility relocation, and which committee gets the required interstate cost estimates. The Trust Fund was not an issue.

The Senate received the House-passed HR 10660 and referred it to its Committee on Public Works for consideration of Title I (old HR 8336). When Public Works reported out the bill (after 10 days and no public hearings), it was then referred to the Committee on Finance for consideration of Title II (old HR 9075 with the Highway Trust Fund). Senator Harry Flood Byrd was Chairman of the Committee on Finance which held two days of hearings on Title II. Practically all of the witnesses directed their comments, objections, and suggestions to the specific taxes from their perspective (truckers, taxicab owners, rubber, air transportation, liquid gas, oil jobbers, etc.). Secretary Humphrey testified on the bill, "heartily endorsing the policy of highway financing contained therein."[17] His principal objection was that the proposed authorizations would produce deficits in the trust fund in later years. He stated "The Amendment I proposed, Senator, is when making an allocation they shall estimate what will be in the fund, and they cannot allocate more for expenditures than the estimated receipts of the fund during the period for which they make the allocation."[18] There was no disagreement on the merits of the Trust Fund concept. The Secretary's proposed amendment was inserted as Section 209(g) of Title II in the Committee mark-up after careful drafting by the Committee and Treasury Department staffs. In reporting out the bill (Senate Report 2054, May 25, 1956) the Senate Finance Committee cited what became known as the Byrd Amendment, saying the proposed amended bill contains a provision which reduces apportionments to the states under the interstate highway system if these apportionments would otherwise have the effect of creating a deficit in the Highway Trust Fund in any year. HR 10660, with its Title I and Title II, was debated on the floor of the Senate May 28 and 29. Actually, Senator Byrd was able to introduce the amendments proposed by his Committee at about midnight the second day. They were agreed to "en bloc" without debate and the bill was passed shortly thereafter. In the conference report, the establishment of the Highway Trust Fund was not at issue and the House receded to the Byrd Amendment. And so the Highway Trust Fund passed both Houses of Congress and became law as the Highway Revenue Act of 1956 on June 29, 1956.

The Birth Was Uncomplicated

The 1956 experience had several interesting aspects. Of course, most striking is the comparative smoothness of the parliamentary processes after the 1955 jurisdictionally plagued and disjointed performance. Also interesting is the complete (official at least) disassociation of the Executive Branch from the legislation as introduced and as eventually passed. Note that Secretary Humphrey and Secretary Weeks made themselves available only for technical support of Congress's efforts. While not a frequent occurrence on major legislative policy developments, the President will call such a signal under various circumstances and motivations. One such circumstance, perhaps this one, is letting Congress take the lead on an alternative after the administration proposal has been defeated. To repeat for emphasis a third point already made earlier, the highway trust fund was created to control, not give a blank check to, the highway interests. One last point is to note how little public debate occurred regarding the principles, problems, and alternatives to a new Federal Government Trust Fund with dedicated user taxes.

The Trust Fund and Highway Program Thrive

Mechanics of the Trust Fund

How does the Highway Trust Fund work? Certain user taxes are designated for highway construction. During debate in 1955/1956, the term used then was *linkage*. While there had been a growing informal linkage of highway-related tax revenues with the authorization and apportionment of highway aid funds, the Highway Revenue Act of 1956 for the first time legally dedicated selected tax revenues for highway purposes. This was the significant policy decision in the Act.

The processes of the resultant Trust Fund are relatively simple. Monies collected are not actually deposited and managed in a separate "pot." The Treasury Department maintains accounting records of the revenues collected through the dedicated taxes. The amount shown on the Trust Fund books as collected but not disbursed for highway purposes becomes a loan to the United States Treasury and "it shall be the duty of the Secretary of Treasury to invest such portion of the Trust Fund as is not, in his judgment, required to meet current withdrawals. Such investments may be made only in interest-bearing obligations of the United States or in obligations guaranteed as to both principal and interest of the United States."[19] The assumption is that the Trust Fund is loaning its balance of funds to the United States Treasury in lieu of Treasury borrowing from the private sector.

The balance of the Trust Fund is reduced only as the Federal Highway Administration (originally the Bureau of Public Roads) draws out funds to pay vouchers for an appropriately related highway program expenditure. The great bulk of these payments is reimbursements to the states for costs already incurred in previously authorized Federal aid highway projects. A policy arrived at many years earlier (with the Post Office Appropriation Act of 1922, 42 Stat 660) had already instituted the practice of "contract authority." It stated that "the Secretary of Agriculture shall act upon projects submitted to him. . .and his approval of any such project shall be deemed a contractual obligation of the Federal Government." The highway program was in the Department of Agriculture at that time. The program committee (Public Works) initiates legislation which authorizes the creation of obligations against the Federal Government by the states without an actual appropriation act. The appropriation, when initiated by the Appropriation Committee, is for liquidating cash to pay the reimbursement vouchers as the states submit their bills. It is when cash is withdrawn to pay the bills under these appropriations that Treasury reduces the Trust Fund account balance. As indicated earlier, this previous usurpation of Appropriation Committee prerogatives added fuel to the jurisdictional fire that sent the 1955 highway legislation down in flames.

The other significant feature of the Trust Fund operation, the limitation on apportioning out the authorizations to avoid a cash deficit in any one year, was described earlier in the development of the Byrd Amendment which became section 209(g) of the Highway Revenue Act of 1956.

Before moving to the mass attack on the policy of funding highway programs through a Trust Fund, a brief review of what happened to and under the Highway Revenue Act of 1956 in the intervening years may be helpful.

The Highway Program Grows in Dollars and Complexity

When the debate began in 1975 over the survival of the Trust Fund, the annual program authorizations (the contract authority) for the interstate system had grown from $1 billion in 1957 to over $3 billion. Other-than-interstate authorizations had grown from intended freeze level of approximately $800 million to $3.5 billion. A significant development regarding the latter was the proliferation of project categories eligible for Trust Fund moneys. A series of "Christmas tree" highway acts during those years had added more than 30 such categories. Opponents of the Trust Fund blamed the increase in total authorizations and the increase in categories on the existence and continuing increase of dedicated monies in the Trust Fund. The Highway supporters responded that "During the past ten years (1965-1975), although the total investment for all highway functions by all levels of government has increased substantially, inflation has eroded the highway dollar so seriously that actual construction activities on highways has decreased."[20]

By 1975, the total estimated cost of the interstate system had increased by $44 billion to almost $90 billion. One third of this was attributed to inflation during the 20-year period and another third to additional mileage (1500 miles), added lanes, and interchanges, along with design upgrading. The bulk of the remaining one third reflects the changing climate in which highway construction was taking place as will be discussed later. (Some highway supporters describe these as extortion costs.) $3.6 billion was identified with "social, economic, and environmental concerns" and $3.8 billion for increased "right-of-way and relocation." Almost $2 billion went for "additional safety elements" and even $125 million for "mass-transit-fringe parking." Of the $44 billion increase, only $257 million was admittedly "project overruns."

The Trust Fund Grows

With respect to the operation of the Trust Fund itself, the changes over the years were relatively minor. Most amendments to the Highway Revenue Act of 1956 dealt with the tax rates and special provisions regarding those rates. The tax on gasoline was raised temporarily from 3 cents to 4 cents in 1960 and continued at that level in subsequent years along with the other 1 cent of temporary gasoline tax which was added at the time the Trust Fund was established. In 1970, the fund itself was extended five years (1972 to 1977) without fanfare in a traditional Federal Aid Highway Act. The Congressional reorganizations discussed later had not yet taken place. The strongmen highway advocates were still in key committee positions, men such as Congressmen George H. Fallon, John C. Kluczynski, Wilbur D. Mills, and Senator Jennings Randolph. Ex-Governor John A. Volpe was Secretary of Transportation and he, rather than President Nixon, made a very low key transmittal to Congress of the traditional administration bill which was silent regarding the Trust Fund. An extension was quietly arranged between highway officials and their friends on the hill.

The health of the Highway Trust Fund was at its peak as the debate began in 1975. Not only had it weathered several financial crises of its own when there were slight deviations (legal) from the pay-as-you build principle, but it was a frequently used tool in support of overall government pump-priming, job-creating, and inflation-fighting policies. While some of these special uses of the Trust Fund required legislation, much of it was accomplished with the imaginative manipulation of us bureaucrats. There was considerable administrative latitude and flexibility in redistributing impounded *obligation authority* (discussed later) and in controlling cash flow.

By the time the renewal issue started to brew in 1975, annual tax revenues exceeded $6 billion, with additional income of over $500 million in interest from the investment of balances in government securities. The Trust Fund balance was approaching $10 billion after nine consecutive years of annual surpluses. At the same time, the fund was obligated to pay over $11 billion to the states for already approved highway projects and had authorized the states to come in with an additional $8 billion worth of projects for a total of almost $20 billion. This $10 billion excess of commitments over the existing balance in the fund was perfectly legal, but became a major issue during the renewal debate. Since it was to become such an issue, it might be helpful to review and clarify two provisions in the Highway Revenue Act of 1956.

A Better Understanding of the Byrd Amendment

Section 209(b) stated in part:

"(b) Declaration of Policy
It is hereby declared to be the policy of Congress that if it hereafter appears
(1) that the total receipts of the Trust Fund. . .will be less than the total expenditures from such Fund. . .the Congress shall enact legislation in order to bring about a balance of total receipts and total expenditures. . .[21]

This bail-out policy implied appropriations of general funds to cover any deficit. As indicated earlier, concern about this possibility generated Section 209(g), known as the Byrd Amendment. Stated simply, it requires the Secretary of Treasury in consultation with the Secretary of Commerce (now Transportation) to determine whether the amounts which will be available in the Trust Fund will be sufficient to defray the expenditures which will be required to be made from such fund as a result of the apportionment to the states of previously legislated authorizations. If insufficient, the interstate apportionments among the states would be reduced proportionate to the percentage of the fund shortfall. The withheld authorizations would be released when the Secretary of Treasury determines adequate funds will be available in the Trust Fund.

Under Section 209(g), the FHWA staff would obtain an estimate from Treasury of anticipated annual revenues into the Trust Fund. After making various adjustments (such as adding estimated interest income), the FHWA staff would deduct year by year the anticipated cash *outlays* (*not* obligations). The highway expertise in estimating the rate of project approval and of project progress payments was just as critical as the Treasury expertise in estimating revenues for determining the annual Trust Fund balance. It is this year-by-year cash balance which had to be a plus or the Byrd Amendment withholding mechanism took over.

As the renewal debate unfolded, it became apparent that major misunderstandings existed regarding the real meaning of this little dance between the Treasury and FHWA staffs before each interstate apportionment. For one thing, the surpluses in the fund were looked upon by many as a juicy melon to be plucked and consumed for other more needy and immediate uses. We bureaucrats added obligations (projects approved) and then total commitments (by including unobligated funds apportioned to the states) to all Trust Fund tables as a way of saying hands off. But the more serious misunderstanding was the belief that the provisions of the Highway Revenue Act of 1956 quoted above meant that funds being apportioned in any year were adequately covered by the Trust Fund balance and additional revenues *that year.* In actual fact, what the Treasury certification meant was that when the payments came due on the interstate apportionments about to be made, there would be adequate funds to pay these bills along with all of the previously apportioned and authorized funds, and that in any one year during this payout period, the total *bills* would not exceed available funds *that year.* The payout curves used to estimate the rate of cash withdrawals show about 80 percent of project costs being reimbursed over a two-year period, with the balance spread over another six years. As will be seen later in the debate, critical to this certification was the life expectancy of the Trust Fund and its revenue-generating taxes.

Another Bit of "Technical" Confusion

The Trust Fund was due to expire on September 30, 1977, under the Highway Revenue Act (as amended in 1970). Section 209(f) of the Act stated: "Amounts in the Trust Fund shall be available, as provided by appropriation Acts, for making expenditures after June 30, 1956 and before October 1, 1977, to meet those obligations of the United States heretofore or hereafter incurred. . .which are attributable to Federal-aid highways."[22]

This raised a very interesting question which was never answered during the debate on the Trust Fund renewal. Did the language in the Highway Revenue Act of 1956 quoted above prohibit *any* further payments from the Trust Fund after September 30, 1977, even though there would be a cash balance of over $10 million and obligations to pay the states of over $12 billion as already approved highway projects progressed? This technical question, while never specifically answered, provided momentum for at least some type of Trust Fund extension. We bureaucrats held to the literal language of the Act in the face of Congressional assurances that it was not the intent of the Act to stop payments on obligations already created.

These types of policy issues over legislative intent occur much more frequently than the public is aware. Sometimes it is due to simple drafting or printing error. Sometimes it is the result of legislative haste and inadequate background record of hearings, reports, or floor debate. Sometimes it is *deliberate* (usually not admitted publicly). It is usually the deliberate ones which give bureaucrats the worst headaches. They normally are the product of a compromise open to interpretations favorable to both sides, or a sneak play by legislators who know that the language literally means something they could not get through if it were generally understood. In either event, the bureaucrat is usually placed in a no-win situation when he begins to administer the legislation.

Impoundment and Obligation Authority

A series of events in early 1975 placed a spotlight on the pent-up demand already existing against the cash balance and anticipated revenues within the existing life of the Trust Fund. The events involved the terms *impoundment* and *obligation authority* used elsewhere in this chapter and added considerable heat to the Trust Fund battle.

As early as 1966 under President Johnson, the Executive Branch began withholding project approval (obligations) even though the authorizations had been apportioned or allocated according to law and represented contract authority immediately available to the states for obligation. At first these impoundments were an across-the-board percentage, but gradually the withholding and releases of *obligation authority* became more varied and sophisticated. In fact, the result was that the administration of highway program priorities and highway construction scheduling (usually for other than highway objectives) grew to be *entirely outside the legislative process.*

That it went on so long without serious challenge by Congress or the states is surprising. By 1973, however, the states were in the courts suing for the release of funds. My staff was heavily engaged in preparing affidavits of fund releases and withholdings and were even called to testify in courts around the country. Things became even more worrisome when individual states began winning their suits. We were having to figure out how to release their funds and still keep overall obligations within national control totals, all without any solid legislative authority.

Congress finally reacted to the entire business of impoundment (in many programs in addition to highways) in budget reform legislation in 1974.[23] The President had to advise both houses of all intended deferrals (impoundments). If either house rejected the impoundment, the funds had to be released. On April 24, 1975, the Senate passed Senate Resolution 69 disapproving the fiscal year 1975 deferrals. Before the door was closed, the states submitted—and their counterpart FHWA Division Offices in each state approved—projects totalling over $3 billion dollars, or almost a year's effort in two months. The concern and distrust this flood generated in the Executive Branch and in Congress placed the upcoming highway authorizations and trust fund renewal in an even more precarious environment.

And The Opposition Grows

Among Interest Groups and their Government Counterparts

The success of the Highway Trust Fund and the Federal aid to highways that it nurtured proved to be its own worst enemy. By the time the 1975 renewal struggle began, a betting man would have thought twice about wagering that the Trust Fund would survive.

First, there was now a large alignment of private interest groups in opposition to or in competition with the highway program and its Trust Fund. Some were new since 1956 and some had previously favored an accelerated program. Their motivations and objectives were varied, but their cumulative heat was awesome. The environmentalists and civil rights activists saw concrete covering the landscape and uprooting the downtrodden. The energy crisis was upon us and the chief culprits were the Arabs and the highway lobby. Transit and railroads had seen the highways steal their passengers and freight and wanted to recapture or attain their rightful role in transportation.

The slaughter on the highways was no longer an acceptable cost for personal transportation. Big government, and specifically the growth of the Federal Government, especially through grant programs such as the burgeoning highway authorizations, were subject to ever-increasing attacks.

Second, these changes had been reflected in the government structure where the initial moves would come regarding the future of the Highway Trust Fund. At the national level, the powerful Bureau of Public Roads had been submerged into a Federal Highway Administration which in turn was part of the Department of Transportation in competition with all its sister modes. Inside and outside the Department of Transportation, Federal entities had sprung up as advocates (or at least representative) of the energy, civil rights, environment, safety, transit, and related outside interest groups. Similar changes had taken place at the state level, leaving considerable question whether the all-powerful American Association of State Highway Officials (AASHO), with its partner, the Bureau of Public Roads, had survived as an effective lobby organization. Trying to keep pace with the changing times, the former had become AASHTO in 1973 by adding *and Transportation* to its title since many of its members also had been submerged in state transportation departments. Even at the local level, the large cities had become major forces in the policy brokerage on national legislation, suspicious of, if not outright hostile to, the cozy Federal/state control and influence over metropolitan transportation through the Highway Trust Fund.

Congress Changes

The situation in Congress had also changed drastically in those twenty years. Committee structure, membership, and jurisdiction had somewhat mirrored the changes discussed above. In the House, the Committee on *Public Works* was now *Public Works and Transportation*, with a Subcommittee on Transportation instead of Roads. In the Senate, the Roads Subcommittee had already changed to Surface Transportation and then to just plain Transportation and the Committee on *Public Works* became *Environment and Public Works* during the renewal battle. While committee and subcommittee chairmen were still those "friendly" (as distinguished from "strongmen highway advocates") to the Federal aid highway program, powerful supporters of other interest groups were now members of the committees with active personal staffs as well as eyes and ears on the committee staffs.

In addition to the realignment of highway/antihighway forces, another significant Congressional change had taken place in the fiscal structure arena where the Highway Trust Fund would ultimately live or die. The budget reform legislation of 1974 had been enacted.[24] This created a Committee on

Budget in both the House and Senate as well as a large and strong Congressional Budget Office to provide budget staff support independent of the Executive Branch. In addition, the Act set up an entire new process and schedule for a unified budget under which the Ways and Means, Finance, Appropriations, and Program Committees would operate within each fiscal year cycle. The Budget Act not only established a structure, process, and philosophy that made the Trust Fund an anathema, but also the Appropriations, Ways and Means, and Finance Committees were now even more agressive to protect or recapture turf to offset losses to the new Budget committees and processes. The Trust Fund, dedicated taxes, and contract authority were obvious targets.

During the passage of the Budget Reform Act in 1974, the Highway Trust Fund was quietly rescued from a premature death by friends who cooperated in drafting a section [401(d)(1)] which stated simply, any trust fund receiving 90 percent of its support from user taxes was exempt from the controls.[25]

This provision produced another interesting bureaucratic interpretation in recent years. As interest rates rose, the percentage of receipts in the Highway Trust Fund from interest approached and by 1979 exceeded 10 percent of the receipts that year. An informal (and unchallenged) administrative interpretation was made that "90 percent or more of the receipts" were from user taxes *over the life of the Trust Fund.*

Concessions Had Already Been Made

This is not to say that all of these forces quietly gathered their strength for one concerted attack on the Trust Fund. They made their voices heard in increasing volume during consideration of highway legislation in the intervening twenty years. Furthermore, they had extracted changes in the Highway Act sections but not in the Highway Revenue Act sections of successive laws. As early as 1966 specific authorizations were included for a safety program. In that same year the Department of Transportation was created for modal balance. By 1969, the environmentalists had their Environmental Protection Agency and subsequent highway acts incorporated specific requirements and sanctions on environmental matters. Special civil rights provisions appeared, both with respect to state and contractor employment and to the impact of highway development on minority and disadvantaged populations. "Decent, safe and sanitary" replacement housing became a must, with generous relocation allowances. By 1970, the Highway Trust Fund was providing two-thirds of the safety funds and such public transit support as bus lanes, fringe parking, and other non-rail highway aids. By 1973, "Urban System" highway funds could be used for transit projects (out of the Trust Fund beginning in 1976) and mass transit projects could be substituted for urban segments of the interstate (using interstate authorized funds, but needing general fund appropriations to pay the bills). Separate authorizations for mass transit had already been initiated and general funded. By 1973, the Federal-Aid Highway Act (PL 93-87, 93rd Congress, August 13, 1973) included section titles such as:

Noise Level Standards
Training Programs [minorities and women]
Public Transportation
Economic Growth Center Development Highways
Bicycle Transportation and Pedestrian Walkways
Development of a National Scenic and Recreational Highway
Metro Accessibility to the Handicapped
Environmental Impact Statements
Highway Litter Study
Prohibition of Discrimination on the Basis of Sex

Highway supporters lumped all of these tacked-on provisions as initiating social legislation through the highway acts and saw the primary job still that of building good, efficient highways.

The Fight for Survival

The Administration Prepares

While there was already jockeying and maneuvering behind the scenes, the open battle began as the First Session of the Ninetieth Congress convened in January of 1975.

Gerald Ford was President at the beginning of the struggle. He had been a strong supporter of the Highway Trust Fund (as will be seen, his words of support were thrown back at his Secretary of Transportation in House hearings while the latter was advocating its immediate curtailment and eventual elimination). The Federal Highway Administration was also led by two strong highway supporters, a former governor as Administrator and a former state highway director as his Deputy. It was difficult to find supporters elsewhere in the administration at the Secretary of Transportation level, the Office of Management and Budget, Treasury, or White House. Some (such as fellow "modal" Administrations within Transportation) were rather schizophrenic. They saw the elimination of the Highway Trust Fund as a way of breaking up the all-powerful highway forces; on the other hand, it would be nice if they could share in its revenues.

In the early stages of policy development within the Executive Branch, the complete abolishment of the Trust Fund held sway. Counseling by the Highway Administrator that the early proposals were unrealistic and unwise was interpreted by the more zealous highway opponents as indicative that he was a captive of the highway lobby and should be kept at arms length. On the other hand, the administration had to rely heavily on the technical expertise and the fiscal data and processes of the highway bureaucracy to develop and support whatever transportation legislation the administration would eventually submit. This put us bureaucrats who were responsible for preparing the required data and legislative language in a rather uncomfortable position, especially since, as will be seen, we were also providing (on request) technical support to Congressional staffs.

The pulling and tugging within the administration continued well into calendar year 1975. The delay was not because of any struggle between pro-vs. antihighway or pro-vs. antitrust fund since the highway types had to tread softly with any advocacy or even advice. Rather, the drafting and redrafting represented attempts at getting the most palliative pill for Congress to swallow. The patience of Congress began to wear thin and threats were made to begin hearings in the House Committees with their own bills. Finally the traditional President's Message and recommended legislation were sent to the Hill on July 8, 1975.

The administration bill as finally submitted reduced the gasoline tax going into the Trust Fund from four cents to one cent and restricted the use of the fund to interstate projects. Two cents would continue to be collected, but deposited in the general fund. The fourth cent would also continue to be collected in each state unless or until that state raised its own gasoline tax by one cent. Authorizations other than interstate would continue to be made with two major changes. First, there would be a consolidation of most of the highway assistance categories into three, with increased flexibility among transportation modes (reflected in new titles such as Urban Transportation Assistance Program). The second major change was that, while the use of contract authority would continue, payments would be made from *general fund* appropriations (the end of dedicated taxes).

President Ford's message which accompanied the proposed legislation stated:

> This Highway Program is a classic example of a Federal program that has expanded over the years into areas of State and local responsibility, distorting the priorities of those governments.
>
> This is consistent with my general philosophy that we should not, at the Federal level, extend our influence into areas which other levels of government can handle better.[26]

Generating Media Hype

Meanwhile the administration orchestrated support for its position and the proposed legislation through press releases and briefing sessions for (mostly favorable) members of Congress, their staffs, private groups, and members of the press. Significant effort was put forth on the last group since there was considerable support among editorial writers and columnists in the general press for the elimination of the Trust Fund and curtailment of the Federal highway programs. Breakfasts, luncheons, etc., were held with the more influential (and favorable) of these, for which the career staff would prepare background facts and figures. The "spontaneous" editorials and columns this produced would, as appropriate, be quoted or printed in hearing records and the *Congressional Record*. Those supporting the highway program status quo (or better) had a little more difficult time finding a national forum, but concentrated more on articles and editorials in more specialized (and supportive) journals and in regional newspapers where highways were still looked upon with favor. They too were quoted, as appropriate, in the printed record. Of course, the highway bureaucracy could only support the administration bill, but many of the facts and figures used in the counterattack were obtained from FHWA, already published or made available under freedom of information rules.

The House Gets to Work Early

To the Federal aid highway advocates, the trust fund crisis would come well before the September 30, 1977, termination date. No sooner had the (approximately) biennial highway authorization bill for 1973 passed on August 13, 1973, than work started on the 1976 authorizations. The committee staffs in Congress began working with agency staffs (Treasury and Transportation) on alternate program levels and revenue projections. On December 11, 1974, the last of the noninterstate authorizations (1976) were apportioned among the states along with the 1976 interstate authorizations. Responding to committee staff requests, we submitted a series of tables and analyses that showed among other things, that the Trust Fund would have to be extended in the next biennial act or the major portion of 1977 interstate authorizations already enacted would have to be held back under the Byrd Amendment. They knew the battle lay ahead. Copies of this analysis went to the Office of the Secretary of Transportation.

The administration bill was referred to both the Ways and Means Committee and the Public Works and Transportation Committee. By the time it arrived on the hill, the impatient highway supporters in the House had introduced (on June 25) a House bill (HR 8235). The introducers were no less than the Chairman (James J. Howard) and the ranking minority member (Bud Shuster) of the Subcommittee on Surface Transportation. This bill is printed on the first pages of the record of the hearings that began July 9, followed by the administration bill (HR 8430) introduced by request by the Chairman and ranking minority member of the parent Committee on Public Works and Transportation. The House-drafted bill contained more and better highway authorizations and continued the Highway Trust Fund to support them. Most of the data on which the bill was based and considerable technical support in drafting the language of the bill were provided by the Federal Highway Administration. The Public Works Committee staffs working on the bill were very knowledgeable about the Federal aid highway program and the operation of the Trust Fund. Fortunately, this permitted them to ask very specific questions to which we could provide the specific answers needed during the drafting. Thus we were able, in the main, both on and off the record, to avoid playing any advocacy role. Committee staffs' understanding of our position was evident in their careful communications, albeit some with humorous tongue-in-cheek. Copies of on-the-record material were dutifully supplied to the Office of the Secretary of Transportation along with the Committee staffs' questions. This did give the administration drafters some ideas about the direction in which the Committee was going, but there were the obvious suspicions and concerns about possible nondocumented exchanges.

As indicated, the House Subcommittee on Surface Transportation began hearings on July 9, 1975, just a day after the administration bill arrived. Twenty-one days of hearings were held producing almost 2,000 pages of records. Chairman Howard made introductory remarks that showed no bias. He stated:

> The hearings of this subcommittee, beginning today, are expected to produce the most comprehensive and complete body of information yet assembled on the subject of transportation in this country.
>
> The hearings will cover all elements of surface transportation under this subcommittee's jurisdiction.
>
> The highway program will be a prime focus on the hearings since this is a normal year for biennial highway legislation.[27]

Congressman Shuster, the ranking minority member of the Subcommittee was a little more biased in his opening remarks, including the statement that "If the faceless, nameless bureaucrats who devised the administration's proposal simply wiped out the Trust Fund and returned the gas tax money to the people, at least that would be honorable. However, to take the gas tax out of the pockets of people who depend on the highways without assuring them that the money will be spent on their roads is unfair, if not duplicitous."[28]

He then quoted "Congressman" Gerald R. Ford as saying just "two years ago on April 19, 1973":

> I believe the integrity of the Trust Fund must be preserved without question. This was the intent of Congress and the Chief Executive in framing the Federal Aid Highway Legislation of 1956 and subsequent acts. In my opinion to divert highway use tax revenues to purposes other than the provision of highways would abrogate a longstanding moral commitment as well as a statutory provision.[29]

Having identified the culprits, the "faceless, nameless bureaucrats" who changed the position of a President, the hearings proceeded. The first witnesses (by design or by calendar coincidence?) were representatives of three of the strongest highway interest groups. They were the American Association of State Highway and Transportation Officials (AASHTO), the American Road Builders Association (ARBA) and the Associated General Contractors (AGC). Needless to say, they were not supporters of the administration bill. The changing character of the Committee membership discussed earlier is illustrated by the challenging questions addressed to these witnesses by Congresswoman Bella S. Abzug. In 1956, a member with her interests and perspective wouldn't even have bothered getting on the old Public Works Committee.

Testimony regarding the Highway Trust Fund ranged from "bigger and better" from the first witnesses to the Sierra Club's statement that "the Highway Trust Fund has outlived its usefulness, and it should be terminated." There was considerable support for continuing the Trust Fund with a one cent gasoline tax until the interstate system was completed, but disagreement about what to do with the other three cents.

On the seventh day of the hearings, Secretary of Transportation William T. Coleman appeared to testify along with other department staff, including several from the Federal Highway Administration. He stated:

> We want to reduce the direct and restrictive linkage between highway tax revenues and highway program levels. In the past, this linkage has forced the program in some years to funding levels higher than we think desirable.[30]

Practically the entire two days of questioning by the Public Works Committee members related to the operation of the Trust Fund even though this was more appropriately the province of the Ways and Means Committee.

The line of questioning indicated strong support among the members for continuation of the Trust Fund with dedicated taxes at current levels. Toward the close of Secretary Coleman's appearance, Congressman Shuster quoted "Congressman" Gerald Ford's support of the Trust Fund two years earlier. The Secretary's response was that "What we ought to admire is that political leaders, whether they be in the executive or in the Congress, have at times gotten more facts, seen different interests, and changed their opinions."[31]

The hearings continued through September, with an August break for vacations. Much of the remaining testimony dealt with other than Trust Fund matters. As the Chairman promised, the hearings covered "all elements of surface transportation" under his Committee's jurisdiction with "the highway program being the prime focus." The pro-highway forces were using the pressure of states running out of Federal aid funds to get through a regular biennial highway bill along with the all-essential extension of the Trust Fund so the apportionments could be made under the Byrd Amendment. The Committee staff approached us highway bureaucrats for data to support this pressure. We could and did provide unobligated balances by state and by category, but would have had to go to the states to get their estimated rate of project submittals which would obligate those balances. While we could justify this for projecting workload, cash requirements, and various other planning purposes, the timing would be very obvious to the administration. As indicated earlier, our sensitive position was understood by the Committee and the estimates to go along with the unobligated balances were obtained through AASHTO which formally submitted them to the Committee.

The House Public Works Committee on December 11, 1975, reported out HR 8235, which carried the number of the bill introduced in June by Congressmen Howard and Shuster. By now it had become a typical biennial highway act including the usual "Christmas tree" special sections which, needless to say, made chances of ultimate passage somewhat better since more Congressmen had a stake in its passage. Titles I and II dealt with program matters and that portion of the report was written by the Public Works Committee. The Ways and Means Committee authored Title III of the bill extending the Highway Trust Fund two years and the related part of the report. No hearings or public record exists of the Ways and Means Committee deliberations. Their part of the report states:

It is clear that if the current construction and safety programs of the States are not to be interrupted, a decision needs to be made expeditiously as to whether the Highway Trust Fund is to be extended beyond the 1977 date. However, since there has not yet been an opportunity to study and reach conclusions as to modifications which are sought, the Committee on Ways and Means believes that only a temporary extension of short duration should be provided for the fund..[32]

The Committee acknowledged that "many would like to have substantial modifications made in the Trust Fund."[33]

Floor debate was held on December 18 and the bill passed 410 to 7. There was considerable discussion of the Trust Fund operations as well as of the size of the proposed authorizations compared to the anticipated Trust Fund revenues. Title III (containing the Trust Fund extension) was not open to amendment, however, under a House Resolution previously approved to avoid rules challenges under the new budget reform procedures.

The Senate Doesn't Wait

While the House had impatiently marked time and pushed the administration for an administration bill until June, the opening guns were fired in the Senate early in the First Session. Senator Robert T. Stafford, a member of the Public Works Committee (and a member of the President's party), introduced on February 19 a traditional authorization bill (S 752) and a bill to extend (for interstate only) the Highway Trust Fund three years (S 753). Then on March 21, Senators Kennedy and Weicker introduced S 1300 which, in addition to drastic changes in the highway program itself, would have abolished the Trust Fund. In remarks by the two Senators, the Trust Fund is blamed for "the air we choke on," the "heart of the problem which we have for our rail system," and denying the "right to mobility of the young, the elderly and the poor." Senator Weicker states "the concept of a trust fund has outlived its usefulness." Senator Kennedy states "We must abolish it at a single stroke."[34]

The Transportation Subcommittee of the Senate Public Works Committee also held comprehensive hearings on all aspects of surface transportation. Senators Baker and Stafford, ranking minority members of the Committee and Subcommittee respectively, introduced the administration bill by request as S 2078 on July 10. The regular hearings began July 14 with Secretary Coleman and Department of Transportation officials appearing on July 17. Chairman Bentsen stated "I would be less than candid if I did not express my distress that the administration, which has been severely criticizing Congress for the absence of an energy policy, failed to submit its highway legislation until a few short days ago."[35] The Committee completed its eight days of Washington, D.C., hearings by July 31. On November 20, 1975, the Public Works Committee reported out a highway bill, S 2711, as comprehensive as House bill 8235, but with many significant differences. There was no provision for extending the Trust Fund. But on December 2 a separate bill to do so was introduced by most members of the Senate Public Works Committee as S 2729 and referred to the Finance Committee. It was very similar to Title III of the House Resolution 8235 which was not to be reported out of the House Public Works Committee for another nine days. Obviously, considerable informal negotiations had been taking place among the Public Works, Ways and Means, and Finance Committees of the two Houses. Floor debate on S 2711 was held December 11 and 12, which did not include the Trust Fund. S 2711 passed 86 to 1 on December 11 but was to be "held at the desk pending a message from the House of Representatives relative to highway authorizations." Then, on January 18, the House-passed HR 8235 was "laid before the Senate," its Titles II and III replaced by S 2711. This made Title III on the Trust Fund identical in the House and Senate versions. The bill was then immediately passed by voice vote with no debate regarding the Trust Fund extension.

The Act Finally Passes

The conference on the House and Senate bills proved very difficult (on Titles I and II, but not Title III, being identical) and a conference report did not emerge until April 8 almost three months later. Both Houses passed the conference product on April 13 and the President signed it into law May 5, 1976. The cause of the gap between Congressional passage and Presidential signature illustrates what little things can cause big problems in the legislative (and policy development) processes. When the bill was enrolled and sent to the President, someone forgot to re-attach Title III which extended the Trust Fund two years. This meant some type of floor action in both Houses was required or the Trust Fund would die. We all kept our fingers crossed against some parliamentary block or delay by the Trust Fund opponents. Fortunately, Concurrent Resolution 618 was quickly and quietly passed, which recalled the bill from the President, invalidated the signatures of the President of the Senate and the Speaker of the House, and directed that the bill be properly enrolled for resubmission to the President.

A Two-Year Reprieve

The *apparent* end result of all the public hearings and debate and all the private maneuvering and negotiations in 1975 and 1976 was a two-year extension of the Trust Fund while its ultimate fate was to be studied. In actual fact, the high water mark of the kill-the-Trust-Fund effort had been reached.

It was now obvious that it had no support among the movers and shakers in the House. Even in the Senate, where there was opposition from strong individual Senators, it was obvious that the Trust Fund would not be killed or even significantly weakened in the foreseeable future.

As we have seen, the establishment of the Highway Trust Fund was a casual, low-key, almost accidental event. Its objective was to keep an obviously exploding Federal aid to highways under some control. By 1976, it had become an institution with large and powerful highway supporters able to withstand forces which would have made its creation almost unimaginable. But since this was identified as a temporary two-year extension until the ultimate fate of the Trust Fund would be determined, it would be instructive to look at what happened two years later.

The Flank Attack

A New Administration Takes Over

The Carter Administration took over the Executive Branch in January 1977. Based on its platform, policies, and appointments, the bust-the-trust proponents had reason to expect an even stronger frontal attack on the Trust Fund. Energy conservation, antipollution, antibig-government, and all the other forces to whom dedicated highway revenues were a prime villain were well represented. President Carter appointed Congressman Brock Adams as Secretary of Transportation and he in turn appointed members of his Congressional staffs (personal and committee) to key positions in the Office of the Secretary. A president of a trucking firm became Federal Highway Administrator and a former state highway commissioner became his deputy. Brock Adams had been Chairman of the House Budget Committee that emerged out of the Budget Reform Act discussed earlier. His previous position made him well aware of the survivability of the Trust Fund. In contrast to 1975/76 when the highway types were kept at arms length, it was a surprise to find the first draft of the administration bill prepared by the Federal Highway Administration (FHWA) based on guidance given by the Office of the Secretary of Transportation (OST) and submitted to the Secretary on July 18, 1977. It contained authorizations for two years and extended the Trust Fund two years. The transmittal from FHWA indicated that "should it be desirable to make this a four-year authorization bill, modification can easily be made." This latter was done, but fine tuning went on until the President's Message and the proposed bill was not submitted until January 26, 1978, for the Second Session of the 95th Congress. The Trust Fund change was a simple extension of four years. On the program side, there was renewed effort to consolidate categories and to permit greater flexibility in the use of the funds within categories, including transit-related projects.

House Public Works Writes Its Own Bill with Technical Support

The House Public Works and Transportation Committee had already held 18 days of comprehensive fact-gathering hearings in May and September of 1977. The administration bill was introduced by request on January 26, 1978, as HR 10578 and the Committee then held one final day of hearings on February 1 to receive testimony from the Secretary of Transportation and staff in support of HR 10578. By that time, the Committee was well along in drafting its own bill and the final day was but a courtesy.

Involvement of the bureaucrats during this period was most challenging. It was not long after the 1976 Act passed that the Public Works Committee staff began working on 1978. As the size of their tentative authorization levels grew, they nervously began to ask us for data on the status of the Trust Fund. At first it was historical data on income, disbursements, obligations, and the payout curves (the rate at which progress payments were made after a project was approved by FHWA). This data was a matter of record and was provided directly with no careful recording or information copies or clearance with OST. By November of 1977, the Subcommittee authorization levels were firming up and the Trust Fund inadequacies were looming ever larger. On November 9, I sent a set of tables (on request) to the Committee staff with an accompanying analysis which indicated what authorizations (over and above the continuing interstate authorizations) the Trust Fund would support without going in the red if extended five years and if extended six years. Copies of this technical assistance were distributed to the FHWA front office and the program offices (all having been previously advised and consulted). Copies did not go to OST (at least not formally).

The next major technical assistance package was sent over to the Congress on January 27, 1978. This request was triggered by a report which demonstrated an interesting change since the 1976 renewal fight. In 1976, the same basic Trust Fund data used by all parties came out of Treasury and FHWA. While the assumptions, interpretations, and significance of the data were subject for debate, the bureaucrats' products from those two agencies provided the grist. As the 1978 battle warmed up, it became apparent that the Office of the Secretary of Transportation, the Office of Management and Budget, and the Congressional Budget Office had all taken the historical data and various projection formulae and cranked them into a computer somewhere. They felt completely free (and knowledgeable) to vary them at will. Further, the energy crisis had opened up wide the range of projections for what had been a very stable estimate of Trust Fund revenues. Our January 27 submission to the Committee staff was the result of their receiving a staff draft analysis entitled *Forecasts of Highway Trust Fund Revenues* produced by the Congressional Budget Office and dated December 1977. This time the Committee staff request was for the revenue available for new authorizations using the FHWA revenue estimates versus the Congressional Budget Office estimates "with President Carter's Energy Program" and "without Energy Program." The internal handling of this analysis was the same as the one in November. (Incidentally, the Congressional Budget Office distributed a very excellent background paper later in February entitled *Highway Assistance Programs: An Historical Perspective.*)

Several days before the Subcommittee sent its proposed bill HR 11733, now totalling $11 billion, to the parent Public Works and Transportation Committee, we sent an estimate for the authorizations contained in the bill showing that both a five-year and a six-year extension would support HR 11733. These data were used in requesting the Ways and Means Committee for a Trust Fund extension.

Variations continued to be provided under a series of assumptions regarding authorization levels, revenue levels, and years of Trust Fund extension. While all of these were handled at my level or even by my division chief with information copies within FHWA, we kept "our skirts clean." The requests and assumptions had to be clearly stated by the Committee staff (and repeated in the analysis). My front office (within FHWA) was advised of the request and precleared the response. The front office assumed the responsibility for informing OST as appropriate. OST during this period was naturally suspicious of this continuing exchange since they saw the assumptions and program levels contained in the requests as endangering the administration bill. They varied their control from nothing, to requiring information copies, to insisting that all deliveries be made by an OST staff member. They realized they could not delay or change any very specific response to a very specific request.

Ways and Means Takes Up the Trust Fund

On February 8, 1978, the Committee on Ways and Means heard testimony on Title V of the administration bill which proposed a simple four-year extension of the Trust Fund. Congressmen Howard and Shuster from the Public Works and Transportation Committee, envisioning a much higher authorization bill, urged the Committee to propose additional taxes dedicated to the Trust Fund.

The witness for the Highway Action Coalition testified that,
    . . . we believe the isolation of highway funding occasioned by the
Highway Trust Fund cannot be rationally supported. Congress cannot
and should not avoid its responsibility of weighing highway costs and
benefits by isolating highway financing from competing considerations
and pretending that societal costs will be reimbursed by the highway
user.[36]

On May 24, the Ways and Means Subcommittee on Oversight resumed
hearings on the fate of the Trust Fund. By now, the Public Works Committee
had reported out its bill with four years of Trust Fund authorizations
increasing almost 50 percent to $11 billion a year. Subcommittee Chairman
Gibbons in his opening remarks indicated that the Chairman of Public Works
had asked Ways and Means to extend the Trust Fund *six years* (as we will see,
this was an alternative to a hard-to-sell tax increase).

Enter the Save the Trust Fund Amendment

The furor about the Trust Fund in 1978 centered around the
Conable-Gibbons Amendment. This was introduced by the Chairman of the
Oversight Subcommittee and the ranking minority member of the parent
Ways and Means Committee. As Chairman Gibbons indicated, "I hope no one
will get too wedded to the Conable-Gibbons amendment; it was something
that was dashed off pretty hurriedly by the Department of Transportation and
at the request of Mr. Conable and Mr. Gibbons, and we certainly have no
pride of authorship."[37] The amendment idea actually generated within the
administration. The drafting was done in the Office of the Secretary of
Transportation (with assistance and push by the Office of Management and
Budget) and we in the Federal Highway Administration were asked for
technical assistance and comments on how it could or would be administered.
Among the prime drafters were those who still thought the best Trust Fund
was no trust fund, but recognized the proposed amendment was the best they
could get. With obvious tongue-in-cheek, their drafts submitted to Conable
and Gibbons carried the heading *Save the Trust Fund Amendment*. They
appreciated our compliments on their humor.
    Very simply stated, the Conable-Gibbons Amendment would restrict the
amount that could be apportioned or allocated (discretionary categories) in any
year to the Treasury estimate of the Trust Fund income *that year*, regardless of-
the legislated amounts authorized for that year. If the income was less than the
authorizations, the distribution of all categories of authorizations would be
proportionately reduced. Others had now become aware of what the House
Public Works Committee and FHWA had known all along. The Trust Fund,

even with the Byrd Amendment, could commit funds to be received in future years so long as Treasury and FHWA estimates showed that the cash progress payments would not put the Trust Fund in the red in any one year. And, of course, so long as the life of the Trust Fund went on long enough to cover the last of these progress payments.

The House Public Works Committee had awakened everyone to this fact by (1) being unable to reduce their proposed authorizations from $11 billion, (2) being unable to get a gas tax increase, and (3) using the alternative of extending the Trust Fund two years beyond what would have been normal (from four years to six years).

Congressman Howard, in introducing HR 11733 back in March (without a Revenue Act section) stated for the record that:

> I went down to resounding defeat last year on five cents (gas tax increase) and was told by the Ways and Means Committee this year that any chance for two cents might be very difficult. I find now that a gas tax increase to finance this bill is unnecessary. Instead an alternative proposal for financing will be proposed which merely builds on the longstanding, highly successful structure of the Highway Trust Fund.[38]

His solution was apparent in his request to the Ways and Means Committee cited above by its chairman for a *six* year extension of the Trust Fund based on the data we had provided.

On May 24, 1978, the Subcommittee on Oversight of the House Ways and Means Committee heard joint testimony by top level officials from the Office of Management and Budget (OMB) and the Departments of Transportation and Treasury. Using basically the same data as we had provided the Public Works Committee staff, the Office of the Secretarty of Transportation staff had developed what we warned them were "bogieman" figures. This culminated in the Secretary testifying "The Trust Fund would be flat out of money in 1985. . .we would have unpaid bills out there of $26 billion."[39] This testimony followed a joint statement by Congressmen Howard and Shuster admitting (more accurately) their proposed $11 billion program and six year Trust Fund extension would "bring us in later years to a decision of whether to increase revenues or drop back the size of the program modestly." The OST's exaggerated picture also suffered in comparison with a very excellent, objective presentation by the Congressional Budget Office. While avoiding specific recommendations, it did point out where the Public Works Committee's $11 billion proposed bill did stretch what was normal. At one point, I was escorted by an OST representative to Congressman Conable's office to describe how the system had been operating in the past. It was obvious from his questions that he too was trying to put the $26 billion OST scare figure into some sort of perspective. My answers, while not specific as to numbers, would probably have reduced this by more than two thirds.

The Trust Fund Survives without Major Revision

I attended a series of legislative drafting sessions with the Ways and Means Committee staff during the summer of 1978. The impression we had was that Conable and Gibbons had held up the OST and OMB end long enough. Finally, the drafting dropped the proposed amendment and concentrated on extending the Byrd Amendment withholding to all categories of funds and not just the interstate. This was easy, and on August 10 the Ways and Means Committee sent a proposed Title V: Highway Revenue Act of 1978 to the Public Works and Transportation Committee for inclusion in the Surface Transportation and Assistance Act of 1978. The accompanying transmittal from Chairman Ullman indicated that the Public Works Committee had reduced their proposed authorizations by $1 billion a year and stated that a five-year extension was adequate (our data again). So the proposed Title V contained the revised Byrd Amendment and a five year extension (1979 to 1984). These provisions survived in the final House passage on September 28 and were the same in the Senate bill passed on October 3. They therefore were not at issue during the conference and were in the final 1978 act signed by the President on November 6, 1978.

Observations Regarding 1977-1978

What was the significance of the 1977-1978 episode insofar as the Trust Fund is concerned? Opponents had given up their efforts to abolish it. Instead, they attempted to get the Trust Fund to serve the purpose for which it was established—to be a rein on Federal aid to highways. Proponents of the Conable-Gibbons Amendment saw a dual control by limiting each year's apportionment of new contract authority to the revenues anticipated in that year. First, it would eliminate the opportunity for higher program levels through the practice of obligating future years' Trust Fund revenue. Second, the proponents of the Amendment anticipated the energy crisis would produce less revenue (and therefore even lower program levels) through fuel-efficient cars and reduced mileage.

The interesting parallel story is the example of Congressmen carrying the torch for an administration proposal. The weak introduction by Congressman Gibbons quoted above is not unusual when the move is made as a courtesy and not as an advocate. And it is not unusual to find Congressmen wary of the supportive data and rhetoric being provided by the administration. Nor is it unusual to find the proposal disappear without the Congressional sponsor "breaking his pick." In other words, this is a good example of what can occur.

A fascinating aspect of 1977-1978, from this writer's perspective, is the involvement of the career bureaucrat when the administration and the Program Committee (in this case House Public Works) are poles apart. There is always the suspicion that the interest groups and their bureaucratic associates lobby intensely to get Congressional support for their mutually agreed upon objections. In the 1977-1978 experience, this suspicion was particularly strong in the Carter administration. Normally, the distrust of the bureaucrats lasts about six months, perhaps a year. Then the administration figures out how to harness the bureaucratic horses to run the government. Three years into the Carter administration, the bureaucrats, more often than not, were still identified in speech and action as the enemy, along with the interest groups and Congress. No wonder the administration was in trouble! In the case of the highway legislative development during that period, the role of the "bureaucrats-in-the-middle" described above was a challenge: responsiveness without advocacy.

In Summary

To sum up, the Trust Fund was born without thorough study and public debate. It munificently supported, and critics would say grossly distorted, the highway role in our national transportation system. It has survived about as formidable an array of opponents as can be assembled against a Federal institution or policy. Why did it survive? It would be easy (but controversial) to say that its merits outweighed its demerits. And it would be easy (and totally incorrect) to say the democratic processes produced a majority favorable decision. The opponents would say that the insidious triangle comprising the interest groups, entrenched bureaucrats, and their Congressional cronies prevailed once more against right *and* the majority. My own personal opinion: without judging the merits of its survival, the Highway Trust Fund is but another example of a policy and process that has become so ingrained in the operation of the Federal Government that radical change is about as likely as a convention to rewrite the Constitution. Just as in the latter case, many who for various reasons might like to see the Trust Fund eliminated are uncertain as to whether they will be better or worse off by what would fill the void. I believe the Trust Fund is now subject to evolutionary change, but not death.

What about the participation of the "experienced, senior participants in the policy decision process" involving the birth, growth and survival of the Trust Fund? For one thing, it was very typical. Those most knowledgeable and most valuable in drafting implementable policies and in providing supportive testimony and data are usually the experienced career staffers in the agency involved. When either Congress or the higher echelons of the Executive Branch are having difficulty in furthering their position on a particular major policy issue, these career staffers are frequently suspect, especially to those whose position would have a negative impact on the agency's programs. The assumption is that such staff are motivated inevitably and entirely by self-preservation and/or personal ambition. In the Trust Fund story, the experienced staff were frequently placed in the position of what someone described as "serving two masters"—Congressional committees and Executive Branch policy workers. I would not accept this description. They recognized as their masters the Executive Branch policymakers, but they were obligated to provide technical support to Congress. In fact, to frustrate or subvert Congressional requests for assistance is a sure way of bringing down Congressional wrath on an entire agency, department, or even an entire administration, a type of sabotage in itself. It would be naive to say the FHWA staff were rooting for the administration's moves to eliminate or emasculate the Highway Trust Fund; and it would be untruthful to say that the technical support was absolutely free of gratuitous tidbits. But it would be equally untrue to say that the technical drafting, counseling on feasibility and strategy, and supportive testimony and data for the administration were in any way less than the best or tainted with subversion. Too often the public, Congress and successive administrations of both parties lose sight of the existence and value of experienced career executives who are fully aware of their role as supporters of government policy development and execution, and conscientious and proud in the performance of that role.

Epilogue

On November 30, 1982 President Reagan sent a message to Congress transmitting "A Proposal for Legislation to Authorize Appropriations for the Construction of Certain Highways in Accordance with Title 23 of the United States Code, and for Other Purposes." Not only did it propose that the Highway Trust Fund be retained, but *extended seven years* and made the recipient of *five additional cents* (making a total of nine cents) of taxes or user fees. One cent of the additional taxes would go into a separate Transit Account, so in effect, public transportation would have its own Trust Fund. There is the promise (or warning) of a Federalism turnback. In his transmittal message, President Reagan states "The administration is consulting with the Governors, affected State and local officials, and the Congress on a bill which will implement the appropriate turnback of highway programs and accompanying revenues." Shades of 1976! Only time will tell.

The House Ways and Means Committee held hearings on December 1, 1982, and reported out the Highway Revenue Act of 1982 which extended the Trust Fund only four years, but provided all of the additional taxes. There were only kind and supportive words for dedicated user taxes to support the highway program (and now transit also). The Highway Revenue Act was incorporated into the Surface Transportation Assistance Act of 1982 which was passed by the House on December 6, one week after receipt of the President's message. The Senate passed an amended version on December 21. The conference report was completed and agreed to by the House that same day and by the Senate on December 23. The President made it law on January 6, 1983. During this compressed legislative process, there were many parliamentary cliff hangers generated by issues other than the Trust Fund (such as the increased truck taxes), but that's another story. The Highway Trust Fund, in danger of abolishment under the previous Republican administration, ends up bigger and better with a new neighbor—the transit trust fund.

Footnotes

1. Constitution of the United States, Article I, Section 7.
2. Dwight D. Eisenhower, *Message from the President Relative to a National Highway Program*, House Document 93, 84th Cong., 1st sess., February 22, 1955.
3. U.S. Congress, House Committee on Public Works, *Hearings, National Highway Program, H.R. 4260*, 84th Cong., 1st sess., 1955, p. 51.
4. *Ibid.*, p. 1189.
5. *Ibid.*, p. 977.
6. *Ibid.*, p. 712.
7. *Ibid.*, p. 619.
8. *Ibid.*, p. 576.
9. *Ibid.*, p. 1105.
10. U.S. *Congressional Record*, House, vol. 101, 84th Cong., July 27, 1955, p. 11690.
11. U.S. Congress, Senate Report 350, *Federal-Aid Highway Act of 1955*, 84th Cong., 1st sess., 1955, p. 19.
12. U.S. Congress, House Committee on Public Works, *Hearings, National Highway Program, H.R. 4260*, 84th Cong., 1st sess., 1955, p. 1210.
13. U.S. Congress, House Committee on Ways and Means, *Hearings, Highway Revenue Act of 1956, H.R. 9075*, 84th Cong., 2nd sess., 1956, p. 26.
14. *Ibid.*, p. 25.
15. *Ibid.*, p. 154.
16. U.S. Congress, House Committee on Ways and Means, Report 1899, *Highway Revenue Act of 1956*, 84th Cong., 2d sess., 1956, p. 45.
17. U.S. Congress, Senate Committee on Finance, Hearings, *Highway Revenue Act, H.R. 10660*, 84th Cong., 2d sess., 1956, p. 66.

18. *Ibid.*, p. 77.
19. Public Law 84-627, Federal-Aid Highway Act of 1956, June 29, 1956, Sec. 209(e)(2).
20. U.S. Department of Transportation, *America's Highways - 1776-1976*, (Washington, D.C.: Government Printing Office, 1977), p. 544.
21. Public Law 84-627, Federal-Aid Highway Act of 1956, June 29, 1956, sec. 209(b).
22. *Ibid.*, sec. 209(f).
23. Public Law 93-344, *Congressional Budget and Impoundment Control Act of 1974*, July 12, 1974.
24. *Ibid.*,
25. *Ibid.*, sec. 401(d)(1).
26. Gerald P. Ford, *Message from the President, Federal Highway Act of 1975*, House Document 94-204, July 8, 1975.
27. U.S. Congress, House Subcommittee on Surface Transportation of the Committee on Public Works and Transportation, *Hearings, Surface Transportation,* 94th Cong., 1st sess., 1975, p. 125.
28. *Ibid.*, p. 127.
29. *Ibid.*
30. *Ibid.*, p. 474.
31. *Ibid.*, p. 576.
32. U.S. Congress, House Report 94-716, *Federal-Aid Highway Act of 1975,* 94th Cong., 1st sess., 1975, p. 104.
33. *Ibid.*, p. 103.
34. U.S. *Congressional Record*, Senate, vol. 121, 94th Cong., March 21, 1975, p. 4644.
35. U.S. Congress, Senate Subcommittee on Transportation of the Committee on Public Works, *Hearings, Future of Highway Program*, 94th Cong., 1st sess., 1975. p. 797.
36. U.S. Congress, House Committee on Ways and Means, *Hearings, Administration's Proposed Extension of the Highway Trust Fund*, 95th Cong., 2d sess., 1978, p. 124.
37. U.S. Congress, House Subcommittee on Oversight of the Committee on Ways and Means, *Hearings, Highway Trust Fund*, 95th Cong., 2d sess., 1978, p. 24.
38. U.S. *Congressional Record*, House, vol. 124, March 22, 1978, p. 2352.
39. U.S. Congress, House Subcommittee on Oversight of the Committee on Ways and Means, *Hearings, Highway Trust Fund*, 95th Cong., 2d sess., 1978, p. 44.

Editorial Note: William C. Valdes has skilfully shown how an outstanding and dedicated appointed official can exercise innovative and powerful leadership in setting policy to solve tough administrative problems. To carry out such daring policy, the help of can-do bureaucrats is necessary. The tone of the Defense Department was set by Robert McNamara as Secretary. He took a broad view of the Department's responsibilities and was deeply concerned not only with defense responsibilities per se but also the societal, economic, and human impacts of military policy. Reduction of military bases involved closing facilities and either transferring or dismissing employees. Previous experience has indicated that such closings had the effect of a stone thrown in a pond of water: the rippling effect impacted all parts of the base and the supporting community. The resistance to closing a base was understandable if the individual and community needs were not recognized and met in a satisfactory way. Before announcing his policy, McNamara asked "Can we guarantee every displaced employee a replacement job?" Over 100,000 employees were involved. The dramatic description of the task and results is rewarding, but the significant policy approach of employer responsibility for what happens to individuals and communities as the result of management decisions can have far reaching implications for all governmental and private organizations. Finding some way to get on top of this policy area is essential to the continuance and improvement of the nation's productivity. Valdes points out that change is continuous and resistance to change is persistent. Tough challenges lie ahead!

CHAPTER 9

THE CHALLENGE OF CHANGE

William C. Valdes

There are some kinds of problems which seem to bring out the best, and the worst, in our system of government. In my experience in the Defense Department one of the most striking examples of such problems is the continuing effort to make needed changes in the numbers and types of military bases that support our armed forces. The struggle to adapt and modernize our military base structure has generated both bold and innovative management on the part of the political and career leadership of the Defense Department and sad examples of frustration and political resistance to needed changes. Modern day armed forces are highly technical organizations and as such either stay abreast of continuing technological change or lose their status as a credible military force. Missiles replace aircraft, nuclear-powered ships replace or supplement conventional power, satellites bring new problems and opportunities, and a seemingly unending string of other technological advances force constant revision in the armed forces.

The changes required are not confined to weapon systems themselves. Frequent adjustments are needed in the support structure, including the bases where troops are trained, where equipment is built, repaired and stored, and where research is conducted. Yet the resistance encountered when management seeks to make the needed changes in the base structure is so potent that sometimes it appears a wonder that the country isn't still dotted with cavalry remount stations.

The basic reasons for the potent resistance to changes in installation structure are economic and political, and jobs are at the heart of the problem. Communities with military bases, especially large military bases, become dependent upon them for jobs, both jobs that are directly on the government payroll and those that are generated in the economy by the presence of the base. Congressmen representing districts where a potential base closure is rumored immediately come under great pressure to protect the jobs of their constituents. "Save the shipyard" campaigns and furious jockeying to assure that whatever happens, happens somewhere else, becomes the order of the day. As often as not, pressure from the Congress prevents the management of the Defense Department from accomplishing what it knows needs to be done (and which Congress knows should be done). This resistance, unfortunately, receives some of its support from allies in high places within the Defense Department itself. Interservice rivalries, role disputes, and political or personal ambitions sometimes result in less than wholehearted support of efforts to consolidate, merge, or eliminate service functions and activities.

Unlike some of his predecessors and successors, Robert McNamara did not shy away from the problem of an obsolete and inefficient base structure, nor did he even choose to skirt around the edges. He took it on directly, by initiating realignments and closures that involved more than 900 installations, billions of dollars in cost savings, and over 200,000 civilian and military jobs. The manner in which he tackled the problem constitutes an informative case study in how strong management leadership by a Presidential appointee can produce the responsiveness many automatically claim is lacking in bureaucracies. Bureaucracies are not without their problems, especially large ones, in attempting to respond quickly to directions from above. The cry of "unresponsive bureaucracy" however, is as often a cover for weak and inept leadership by inexperienced or incapable Presidential appointees as it is a valid criticism of the bureaucracy.

Whatever one may conclude about the policies and practices of Secretary of Defense Robert McNamara, the one thing his critics never accused him of was weak leadership or unwillingness to take on problems. He said:

> I see my position here as being that of a leader, not a judge. I'm here to originate and stimulate new ideas and programs, not just to referee arguments and harmonize interests. Using deliberate analysis to force alternative programs to the surface, and then making choices among them is fundamental.[1]

For starters, he usually understood the problem. He recognized that realigning the support structure was not simply a technical exercise in determining, for example, whether the Navy's needs could be met as well with one less shipyard or whether the Air Force could consolidate its repair depots and manage the total maintenance operation more efficiently. He understood that jobs and payrolls were involved and were at the heart of the resistance to change. He understood that he had to get involved in the process of finding ways to ease the impact of realignment and closure decisions on the people and communities affected or those decisions might never be carried out.

Previous secretaries tended to believe that if adjustments within the huge defense establishment had adverse impacts upon jobs and communities, this was not the concern of the Department of Defense. Under the government structure, according to this line of reasoning, job assistance was a concern of the Civil Service Commission and the U.S. Employment Service. The adverse economic impact of closures on communities were problems to be handed over to Commerce, Labor, and the other agencies concerned with managing programs of economic assistance. The Department of Defense, it was argued, had enough to do in organizing and running the defense of the country and it was unwise to get involved in other matters.

This line of thinking did not fit in well with the McNamara style of active leadership, nor did it fit in at all with his philosophy concerning the management of change. That philosophy, reflected repeatedly in his official statements (and actions), was that management could not afford to let the full burden of technological change fall upon the people affected by it. Failure to help ease the burden for those adversely affected, he believed, very well might result in little or no change being accomplished. He was unwilling to accept the assumption that someone else should assume the primary responsibility for a problem generated by Department of Defense management. This philosophy of shared responsibility is succinctly summarized in a prophetic statement he issued in 1965:

> ...obsolescence occurs continuously throughout our economy as technology advances and needs change. Should our major institutions, either public or private, fail to adjust to such changes, we would shortly face the unacceptably low levels of economic growth which today plague so many nations of the world, limiting their power and restricting their freedom.
>
> * * *
>
> It has long been my contention that the burden of major dislocations caused by our dynamic economic growth should not rest solely upon the people immediately involved. Our entire society should help to carry that burden.[2]

Job Guarantee

In accepting this special responsibility for the Defense Department, McNamara learned after an initial skirmish or two that vague talk about providing the people losing their jobs in a base closure or consolidation with "placement assistance" wouldn't satisfy either the people involved or the Congressmen under heavy pressure from their constituents. He asked his staff whether there wasn't some way that when he made his next major base closure announcement, he could temper the shock by also guaranteeing that all of the employees at the bases affected would get another job offer.

When that question hit my desk as Deputy Director, Office of Civilian Personnel Policy, as much as I wanted to respond yes, I had to consider fully what yes really meant and be prepared to back up the decision reached. *Yes* meant that jobs would be promised to over 100,000 people in hundreds of different occupations, from young people, old people, people who were blind and otherwise handicapped, to people with sometimes narrow skills in shipyards, repair depots, offices and some kinds of exclusively military activities. Considering the complexity of this task, it would have been easy to respond that such a guarantee could not be offered and to produce many persuasive reasons why it could not be done. But this is not the way I decided to respond, for very good reasons. Here was a classic opportunity to weld the skills of a strong and able politically appointed manager with those of skilled career professionals to hammer out a solution that would fundamentally change things for the better for thousands of people and their communities.

What was needed was some give-and-take between program demands and personnel management considerations for the ultimate benefit of both. It required an understanding by all involved that advance planning for management actions must include consideration of their effects on people if unnecessary hardships were to be avoided. And this advance planning had to start with the analysis needed to provide a reasoned response to McNamara's question "Can I guarantee them all another job opportunity?" As a first step in this analysis, the bases under consideration for closure or consolidation were reviewed as to the numbers and types of skills in the affected work forces. Anticipated turnover and projected manpower requirements elsewhere in the Defense Department were studied and related to the planned reductions. Based on this analysis, my response to McNamara's question then was phrased in a way that said "Yes, we can deliver on your guarantee provided you are willing to do certain things." These "certain things" included: providing an extended time for phasing out large activities (rather than closing them quickly "to get it over with" as some urged), agreeing to pay the transportation expenses of the people affected to other locations (so that meaningful job offers could be made), and supporting a rule which would require that the displaced employees be given firm priority placement rights to position vacancies for which they were qualified and willing to accept (so that subordinate managers would be required to support the established policy objective).

Clearly, it was a gamble for the Secretary, my bosses, me and the staff. On his part, it required considerable faith in the capability of others to deliver on his personal commitment. On the part of the staff, it required a willingness to undertake some sleepless nights while going down a road never before traveled by anyone in or out of government.

When an official as prominent as the Secretary of Defense, in writing and before the television cameras, guarantees over 100,000 people that they will receive another job offer, his personal integrity is directly involved. Not one of the 100,000 people is likely to forget *that* commitment and go quietly onto the unemployment rolls! With the intense local and national press interest in developments affecting the defense structure and in the effect of base closures on the economies of the hundreds of communities in which they were located, I could be sure that any failure to live up to the guarantee would not escape the public eye.

The job guarantee was incorporated initially in a December 1963 press release and it read as follows:

> Every employee whose job is eliminated will be offered another job opportunity. If the new job requires a move to another government installation, the expenses involved—in the case of career employees and their families—will be borne by the government.[3]

This commitment subsequently was incorporated in a series of additional closure and realignment decision announcements made throughout the next six years. These necessary decisions affected many thousands of jobs in almost the whole range of skills used in the U.S. economy and in locations throughout the country, from isolated rural areas such as Presque Isle, Maine, to inner city locations such as the Brooklyn Naval Shipyard.

Having decided to offer a job guarantee, it was obvious that the existing administrative machinery would have to be revised to cope with placement problems of a size and diversity not previously encountered. It also was clear that no one measure or program could be relied upon to resolve all the difficulties involved in placing over 100,000 employees in different positions throughout the country.

A global plan was developed which included phasing out activities over extended periods of time to make maximum use of attrition and to provide time for "out-placement" processes to work: freezing outside employment in order to stockpile vacancies into which employees at activities being closed or reduced could be reassigned; giving employees longer advance notice of impending actions; establishing a clear system of priority rights to vacancies; creating a placement system which would rapidly and accurately match surplus employees with vacancies occurring anywhere in the many different components of the Department of Defense; creating an improved set of policies for payment of transportation expenses and the expenses of buying and selling homes; creating a system of early retirement and of severance pay for employees choosing not to relocate; and initiating programs of job retraining for employees whose existing skills were not in demand.

Department of Defense
Priority Placement Program

Many of the administrative programs and statutory authorizations needed
to initiate these measures were not in existence and had to be generated from
scratch. Some useful administrative programs, however, did exist and these
provided a base from which to start. Past international crises such as the
Korean conflict required a large scale buildup and subsequent phase-down of
civilian support personnel as well as military personnel. In the process of
coping with these changes, various components of the Department of Defense
had used employment freezes, attrition, and reassignment of surplus personnel
to ease the impact. A number of commands had particularly effective
programs for their employees, but each was pretty much in business for itself.
Since the adverse effect of realignments did not fall equally upon all
components and some had no effective placement programs at all, the
commands could not be relied upon to deliver on a job guarantee. What was
clear to me was needed and didn't exist was a comprehensive program that
reached across the work force of over one million civilian employees located
throughout the Department of Defense agencies.

The sheer size of this huge placement potential virtually guaranteed that
an effort based on conventional methods of passing around job applications
and lists of job vacancies was bound to bog down in a mass of outdated
information and frustration. I decided, therefore, to establish what in effect
was a centralized, computer-assisted job clearinghouse for the entire
Department of Defense in which available people could be rapidly matched
with available jobs. The Department of Defense Priority Placement Program,
as it came to be known, was created to do this job. The concept on which it
was based was fairly simple. All Defense activities with employees facing the
loss of their jobs were required to promptly register them in one central
computer bank and other Department of Defense activities with vacancies
were required to fill those vacancies from this central bank.

Translating the concept into a workable system that would both place
employees and yet not tie up normal employment processes was far from
simple. Little experience existed with anything of this scale in personnel
management, so I decided to draw upon experience which existed in the
supply management field. Computers were being used to match supply
requisitions with the nuts and bolts needed by the armed forces throughout the
world. While people and jobs are inherently more difficult to match and move
than nuts and bolts, at least the concepts are similar.

A Defense Supply Agency activity, the Defense Electronics Supply Center
in Dayton, Ohio, was selected to help design and operate the computerized job

bank. Supply center computer and personnel specialists worked closely with me to develop the Priority Placement Program. An effort was made in its design to keep the system as simple as possible and to minimize the disruptions to ongoing activities that in the past had characterized general employment freezes. It was determined that with some exceptions, hiring would be frozen only in the specific positions at specific installations where qualified displaced employees were registered for placement. This was done by having employees indicate the specific activities or areas to which they were willing to transfer. A computerized list known as a Priority Placement Certificate was then forwarded on a regular cycle to each individual activity listing the job skills of the displaced employees who had registered for placement at their particular base or office. Simultaneously, the organizational unit receiving such a certificate was required to stop hiring for those skills and to use the Centralized Referral Activity as the sole source of applicants. Upon receipt of a Priority Placement Certificate (quickly nicknamed the "stopper list"), the unit submitted a requisition to the Centralized Referral Activity and received a computer printout summarizing the education and experience of available registrants. The unit then selected an employee to fill its vacancy and entered into direct negotiations with the releasing unit for transfer of the employee.

To make this relatively simple procedure work effectively did require development of many detailed policies concerning such matters as registration, zone of referral, order of selection, timing of releases, and the other nitty-gritty details that can make a program work or fail. It was observed early, for example, that hiring activities were often deterred from selecting a person because of the transportation costs involved. To avoid this problem and to gain greater acceptance for the program, it was required that releasing activities budget for these costs and pay the transportation expenses of the employees to the new location. Also, in the interests of the general acceptability of the program, it was stressed that releasing activities register their employees only for skills for which they were fully qualified.

To oversee the operations and to referee disputes over qualifications and other matters, the country was divided into four zones and a Department of Defense Zone Coordinator was appointed in each to serve as the representative of the Secretary of Defense in assuring that the system worked as was intended. Regular reports of progress were furnished to Secretary McNamara by his personal request.

The reception to the Priority Placement Program, as could be expected with any directed placement program, was mixed. Units being closed loved it. Those on the receiving end were less enthusiastic, but gradually accepted the basic concept. It became widely recognized that with the major changes taking place in the Department of Defense, almost anyone could be affected tomorrow. The old feeling that if a person lost his job, it was a sign that he or she was somehow incompetent faded to one of recognition that most of the people being registered for placement were guilty of nothing more than standing on the wrong rock at the wrong time.

The overall placement system not only gained acceptance, it worked. In a December 8, 1965, press release Secretary McNamara took note of this fact:

> I am pleased to report that since our 'guaranteed job opportunity' program was initiated, no career employee has been separated without having received a valid job offer. More than 97% of those who accepted offers are still with the Federal Government.[4]

Local efforts to place employees, undertaken primarily by the activity being closed, remained a key ingredient of the total program. These efforts received reinforcement from the Defense-wide Priority Placement Program because hiring activities were aware that, one way or another, vacancies occurring at their activity would have to be filled first with employees being laid off.

The end result of these combined efforts was that, as promised, not one of the over 100,000 employees involved in base closure or reductions during the period from 1963 through 1969 was separated without another job opportunity.

As Table 9.1 indicates, over the 4½ years when about 127,000 career employees were displaced by base closures and consolidations, almost three quarters continued to work, the largest majority in other jobs in the Department of Defense (66 percent), smaller numbers in other Federal agencies (3.8 percent) and a few thousand were placed in non-Federal jobs through outplacement efforts (2.3 percent). The largest category of employees who didn't continue their careers in other Federal jobs were those who rejected valid job offers and eventually had to be separated (10.2 percent).

In July 1965, McNamara summarized the results as follows:

> Since 1961, the Defense Department has closed or substantially reduced activities at over 700 installations, with an annual saving to our taxpayers of more than $1 billion each year, every year. These monetary savings are impressive in themselves, but the closing of surplus and obsolete military facilities promises an even greater benefit to our nation. Valuable resources which would otherwise remain idle are freed for more productive purposes—property which was tax-consuming becomes tax-producing.[5]

Although it was not considered feasible to continue the absolute guarantee of another job opportunity for everyone indefinitely, the programs put in place

Table 9.1

Department of Defense
Summary of Personnel Actions
Base Closures-Major Reductions
(January 1, 1964-June 1, 1969)[5]

	Number	Percent
Moved to another Department		
of Defense job	84,058	66.0
Placed in another Federal job	4,877	3.8
Placed in a non-Federal job	2,986	2.3
Total placed	91,921	72.1
Retired	12,115	9.5
Resigned	7,314	5.7
Separated due to declination of jobs	13,063	10.2
Other separations	3,123	2.5
Total	127,536	100.0

to assure that displaced employees got priority reassignment rights to vacant positions have been continued to this day, and most employees who are mobile. receive an opportunity to be reassigned to another job.[6]

Experience with the Priority Placement system suggests that it is not self-maintaining. For a directed placement system and related employee-oriented measures to work successfully in an organization, three essential ingredients must be present: firm top management interest and support, continuing emphasis on assuring that employees are referred only to jobs for which they are qualified, and acceptance throughout the organization of the concept that management has a significant degree of responsibility to minimize the adverse impact of its decisions upon career members of the work force.

Retraining

In the base closure announcement of December 8, 1965, Secretary McNamara personally expanded on the usual statement of a job guarantee by adding another statement which reflected a special interest of his own: "We also arrange for retraining at our expense and continue employees' salaries while they are being retrained."[7] Although I knew he had a strong feeling that many of the problems of job dislocation could be resolved through the retraining of workers, I deliberately had not included reference to retraining in the press release and winced when I saw it in the final draft. Not because I was opposed to retraining, and not because we weren't trying to retrain workers, but because this was one aspect of our program that really wasn't working very well.

Despite this special interest of McNamara's which kept popping up to my consternation, retraining never became a major weapon in the total agency program to deal with job dislocation. We issued special guidance on developing such programs, we obtained waivers which permitted employees to be reassigned to positions for training, and we undertook a number of retraining programs.[8] Some were successful, but in practice other measures proved to be more practical and more acceptable to employees. In retrospect, those retraining programs that were successful took place in circumstances where there were readily identifiable target jobs in the immediate geographic area in which the employee could be placed at the end of a limited period of retraining. Those programs that were not very successful were designed to give employees new and more marketable skills which, upon completion of training, would be used in a subsequent job search.

Instances where circumstances were right for retraining occurred most frequently at activities where some functions were being phased out and new ones undertaken. It was possible under these circumstances to plan a retraining program which gave employees the skills they needed in order to be reassigned into the new functions coming into the base. In a few situations, it was also possible to work out retraining programs that placed employees in known positions outside the Department. One military installation, for example, collaborated with a nearby Federal agency to train displaced employees to fill card punch operator positions for which that agency had a continuing need. Problems of timing, however, limited the number of situations in which this could be done. The timing of one function to be phased in and another moved out often was driven necessarily by factors other than staffing.

Retraining was tried, not too successfully, in other circumstances where the objective was to give the employees skills that were more marketable than their present ones. The assumption was that, upon conclusion of retraining, other jobs eventually could be found for them in their newly acquired skill area. A program was established at the Brooklyn Navy Shipyard, for example, to train sheet metal workers in how to work with types of metal other than those they were accustomed to handling in the shipyard environment. Some limited success was achieved with this and other programs of this type, but for several reasons related primarily to the wishes of the employees themselves, the results generally were not worth the effort involved.

Most employees did not want to move into a different occupation if they could find some kind of position which used their present skills, even if the position was at a lower grade. Most also did not want to stay in training programs when they did not know precisely when and where a job which could utilize that new skill would be available. As a result, many would enter a training program but then drop out as soon as a concrete job opportunity became available, even if the job wasn't as wellpaid as the target jobs for which they were in training. One can only surmise from this experience that workers who are established in their occupations feel both uncomfortable with the prospect of change and also pressured to accept a bird in the hand rather than to wait for one to appear in the bush.

Severance Pay

Some workers also preferred to quit or retire rather than move to another location where a job was available. Sometimes such decisions were based on sound economic reasons, such as two-worker households; others based their decisions on the understandable and widespread reluctance of many people to pull up roots from communities in which they have lived all or most of their lives. Whether it be Brooklyn, New York, or Macon, Georgia, it is home, and most workers other than those in professional and managerial jobs will leave home only as a last resort.

One measure undertaken to ease the plight of those who could not move and who were not eligible to retire was to seek legislation to provide them with severance pay to ease their transition to other careers. In common with many other issues, McNamara took such an active part in the drafting of this legislation that it became known as McNamara's Bill. As finally enacted, the statute contained a liberal formula based on age and length of service which entitled an employee who was separated but not eligible for an immediate retirement annuity to receive up to the equivalent of one year's pay. During the development of the legislative proposal, McNamara rejected several formulas as not sufficiently liberal and insisted that the age of the employee as well as his or her length of service be taken into account. He recognized that older workers encounter extra problems when seeking other employment and sympathized with their plight—an interesting perspective on a man sometimes referred to by his critics as a "kindly computer." As finally enacted, the severance pay formula provided one week's pay for each year of service up to ten years and two weeks pay for each year of service beyond ten years, plus an additional ten percent severence pay for each year beyond forty years of age, up to a total of one year's pay (5 USC 5595).

Homeowner's Assistance

As the base closure and consolidation program proceeded, other problems developed which demanded attention if the objective of minimizing the impact of closures on employees and communities was to be achieved. In some locations, where a large military installation had been the primary employer, the bottom fell out of the housing market when the closure was announced. Among other things, this meant that homeowners among the military and civilian personnel stationed at the base would have to sell their homes at catastrophic losses in order to move to another location.

It was decided, therefore, to seek Congressional support for a homeowner's assistance program, a program which would help both the people involved and, indirectly, the community itself while it made the transition to a new economy. The program was enacted into law as PL 89-754 in November 1966 and retroactively covered all base closures occurring after November 1, 1964. The statute provided that employees and military personnel located in an area where it was determined that a base closure was responsible for a substantial drop in the community housing market could sell his or her home to the government essentially at the market value that existed before the closure announcement. Since the average employee's single largest investment is his home, this legislation proved a godsend to many who were forced to move in order to continue their careers.

Travel Allowances

Another area that obviously needed fixing was an obsolete system of travel and transportation allowances. In some cases, displaced employees did not qualify or the allowances were clearly inadequate. A greatly liberalized statute was drafted and the Congress persuaded to enact it in July 1966.[9] The result was that it became economically feasible for more employees to accept job opportunities that involved moving their households to other geographic areas.

Included among the new provisions were such benefits as authorization of travel for the employee and his wife to the new job location to find a home, an increase in the weight allowance for household goods, reimbursement for the expenses of selling a home and purchasing a new one, and a thirty-day subsistence allowance during the period an employee was in the process of relocating.

In a number of other program areas, quirks and gray spots in existing statutes and implementing regulations were found to be interfering with the readjustment program. Normal bureaucratic caution, however, did not prevail when it came to decision making in grey areas. The word was to push ahead, devise alternatives, and get results. The use of early retirement and saved pay illustrate this activist management approach.

Early Retirement

Civil service laws contained provisions for a discontinued service annuity which can be most helpful in bringing down the size of an activity with minimum pain. But the interaction between the seniority-based reduction-in-force system and the retirement system was limiting the usefulness of the early retirement provisions. On many occasions this interaction produced a result desired by no one, including both the employee being laid off and those being retained.

The discontinued service retirement option permitted employees 50 years of age with 20 years of service or, regardless of age, with 25 years of service, to receive a discontinued service retirement annuity if they were involuntarily separated. Although retirement annuities are substantially reduced under this provision, frequently employees would decide that this was the best option for them. But these were the more senior employees and often not the ones being separated (unless an employee received a reduction-in-force notice, he could not elect to retire). Meanwhile, in the same job category, the less senior employees who needed to continue to work were the ones receiving the reduction-in-force notices (and for whom other jobs had to be found).

To produce a more satisfactory result, I undertook negotiations with the Civil Service Commission which managed the retirement system. The Commission was most responsive and worked out with us a "resignation requested" procedure that made it possible for employees high on the retention register to forego their seniority rights and retire on a discontinued service annuity when this would save the jobs of employees lower on the retention register. Thousands of involuntary separations were avoided in this manner.[10] While this procedure was effective and was believed to be consistent with the intent of the statute, it was not entirely clear that the language of the law permitted it. Congress was advised of the problem and subsequently revised the law to clearly authorize use of the involuntary retirement options under these circumstances. While this legislative action moved slowly forward, thousands of persons were saved from displacement because management was willing to take a chance on having its actions sustained.

Saved Pay

A similar situation arose in connection with the statute which authorized management, within certain limits, to keep an employee's pay at the same rate for two years when that employee was involuntarily reassigned to a lower graded position. The language contained an exception, however, that stated it would not be applicable when the reduction was caused by lack of work or shortage of funds. Nobody knew what that language really meant because when actually applied to specific cases, reasonable people could reach different conclusions about the underlying cause for the reduction. Making distinctions among individual actions in this vast complex of realignment decisions seemed almost impossible and was bound to result in inequities. I decided, therefore, with the concurrence of the General Counsel, to simply declare that the base closure and reduction program in its totality was not caused by lack of work or shortage of funds. This eliminated the need for individual determinations and greatly eased management's task of reshuffling the work force. Lawyers could debate endlessly whether a particular action was due to lack of work or shortage of funds, but it was decided to act and not debate. It was also decided not to wait for Congressional clarification and that too was a wise decision—the clarification did not come until the Civil Service Reform Act of 1978 (which finally supported the approach taken by the Department of Defense in 1965).

Economic Adjustment Program

Dealing with the problems of readjusting the Department of Defense civilian work force and finding other jobs for the people affected was recognized to be only half of the problem. The other half was helping the community readjust to the loss of Department of Defense payrolls, to bring in new industry, and to make productive use of the often-valuable Defense land, buildings, and equipment which in many cases ended up as surplus to the government's needs.

Economic adjustment assistance to communities would not normally be considered a function of the Department of Defense, but McNamara was not willing to sit back and leave the problem to others who might or might not provide the assistance needed. He established in the Office of the Secretary of Defense an Office of Economic Adjustment and offered its services to the communities affected by base closures.[11] This office took the leadership in pulling together the resources of various Federal agencies that had responsibilities for economic development. Upon request of the communities involved, teams would study the community's economic problems, the potential use of any surplus facilities, the possibilities of attracting new industry, and other recovery possibilities. With community assistance, an economic adjustment plan would be developed and the resources which might be available from Federal agencies to carry out the plan identified.

Just providing local officials with knowledge of the possible sources of assistance, given the complexities of the Federal Government, was a major contribution in itself. At various times direct assistance proved to be available in carrying out an economic adjustment plan from the Economic Development Administration, the Small Business Administration, the Federal Housing Administration, the Federal Aviation Agency, the U.S. Office of Education, the General Services Administration, the Urban Renewal Administration, the Manpower Training Administration, the U.S. Employment Service, the Office of Economic Opportunity, and others. Many communities were receptive to this assistance, although some were so busy fighting the base closure that they were unwilling to take any steps that would suggest they were acquiescing in the decision to close the base.

As might be expected, there were successes and failures in this readjustment effort, but some success stories were truly remarkable. To encourage other communities, these successes were dramatized in a slick multicolored brochure called *The Challenge of Change*. The following two examples of effective conversion of agency facilities to industrial uses and civic uses are drawn from that brochure.[12]

Industrial Use

Donaldson Air Force Base, situated on about 2,500 acres of land in Greenville, South Carolina, was a major economic force in the community, providing some 4,100 military and civilian jobs. After strong initial resistance to the closure, the community turned its energies to developing the base into an attractive industrial park renamed the Donaldson Center. Vigorous efforts were undertaken to entice industries to make use of the facilities available. Businesses from large corporations to home-grown industry rose to the bait. As a result, over 7,000 new civilian jobs were created, exceeding the level of employment that existed at the base when it was closed. The spectrum of products subsequently produced at the Donaldson Center included chemicals, textiles, tools, electronics, trailers, furniture, business forms, bedding, power, and a variety of services. The community's prosperity is no longer dependent on having a military installation in its midst.

The Presque Isle Air Force Base meant even more to the economy of the rural community of Presque Isle than Donaldson did to Greenville, South Carolina. The total work force in this small community in the northern part of Maine was around 4,500 and of this number 1,500 represented civilian and military jobs on the Presque Isle Air Force Base. Faced with this blow to the economy, the community knew it had to diversify to survive. The city acquired the entire portion of the base suitable for industrial development and with the assistance of various Federal agencies attracted nineteen firms to buildings leased by the city. Some 2,400 new civilian jobs were created to replace the 1,500 lost. A new wood veneer plant, three new potato processing plants, a new sugar refinery, a new shoe plant, a corrugated shipping container plant, a propane gas plant, and a modern wholesale grocery distribution center all added to the industrial diversification effort. One of the earliest bases to be closed, the conversion of Presque Isle from dependence on a military base to a thriving civilian economy proved to be a model which many communities sought to emulate in subsequent years.

Civic Uses

The town of Salina, Kansas, where Schilling Air Force Base was located, determined that the facilities of this large Strategic Air Command base could be effectively used to meet its educational and transportation needs. With the assistance of the Office of Economic Adjustment, a Schilling Development Council was formed, a regional economic development plan worked out, and the full resources of a number of Federal agencies mobilized to assist Salina in its adjustment problem. Salina was able to drop plans to sell $750,000 in bonds to finance the construction and equipping of a needed Vocational Technical School. With the use of Schilling facilities and the assistance of the Department of Health, Education and Welfare, a technical school was established to help develop the skills in the Salina work force that were badly needed in order to attract employers to the area. The Schilling runways were converted to a municipal airport and Kansas Wesleyan University, needing room for expansion, also moved to the base.

Similar adaptation of unneeded military facilities to educational purposes occurred at many other locations. At Waco, Texas, for example, where the Air Force closed a large navigator training school, the Texas A&M University established in its place a technical training institute. The modern air-conditioned barracks with separate rooms, lounges, and office space made possible the enrollment of over 3,000 students and full utilization of the base for its new civilian training function.

These kinds of readjustment efforts, to be successful, required the combined efforts of many Federal, state and local organizations as well as private community groups. It would have been easy for the Department of Defense to turn the job of coordinating these diverse groups over to others, but that was not the McNamara philosophy. The impact of that philosophy was a lasting one. Today, the Secretary of Defense remains the chairman of the President's Economic Adjustment Committee comprised of 17 Federal agencies. The Committee, for which the Defense Office of Economic Adjustment provides the staff, continues to assist communities faced either by closures or by increases in Department of Defense activity which place new demands on communities for more public services. A fuller account of these economic adjustment activities can be found in the 1981 report of the President's Economic Adjustment Committee[13] and the Committee's brochure *Communities in Transition.*[14]

Today's Realities

With all of the effort and constructive thinking that has gone into minimizing the adverse impact of base closures and realignments, it would be nice to conclude that today it is now easier to keep the military base structure abreast of technological change, to reduce nonessential overhead, and to use the limited personnel and financial resources available to meet the real needs of the combat forces. Unfortunately, nothing could be further from the truth. The momentum generated during the McNamara period carried forward for awhile into later years, but it appears that the very success of the effort stimulated the opposition forces to assure that it could never happen again.

Congress began insisting on more advance notice and more and more complicated procedures before the Executive Branch could take any significant action affecting a base. Provisions were inserted in the Military Construction Act in 1966 requiring advance notice to the Congress of any closures affecting 250 persons and specifying that no action could be taken until 30 days after notification of the Congress. One major purpose served by this notification was to give any Congressman who did not want a base closed in his district time to prevent it from happening, something at which many Congressmen have excelled.

The advance-notification-to-Congress provision was relatively mild compared to what came later. Title X of the U.S. Code was amended to establish a procedure that not only requires prior notification to the Congress, but to the public as well. Announcements of proposed studies of candidate actions must be made before a study is even begun. The procedures require that when a major action is contemplated, an environmental impact statement also will be prepared. A typical announcement of "candidate actions" drawn from a 1976 press release, explains what is involved in an environmental impact statement:

In those cases where it is determined that the candidate is a major action which could significantly affect the quality of the human environment, the Army will prepare environmental impact statements as required by existing regulations. These statements will include consideration of such environmental factors as pollution, population and traffic conditions together with any related socio-economic impact of the realignments on employment, housing, public schools, recreational activities, etc. Pursuant to the National Environmental

Policy Act (NEPA) the environmental statements will be filed with the Council on Environmental Quality and disseminated to all interested agencies and parties for comment. Notice of the availability of these statements will also be published in the *Federal Register*. It is anticipated that the complete process for such actions will require a period of four to nine months to complete.[15]

If the impact statements are challenged in the courts, as they often are, the process can take not four to nine months, but years to complete. Under the provisions of this statute, if a base with as few as 300 employees authorized (not necessarily employed) desires to reduce the number authorized to 150, all of the required public announcements, environmental impact assessments, and detailed justification requirements come into play. An understanding of the complexity and rigidity of these statutory procedures can only be gained by reading them:

(b) No action described in subsection (a) with respect to the closure of, or a realignment with respect to, any military installation may be taken unless and until—

(1) the Secretary of Defense or the Secretary of the military department concerned publicly announces, and notifies the Committees on Armed Services of the Senate and the House of Representatives in writing, that such military installation is a candidate for closure or realignment;

(2) the Secretary of Defense or the Secretary of the military department concerned complies with the requirements of the National Environmental Policy Act of 1969 with respect to the proposed closure or realignment;

(3) the Secretary of Defense or the Secretary of the military department concerned submits to the Committees on Armed Services of the Senate and House of Representatives his final decision to carry out the proposed closure or realignment and a detailed justification for such decision, including statements of the estimated fiscal, local economic, budgetary, environmental, strategic, and operational consequences of the proposed closure or realignment; and

(4) a period of sixty days expires following the date on which the justification referred to in clause (3) has been submitted to such committees, during which period no irrevocable action may be taken to effect or implement the decision.[16]

Managers must have stout hearts and a zest for hoop jumping to even initiate the process outlined above. Particularly frustrating to many is the fact that even after compliance with this detailed and lengthy procedure, the action still can be stopped by an influential Congressman who just doesn't want it to happen. Through the familiar process of back scratching, it is not too difficult for a Congressman to gain the support of his colleagues when a base in his district is threatened.

An effort initiated in 1976, for example, to consolidate at Fort Meade, Maryland, intelligence functions spread out among a number of different locations met this fate five hard years later. The proposal involved closing two installations and consolidating all the intelligence activities into a new building at Fort Meade for an annual net savings of 7.1 million dollars. After all the necessary notifications and an elaborate environmental impact study, a final determination in full accordance with the law was made in 1981 to proceed with the consolidation. When this decision was announced, a brief one-paragraph letter was received from the House Armed Services Committee announcing that the Subcommittee on Installation and Facilities had voted to disapprove the award of the architect-engineering contract for the design of the facility needed to house the consolidated functions at Fort Meade. End of project; end of 7.1 million annual savings for the taxpayer!

Conclusion

What is one to conclude from this experience? It would be easy to simply decide that there is no way to get there from here, and give up; some have. But a more considered view is that, while the workings of our democratic form of government have their drawbacks in trying to manage programs efficiently and effectively, they also have their advantages.

Some positive things have come out of the give-and-take of the process of closing and realigning bases that might never have happened otherwise. A great deal more attention is being given to the effects of government decisions upon people and communities and effective programs have been developed to deal with the problems. It is a definite plus that people whose jobs and careers are affected are not simply shoved aside and forgotten when changes must be made. It is good that consideration is being given to the impact on the environment of major changes brought about by government decisions. It is right that the government should do what it can to help communities deal with the economic hardships resulting from decisions to withdraw governmental organizations that the community has come to depend upon. The procedures developed to deal with these problems may be overly elaborate, but they have sound objectives and have produced much that is good.

The darker side is that these procedures lend themselves to manipulation and misuse, and they are being misused. Actions needed in the interest of the nation as a whole are being sidetracked in order to satisfy the narrow, partisan interests of some. This should surprise no one and there is no simple counter to it. In the last analysis, it's up to the public. Progress depends upon a willingness of the leadership in both the Executive and Congressional Branches to stand up to those who would misuse the process. But they will do this only if the public recognizes that painful changes are sometimes necessary and supports them. The cost of obsolescence is high and the American public is paying the price in waste and inefficiency. To repeat Robert McNamara's 1965 statement:

> ...obsolescence occurs continuously throughout our economy as technology advances and needs change. Should our major institutions, either public or private, fail to adjust to such changes, we would shortly face the unacceptably low levels of economic growth which today plague so many nations of the world, limiting their power and restricting their freedom.[17]

And which in 1984 now plague the United States.

Footnotes

1. Joseph Kraft, "McNamara and His Enemies," *Harper's Magazine*, August 1961, p. 142.
2. "The Challenge of Change," (Washington, D.C.: U.S. Department of Defense, July 1965), p. 1.
3. Department of Defense News Release, No. 1562-63, "Department of Defense to Reduce, Discontinue Certain Activities," December 12, 1963, p. 1.
4. Department of Defense News Release, No. 879-65, "Statement of Secretary of Defense Robert S. McNamara," December 6, 1965, p. 2.
5. "The Challenge of Change," *op. cit.*, p. 1.
6. Department of Defense Nation-wide Priority Referral System Manual 1400, 20-2M, April 1980.
7. Department of Defense News Release No. 879-65, *op. cit.*, p. 2.
8. Department of Defense Instruction 1430.9, Subject: Department of Defense Policy for Retraining of Career Employees, June 4, 1964.
9. P. L. 89-516, "Administrative Expenses Act of 1966."
10. William C. Valdes, "Perspectives on Reduction-in-force," *Defense Management Journal*, Vol. VII, Issue No. 1, Spring 1971.
11. Department of Defense News Release, No. 822-64, "Department of Defense Announces Actions to Discontinue, Reduce or Consolidate Activities," November 19, 1964, p. 4.

12. "The Challenge of Change," *op. cit.*
13. Department of Defense, "1961-1981 20 Years of Civilian Reuse," Nov. 1981.
14. Department of Defense, "Communities in Transition," June 1978.
15. Department of Defense News Release No. 129-76, "Army Announces Plans for Installation Realignment Studies," April 1, 1976, p. 2.
16. 10 USC 2687, par. (b)(1).
17. "The Challenge of Change," *op. cit.*

Editorial Note: Theodore W. Taylor identifies and describes some of the dynamics of various policies developed as the Federal Government worked in cooperation with the private sector in the electrification of rural America, the World War II joint effort in building ships, and the interfacing of electric utilities and government civil defense operations. Taylor also emphasizes the importance of competent leaders and innovative personnel in developing and following through on policy in the foregoing areas as well as in his accounts of the decisions concerning James Smithson's legacy to the United States and the operations of the trustee relationship between the American Indians and the Federal Government. He provides clarifying examples of the dilemmas which policy makers and administrators often face when issues may be fuzzy, controversial, unpopular or moot.

CHAPTER 10

PERSPECTIVES ON POLICY

Theodore W. Taylor

Introduction

From an early age I had in mind entering the government service. My father, Walter Penn Taylor, was a biologist in the U.S. Biological Survey which was later merged with the Bureau of Fisheries into the Fish and Wildlife Service. As a boy, on trapping and specimen collecting trips with my father, I enjoyed the semidesert country around Tucson, Arizona, and met forest rangers when we trapped on forest range reserves. A forest ranger's life seemed to me to be the best of all worlds. Therefore, when I entered the University of Arizona in 1931, my objective was to major in forestry. However, my first botany course turned me off.

Although in high school I disliked civics which was taught by the track coach who generally stayed about one page ahead of the class, I enjoyed my first course in political science at the University. It was taught by Neal Doyle Houghton who made the government come alive as a living, vital part of our democracy. So I majored in political science though I had some misgivings since the only future I saw with such training seemed to be law or teaching. I was sorely tempted by the agricultural economics professor who said if I majored in his field he could guarantee me a job upon graduation! This was the time of the great depression—my dad had received a 15% pay cut and wondered whether the next step would be to lose his job. But I reasoned if I were going to spend four years in college, I might as well study something I liked.

In my senior year I applied for and received a graduate residency at Syracuse University. My master's thesis, under faculty advisors William E. Mosher and Herman C. Beyle, was a study of the "Predictive Value of Civil Service Examinations in the Syracuse Fire Department." It was disillusioning to discover little correlation between the written exam and success as a fireman. The results of the exams were accepted by the applicants and the public, so they were an effective way of selecting a few persons from the large number of applicants without too much flack. Since then I have always had a suspicion that many examinations and selection criteria have little predictive value and may be primarily acceptable elimination devices.

While at Syracuse I applied for an internship with the National Institute of Public Affairs (NIPA) and for a Rhodes Scholarship. I did not get to England, but after interviewing Frederick Davenport at his home in Hamilton, New York, I was selected as an NIPA intern.

Many of us who entered the Federal service in the 1930s were motivated by at least two factors: (1) jobs were scarce and any job was like manna from heaven and (2) many of us were service oriented, that is, we wanted to work in some way that would benefit society and we considered government as a preferred option for this objective as compared with the private sector. A Brookings Institution roundtable of top career and political executives held in 1957 indicated that many key personnel were interested in making life a little better for the nation. Political appointees from business sometimes found government service more rewarding than their business careers even though they received far less pay and suffered considerable frustration.[1] This was often because they found they had a potentially greater impact on policies that were of importance to the country in government than in their presidencies or other key positions in a private firm.

What follows is a personalized view of some aspects of policy and the policy process in various agencies in which I have worked.

Changing the Life Style of Rural America: The Rural Electrification Administration

The New Deal was a time of ferment growing out of the economic crisis of the depression. Innovative ideas were sought and some were bought. When I arrived in Washington, D.C., as a National Institute of Public Affairs Intern in 1936, I was fortunate to draw an assignment with the Rural Electrification Administration (REA).

In 1935 approximately 10 percent of the farms had electricity and Franklin D. Roosevelt wanted to help the other 90 percent get electric power. Private utilities had not served rural areas except in the few instances in which farmers could pay the high cost of extending a utility line to their farms. Furthermore, few farmers could afford the high rates for electricity normally charged by private companies at that time. The view of the private utilities was that "the national level of farm income must be raised to a point where we can profitably serve agriculture."[2]

In contrast, the President, leading farm organizations, and authorities on agriculture proposed that "the costs of electrical service must be lowered to a point where farmers can pay for it out of their present incomes and thus help increase those incomes."[3]

Roosevelt, by Executive Order, established REA on May 11, 1935, to tackle the problem of "generation, transmission, and distribution of electric energy in rural areas."[4] The grand strategy or general policy goal was electrification of rural areas. What were the alternative options for achieving this goal? In addition to the two opposite economic policy approaches of the private utilities and the President indicated above, there were two administrative or procedural options for achieving Roosevelt's objective: (1) for REA to engage in direct construction activity, or (2) for REA to make loans for construction to private utilities, municipalities with publicly owned plants, and nonprofit cooperatives. A loan program was decided upon as the best approach.

One of the reasons for deciding on the loan approach was the hope that private utilities would apply for loans to do the construction of rural lines. They had the know-how and experience and they could do it faster since it would take time either to staff REA to do the job or to organize and train rural cooperative personnel. However, an electrical industry committee concluded that most farms having a real need for electricity were already being served![5] In September 1935 no requests for loans had been received from private utilities and the first loans went to a municipality and three electric cooperatives.

In the summer of 1936 when I became a clerk in REA's personnel office, as my first intern assignment, the private utilities were beginning to worry about REA's effect on their potential rural market. So they started to build more lines, but tended to "cream" the rural territory and not emphasize area coverage. This made co-op or municipal service for the rest of the area less feasible economically. In some instances, private utilities even paralleled REA lines to try to sabotage an economic load necessary for a co-op to pay off the REA loan. Still they did not seek REA funds with which to build lines to serve rural areas.

Since the private utilities were not going to help, REA had to adjust its strategy. REA personnel worked with farmers and state legislatures in developing legislation authorizing rural electric cooperatives, made economic feasibility studies, and helped organize and assist new REA cooperatives. The engineering section developed less costly distribution lines, reducing the $1200 to $1800 cost per mile prior to REA to $720 per mile in 1940. REA also had to work with farm market cooperative leaders who were worried that the Federal involvement in rural electric cooperatives would endanger the cooperative movement.

The number of farms served with electricity went from approximately 10 percent in 1935 to 97 percent in 1960! Keeping its eye on the overall goal REA had helped change the life style of rural America. This example illustrates the process of deciding upon a goal, selecting the best implementation options available, and achieving success.

Not envisioned by the REA or TVA policy makers, as far as I know, was the magnitude of the side effect of the rural electrification policy on the electrical equipment industry. Farmers and farmers' wives were not content with electric motors for pumps, loading hay into the barns, and electric lights. They wanted electrified feeding, grinding, and cleaning equipment, milking machines, refrigerators, stoves, toasters, clocks, blowers for the furnace and air conditioning, washing machines, dryers, and the myriad of other products produced by electrical equipment manufacturers. Inside toilets took over from the privy and life on the farm became less onerous with many of the comforts of the city. It was indeed a revolution in farm life based on a government policy initiative to electrify rural America in the face of opposition from the private utility electric power industry.

REA was fortunate to have Morris L. Cooke, a private engineering consultant from Philadelphia, as its first administrator. He was acquainted with the President, and held to the overall policy goal of electrifying rural America no matter what the pressure from the utilities and members of Congress. He cut to the core of each issue involved in implementing the policy and supported his staff in carrying out their assignments. Innovation was encouraged and many breakthroughs accomplished in organizing cooperatives, construction of durable and cheap transmission lines, and purchase of or generation of inexpensive power. The result: electricity at a low rate to the farmer, payout of loans ahead of schedule in many instances, very few defaults, and the opening of an immense market for electrical appliances.

As an intern at a GS-3 grade, obviously I was not directly involved in the grand policy and implementation decisions. However, Congressmen did not call up the Administrator and order him to the Hill to interview a Congressman's constituent who wanted an engineering job. The Congressman would call me, a personnel interviewer, for an appointment and bring his constituent to my office. That's what real unemployment means! I will never forget the desperation of many highly qualified individuals who could not find jobs! Since there were few jobs available for engineers, REA recruited the cream of the graduating classes, put them through a rigorous training program, and they became the leaders in the REA movement.

The innovative challenge of the agency goal, the newness of the program, the appreciation of the staff that they had a worthwhile job to do, and the strong leadership of the Administrator resulted in high morale and prodigious results.

This experience demonstrated to me that a government agency can be productive, efficient, and accomplish a social goal under the right circumstances. During my approximately four years at REA I had various assignments, ending up as Management Officer in charge of administrative services—administrative accounting, mail, messengers, space, and the like.

REA also granted me leave without pay for 18 months to do graduate work at Harvard.

Federalism in Operation: The Cooperative Extension Service, U.S. Department of Agriculture

From 1940-1942 I was administrative assistant to Milburn Lincoln Wilson, Director of the Extension Service, the author of *Democracy Has Roots*, and former Undersecretary of Agriculture. Although I had graduated from a land grant college, I did not fully appreciate the significance of the Morrill Act of 1862 which provided for the granting of public lands for the establishment of the land grant colleges. Representative Justin Smith Morrill, instrumental in the passage of the Act, laid the foundations and started the chain of events that led to the Agricultural Experiment Stations and the Cooperative Extension Service (1914) headquartered at the land grant colleges throughout the nation. The well-known county agent was the local man representing the extension service. His salary was often supported by three governments— Federal, state, and county.

The results of agricultural research were translated to the farmer by the extension service through specialists and the county agent. Many have attributed the agricultural revolution in this country, leading to development of the world's most productive agriculture, to the research of the experiment stations and the educational efforts of the extension service.

It was here that I learned that grants to states or to land grant institutions by a Federal agency, in this case the Federal extension service, may, in large measure, turn the actual determination and execution of policy over to the grantee. The grants to the state extension services at the land grant colleges were based on work plans submitted by the states and approved by the Federal office. I believe this is still the procedure. But I learned that although the Federal director and his aids had the opportunity to discuss and achieve mutually agreed to adjustments in the state programs, were there an impasse, the state would often come out on top. Although the Federal director had the authority on paper to approve or not approve a state plan, if he decided to not approve the plan, say, for Pennsylvania, he was soon straightened out by the state director and the state's Congressional delegation on the Hill. State plans were also subject to accounting audits and these were effective. The Federal office was basically a conduit for funds for programs authorized by legislation. To a large extent, details of policy and implementation were determined in the field.

At the time, my reaction was that the Federal office was toothless and not of much use. But in retrospect it seems to me the procedure tended to force a consensus in most instances. This probably resulted in a more effective policy impact than might otherwise have been the case. Certainly central determination of policy detail, especially in the social field, has been fraught with difficulties and often negative results in the varied circumstances found throughout the nation.

The Extension Service Director, M.L. Wilson, had arthritis in his arm, ate at least one banana a day, took vitamin B1, and was interested in nutrition. He headed a nutrition committee within the government. The Surgeon General of the United States and Wilson, impressed by surveys indicating inadequacies in American diets, were "convinced that the improvement of the quality of bread was basic to any nutrition program that might be considered for national defense."[6]

The American Medical Association, Food and Drug Administration, Food and Nutrition Board of the National Research Council, American Baker's Association, professors, and nutritionists were all involved, and many representatives of these groups met in M.L. Wilson's office. The bread and flour enrichment program began in May 1941.[7] Although there was much controversy, nonetheless, this was an example of what a few leading and interested individuals in government and industry could do in establishing a goal that would have impact on millions of Americans and help achieve a consensus for implementation which then led to appropriate action to achieve the goal.

Just before I left the Federal extension office, Milton Eisenhower become Associate Director for a short time. Things were heating up in Europe and Milton's brother, Ike, was an army officer stationed in England. I can remember Milton Eisenhower standing with one foot on the windowsill in the South Building of the Department of Agriculture looking out toward the Potomac and commenting that he envied Ike's profession and location at that juncture in world affairs. He was prophetic.

Line and Staff: The Navy

From 1942-1946 I was assigned to the civilian personnel office for the Washington headquarters of the Bureau of Ships, Navy Department, which was headed by Commander Carl E. Haglund. By the end of the tour, I was the officer in charge of the civilian personnel office with the rank of lieutenant commander. It was the most challenging assignment I had had up to that time.

We had some interesting sessions on classification of positions. A senior admiral (division head) would be unhappy with the classification of his civilian secretary or civilian engineer. The ensign or lieutenant (jg) classification officer and I would be called to his office and raked over the coals. Unless he shed new light on the position, we generally stood our ground on the merits of the situation, but it was not comfortable. On one such occasion the division head complained to the assistant chief of the bureau, Admiral Earle Watkins Mills. Mills supported us, but he was not very happy. He was gruff, positive, direct, and made a lasting impression on me with this statement: "Remember, Taylor, the personnel function is a staff activity to support the work of the bureau. Personnel rules are necessary but use them to help the bureau accomplish its job." The implication came over loud and clear that life would be unpleasant for me if I did not follow that injunction.

This incident was burned vividly in my mind and it reinforced the guideline for staff to put priority on serving the line. It has been my experience that if staff is helpful and competent, the line will often ask for assistance. Staff is ill advised to take credit, even if warranted, for a suggestion that works. Let the line official have the glory, and if he or she voluntarily gives the staff credit, fine. But if staff threatens the line official's confidence and security, he or she may be hostile.

Another lesson learned was that many supervisors do not like the responsibilities of supervision. They like the status, but not the difficult, hard work of making clear-cut assignments to subordinates, insisting on performance, helping with suggestions and guidelines, rewarding high achievement, penalizing poor performance, and firing incompetents and sloths. When a supervisor was moved by desperation or anger to fire an employee, we often found that the employee was unaware of the depth of the supervisor's displeasure and the reason for it. Often the employee had a "Very Good" or "Excellent" efficiency rating, no job goals had been set, the supervisor had not talked to the employee about the shortcomings of his job performance, and the supervisor had no record of performance that could be compared with reasonable requirements to be met for satisfactory job accomplishment. So it was necessary to work with such supervisors to help them to do their job properly. Most employees want to do a good job and will respond to goals and guidelines and firm supervision. Although we fired both poor employees and poor supervisors, helping individuals perform well is the objective of supervision and personnel assistance.

Supervisory practices ran the gamut from nonsupervision to autocratic control. Hyman G. Rickover (later the Admiral who fathered nuclear submarines), then in charge of the electrical section, was arbitrary, demanding, feared, often disliked—but respected. If a tough job had to be done, the chief of the bureau would often assign it to Rickover whether it fit into the electrical section or not. He would get it done and on time. I was rudely shaken from my previous belief that autocratic supervision would not be productive. It was, in Rickover's case.

Different supervisors get different results with different methods. Vice-Admiral Edward Lull Cochrane, Chief of the Bureau of Ships, and Rear Admiral E.W. Mills, Deputy Chief, had both been captains before the War began. President Roosevelt, who had previously been in the Navy Department, knew how to find out who the good men were. So he appointed Cochrane and Mills to their jobs as chief and assistant chief over the heads of senior captains and admirals. Cochrane and Mills were tops. In my judgement about ten of the key regular Navy captains and admirals in the Bureau of Ships were as good as any supervisors or leaders I have ever known. They, along with some excellent top civilians in the various sections, led the agency to fantastic feats of design, contracting to private industry, and supervision of the construction of more than 100,000 ships and landing craft in a remarkably brief period of time.[8]

Captain Edward Ellsworth Roth was the head of the Division of Administration and junior to all other division chiefs. Most of Roth's section chiefs were reserve officers from civilian life, such as myself. The regular navy admirals and captains who headed other divisions and sections sometimes found it difficult to accept personnel regulations and other staff services and requirements from junior reserve officers. They gave Roth a hard time and referred to his division as "Boy's Town." Roth stuck to his guns and backed us up. I am an admirer of Captain Roth.

Government Business Operations: The Office of Territories and Island Possessions, U.S. Department of the Interior

When at the University of Arizona, my political science professor Neal D. Houghton, in addition to regular course work, required students to read a book for each course to broaden our knowledge and background from a list of over 100. In one of these classes I chose *The Public Pays* by Ernest Gruening, a summary of the financial havoc created by the collapse of the electric utility holding company empires in the 1920s. Demonstrating that this is a small world, in 1946 when I became Executive Officer of the Office of Territories and Island Possessions then headed by Edwin Arnold, it turned out that Gruening was the appointed Governor of Alaska with whom I worked in connection with the Territory's budget and other administrative matters. Gruening was elected Senator when Alaska became a state.

The Alaska Railroad and the Virgin Islands Company (VICO) were two business-type operations under the office at that time. VICO raised sugar cane and made and marketed Government House Rum. The Bureau of the Budget (BOB) was converting many business-type budgets to corporate accounting practices with balance sheets and profit and loss statements. Harold Seidman was the BOB examiner who worked with the VICO and railroad accountants and myself on this conversion. The business-type budget was a great help as it concentrated attention on profit and loss. If there was a loss, an appropriation subsidy was sought from the Congress. All annual financial statements were, of course, submitted to the BOB and the Congress for review.

The Alaska Railroad was unprofitable because it had only a one-way haul from the coast to Fairbanks. It was a constant struggle to obtain funds from Congress for adequate maintenance and operating funds. There were many wooden trestles and they rotted. Colonel John P. Johnson, then General Manager, once stated to the House Subcommittee on appropriations: "Those trestles are so bad the engineer stops before each trestle and blows his whistle three times so the termites can lock arms!"

After World War II, the United Nations assigned portions of Micronesia to the United States to administer as a trusteeship. The Department of the Navy was the first administering agency, and then the responsibility was transferred to the Office of Territories in the Department of the Interior.

What a contrast in budget and allocation magnitudes between the Departments of Navy and Interior! Under the Navy, it was difficult to determine specific funding assigned to trust territory support in the budget and program allocations. Ship and air transportation were simply parts of larger Navy programs, as were public works, health, education and other activities. In the Interior Department, budget estimates based on analysis of trust territory programs in place were made during an on-the-spot survey in the South Pacific. I headed a team concerned with all administrative and program activities except transportation. Our estimates were crucial as the Department of Interior budget for the trust territory, in contrast to the Navy period, would be reviewed in every detail and every penny by the Congressional Subcommittees responsible for Interior.

This policy decision by the United States to transfer the administration of the trust territory from military to civilian control was in part to indicate to the rest of the world a nonmilitary orientation in carrying out the trusteeship, but it also had other policy implications and results. One was that Congress paid much closer attention to trust territory policy and funding than when under Navy, and another was that the costs of the trusteeship became much clearer.

In the trust territory, the burgeoning population resulting from playing "half-god" by the policy of decreasing the death rate through public health measures but doing nothing about the birth rate was beginning to cause real economic problems even in the late 1940s.

Decentralized Operations
for Emergency: Defense
Electric Power

The goal of the civil defense effort to provide for the safety of the civilian population required the continuance of necessary services. One of these key services is the provision of electric power. From 1956-1959 I was a mobilization officer in Defense Electric Power, Office of the Assistant Secretary for Water and Power, Department of the Interior. In the event of an atomic attack which might knock out portions or all of the central government and possibly the headquarters of some utility companies, a plan of operation was needed for those utilities still capable of generating and delivering electricity. The policy was to develop voluntary local and regional organization and procedures to automatically go into effect in the event of such an attack.

An official of a local electric utility would be designated as the coordinator for a given area and procedures developed for cooperation with other electric utilities that tied in with the local system. The advantage of this voluntary decentralized approach was that it was always in place and ready for action. It was to be self-initiating if communications were destroyed. Procedures were developed too for coordinating efforts with mayors, other local officials, and the local representatives of other resource activities such as coal, oil, natural gas and communications.

Taking the objective as a given, the organizational aspects of this policy made a great deal of sense. It required a minimum of government staff to initiate the organizational arrangements and preparation of manuals and training procedures. Conferences with private utility personnel not only helped work out procedures, but offered an opportunity to train them in the basic effects of atomic bombing—blast and radiation—including the influence of prevailing winds. The main objective was to have a clear-cut and understood action plan with specific individuals who had clearly defined responsibilities. Backup personnel were also designated as well as alternative options for delivering electricity under varying damage assumptions. Industry and government cooperated to achieve the policy goal of developing contingency procedures to provide electric power in the event of an emergency.

As a result of the private electric utility opposition to the Rural Electrification Administration, I had formed a low opinion of the social attitudes of private utilities and their officials. Working with utility officials on defense electric power, I found them to be fine human beings, just like most people, with a strong sense of public service and responsibility. Institutions seem to get locked into stereotyped attitudes and employees are generally brainwashed into accepting the institutional view.

Private Benefactor Stimulates Government
Policy: The Smithsonian Institution

One would not suspect that the will of an English scientist, the natural son of the Duke of Northumberland who died in Genoa in 1829 would result in the establishment of one of America's better known scientific organizations—The Smithsonian Institution. James Smithson left over $500,000 to the United States of America "to found at Washington, under the name of the Smithsonian Institution, an establishment for the increase and diffusion of knowledge." The gold coins arrived in 1838. Congress engaged in eight years of debate. Should the funds be accepted at all, should they be used for a national library, the promotion of literature and science, an agricultural school, a women's seminary, or in some other educational or research enterprise? John Quincy Adams favored an astronomical observatory, believing that no school or college should be supported by these funds as education was "a sacred obligation binding upon the people of the Union themselves."[10] The widely varied proposals, hotly debated, led to compromise and not very precise definition of how the purpose would be carried out. This is often the result in setting goals when widely divergent views in our pluralistic society have to be considered and a consensus achieved.

The institution created in 1846 was unique in governance and in funding. In his book *Politics, Position and Power*, Harold Seidman discusses the Smithsonian's organizational arrangements and policy impacts. He states: "Purists would find it difficult to reconcile the organizational arrangements established for the Smithsonian with the constitutional doctrine of separation of powers."[11] The President and members of the cabinet are the members of the Institution, but it is governed by a Board of Regents made up of the Vice President, Chief Justice of the Supreme Court, three members of the Senate, three members of the House, and six citizen members, with the Secretary of the Institution to also act as Secretary to the Board of Regents. The Act provided for a museum to contain objects of art, research activities, objects of natural history, plants, geological and mineral specimens, and a library. The Institution was to live on the interest of the bequest and not use the principal fund.

The regents elected Joseph Henry as first Secretary. Henry, a Princeton professor known for his work in electricity, developed the principles that have guided the Institution to this day.

Smithson's bequest, shepherded by such as John Quincy Adams and Joseph Henry, has contributed considerably to science and the spread and diffusion of knowledge. The origins of the Weather Bureau, Fish Commission, the forerunner of the Geological Survey, and the National Advisory Committee for Aeronautics were among the developments stimulated by the Institution.

Robert Hutchings Goddard's rocket experiments, supported in part by the Institution, provided much of the foundation for the explosion of rocket development in World War II and since.[12] Satellites and the communications and observational revolution they have stimulated would have been impossible without some means of placing them in orbit.

First as administrative officer and then as assistant to the Secretary, I had the opportunity (1959-1966) to work with many of the activities of the Institution. The museums and the exhibits are the obvious activities, but research is the priority program, with education a close second. The curators are physical, natural, and social scientists. The Smithsonian has some of the best research collections in the world. As a result, my brother-in-law comes from Canada to study the moose and bat collections, for example. The Smithsonian Astrophysical Observatory is located in Cambridge, Massachusetts, and cooperates fully with the Harvard College Observatory. All secretaries of the Institution have been scientists, most of them members of the National Academy of Sciences.

The Smithsonian Institution was also a participating agency in the Science Information Exchange (SIE), which various agencies with grant funds for research banded together to create and operate. The primary purpose was to make information available concerning research that was funded by the several agencies so that panels awarding funds could determine what other projects a particular applicant had as well as discover whether there were other projects with the same research focus. This helped limit research contract brokering by prominent scientists and unknown duplication of research effort. Each participating agency contributed funds for support of the SIE staff, space, and equipment. For a while the Smithsonian was the administering organization and during part of this period I was the coordinator from the Secretary's office to work with the director of the Exchange on policy issues and administrative matters. As Smithsonian's representative, I sat in on the meetings of agency representatives supporting the Exchange, sought out and recommended candidates to the Secretary for director when a vacancy occurred, and represented the Smithsonian's point of view on Exchange policy.

One personnel matter was very discouraging to me. J. Edgar Hoover sent a personal note to the then Secretary, Leonard Carmichael, calling his attention to the homosexual activity of a key clerical worker at the Exchange and suggesting, as I remember it, that Carmichael might want to drop this person from the payroll. This employee had worked faithfully and with excellent performance and had engaged in no improper advances on the job and apparently limited homosexual activity to other consenting adults during off-duty hours. No one at the Exchange had any idea that the individual was a homosexual. On the basis of Hoover's suggestion, Secretary Carmichael dropped this employee from the payroll. This economic persecution of a person whose behavior on the job was exemplary but whose personal life deviated from the then-accepted norm bothered me a great deal.

The decision by Congress to accept Smithson's bequest, the basic broad goal posed by Smithson and incorporated in the authorizing statute, the implementing guidelines of Henry and subsequent secretaries, and generous support by Congressional appropriations committees have been fruitful indeed for the "increase and diffusion of knowledge."

Indian Policy, U.S. Department of the Interior

The romantic and thrilling history of the Indians and their encounters with the whites was all around me as I grew up. The tuba player in the high school band in Tucson was a Pima Indian. Indian wagons with no lights were a hazard at night on the highways in the 1920s. I spent three weeks at a ranch in Cochise Stronghold one summer when in high school. The study of anthropology was an important part of the University of Arizona curriculum. So after World War II, I sounded out the Bureau of Indian Affairs for a job. No success, so I went with the Office of Territories.

However, I worked in Indian Affairs for two different periods: (1) from 1950-1956 as management planning officer advising the Commissioner on organization, procedures, land and other policies, and performing special assignments, and (2) as deputy commissioner from 1966-1970, and after Nixon, Assistant to the Commissioner for policy research from 1970-1974.

Difficult policy issues are still with us today in Indian affairs.[13] Since much of my recent experience has been in this area, I present several examples of policy issues and the policy process.

Tribal Attorneys

In 1950 Dillon S. Meyer was Commissioner and, as trustee for Indian trust resources, he took his responsibility seriously. Therefore, he insisted that he approve the contracts of attorneys employed by the tribe to work on tribal claims or other legal matters. Some tribes and their attorneys did not like this. The American Civil Liberties Union (ACLU) thought it involved a conflict of interest. Myer maintained that if he was responsible for Indian trust lands and funds, he had to have the ability to control them. If tribes were permitted to draw up valid contracts with attorneys to be paid from tribal funds or percentages of judgements received without the approval of the Bureau of Indian Affairs, tribal assets might quickly be dissipated. Myer believed that though he was responsible for the whole bucket of trust assets, the hole in the bottom of the bucket caused by unapproved attorney contracts could leak out all of the assets without his being able to do a thing about it. On the other hand, the tribal attorneys and the ACLU pointed to possible legal issues involved in the way in which the agency carried out its trust responsibility, and claimed it would be a conflict of interest if the Bureau of Indian Affairs could control these contracts through its approval power.

Secretary of the Interior Oscar Chapman held a hearing in which all parties had their say. The Secretary's decision endorsed the position of the Indians' attorneys and the ACLU. As a result, there was exploitation of some tribes by unscrupulous attorneys through brokerage of contracts which built up costs, and through contrasts that could never be carried out because of the inadequate resources of some attorneys. The Commissioner had to sit by and watch this happen.

This case illustrates the fuzzy and conflicting nature of many policy issues. Both views were essentially valid. One or the other had to be subordinated. In keeping with the objective of transferring as rapidly as possible the responsibility to the Indians for their own affairs, the Secretary's decision may have been the best, although I did not think so at the time. It raised the whole question of competency: if the Indians were capable of negotiating legal contracts, why were they not also just as capable of handling their other business? However, the Indians did not want a general transfer of all responsibility for reasons that will be indicated later.

Conflict Between Trust Responsibility
to the Individual and to the Tribe

Another tough issue is individual versus tribal goals. On reservations where land was allotted to individual Indians, frequently the individual Indian owner sold his land when he could get permission from the Indian superintendent to do so. In some cases, the tribes desired to acquire this allotted land if the Indian owner wanted to sell. This posed a conflict of responsibility for the trustee: (1) if the Bureau of Indian Affairs provided that the tribe be able to meet the high bid and have priority for purchase, it might lower the number of bids and the amount bid, either of which would be disadvantageous to the Indian owner; (2) if the individual seller and the tribe were permitted to agree upon a negotiated sale price without bidding, there might be the problem of exploitation of the individual by the tribe; and (3) if the Bureau of Indian Affairs insisted on advertising and let the high bidder buy the land with no tribal preference, this would often mean that the land might go out of Indian ownership, but the individual Indian would maximize the amount received for the sale of his land.

The Bureau's responsibility was to both the individual and the tribe. Which should take precedence? The Bureau's position varied from time to time, but in general provided the tribe the opportunity to meet the high bid.

Tribal Elite: Trust Responsibility Puzzle

On the Cheyenne River Indian Reservation in South Dakota and on other reservations with tribal land held in trust by the Federal Government there were a few dominant Indian ranchers. They did not own most of the land on which their cattle grazed. A good percentage was tribal land. Something like the following dialogue has taken place many times:

"But isn't tribal land owned by all members of the tribe?"
"Well, yes, to be sure."
"Did the ranchers pay fair market rent for use of the common land?"
"Well, no."
"But wasn't the government the trustee for individual Indians as well as the tribe?"
"Ah-a-a, yes."
"Then how come the subsidy of the few by the many?"

The Bureau of Indian Affairs and the reservation superintendent are in a constant vortex of competing and conflicting interests and requirements of the trust law. If the big Indian ranchers were required to pay fair market rent, they might go broke. If they did not pay fair market rent, a majority of the owners did not receive their fair share of the income from the jointly owned land assets which they might have received if rented to a non-Indian rancher with an economic ranching operation.

Due to Indian culture this situation was accompanied by minimum complaint by the Indian owners. Traditionally, land was available to those who would use it. Tribal land was also considered available for use by any member of the tribe. However, unregulated use and inequitable assignments or leases in which a few members use most of the tribal land poses a problem of equity. For many years the tribal owners received no payment from the users on many reservations. Lately, however, most tribes provide for a leasing fee for individual use of tribal land, which does yield income to the tribe for the benefit, hopefully, of all members although it may not be at the market rate. As in most societies, the aggressive and well-to-do become the leaders and, in case of American Indians, frequently dominate the tribal council.

Trustee or Indian Decisions

The fact is that although the Bureau of Indian Affairs has trust responsibility, it has largely let the tribes and individual Indians make their own decisions for their respective land. This applies to almost all forms of land use. When the agency has to approve a use, it frequently is a rubber stamp operation, except for insistence on at least minimal lease rates if leasing is involved. The Indian owner often fights this because he fears that the lessee may not be willing to go that high. The Bureau of Indian Affairs must approve a sale of individually owned land or it is not valid. The approval of Congress must be obtained for the sale of tribal land or removing the trust from tribal land. Other than for these actions, the Indians largely decide even on mineral leasing which can involve billions of dollars worth of assets and millions of dollars of income.

The Navajos and Papagos heavily overgraze their land, while the trust requires the trustee to prevent damage to the land. Overgrazing is damaging the land and a large portion of the best top soil of the Navajo reservation is ending up in the Colorado River and lowering the water storage capacity of dams. In the 1930s, the Bureau of Indian Affairs tried to restrict Navajo grazing, but the protest was so great that the government gave up. However, the government did not thereby release itself from the trust responsibility for protection of the land. I am informed that the Navajos have considered suing the government for allowing them to abuse their land. They would probably win such a suit and be awarded millions of dollars in damages which the general taxpayer would have to pay.

Why haven't they sued? Consider the possible consequence. If the present arrangement were forcibly thrust into the limelight through a large judgement, the public might think the situation did not make much sense. What is the logic of the government having responsibility for controlling use of Indian land, not exercising that responsibility because of Indian pressure, and then having to pay damages for letting the Indians have their way? The resulting public pressure might stimulate Congress to modify or repeal trust statutes. The Indians do not want the trust lifted. They chafe under government kibitzing, but enjoy the tax-free status of the land as long as it is in trust, the free management of the land by the government in many instances, the possibility of suing of government if a mistake is made with the use of their land, as well as the symbolism of the trust status as recognition of their original sovereignty.

Secondly, the Indians might well lose some of their land for nonpayment of taxes if it were subject to a state real estate tax as is other land. Much Indian land is not used in an economically productive fashion by its owners. Land might also go out of ownership by sale. Although removal of the trust would not change ownership, it would remove the Bureau of Indian Affairs brake on disposition of Indian land to non-Indians. The Superintendent or Congress would no longer have to approve a sale. Since many Indians might prefer the cash value of a piece of land to the land itself, as often is the case with non-Indian landowners, some, perhaps a great deal of land might be sold and go out of Indian ownership.

One of the favorite battle cries of the Indians is the perfidy of the whites in the loss of Indian land. Much Indian trust-allotted land has gone out of Indian ownership because the Indian wanted to sell it and get the cash. But they collectively blame the government for letting this happen.

It is true that in the past our ancestors, in effect, forced land cessations by many tribes and many citizens have a guilt complex because of this. But no one alive today was responsible for such actions. Since 1924, all Indians have been U.S. citizens. The trust was placed on Indian land because they were considered incompetent to manage it themselves. Times have changed. Many Indians are as competent as anyone else and most tribal leaders are quite sophisticated.

Individuals, Innovation, and Population Pressure

Individuals can have an impact on policy. Americans feel uncomfortable about welfare payments to able-bodied adults who are not working. Many recipients also are not comfortable. In striving to resolve this problem on Indian reservations, Charles B. Rovin, chief of the social services branch, proposed an innovative Tribal Work Experience Program (TWEP). In essence, the program provided the welfare payment plus $30 (now $45) a month and, work related expenses to an Indian adult qualifying for welfare if he worked on projects for the tribe. This provided an alternative to idleness and proved to be very popular. The objective was to have the tribe administer the program and determine the projects of greatest priority to themselves. Assignments could vary from storytelling and relating oral history by an adult to Indian children to construction of needed public facilities. In the process, too, many would learn work habits which might help them later in getting off welfare. Congress approved the idea and supplied the extra money required. The psychological impact on the participation is illustrated by one Navajo going to the welfare office and saying: "You can take me off of welfare. I am working in the Tribal Work Experience Program."

This program, of course, is not a solution to the unemployment problem. It is a subsidized activity. But it gives the recipients a degree of dignity and helps orient them toward the world of work while other efforts are made to resolve the basic economic issues involved.

One of the dangers of this approach is that the Indians and the tribal governments may come to regard the work as regular employment, as for a gas station or a lumber company. The Navajo quoted above apparently did not realize that the Tribal Work Experience Program was another "welfare program."

There has been pressure from the beginning to expand the program and make it a general works program for which any Indian would be eligible, whether above or below the poverty line. Although Congress does not seem to favor this, the Comprehensive Employment and Training Act (CETA) to some extent fits this pattern. This pressure to extend the program raises the question of the relationship of means to ends. If the ultimate objective is Indian self-sufficiency, as in the rest of society, would a subsidized general works program promote or sabotage this objective? It might encourage Indians to stay where they are when resources are not adequate to support them without a subsidy. It might eliminate some stimulus to get education and training to help them become competitive for real jobs. Thus, it might lead to ever-increasing subsidy requirements as the Indian population expanded (at a 2.5 percent annual rate). Reservation resources in most instances will not support a viable economy which provides an opportunity for employment to all potential Indian workers. Unemployment on many reservations is 50 to 75 percent (1983). Along with the development of the maximum productive economy on or near Indian reservations, the practice of many Indians going to where the jobs are in nonreservation communities will be necessary if all are to have an opportunity for productive employment.

Castration, Windmills and Charcos

The following is a reconstruction of events as related to me by Russell Kilgore and Evan Flory many years ago, with no certification as to its accuracy in detail. Indian farmers and livestock men were sitting around the corral in Oklahoma. They were mostly owners of hogs that needed castration. While waiting for the new Indian agricultural extension agent to show up, they were engaged in tribal gossip and good natured banter. The agent, Russell Kilgore, arrived at the appointed time and made preparations. When he was ready, he spoke to the group.

"I'll show you how this is done with the first animal. Then I will watch you do it on the second animal and give you any help you need. After that you will be on your own to finish the rest of the job."

"Hold on, Mr. Kilgore," said one Indian. "You are paid by the government to do this for us."

"Nope," responded Kilgore. "I'm paid by the government, all right. But I am not paid to castrate for you. I'm paid to teach you how to castrate so that you can do it yourself."

"You're talking through your hat," said another hog owner. "The former agent did this for us."

"I'm not the former agent and I do not intend to do this for you. I will show you how to do it. Let me have a hog and we will get started."

There was much grumbling, threats to appeal to the agency Superintendent, perhaps even castrate Kilgore, but finally one hog was brought forth for the operation. Indians helped hold the hog while Kilgore performed the operation, explaining each step as he went along.

"Watch carefully. I will explain each step. If you have any questions, ask them. That is what I am here for." And Kilgore proceeded to castrate the animal. "O.K." said Kilgore, "Now the owner of this hog will castrate another of his hogs and I will stand by as coach."

Amid muttering of resentment and comments about Kilgore being too lazy to do his job, the owner brought forth another of his hogs and proceeded under the agent's direction to castrate the animal. Each of the other owners present did one of their animals under the agent's supervision and when each owner had demonstrated that he could do the job, Kilgore said "You all have done good work. You can finish the rest of the job without me." He left.

Kilgore also related another incident that occurred when he was an extension agent assigned to a New Mexico group of Indians. With these Indian cattle ranchers, he took the same attitude of showing rather than "doing for" on one roundup. As a result, the cattlemen got angry and seemed intent on man-handling the crazy agent. Kilgore said he retreated up a windmill until they dispersed.

*   *   *

On the Navajo reservation, the government put in windmills to provide water at various points on the range for cattle and sheep. In this process, the agency used government funds, bought the windmills, and hired local Indians to put them up, dig wells, and do other work required to get the windmills operational. The beneficiary Indian stockmen did not contribute anything. If they worked on the project at all, they were paid for their labor. When a windwill malfunctioned, an Indian sheepherder would call the agency and say "Come fix your government windmill" even if a simple operation would have solved the problem, such as replacing a bolt or plugging a leak in the trough.

When Evan Flory, head of Water and Soil Conservation in the Bureau of Indian Affairs, got some money from Congress to build charcos for stock water, he took a different approach (charcos are deep holes in the ground with a dam on a wash with the object of having as little surface water exposed as possible for the amount of water stored so as to cut down on evaporation). He personally held the first meeting with the stockmen in several Navajo grazing areas.

"These charcos will greatly increase water availability," he told the first assembled group in a picturesque setting on the reservation. "Of course," he continued, "this will help achieve more balanced grazing of the range because there will be more places for the stock to get water."

The stockmen liked this. It would mean less miles for animals to go for water and possibly the ability to graze more animals in a given area.

"The program for building charcos will be a cooperative effort between the communities concerned and the agency," continued Flory. "We will provide materials, you will contribute the labor and horses."

One stockman said "The government put in the windmills. They paid us to work."

"This charco is for your benefit. So we think it proper for you to use your horses to scrape and haul dirt, your hands on the shovels, your labor on necessary concrete work for the spillways—with no pay. The government will furnish cement and a bulldozer and operator when necessary," responded Flory.

"This is a cheap program," commented one Indian leader. "You are supposed to do these things for us. That is what you are paid for. We will work on the charcos if you pay us and rent our horses."

"That is not the way this program will be developed," responded Flory. "You do not have to have a charco, although I believe you would benefit from it. If and when you think it is worth your while to contribute your horses, time, and labor, let the agency know."

Flory had this same experience in each community he visited. None agreed to the cooperative proposal. It looked for awhile as if no charcos would be built. In fact, as Flory reported it, almost a year passed before one community said it was ready and the charco was built with contributed community labor.

This kind of delay is generally risky, given the government appropriation process. If the agency does not spend the money appropriated for a given year, Congress may well take it away the following year. So the agency incentive is to spend the money whether it will achieve the maximum results or not in order to justify the funds again for the next year—a perverse incentive if there ever was one!

However, soon other charcos were built.

When a charco develops a leak, the Indian who discovers it grabs a shovel and fixes it himself, or, if it is too big a job for one man, calls on his neighbors. "Come, we've got to fix *our* charco," he will say. It is not the *government's* charco, it is *their* charco. They take the responsibility for protecting their investment in time and labor.

                    *   *   *

The windmill, hog castration, and charco building incidents illustrate different aspects of policy. Helping the Indian use his resources to the best advantage was achieved by installing the government windmills and by castrating hogs for Indians. The other practice, under the same general policy, of showing the Indian how to do given tasks and requiring his participation also helped in best use of resources, but had an additional dimension: the Indian learned to do for himself, and developed a different attitude toward his own responsibility.

If efficient use of resources and avoiding friction with clients is dominant, education may be deemphasized. If growth of the Indian and his eventual ability to stand on his own feet is dominant, some management actions such as the hog castration or charco building procedures cited above may not be done as efficiently at first, but the long run effect may eliminate the need for any subsidy as well as result in an increase in human dignity and productivity.

In the charco case, Flory did not fear losing his appropriation, even if no funds were used during the first year. He had carefully briefed the Bureau of Indian Affairs, the Office of the Secretary of the Department, Bureau of the Budget, and Congressional Subcommittees, all of whom subscribed to his approach. Further, one of the senior Subcommittee members in the House, a strong supporter of soil conservation, believed in Flory. So in this instance, with appropriate communication and rapport, the possible perverse incentive related to spending within a budget year was not as great a factor as it may be in other settings.

Who is an Indian?

Edison Ward, fair skinned, blue eyed, red haired, and of one-quarter Indian blood considered himself an Indian. In fact, he was a member of the Ogalala Sioux Tribe on the Pine Ridge Reservation in South Dakota.

Some tribes have recognized members with as little as 1/32 degree of Indian blood. Biologically, who is an Indian? Does any degree of Indian blood, no matter how small, make a person an Indian?

There is a cultural dimension to the question. A person with little Indian blood who lives in an Indian community and is part of that community's culture may be culturally and psychologically an Indian. Even persons without any Indian blood can be Indian in a cultural sense. On the other hand, some individuals with 100 percent Indian blood may be culturally and psychologically non-Indian. Certainly there are many with some Indian blood who do not identify themselves as Indian. Some may not know that they have Indian blood.

It is estimated that there may be 20 million persons with some Indian blood in the United States. Only a few over 1,400,000 identified themselves as

Indian in the 1980 census. Only 53 percent of these had any relation to Federal reservations or the Bureau of Indian Affairs.

The question of who is an Indian is more than esoteric under current law. Indians have, as a racial matter, been given certain benefits and subsidies. Some on Federal reservations have special provisions for law and order, justice, taxes and the like, plus subsidized education, health care, roads, and houses. So whether a person can be classified as an Indian has a fiscal impact on the Federal and state budgets as well as placing that person in a minority racial group with a special, privileged legal position. It has been jokingly said that if a person commits an offense on an Indian reservation, the site of the offense has to be surveyed to see if it was on Indian or non-Indian land to determine jurisdiction, and a blood sample has to be analyzed to determine whether the culprit is Indian or non-Indian and thus subject to state or tribal law and courts. Legal distinctions by race cause all kinds of difficulties if benefits, privileges, or other matters of concern hinge on racial definition.

Most persons of Indian blood do not live on reservations. Do special benefits follow an Indian to the city? In the 1970 census 37 percent of those calling themselves Indian lived in metropolitan areas such as Los Angeles which has 25,000 Indians. In view of this situation and the fact that all Indians are citizens of the U.S. and the state in which they live, one might ask why not forget race and provide assistance or subsidy on the basis of need?

Summary Observations

In all of my jobs, the character and ability of persons, both political appointees and career employees, have been crucial.

This is true of Morris L. Cooke in the Rural Electrification Administration, Milburn L. Wilson in the Federal Extension Service, Dillon S. Myer and Charles Rovin in the Bureau of Indian Affairs, and E. Ellsworth Roth in the Navy's Bureau of Ships. These are but examples. There were many able and dedicated people along the way emphasizing that the character and ability produced in our homes, churches, and communities have an impact on government as well as all other societal institutions. It is clear to me that government through its various agencies and employees can be effective and often is.

It is obvious that Congress, pressure groups, and the general public have great impact on the entire system. In the case of the Rural Electrification Administration, the support of the President and leaders of Congress overcame the opposition of the private electric utility industry in electrifying rural America. The influence of local county agents and state extension officers in Federal extension work probably resulted in a more effective educational effort than would have been the case with strong central direction. Active Indian advocates have had great impact on Federal Indian policy.

The complexity of policy decisions is illustrated in almost all the examples presented. The impact of policy options in terms of long run development of self-sufficiency or increased dependency are evident in the Trust Territory and Indian examples. The Experiment Stations and Extension Service relate to the basic productivity and self-sufficiency not only of farmers but the nation. The policy of cooperation between the private and public sectors is demonstrated in the World War II shipbuilding effort and the Defense Electric Power program. The balance of power in the policy realm between the central government, the states, and counties is a factor in the Federal Cooperative Extension Service discussion.

One of the exhilarating aspects of reflecting on these experiences is the positive contribution to the citizens of this country by Federal policies and their application as described above: electrification of farms, increased agricultural production, ships with which to win World War II, aiding Micronesian and Indian minorities adjust to their new environments, and contributing to increase and diffusion of knowledge through a research and museum complex serving millions of persons each year.

It was very rewarding to participate in and contribute to the success of these beneficial governmental programs.

Footnotes

1. Marver H. Bernstein, *The Job of the Federal Executive* (Washington, D.C.: Brookings, 1958).

2. Harry Slattery, *Rural America Lights Up* (Washington, D.C.: National Home Library Foundation, 1940), p. 26.

3. *Ibid.*

4. E.O. 7037, May 11, 1935, based on authority of the Emergency Relief Appropriation Act, 49 Stat 15.

5. H.S. Person, "The Rural Electrification in Perspective," *Agricultural History*, April 1950, p. 73.

6. *Enrichment of Flour and Bread*, Bulletin of the National Research Council, National Academy of Sciences, Washington, D.C.: No. 110, Nov. 1944, "A History of the Movement," p. 4.

7. "To Enrich or Not to Enrich: A Symposium," *Journal of Home Economics*, Vol. 37, No. 7, September, 1945.

8. Herman Wouk's novel, *The Winds of War,* dramatizes the importance of this shipbuilding effort.

9. On the way to and from the Trust Territory we stayed at Pearl Harbor, as the High Commissioner of the Trust Territory, Admiral Leon Sangster Fiske, was stationed there. It was a strange feeling to see the harbor with its sunken battleships, that had

been the scene of catapulting the United States and Japan into war. The remains of bombed installations throughout the islands, abandoned tanks in the surf, a rusted Japanese locomotive were all reminders of the recent war in the Pacific.

10. Bessie Zaban Jones, *Lighthouse of the Skies* (Washington, D.C., Smithsonian Institution, 1965), p. 15.

11. Harold Seidman, *Politics, Position and Power,* 2nd ed. (New York: Oxford University Press, 1975), pp. 245-246.

12. "The Smithsonian Institution," Pamphlet, S.I., 1959.

13. For a full discussion, see Theodore W. Taylor, *American Indian Policy* (Mt. Airy, MD: Lomond Publications, Inc., 1983).

AFTERWORD

Theodore W. Taylor

The foregoing pages presented examples of the various forces involved in the production of policy. Whether a statement of policy is in a statute or a government regulation, the actual policy depends on its application. What the individual citizen encounters in relation to government programs is the governmental policy whether or not it bears direct relationship to undergirding statutes or regulations.

Obvious, too, is that the term *policy* is not very precise. The larger, over-arching policies stated in a major statute such as that establishing the Highway Trust Fund or the G.I. Bill generally are equivalent to grand strategy or setting of broad overall goals with very general outlines of how to carry out such policy. These major policies are amplified by numerous layers of lesser policy down to field operations.

The discussion in these pages is illustrative of the infinite variety of goals, values, and environmental challenges in which policy is formulated and executed. The governmental process is not always neat and orderly and policy statements are not always followed. Nevertheless, policy is always being applied whether or not it is stated in writing or referred to as policy.

The major affective element in the policy process is the cadre of responsible public officials. The quality of government depends on people of principle, ability, understanding, and initiative such as those represented here.

WORK EXPERIENCE OF AUTHORS

The work of the authors collectively covers a great variety of governmental responsibilities, including experience in:

Executive Departments of:

    Agriculture
    Defense
    Energy
    Health, Education, and Welfare
    Interior
    Labor
    Transportation
    Treasury

Other Governmental Agencies and Organizations:

    Agency for International Development
    Bureau of the Budget
    Federal Aviation Agency
    Federal Civil Defense Administration
    Federal Council on Science and Technology
    Federal Mediation Service
    Hoover Commission Task Force
    National Aeronautics and Space Administration
    National Council of Marine Resources and
       Engineering Development
    Office of Management and Budget
    Smithsonian Institution
    States of Ohio and Pennsylvania
    Veterans Administration
    War Labor Board

Private Sector:

    McKinsey and Company and other consulting firms
    Population Reference Bureau
    Various universities

BIOGRAPHIES OF AUTHORS

David S. Brown

David S. Brown, Professor of Management, George Washington University, has had service in Federal and state governments and the private sector, and has spent two years in developing countries.

In 1940 he became a personal assistant to W.A. Jump, Budget Officer and Director of Finance in the U.S. Department of Agriculture.

Brown received his A.B. degree from the University of Maine and his Ph.D. degree from Syracuse University.

Brown has written over 150 professional articles and two books: *Federal Contributions to Management* (1968) and *Managing the Large Organization: Issues, Ideas, Precepts, Innovations* (1982).

James W. Greenwood, Jr.

James W. Greenwood, Jr. is a writer. He has served at the local, state, Federal, and international levels of government (as well as in private enterprise). From 1950 to 1953 he served as associate director of FMCS. Prior to retirement he was director of Management Policy, Office of the Secretary at H.E.W.

Greenwood has the B.S. and M.A. degrees in public administration from American University.

He is co-author with his son, James W. Greenwood III, of the recently published *Managing Executive Stress*. Both are working on another volume, *Systems Thinking for Managers*, based on a course they jointly developed for the IBM Systems Science Institute.

Martin Kriesberg

Martin Kriesberg is a Deputy Administrator of the Office of International Cooperation and Development (OICD) in the U.S. Department of Agriculture (USDA). OICD is a sister agency of the Department's Foreign Agriculture Service (FAS) which has line responsibility for international food aid programs. Both agencies report to the Undersecretary for International Affairs and Commodity Programs. Kriesberg has served OICD and its predecessor agencies for over 15 years.

Currently, Kriesberg is the principal officer for USDA in its relations with the UN system and its agencies such as the World Food Council and the Food and Agriculture Organization.

Kriesberg received a B.S. degree in marketing and economics from Northwestern University and his M.A. and Ph.D. degrees from Harvard in public administration, international affairs, and economics. He has been Adjunct Professor at American and George Washington Universities.

Kriesberg has written widely in the field of public policy, particularly in the area of international economic development.

Michael S. March

Michael S. March is a Professor of Public Affairs in the Graduate School of Public Affairs, University of Colorado, formerly serving as Assistant Vice-President at its Medical Center. He served for 33 years in 8 different Federal agencies, including 28 years in 6 different administrations as an analyst on a wide range of programs with the Bureau of the Budget and the Office of Management and Budget. He played key roles in many Federal policy reviews. In 1967 he received the Bureau of the Budget's Exceptional Service Award.

March holds a B.A. in economics from the University of Colorado (Phi Beta Kappa and magna cum laude) and a Ph.D. in political economy and government from Harvard University. He has published numerous articles and reports.

Rufus E. Miles, Jr.

Rufus E. Miles, Jr., is a writer and consultant and has served as Senior Fellow and Lecturer at the Woodrow Wilson School of Public and International Affairs, Princeton University; Assistant Secretary for Administration, Department of Health, Education, and Welfare; Division Chief in the Bureau of the Budget; Lt. Commander in the Naval Reserve, and various other positions in the state of Ohio and the Federal Government. He has also been President of the Population Reference Bureau, Washington, D.C.

Miles received his A.B. from Antioch College and did further studies at the University of Berlin and Ohio State University.

Besides articles Miles has written two books: *The Department of Health, Education and Welfare* and *Awakening from the American Dream: The Social and Political Limits to Growth.*

Miles awards include: Superior Service Award and Distinguished Service Award (HEW), the Rockefeller Public Service Award, and the National Civil Service League Award. He is a member of the National Academy of Public Administration. In addition, he is on the Visiting Committee, Kennedy School of Government, Harvard University and the Advisory Council of the Woodrow Wilson School of Public and International Affairs, Princeton University.

John R. Provan

John R. Provan retired in December 1978 after ten years of service as Associate Administrator, Federal Highway Administration, Department of Transportation. His experience includes similar positions in the Federal Aviation Administration and the Veterans Administration, with earlier assignments in the Bureau of the Budget, Department of Defense, Hoover Commission Task Force, Federal Civil Defense Administration, and the United States Air Force. For ten years, Provan was Associate Professorial Lecturer at George Washington University.

Provan received his A.B. in political science from the University of Pittsburgh and his M.S. in public administration from Syracuse University.

Theodore W. Taylor

Theodore W. Taylor, a consultant and writer, has served in the Bureau of Indian Affairs, Office of Territories and Island Possessions, and the Office of the Assistant Secretary for Water and Power, all in the U.S. Department of the Interior. In addition, he has been Assistant to the Secretary of the Smithsonian Institution, served in the Office of the Director of the Cooperative Extension Service, worked for the Rural Electrification Administration in the Department of Agriculture, and served as Lt. Commander in the Bureau of Ships, U.S. Navy Department. For ten years he was Professorial Lecturer in Public Administration at George Washington University.

Taylor received a B.A. from the University of Arizona, M.A. from Syracuse, and Ph.D. from Harvard.

Taylor has written three books: *The States and their Indian Citizens* (1972), *American Indian Policy* (1983), and *The Bureau of Indian Affairs* (1984).

William C. Valdes

William C. Valdes is a consultant, Professorial Lecturer at George Washington University, and Lecturer in Government and Politics at George Mason University. He retired in 1981 as Deputy Assistant Secretary in the Department of Defense and has held various personnel management positions in other Federal agencies and in private industry. He is currently a consultant to the National Academy of Public Administration and a Trustee of the National Capital Medical Foundation.

Valdes received a B.A. degree from Yale University, a M.A. from George Washington University, and a Ph.D. in public administration from American University.

Valdes has published many articles on public administration.

Edward Wenk, Jr.

Edward Wenk, Jr. is engaged in consulting in science policy and futures studies and is Emeritus Professor of Engineering, Public Affairs, and Social Management of Technology at the University of Washington, Seattle. He has served 26 years in government including two tours at the Congressional Research Service and positions on the science advisory staffs of Presidents Kennedy, Johnson and Nixon.

Wenk received his B.E. and D.Eng. from Johns Hopkins, and his M.S. from Harvard.

He is the author of *The Politics of the Ocean* (1972), *Margins for Survival* (1979), and was consulting editor of *The Undersea* (1977).

Wenk has been elected to the National Academy of Engineering and the National Academy of Public Administration.

John D. Young

John D. Young, Professor of Public Management at American University, served as Deputy Undersecretary of the U.S. Department of Energy; Assistant Secretary, Management and Budget, Department of Health, Education and Welfare; and Assistant Administrator for Administration, NASA. He held other senior Federal posts, and in the private sector was a principal of McKinsey and Company, consultants.

He received his A.B. from Colgate, M.S. from Syracuse, and Ph.D. in public administration from American University.

Young's awards include: election to the National Academy of Public Administration; Maxwell School Distinguished Alumni Award; National Civil Service League Award; Distinguished Service Award, H.E.W.; Distinguished Service Award, American Association for Budget and Program Analysis; Award for Outstanding Contributions to U.S. manned space flight, NASA.

PUBLISHER'S COMMENT

One afternoon, as a Professor of Management, I was sitting quietly at my desk in my downtown Washington, D.C. office when I received a telephone call from a mid-level administrative functionary in the U.S. Department of State. His voice was excited as he said "Professor Hattery, I have a two million dollar idea and I must talk to you about it. Can you see me right away?" I said O.K. and thought to myself, another capable Federal Administrator is going to leave for greener, money-making pastures in the private sector.

When he arrived, breathless and still excited, he sketched for me his idea. It was not how to patent a new gadget or set up a new business to make a personal fortune, but a plan for a new mangerial procedure in the Department of State which would save the taxpayers of the United States two million dollars and at the same time improve the functioning of the Department. A telerecording of the conversation would be an eye-opener and an important educational experience for the many who think of Federal civil servants as passive persons simply feeding at the public trough.

The statements in this book by ten former bureaucrats, most of whom spent the greater part of their careers serving the public through Federal assignments, give impressive evidence of the degree to which there is dedication by Federal civil service officials to the public trust in serving the citizens of our Democratic government. Their alertness, imagination, perceptiveness, industry, and courage are likewise evident and a key to why, despite weaknesses, the United States political and governmental system has served us well for 200 years as a vital, driving, leader among nations.

These ten reports by and about dedicated and able civil servants are productive reading for two reasons. First, they provide the evidence which should be comforting to the American public that there is a strong inner fiber in governmental administrative institutions. Second, they reveal insights into the nature of governmental administration and policymaking which ought to be known and understood by policymakers, teachers, students, and citizens everywhere, but for which the documentation is so rare. The "doers" illustrated by these ten authors seldom write about their experiences for the very reason that they are so actively involved in carrying out policy and plans.

One of the dominant characteristics of the contributors' stories is that they do not hesitate to cite both the good and the bad, the bitter and the sweet, the successes and the failures. That they do not sugar-coat experiences is a very great value; nevertheless, it seems to me, all the writers provide an upbeat note about the possibilities of achievement within the often frustrating and imperfect policy-making and administrative dynamics.

Until only a few years ago, the literature about government and the teaching of government was almost exclusively theoretical and legal. Through the special vision and conviction of political science professors, first at the University of Chicago and later at Syracuse University, followed by many universities throughout the country, there was a new message about understanding government which was based on the assumption that government is first and most importantly the sum of the behavior of the participants. In other words, the impact of government is not what the theory of democratic institutions says government should be, not what the laws and regulations say it shall be, but rather what officials actually do in carrying out democratic, representative government and its laws and regulations. This view is strongly supported by the experiences described in this book. No one can come away from its reading without a sharpened understanding and belief that the nature and quality of government is defined in large degree by officials and what they do rather than by theory or legal rules.

These officials are the people who make the system work. They are intelligent, knowledgeable, devoted, persistent. These are the stalwarts of the system who have been underrated, sometimes berated, but most of all, misunderstood by those who do not understand their functions. Unfortunately, this includes our last two Presidents and much of the personal staff they chose from state governments and business. Carter and Reagan had little knowledge of the Federal policy and administrative system and were slow to learn. Carter's and Reagan's failure to utilize effectively this most essential resource has caused an out-migration of many of the best Federal Administrative professionals. In a huge bureaucracy with an often idiosyncratic and whimsical policy-making authority in Congress and a mass turnover of upper-level political appointments every four years, a stable, capable "under-executive" corps of senior career officials is absolutely essential.

Each one of these essays gives only a glimpse of the senior civil servant role. Together, they provide as nothing else does an illuminating depiction of the human element which offsets deficiencies in the system and supports both policymaking and administration.

Sparked by discussions with Michael S. March and others, in 1979 I proposed to several experienced, senior paticipants the idea of developing a book on the policy decision process in the U.S. Government. The response was very favorable. This book is the result. I am stimulated by the quality and tone of the ten accounts, as I think all readers will be. Developed under the sensitive editorship of Theodore W. Taylor, *Federal Public Policy* shows the vital importance of persons of character and ability in government who have the motivation, stamina, ability and courage to serve the people of this country wisely and well through their government. The future of our country depends in large measure on continuing to attract and retain such persons as these to Federal government service.

Lowell H. Hattery
Publisher
Professor Emeritus of Management
and Public Administration,
American University

INDEX